OUR OWN DE

National Symbols and Political Conflict in Twentieth-Century Ireland

EWAN MORRIS

IRISH ACADEMIC PRESS
DUBLIN • PORTLAND, OR

First published in 2005 by
IRISH ACADEMIC PRESS
44, Northumberland Road, Dublin 4, Ireland

and in the United States of America by
IRISH ACADEMIC PRESS
c/o ISBS, Suite 300, 920 NE 58th Avenue
Oregon 97212

Website: www.iap.ie

British Library Cataloguing in Publication Data
An entry for this title is available on application

ISBN 0-7165-2663-8 (cloth)
0-7165-3337-5 (paper)

Library of Congress Cataloging-in-Publication Data
An entry for this title is available on application

Typeset by FiSH Books, London
Printed by MPG Books Ltd, Bodmin, Cornwall

Contents

List of Illustrations

Acknowledgements

It is a great pleasure to be able at last to acknowledge all those who have contributed to the writing and publication of this book –

At the University of Sydney, I received valuable support and guidance from Tony Cahill, Oliver MacDonagh and Richard White. David Fitzpatrick provided very useful advice at various points along the way, and was kind enough to talk to me when I first conceived of the idea of doing research in Irish history. Dan Collins and Michael Laffan also assisted me during my research in Ireland, and Colm Gallagher generously shared his knowledge of, and sources relating to, the 1928 coinage designs.

Thanks to the staffs of the National Archives of Ireland, the Military Archives of Ireland, the University College Dublin Archives Department, the Trinity College Library Manuscripts Department, the Public Record Office of Northern Ireland, the National Library of Ireland, the University College Dublin Library, Fisher Library at the University of Sydney, the Grand Orange Lodge of Ireland in Belfast, and Niamh O'Sullivan of the Kilmainham Jail Museum, for their assistance.

I also wish to thank the following individuals and institutions for permission to use quotations or to reproduce images in this book: Director of the National Archives of Ireland and the Deputy Keeper of Records of the Public Record Office of Northern Ireland for permission to quote from documents in their respective collections; David Higham Associates for permission to quote from 'Autumn Journal' by Louis MacNeice; A.P. Watt Ltd on behalf of Michael B. Yeats for permission to quote from 'The Man and the Echo' and 'September 1913' by W.B. Yeats; the Department of the Taoiseach for permission to reproduce the Great Seal of the Irish Free State; An Post for permission to reproduce the Irish Free State stamps; the Central Bank of Ireland for permission to reproduce the Irish Free State banknotes; the Department of Finance for permission to reproduce the Irish Free State coins; Bill Rolston for permission to reproduce his photographs of wall murals; the Police Service of Northern Ireland for permission to reproduce the crests of the Royal Ulster Constabulary and the Police Service of Northern Ireland; and Martyn Turner for permission to reproduce his cartoon.

I am eternally grateful to Keith Jeffery for recommending this book for publication, and for his invaluable help and encouragement over a number of years. At Irish Academic Press, Linda Longmore initially took the book on. More recently Jonathan Manley showed great patience in dealing with my many queries, Rachel Milotte kindly obtained copies of illustrations, and Lisa Hyde has overseen the book during the final stretch, helping to nudge it over the finish line. Many thanks to the whole IAP team.

Many friends have supported me and helped to keep me sane through the long process of working on this book. In particular, Melissa Harper, Kate Jackson, Hsu-Ming Teo and Stuart Ward have been there from the start of this project, or near enough to the start, and I have benefited hugely from their friendship, support and suggestions. I am indebted to them, and to all my other friends who have continued to ask about the book even when I was heartily sick of it.

Finally, Mum, Dad and Meredith have kept me going with their love and support, and I am grateful to them beyond measure. I dedicate this book to the newest member of our family, my niece Abigail, and hope that she will not respond by asking for 'More!'

Go raibh míle maith agaibh go léir

Ngā mihi nui ki a koutou katoa

Good on youse all!

Ewan Morris
June 2004

Foreword

In the early days of the Northern Ireland 'peace process', when the issue of the IRA decommissioning of arms was an especially fraught topic, the consistently stimulating Derry commentator Eamon McCann remarked in a radio interview that the Provos would not release even so much as 'a smidgeen of Semtex'. Those of us who regarded the whole exercise as merely symbolic were greatly dismayed by this assertion. All PIRA needed to do, we thought, was give up a few weeping bars of elderly explosive, and a rusty Thompson machine-gun or two. But, as we soon came to appreciate, McCann was absolutely right and no movement was possible precisely because any surrender of arms, however small, would be a *symbolic* gesture, and therefore pregnant with political meaning. Quoting Adolf Hitler, no less, who had a shrewd appreciation of national symbolism, Ewan Morris reminds us that there are 'very important matters in these apparent trifles'.

This book engrossingly explores the 'branding' of the two post-partition Irish states. Independent Ireland was, naturally, quicker off the mark than the North. By April 1922 the red British pillar boxes, royal cipher and all, were being painted green, a cheerfully pragmatic demonstration of the regime change. The green, white and orange tricolour was adopted from the start, despite republican objections that the Free State government had no right to sully the pure republican symbolism of a flag which had, apparently, flown over the GPO in 1916. But there was another Irish flag, a green standard, bearing the words 'Irish republic' in gold, which had certainly flown over the GPO and had been seized as a battle trophy by the British. In 1966, as a gesture of reconciliation, it was decided to give this flag back. A curator at the Imperial War Museum was sent to get the 'Irish flag' out of the safe where it had lain for half a century (it having been thought far too provocative to put it on display). But there was consternation when a tricolour was presented to the Irish ambassador, for he was expecting the green one, and the poor curator had to rush back and find the correct flag. Thus it was that a well-intentioned symbolic gesture, itself involving a sacred national symbol, nearly turned into a very real diplomatic incident. Tread softly, one supposes, for you may tread on our symbols.

Ewan Morris tells the story of the Irish, and Northern Irish, flags, seals, stamps and songs, and tells it very well. From the wolfhounds and round towers of the nineteenth century to the re-badging of the Northern Ireland police in the late twentieth century, he deftly unpicks the sometimes very passionate debates which accompanied the adoption (or not) of precious party symbols. By dispassionately illuminating this important topic, Ewan Morris, himself a New Zealander, has done us Irish a great service.

Keith Jeffery
University of Ulster at Jordanstown
September 2004

Introduction

Mr. Healy: Are the people of Northern Ireland not tired of this question of flags – (Hon. Members: No, no) – and are they not more concerned with rates and taxes? (Hon. Members: No, no).[1]
(Cahir Healy speaking in the Northern Ireland House of Commons, 1928)

What did politics mean? Flags, parades, the red, white and blue: that's what you remember.[2]
(An old Belfast shipyard worker recalling the years of devolved government in Northern Ireland)

There is a curious ambivalence in much contemporary thinking about symbolism, a tension between passionate attachment to symbols and blithe dismissal of their importance. It is often assumed that questions of symbolism are peripheral, if not irrelevant, to the 'real' business of politics: struggles for power and the distribution of resources (rates and taxes). We have become used to associating the symbolic with the ineffectual; 'It's purely symbolic', we say dismissively of changes which we believe will have no practical consequences. Yet at the same time many people continue to care deeply about symbols: a proposal to change the Australian flag or anthem is sure to provoke a flood of letters to the editor;[3] the Greek and Macedonian governments can spend several years in a hostile stand-off over the question of the Republic of Macedonia's name and flag;[4] and in Northern Ireland, the display of national symbols can still spark conflict between nationalists and unionists.[5] Such conflicts over symbols occur because, far from being incidental to politics, symbols are intrinsic to it. Symbols make it possible to imagine abstract entities such as nations and states, and they play an important role in creating emotionally charged bonds of social solidarity. However, symbols can also be a source of dissension. Groups are distinguished from each other by their attachment to different symbols, and even within groups disputes can break out about the meanings of symbols. This book focuses on conflicts over, and debates about, official symbols of state in Ireland.

Despite the general tendency to dismiss the importance of symbols, few people who are familiar with the politics of Northern Ireland would dispute the important role of symbols in the conflict there. A newspaper headline declares 'In Northern Ireland, symbols can be a matter of life and death',[6] and the most obvious symbolic trappings of conflict – tricolours and Union Jacks, political murals, painted kerbstones, Orange banners – have become standard reference points for reports on Northern Ireland by the international media. Symbols even rate a special mention in the Good Friday Agreement signed in 1998 by representatives of the various parties to the conflict (see Chapter 7). Yet there has been little attempt to provide a historical context for the continuing importance of symbols in political conflict in Ireland. This book shows how some of the national symbols which are the subject of dispute in Ireland today came into being and were given official recognition. It also examines the ways in which national symbols have, throughout the twentieth century, been the subject of political debate and contestation. Before looking at the specific case of twentieth century Ireland, however, it is important to explain the crucial part that symbols play in the imagining of nations.

Symbols and nations

In common usage, a symbol is simply something which stands for something else. However, it is useful to draw a distinction between this general category, which many theorists refer to as signs, and the more specific category of symbols.[7] Symbols are distinguished from other signs by three important characteristics: the emotional charge which they carry, the complex web of associations attached to them, and the fact that they represent ideas or emotions which are difficult, if not impossible, to express in words alone.[8] Raymond Firth illustrates the distinction between symbols and other signs by using the example of the red flag. A red flag placed in the middle of the road as a signal to traffic is not a symbol; it has a simple message which is easily expressible: 'Slow down, obstacle ahead.' However, a red flag on the Parisian barricades in 1968:

> stood for a complex, not very specific set of ideas and actions. In an immediate general sense it stood for a simple attitude – defiance of established authority. But behind this, or side by side with it, were much more elaborate, much more vaguely delineated ideas of moral values and political freedom. It was a political symbol. Moreover, as with many symbols, strongly emotional attitudes were mingled with intellectual concepts.[9]

It is partly because of their strongly emotional character that symbols have often been viewed with suspicion by intellectuals. The origins of the modern ambivalence about symbolism can be found in the early modern period when, according to Peter Burke, 'educated Europeans first drew a firm distinction between what was real and efficacious on the one hand and what was "mere" symbol or ritual on the other'.[10] This 'rise of literal-mindedness' was associated with the Protestant insistence on interpreting the Bible literally, with the development of a mechanistic view of nature by scientists, and with the move towards realism and positivism in philosophy. It had important political repercussions, since it undermined the authority of rulers who had relied on ritual and symbolism for legitimation, and in France it helped pave the way for revolution.[11] As the French Revolution proceeded, some ultra-rationalists argued that the new republic should not need symbols at all; that symbols were relics of a past age when the people had been kept in ignorance, and that 'a people with access to print and public discussion needed no icons'.[12] Most revolutionaries, however, accepted the use of symbols both as representations of public authority and as tools of propaganda.[13] French revolutionaries could not do without symbolism, for now the legitimacy of the state rested not on the king but on the nation, and the nation is an abstraction which can only be imagined through symbolism. In the course of the revolution, therefore, quite elaborate systems of symbol and ritual were created to represent the nation.

Much of this symbolism failed to outlive the revolution, but a few key symbols survived, most notably the flag (the tricolour), the anthem ('La Marseillaise'), and the personification of the nation (Marianne).[14] The novelty of the French symbols was that they had no association with a ruling dynasty: they represented the idea that the nation was equivalent to the people. They also set a precedent that other states (monarchies as well as republics) would follow: it came to be expected that every state would have a flag, an anthem, and some sort of visual emblem or emblems which would represent the nation on coins, state seals and so on. Democratisation was generally accompanied by a simplification of the symbolism of the state: in comparison to the symbolic panoply of royalty, the symbols of republics were few. However, these official symbols took their place alongside a host of other national symbols and a variety of newly invented national traditions: language, dress, music, literature, architecture and folklore all came to be seen as part of the nation's unique 'way of life'; distinctive aspects of the landscape became emblematic and were linked to 'national character'; and history was a source of such symbols as national heroes and founding documents.[15]

The proliferation of national symbols occurred despite the continuing suspicion of symbolism on the part of rationalist liberals, some of whom only tolerated it 'as a reluctant concession to the irrationalism of the lower orders',[16] but by the late nineteenth century there was widespread recognition by intellectuals 'that whatever held human collectivities together it was not the rational calculation of their individual members'.[17] Nevertheless, the idea that only 'backward' and possibly irrational people attach great importance to symbols remains influential today. When parts of Europe such as Northern Ireland or the Balkans are said to be afflicted with tribalism,[18] the implication is not just that ethnic loyalties in these regions are too strong but also that the local people exhibit an excessive attachment to myths, rituals and symbols, comparable to that of supposedly 'primitive', 'tribal' societies in Africa and elsewhere. 'Civilised' people, in this view, should be able to conduct politics through reasoned debate, on the basis of rational assessments of their interests; they should not be stirred by atavistic appeals to rally round the totems of the tribe.[19] This dismissal of symbolism underestimates the extent to which, unavoidably, people understand the world through symbols. Nations and states, in particular, are entities which cannot be perceived or represented except in symbolic form. These 'imagined political communities', as Benedict Anderson calls them,[20] are imagined by means of symbols. Groups of people become nations by identifying with common symbols, and individuals become aware of their membership in the nation as they become conscious that they share their attachment to certain symbols with others. They generally also imagine that these symbols mean the same thing to all members of the nation, but in fact common symbols do not necessarily indicate common beliefs. On the contrary, they are useful precisely because they make possible what David Kertzer calls 'solidarity without consensus'.[21]

Symbols and solidarity

It is the ambiguity of symbols that gives them such an important role in the creation of social solidarity. They are ambiguous both because the same symbol can be interpreted by different individuals in different ways, and because for each person a given symbol will represent diverse ideas which interact in the individual's subconscious and become associated together in her or his mind.[22] This ambiguity works on two levels. There may be different ideas about what a symbol stands for: whether it stands for the nation, the state, or a particular political party, for example. But there will also be different ideas about the nature of the thing symbolised; so, in the case of national symbols, there will be a variety of interpretations of the values and ideals of the nation for which they stand. Symbols gain much of their power from the rich mixture of meanings and associations which they evoke. Different meanings may come to the fore in different contexts,[23] while both the symbol itself and the thing for which it stands will have very individual histories of cognitive and emotional associations. The associations of a particular symbol for each individual are the result of that person's unique life experiences, but, at the same time, they are learned socially. People learn about the importance of symbols, and gain ideas about their meanings, through collective activities and forums (rituals, school lessons, parental homilies, the mass media). As a result, the individual's interpretation of symbols is strongly influenced by the views of other members of social groups to which he or she belongs.

The range of possible meanings of symbols, then, is somewhat circumscribed, but their degree of ambiguity is nonetheless considerable. Because of this ambiguity, people can identify with a common symbol while disagreeing about precisely what it stands for.[24] The only point on which members of the group need to agree is that the symbol does in fact represent them. Social cohesion can be threatened, however, if ambiguity gives way to open conflict over meaning.[25] It is not unusual for social groups to go through periods in which the meaning of their symbols is openly debated, and this book concentrates on one such period. In the long term, however, no group can maintain cohesion if the meaning of its symbols is continually contested from within the group. Such ongoing contestation destroys the illusion of consensus on fundamental values, leading to fragmentation and schism.

As Eric Hobsbawm argues, it is 'the invention of emotionally and symbolically charged signs of club membership rather than the statutes and objects of the club' which is important in developing social solidarity.[26] The shared sense of identity of 'club' members is reinforced not only by their attachment to common symbols, but also by the knowledge that those who are excluded from the club do not share this attachment: 'they' are distinguished from 'us' by the fact that their symbols are different from ours. In this way symbols act as boundary markers, dividing at the same time as they unite. Where social groups are in conflict, their respective symbols will be placed, rhetorically, in opposition to each other. In such situations symbols become a focus for conflict, as members of each group denigrate or even physically attack the symbols of the other, and in the process divisions between the two are perpetuated. This has been the situation in Ireland, where nationalist and unionist identities developed in opposition to each other, and where these oppositional identities have been reinforced by the fact that each group takes offence at the other's symbols. 'In Ireland', the narrator of G.A. Birmingham's satirical novel *The Red Hand of Ulster* (1912) observes wryly, 'we only hoist flags with a view to irritating our enemies'.[27]

The power of symbols both to unite and to divide comes from their strong emotional associations. People feel strongly about national symbols because they feel strongly about the nation for which those symbols stand, but symbols also play an important role in allowing people to imagine the nation as an entity towards which emotion is properly directed. The strength of emotional response to a symbol is, like its meaning, highly contextual and individual. Even the most hardened cynics may find themselves overcome with emotion when they see a symbol of their nation in time of national crisis, at an exciting international sporting event, or when travelling abroad and feeling homesick.[28] Likewise, an individual memory of seeing a particular symbol at a time of great emotion in the past may re-evoke those feelings in the present, giving a very personal charge to the collective experience of viewing the symbol. It is because strong emotional associations are such a defining characteristic of symbols that I include national anthems in the category of national symbols. The mood of a song's music, combined with its lyrics, can convey a much clearer message than is possible with simple visual emblems. However, while the musical and lyrical messages are certainly important, they take second place, in the case of national anthems, to emotional associations, and this is what gives them symbolic status. As the French nationalist ideologue Maurice Barrès wrote in 1902: 'One sings "La Marseillaise" for its words, of course, but [especially] for the mass of emotions that it stirs in our subconscious!'[29] The tune of the anthem alone is usually enough to evoke these emotions, and Ireland is not the only country where many people are unsure of their anthem's lyrics.

As David Kertzer argues, the emotional investment of individuals in symbols is partly a result of the important role which symbols play in providing people with a continuous and stable sense of identity.[30] Continuity in the symbolism of groups to which individuals feel they belong can provide a comforting sense of continuity and coherence of individual identity. People may find changes in national life, and consequent changes in the relationship of individuals to the rest of the national community, unsettling. If the symbols of the nation remain the same, however, those individuals may feel reassured that the essential meaning of their membership of the national community remains unchanged. This link between group symbolism and individual identity helps to explain the vehemence with which some people oppose changes to national symbolism; indeed, people often find it easier to change their beliefs than to change their symbols.

A sense of continuity, so important to individual identity, is also crucial to the imagining of national identity. Just as the knowledge that people throughout the country are saluting the same flag and singing the same anthem helps individuals to imagine themselves as part of a present-day national community, so, too, the knowledge that people in the past saluted this flag and sang this anthem makes it easier to imagine that previous generations belonged to the same national community. Although all symbols are devised at particular points in history, they can, within a generation of their invention, begin to link the living and the dead. More-over, the mystique of antiquity is such that people may make extravagant claims about the age of their symbols, if only in rhetoric; they may claim, for example, that their flag has 'braved a thousand years/The battle and the breeze'.[31] The symbols themselves may also point to the distant past, as in the case of the Cambodian flag, emblazoned with the image of Angkor Wat. Likewise, people can imagine that their symbols provide a link to the future of their nation; that generations to come will be honour-ing the same symbols and thereby keeping the nation's identity intact. The importance of symbols in making possible a sense of historical continuity is another factor which creates resistance to changing the group's symbols. Even political radicals can be remarkably conservative about their symbols, so that socialists sing of the red flag: 'It witnessed many a deed and vow – / We must not change its colour now.'[32]

Symbols of state

Symbols, then, make possible the imagining of nations, the marking of inclusion in and exclusion from the nation, and the development within nations of solidarity without consensus. This book is not concerned with the full range of national symbols, however, but deals principally with official symbols of state: symbols chosen by governments and given offi-cial sanction by legislation or usage. A state is a political community liv-ing within a defined territory under the authority of a government. States are also imagined communities, and they are usually imagined in terms of their relationship to a particular nation, although some are explicitly multinational. Most, if not all, governments rely on the idea of the nation to legitimate the state. In some cases, as in both parts of Ireland, a partic-ular ethnic or national group is dominant within the state, in which case the symbols of that group are likely to be used to represent the state. In other cases, as in Indonesia, for example, governments try to use symbols to create a nation out of the diversity of ethnic or national groups living within the boundaries of the state. Either way, official symbols of state are a point at which nation and state intersect, so debates about state symbols often focus on the relationship between the state and people's ideas of the nation.

Every state in the modern world must select certain official symbols to show that it has joined the 'club' of states. In choosing official symbols, a government proclaims the uniqueness of the state, but simultaneously conforms to universally recognised conventions of statehood.[33] Furthermore, the symbols themselves tend to fit common patterns: flags are rectangular in shape and are unlikely to include either drab browns or shocking pinks among their colours;[34] anthems are frequently militant in their lyrics and have a solid rhythm in their music (either the stately rhythm of hymns or the brisker rhythm of military marches);[35] state seals or coats of arms often follow the conventions of European heraldry, even in countries with no heraldic tradition, or with separate heraldic traditions of their own. As Raymond Firth explains, this similarity in diversity is due to the fact that such symbols are 'not autonomously conceived, but [derive] much of their meaning from the contrast that each presents to others of the same general class'.[36] The principal symbols of the state are the flag and anthem, and the emblems which appear on the state seal or coat of arms, the coinage, banknotes and stamps. Seals, currency and stamps are appurtenances of states, not of nations; even when they are issued by rebel movements, this is done in an attempt to create an embryo state within the existing state. Flags and anthems, however, can belong either to states, or to nations, or to both; the fact that they are routinely referred to as *national* flags and anthems only heightens the confusion. For example, the Welsh flag represents a nation to which no state corresponds; the Union Jack is the flag of a multinational state, and was once the flag of a multinational empire; the Irish tricolour is used not only as the flag of a state (the Republic of Ireland) but also by nationalists in Northern Ireland as the flag of a nation (Ireland). This ambiguity is the source of some of the conflict over flags and anthems which I will explore in this book.

In politically stable states, based on a widely accepted sense of nationality, state symbols are part of what Michael Billig calls 'banal nationalism'. Banal nationalism is the nationalism of the status quo. In contrast to the self-conscious assertions of nationality characteristic of separatist, expansionist or fascist nationalisms, banal nationalism depends on the continual reinforcement of national identity by symbols and practices which are part of everyday life.[37] As a state becomes established there will be a diffusion of the dominant national symbols: the national flag will fly from government buildings, the national anthem will be played on radio and television, the coat of arms or some other national emblem will appear on public buildings and official documents. In time, these symbols are no longer consciously noticed in the ordinary course of everyday life, but they remain important, acting as 'reminders of nationhood [which] serve to turn background space into homeland space'.[38] People do not stop caring about national symbols just because they no longer consciously notice them, and even when nationalism has become banal, national symbols can still stir emotions, particularly on ritual occasions. These latent emotions can be roused, too, by politicians and others who manipulate symbols.

Debates about national symbols

Nationalism and national symbols may, in the long run, become banal, but this does not mean that such symbols are politically neutral or simply an expression of 'national spirit'. As Geoffrey Cubitt reminds us, 'Repertoires of national symbols do not arise painlessly from consensual reflection on a naturally homogeneous national experience; they are forged in conditions of contest between different political and social as well as cultural interests.'[39] There are times in the history of all states and nations when nationalism is far from banal, and when people's feelings about national symbols are not latent but widely displayed and articulated. At such times, the meaning of national symbols, and their appropriateness as representations of the nation, is actively debated. Obvious examples are the periods immediately following radical changes in political structures, such as the French and Russian revolutions, and times of political upheaval and intense competition over the future direction of the nation, as in Weimar Germany. This book deals primarily with a period in the history of the two Irish states which took them from their formation to their political stabilisation.[40] The period of formation and consolidation of a new state is an ideal one for the historical investigation of national symbols. The government must select official symbols to represent the newly independent polity, and this not only leads to the production of official documents about national symbols, but also provokes discussion in the general community about these symbols. Moreover, uncertainty and insecurity about the future, amidst the turmoil that almost inevitably accompanies the formation of a new state, give such debates an emotional charge which is usually greater than in more stable societies.

There are a number of reasons why the selection of official symbols can become the subject of passionate debate. The ambiguity of symbols, the fact that they have no agreed meaning, except perhaps in very general terms, leaves scope for conflict. At the same time, the concreteness of symbols, the fact that they have a single, unchanging form, leads people to believe that they have a single, unchanging meaning. In debates about symbols people tend to argue as if the symbol can only mean one thing, and the fact that other participants in such debates clearly think it means something else can be attributed to self-deception or to a lack of understanding of the true meaning. People also care about official symbols because they have an emotional attachment to the nation with which the state seeks to associate itself (or, if they are members of a minority nationality within the state, they may have an emotional antipathy towards the dominant nation). Moreover, because official symbols are meant in modern democracies to represent the people of the state, every citizen can feel that she or he has an equal stake in this symbolism. Finally, it is easier to argue about symbols than about more abstract issues of national identity and purpose. It is easier to talk about changing a flag than about changing a complex network of beliefs, values and allegiances. Nevertheless, in arguing about official symbols, people do reveal their underlying ideas, hopes and concerns about state and nation, and this is what makes such debates of interest to the historian.

The two decades following partition which are the focus of this book saw heated debates about official symbols in Ireland. This book looks at the selection of official symbols – flags, anthems, designs on state seals or coats of arms, coins, banknotes and stamps – by the governments of the two newly formed states. It also examines public responses to these symbols in the period from 1922 to 1939. This was a time of bitter conflicts, and the symbols of both states became caught up in these conflicts. In the Irish Free State, conflicts over symbols gradually subsided, but in Northern Ireland symbols have remained extremely divisive up to the present day. The very different official symbols in the two parts of Ireland have also played an important role in both marking and maintaining the division between the two states.

The role that symbols played in perpetuating partition is a particularly clear illustration of the point that symbols are not distractions from the real business of politics, but rather, an integral part of political life. The selection of official symbols can have very real political consequences, and debates about those symbols can bring to light very real concerns and emotions. People care about how nation and state are represented symbolically because these abstractions can be represented in no other way. As David Kertzer puts it, 'Far from being window dressing on the reality that is the nation, symbolism is the stuff of which nations are made.'[41] To contribute to debates about national symbols, then, is to participate in the imagining of the nation, and people will not grow tired of such debates until they grow tired of nations.

Chapter 1
'The wolf-dog lying down and the harp without the crown': Irish national symbols to 1922

By the mid-nineteenth century the Irish were in possession of a well-established set of national symbols. Although the use of some of these symbols can be traced back many centuries, the development of a widely known and accepted group of national symbols was a product of the late eighteenth and early nineteenth centuries, when modern nationalism took root in Ireland. While nationalism created the conditions in which a standard set of national symbols could emerge, the symbols also aided the consolidation of nationalism by providing a focus for national identity. This national identity was not restricted to nationalists, since unionists, too, thought of themselves as Irish, and some national symbols were shared by nationalists and unionists. Others, particularly the green flag and certain anthems, were associated more exclusively with the campaign for some form of Irish self-government. There were also symbols of the United Kingdom which were used mainly by unionists, as well as symbols associated particularly with the Protestant and unionist people of Ulster, which will be discussed in Chapter 4. This chapter deals only with symbols seen as representing Ireland, examining their origins, their rise to popularity, and the meanings associated with them. In the aftermath of the First World War and the Easter Rising these meanings changed for some people, and some previously marginal symbols came to prominence during the political struggles which led to the creation of the two Irish states. The people of Ireland came out of the revolutionary period deeply divided, as old divisions were reinforced and new ones created, and in the new political order these divisions would be manifested partly in the debates about symbols discussed in later chapters.

Emblems of Ireland: origins and popularisation

Writing to the *Cork Examiner* in 1928 to protest at the absence of traditional national symbols from the new coins of the Irish Free State, an

Irishman quoted a verse which he said had been known in his youth by
most schoolboys:

> There is glory in the round towers of Ireland,
> The pretty little shamrock so green;
> The wolf-dog lying down,
> And the harp without the crown
> With the sunburst of Ireland between.[1]

Even if the rhyme itself was not as widely known as the letter-writer
claimed, there can be no doubt that all Irish people were familiar with the
national emblems mentioned in it. The nineteenth-century iconography of
Irish nationalism overflows with harps, shamrocks, round towers,
wolfhounds, sunbursts and Celtic crosses. These emblems were seen as
symbols of Ireland's traditions, particularly its Gaelic traditions, linking
modern Ireland with a distant past. Yet all of them have histories; they
came to be seen as symbols of Ireland at particular times, they were pop-
ularised for particular political reasons, and they gathered about them particular associations.

The harp is the oldest Irish national symbol still in use, and ironically,
in the light of its later associations with Gaelicism and republicanism, it
was an English king who made it an emblem of Ireland. For reasons
unknown, the harp appeared on Henry VIII's Irish coinage around 1534,
surmounted by a crown, and it went on to be used as an Irish device on
maps, charters and coins in the remainder of the sixteenth century and the
beginning of the seventeenth. Its status was confirmed when, in 1603,
Ireland was represented in one quarter of the new royal arms by a golden
harp on a blue field. The use of the harp by the Catholic and Gaelic Irish
dates from 1642, when Owen Roe O'Neill became the first to fly a flag
showing a harp on a green field. In that same year, the harp appeared in
the seal of the Confederate Catholics of Ireland. However, to confuse matters somewhat, a harp on a green field had also been established as the
arms of the province of Leinster by the seventeenth century, and this
usage has coexisted ever since with the use of the harp as a symbol of
Ireland. The harp as an Irish emblem was initially depicted with a plain
forepillar, but in the course of the seventeenth century the forepillar was
increasingly given female form in heraldic usage. Gradually the figure of
the 'maid of Erin' was standardised, and the harp was frequently, though
by no means universally, shown with a forepillar in the shape of the head
and torso of a woman, represented in profile, naked, and often winged.[2]

The harp was well established as an emblem of Ireland by the end of
the seventeenth century, but it was not until the end of the following century that it was transformed from a heraldic into a popular national

symbol due to its association with mass political action and with the increasing tendency to look for inspiration to a romanticised Gaelic past. The Volunteer movement of the late 1770s and early 1780s, whose members were largely Protestant and loyalist but many of whom also supported legislative independence for Ireland, depicted harps on their banners and medals. These banners and medals commonly showed harps surmounted by imperial crowns, but many others showed harps with antique or 'Irish' crowns, and some even abandoned the crown altogether. The widespread use of the harp without the crown, however, began with the birth of Irish republicanism. The republican Society of United Irishmen adopted a seal depicting a harp, surmounted by a liberty cap on top of a pike, and accompanied by the words 'It is new strung and shall be heard'. The green flag bearing an uncrowned golden harp was flown in the rebellion of 1798, and its adoption as the national flag of Ireland dates from this time.[3]

Simultaneously, there was a renewed interest in the harp as a musical instrument. The Belfast Harpers Festival of 1792 brought political radicalism and Gaelic revivalism together: it concluded on Bastille Day and was used as a cover for a meeting of the United Irishmen, but its organisers were genuinely interested in preserving Irish harp music.[4] The music of the few remaining Irish harpers was transcribed and published, and harp societies were established in Dublin and Belfast, precisely because harping had almost ceased to be a living tradition, leaving the harp open for romantic appropriation. At this time the figure of 'the last of the bards' had become popular with romantics throughout Europe as a result of Thomas Gray's poem *The Bard* (1757). The lone bard may have been seen as representing the romantic ideal of the artist following his individual genius, but he also represented the 'traditional' culture that was thought to be disappearing even as intellectuals tried to preserve it.[5] In Ireland, Turlough Carolan (1670–1738), who was commonly though incorrectly known after his death as 'the last Irish harper', 'became the prototype for the romantic image of the Gaelic artist' from the second half of the eighteenth century. The first decades of the nineteenth century saw the harp brought into even greater prominence by Thomas Moore, who used it as a symbol of Ireland's lost golden age, and of its ongoing 'struggle against muteness and cultural amnesia', in enormously popular ballads such as:

> The harp that once through Tara's halls
> The soul of music shed,
> Now hangs as mute on Tara's walls
> As if that soul were fled.[6]

During the nineteenth century the so-called Harp of Brian Boru,[7] its very name reminiscent of Gaelic heroism (though in fact it was made many centuries after the death of the historic King Brian Bóruma), became the preferred model for symbolic harps. It was made popular as a brooch design by Dublin jewellers from the 1850s onwards, and its familiarity was further increased when it was used as the model for the Guinness Brewery trademark.[8]

The harp was often depicted during the nineteenth century twined with another popular national symbol, the shamrock. The shamrock began to be associated with Ireland in the sixteenth century, when English writers noted that the Irish ate shamrocks and other herbs. The practice of wearing shamrocks on St Patrick's Day is first recorded in 1681, and in 1726 a book on the wild plants of Ireland mentioned for the first time the legend that St Patrick used the shamrock to explain the doctrine of the Trinity to the pagan Irish. In the late eighteenth century it was used in the symbolism of both the Volunteers and the United Irishmen, and the adoption of green as the nationalist colour by the United Irishmen no doubt added to the shamrock's appeal to nationalists. 'The wearing of the green' was seen by Ireland's rulers as seditious, but wearing shamrocks was a safe way of displaying national pride, because the shamrock was an acceptable emblem to Catholics and Protestants, nationalists and loyalists alike. The militia and yeomanry forces which fought against the rebels in 1798 used shamrocks in their banners and medals, and the shamrock was commonly shown in loyalist symbolism entwined with the English rose and Scottish thistle, particularly after the passing of the Act of Union in 1800.[9]

In the early part of the nineteenth century, however, the shamrock became caught up in the conflict between liberal and conservative Protestants over Catholic emancipation. One result of this split was that liberal Protestants turned away from the Williamite anniversaries, seeing them as sectarian and divisive, and embraced St Patrick's Day as the national day. They also accepted the symbols of the Patrician tradition (most notably the shamrock) as *the* Irish national symbols, which in turn caused conservative Protestants to regard these as party rather than national symbols. In the 1820s the state came down on the side of the liberals, beginning with the visit of George IV in 1821, when the King repeatedly pointed to the shamrocks on his hat during his progress through Dublin. From 1829, the year of Catholic emancipation, the public appearance of the viceroy, wearing shamrocks, on St Patrick's Day became a popular annual event, and the state's acceptance of the shamrock as an Irish national symbol was confirmed.[10] By 1914 the custom of wearing shamrocks on St Patrick's Day was so politically innocuous that Belfast's unionist *Northern Whig* could observe: 'Irishmen, whatever their creed or politics have an affectionate regard for St Patrick's Day and yesterday the shamrock was worn in honour of the festival by fully nine tenths of the population of the country.'[11] Shamrocks also became a conventional decorative motif in the nineteenth century, used on harps, coins, buildings, gravestones, street lamps, jewellery, pottery, glassware and book covers, and by mid-century, if not before, 'the shamrock shore' was an established name for Ireland.[12]

The harp and shamrock were probably the two most widely used national symbols in nineteenth century Ireland, but there were a number of other well-known Irish emblems. The Irish wolfhound was being used as a national symbol by the late eighteenth century, though by the early nineteenth century the breed itself had almost died out. However, its popularity in nationalist imagery kept interest in the wolfhound alive, and led to the founding of the Irish Wolfhound Club in 1885, which successfully re-established the breed. The wolfhound could act as a national symbol because it was considered native to Ireland, and it may also have been associated with the hounds which appear in Irish mythology. It seems to have been linked, too, to the Gaelic aristocracy, as in Lady Morgan's novel *O'Donnel* (1814), in which a descendant of the chiefs of Tirconnel finally returns to his inherited domains, where 'his faithful Irish wolf dog lay at his feet, and his affectionate Irish follower stood proudly by'.[13]

Round towers came to be seen as representing Ireland because of their antiquity and their distinctiveness: they are found almost exclusively in Ireland and do not resemble buildings elsewhere in Europe. They seem to have become national symbols in the early part of the nineteenth century, a time when the towers were the subject of a major scholarly debate between those who saw them as pre-Christian structures linked to various Eastern religious practices and others who believed them to be ecclesiastical buildings constructed after the introduction of Christianity to Ireland. The mystery was solved to the satisfaction of most Irish scholars following the publication in 1845 of a book by the prominent antiquarian George Petrie, who established that the round towers dated from the Christian period and had been used as belfries and as refuges in case of attack. Despite Petrie's demystification of the towers, they remained important at a popular level because, as Joep Leerssen points out: 'Unlike the mysterious and the irretrievable disparition [sic] of ancient Irish culture, lost, inaccessible and largely unknown, the Round Towers were still part of the here and now; they formed a physical link with a past that was so mysterious and unknown that it may just as well have been wholly non-existent.'[14] Thus, the Dominican preacher the Reverend Thomas Burke told an audience in 1872 that the round towers were 'the strongest argument for the ancient civilization of our race', while initiates into the Ancient Order of Hibernians in America were brought face to finial with a facsimile round tower and instructed to 'read the lesson of the Tower. Time must not change the Irishman'.[15]

By establishing the Christian origins of the towers, Petrie's research paved the way for the incorporation of newly constructed round towers into churches, probably as part of the competition between the Roman Catholic church and the Church of Ireland to claim continuity with the ancient Celtic church. Petrie himself was involved in planning a memorial to Daniel O'Connell in Glasnevin cemetery, Dublin, which eventually took the form of an enormous round tower. Much more common in cemeteries than round towers were Celtic crosses. Based on another relic of early Celtic Christianity, the high cross, Celtic crosses proliferated in Irish graveyards during the nineteenth century, and also came to be regarded as national symbols.[16]

Finally, the sun came to be considered a distinctively Irish emblem, though such symbolism was by no means unique to Ireland, and was probably introduced into Irish symbolism by way of Freemasonry.[17] However, the idea that the sun was a Masonic symbol would have horrified most Catholic Irish nationalists, who preferred to believe that it was an ancient Irish device. Rising suns and 'sunbursts' (the sun appearing from behind a cloud) were employed in some eighteenth century Volunteer and United Irish symbolism, on a membership card of the Repeal Association in the 1840s, and in the poetry of Young Ireland writers, and the sunburst was adopted by the Fenians as one of their principal symbols.[18]

National symbols, popular politics and Gaelic revivalism

By the 1830s a set of national symbols had developed, and over the following decades their use individually and, increasingly, in combination with each other became commonplace. Two developments in Ireland in the 1830s and 1840s contributed to the standardisation of the set of national symbols: Gaelic revivalism and popular nationalist politics. Interest in the Gaelic past had begun in the eighteenth century, when Protestant antiquarians began studying Irish archaeology, language, folklore and poetry. Their activities culminated in 1785 in the establishment of the Royal Irish Academy, which became the centre of research into Irish civilisation, but such research had little immediate impact on Irish culture or politics.[19] However, antiquarian study continued, as did research into the Irish language, and it prepared the way for another round of Gaelic revivalism in the 1830s which was to have greater impact outside the ranks of scholars. The key figure in this second wave of Gaelic revivalism was George Petrie, whose important work on round towers has already been mentioned. Petrie was personally involved in almost every aspect of the renewed interest in Celtic civilisation: as a researcher, as a promoter through his journalism and his paintings, and as a prodigious organiser of others who shared his interests.

For Petrie and his colleagues it was in the Irish past, and particularly in the golden age of the early medieval period, that Irish people could find inspiration and common cause despite their political and religious differences.[20] The *Dublin Penny Journal* (1832–3), which Petrie co-edited, declared its intention to promote 'a national concordant feeling in a country divided by religious and political discord' and to seek in Irish history examples which could effect 'a moral and practical improvement' in national life.[21] It was in this journal that a very influential woodcut appeared in 1832 showing an assemblage of the established national symbols: harp, seated wolfhound, shamrocks and Milesian crown in the foreground, and a round tower in the distance.[22] It seems likely that these national symbols were increasingly seen as a set, and depicted together, because they were now being thought of as emblems of the Gaelic past. Thus, the harp was the instrument of the Gaelic bards; the shamrock was the plant used by St Patrick to explain the doctrine of the Trinity to the pagan Celts; the wolfhound was the faithful companion of Finn Mac Cumhaill in Irish legend; the round tower represented the glories of Celtic Christianity; and the sunburst was the device which had appeared on the ancient banners of Gaelic Ireland.

If Gaelic revivalism caused people to see the existing national symbols as a set, Daniel O'Connell's campaign for repeal of the Union and his carefully staged 'monster meetings' in the 1840s provided both a reason and an opportunity for popularising this set of symbols. Having won Catholic emancipation, O'Connell's cause was now an explicitly nationalist one, so it was important that he associate himself with the emblems of Irish nationality: hence, the harpers in 'Celtic' costume at his monster meetings, the 'repeal cap' supposedly based on the Milesian or Irish 'crown' which he wore, and the portrait of him with wolfhound and what may be the ruin of a round tower in the background. This was perhaps an attempt to equip O'Connell with the real or imagined accoutrements of Gaelic chieftainship, and it is significant that the 'Irish crown' largely disappeared as a national symbol after his death, presumably because it had become too closely associated with O'Connell personally. A song mourning O'Connell's death even had the national symbols joining in the lamentation:

> Poor Granu sleeps while her wolf dog's stolen,
> Her harp string's broken to sound no more,
> And the Irish tower seems to rend asunder,
> From Derrynane down to Derry shore.[23]

However, with the exception of the Irish crown, these symbols were sufficiently well established at a popular level to outlive O'Connell. The
repeal campaign relied heavily on visual symbols: in a society where
many people were still illiterate, and where many in the huge crowds
which attended political meetings had no hope of hearing the speeches,
symbolism and ritual were crucial means of political communication. The
use of national symbols was part of this system of visual communication,
and they began to appear not just singly, but as a group in repeal banners
and the banners of pro-repeal trade guilds.[24]

The relationship between Gaelic revivalism, the development of popular nationalist politics and the standardisation of the set of national symbols is by no means straightforward. Neither Petrie and his colleagues nor
O'Connell and his lieutenants were revivalists in the sense of seeking to
preserve Gaelic civilisation as a living culture. The antiquarians wished to
revive an interest in Irish civilisation, but they fully expected the Irish language and other aspects of Gaelic culture to die out. They merely sought
to collect as much information as possible about this culture before it disappeared, so that future generations could be inspired by it. As for
O'Connell, though a native Irish speaker himself, he was philosophical
about the displacement of the Irish language by English and indifferent to
antiquarian research into the Irish past. He might curse the day the
invaders disrupted the pious and heroic Gaelic civilisation, and dream of
reviving the period when Ireland was a centre of learning and religion, but
his attachment to the Irish past found expression only in his love of
Thomas Moore's ballads, in which the disappearance of Ireland's ancient
civilisation was contemplated with equal parts nostalgia, mourning and
resignation. O'Connell was a moderniser, more influenced by liberalism
than by romanticism, and it may have been precisely for this reason that
he felt the need to appeal to his more conservative followers by using
symbols which had come to represent national traditions. Furthermore,
the use of such emblems of tradition was part of what George Mosse has
called 'the nationalisation of the masses'. By mobilising the Catholic
peasantry, O'Connell had created mass politics in Ireland, and as in other
European countries the development of a new politics required the development of 'a new political style which would transform the crowd into a
coherent political force'. The use of national symbols was part of this new
style; by giving a prominent place to symbols of the nation, the crowd was
reminded that their identity as members of the Irish nation was more
important than their other allegiances to class, region or (somewhat more
problematically) religion.[25]

Also crucial to the nationalisation of the Irish masses was the Young
Ireland newspaper, the *Nation*, founded in 1842. It quickly achieved a circulation of over 10,000 with an estimated readership of over 250,000, and

its impact was not restricted to the literate, thanks to public reading and discussion of its contents.[26] The *Nation* was not illustrated, but its poems and stories mentioned national symbols and celebrated the glorious past with which these symbols were associated.[27] Its writers looked to this past for inspiration to strive for an equally glorious future, a view of the past exemplified in D.F. McCarthy's poem 'The Pillar Towers of Ireland', which called the round towers 'Bright prophets of the future, as preachers of the past!'[28] The Young Irelanders (particularly their leading figure, Thomas Davis) were influenced by romantic nationalism and were more insistent than earlier Irish nationalists that political independence must go hand in hand with the cultivation of cultural distinctiveness. In this way, they helped to create a climate of opinion in which emblems of this distinctiveness could flourish, and it is little wonder that in later years W.B. Yeats associated clichéd harp-shamrock-wolfhound-and-round-tower imagery with Young Ireland.[29]

Such imagery became all pervasive in Ireland from around the middle of the nineteenth century, as mass production aided both the standardisation and the dissemination of these symbols, bringing items on which they were emblazoned into the homes of people of all classes. The symbols appeared in various combinations with each other, but a typical depiction of the full set of symbols would show the figure of Erin, seated and resting one arm on a harp, a wolfhound lying at her feet, shamrocks strewn around, a round tower in the distance, and on the horizon, probably across the ocean, a rising sun representing the long-awaited dawn of Irish freedom. These symbols were used as decorative motifs on the fronts of pubs and shops, in churches, on gravestones and funerary monuments, on furniture, in jewellery and ornaments carved from bog oak, on glassware, pottery and porcelain. Belleek Pottery, manufacturers of pottery and porcelain which was often decorated with national symbols, adopted a trademark around 1857 consisting of a harp, wolfhound, round tower and shamrocks.[30]

In addition to their decorative uses, these national symbols continued to have political meaning. The nationalist newspaper *United Ireland* in 1881 called the wolfhound and round tower emblems of 'our sleepless fidelity' and 'our unbroken traditions',[31] and given that these emblems represented continuity with Ireland's past it is not surprising to find them appearing on political monuments and patriot graves, from the O'Connell monument in Dublin (completed in 1882) to the memorial erected in Waverley cemetery, Sydney, Australia, to commemorate the centenary of the 1798 rebellion. They were also used by nationalist brotherhoods such as the Ancient Order of Hibernians and the Irish National Foresters, and appeared on nationalist banners during the long campaign for Irish Home Rule. As late as the First World War, Irish Parliamentary Party leader

John Redmond was addressing public meetings beneath banners depicting round tower, Celtic cross, wolfhound, harp and shamrocks.[32] Nor was the use of such symbols restricted to constitutionalists: even the Irish Republican Brotherhood's newspaper, *Irish Freedom*, carried advertisements for such items as 'Very pretty Silver Brooch of ROUND TOWER, HARP AND WOLF DOG. Word "Erin" embossed and Shamrocks'.[33] Thus, it might have been expected that when Ireland achieved self-government its politicians would continue to surround themselves with these symbols, in the manner of the candidate depicted in a *Dublin Opinion* cartoon in 1923.[34] The rise of Sinn Féin, however, was to confound such expectations.

Personifications of Ireland

Although the female personification of Ireland was often depicted together with the other national symbols discussed above, the tradition of using a human figure to symbolise the nation deserves to be treated separately because of its complexity. Many nations possess both female and male personifications, and this gender division is as important in symbolism as it is in social life. As Marina Warner explains:

> The female form tends to be perceived as generic and universal, with symbolic overtones; the male as individual, even when it is being used to express a generalized idea...John Bull typifies the Englishman; Uncle Sam and Brother Jonathan the US citizen. But Liberty can hardly be said to represent the typical American woman, or Britannia the Englishwoman of collective consciousness. Men are individual, they appear to be in command of their own characters and their own identity, to live inside their own skins, and they do not include women in their symbolic embrace: John Bull, however comic, can never be a cow. But the female form does not refer to particular women, does not describe women as a group, and often does not even presume to evoke their natures. We can all live inside Britannia or Liberty's skin, they stand for us regardless of sex, yet we cannot identify with them as characters. Uncle Sam and John Bull are popular figures; they can be grim, sly, feisty, pathetic, absurd, for they have personality. Liberty, like many abstract concepts expressed in the feminine, is in deadly earnest and one-dimensional. Above all, if John Bull appears angry, it is his anger he expresses; Liberty is not representing her own freedom.[35]

The essential characteristics of the gender division outlined by Warner, between the male figure as individual and active, and the female as generic or universal and passive, holds true for Ireland.

The creation of a figure representing the 'typical' man of his nation requires the development of at least a proto-national consciousness, so it was not until the late seventeenth century that such a figure appeared in Ireland. He came on the scene at a time when the Gaelic Irish had been made conscious of their religious and cultural distinctiveness as a result of the extensive colonisation of Ireland by English and Scottish Protestants. It was also a time when Irish Catholics were united as never before following the accession to the throne of the Catholic James II. Gaelic poets, anticipating and exulting at the impending triumph of the Gael, began to refer to the Irish people by the common male name 'Tadhg'. At the same time, the character of the stage Irishman in English drama was being given the names 'Teague' or 'Teg', a usage which survives in present-day Northern Ireland, where 'Taig' is a derogatory term for a Catholic.[36] By the nineteenth century the typical Irishman was usually known as 'Paddy' or 'Pat', and standard visual representations of him had developed. In British cartoons he was equipped with various stereotypical attributes of Irishness (pipe, shillelagh, and tall, brimless hat). He could be seen as a harmless, comical figure or, when representing Fenianism or other threats to law and order, as an ape-like monster.[37] In Irish cartoons, by contrast, he was:

> the epitome of Irish masculinity. His face was long but full, his forehead high, his chin square, and his nose and mouth straight and firm. There was a twinkle in his eyes and an easygoing smile, marking him as a man prepared to trust anyone of equal good faith...His clothes and bearing signified a respectable tenant who farmed upwards of fifteen or twenty acres.[38]

However, in trying to avoid perpetuating Irish stereotypes, Irish cartoonists gave 'Pat' few, if any, obvious national characteristics, so that it was difficult to distinguish him from an Englishman. There was not, therefore, a distinctive male character like John Bull or Uncle Sam who could have been used in the official iconography of the Irish Free State. In any case, such figures are rarely given official status because, as Marina Warner points out, they are too individual, and too specifically male, to allow all citizens to 'live inside their skins'. The only other type of male figure which might have been used by the Free State was the warrior, either real (the pikemen of 1798 or the Volunteers of 1916–22, who appeared on monuments around the country) or legendary (Cúchulainn).[39] A statue of Cúchulainn by Oliver Sheppard was placed in the General Post Office in Dublin in 1936 as a memorial to the Easter Rising, and this statue provided the model for a medal issued in 1941 to veterans of the rising and war of independence. But apart from memorials and medals, it was perhaps too dangerous to use images of warriors in official designs when the state was still under threat from would-be Cúchulainns.

The female personification of Ireland can be traced back much further than the male. In Old and Middle Irish literature, the inauguration of kings was described as a marriage between the king and a goddess representing the land, and this marriage was said to make land and people fertile. Another version of this idea appeared in the 'Loathly Lady' stories in which the sons of a king are confronted by a hideous old woman who demands that one of them sleep with her. When one of the sons agrees to do so, he is rewarded by the transformation of the hag into a beautiful woman who announces that she is 'the Sovereignty of Éire'. Despite the abolition of Irish kingship in the twelfth century, this idea lived on in Gaelic poetry, and the poets worried that without a mate Éire would lose her beauty and her fertility. Following the 'flight of the earls' and the rapid increase in British settlement in Ireland at the beginning of the seventeenth century, the concern of the poets turned to despair. Now Ireland began to be depicted as a whore or a mother who had abandoned her children, or alternatively as a woman deserted by her husband and sons. In a poem by Aogán Ó Rathaille (*c.* 1675–1729), Ireland is:

> Tír bhocht bhuaidheartha, is uaigneach céasta,
> Tír gan fear, gan mac, gan chéile
>
> (A poor, afflicted, lonely and tortured land,
> A land without a man, without a son, without a spouse.)[40]

In the eighteenth century, Jacobitism gave the poets renewed hope, and more optimistic female personifications of Ireland appeared in the aisling or vision poems. In these poems a beautiful woman appears to the poet in a dream; she reveals that she is Ireland and tells him of her woes, but ends by reassuring him that the triumph of the Irish is coming. Aisling poetry had largely died out by the end of the eighteenth century, but the idea was brought into literature in the English language in the 1840s by James Clarence Mangan, whose translations and adaptations of aisling poems became widely known. The tradition also continued in popular ballads in English, in which Ireland may appear either as a beautiful young woman or as a grey-haired old lady, often called the Shan Van Vocht (seanbhean bhocht, poor old woman). The allegorical female figure is often given a name such as Caitlín Ní Uallacháin (anglicised as Cathleen ni Houlihan), Róisín Dubh (who became 'Dark Rosaleen' in Mangan's most famous adaptation of an aisling) or Granuaile. In most cases the name itself probably had no significance initially, but was simply the name of a woman in a conventional love song whose tune was used for a patriotic song. Granuaile, however, was originally a historical figure, Gráinne Ní Mháille (Grace O'Malley), a woman who fought the English in County Mayo in the late sixteenth century, and hence had obvious patriotic associations.[41]

Apart from the Gaelic tradition, there are two other important strands which contributed to the image of Ireland as woman. The first was the post-Counter-Reformation cult of the Virgin Mary. Not only was the Virgin seen as Ireland's protector, she also provided a model for the image of Ireland itself as virgin. In 1618, Aodh Mac Aingil wrote that Ireland was 'a pure maiden in the faith, and kept her maidenhood for Christ since the time she accepted the faith through the preaching of our noble apostle, nor ever yielded to any kind of error or heresy'.[42] If Ireland's steadfast adherence to Catholicism was equated with virginity then, by implication, attempts to convert Ireland amounted to seduction or rape. Needless to say, the potential seducers or rapists were the English, and determination to resist English domination could also be likened to the preservation of virginity. Like Mary, Ireland was both virgin and mother,[43] a mother whose purity could be a source of pride to her children. The Reverend Thomas Burke saw on Mother Ireland's brows:

> a crown of thorns and on her hands the time-worn chains of slavery. Yet upon that mother's face I see the light of faith, of purity, and of God; and far dearer to me is my mother Ireland, a nation in her sorrow to-day, than if I beheld her rich, and commonplace, and vulgar, and impure, and forgetful of herself and of God.[44]

Here the image of Ireland as woman fuses the Christian tradition of virgin saints, martyred for the faith, with the Gaelic tradition of sorrowful Éire.[45]

The other influence on the image of Ireland as woman was the classical tradition of personifying countries, and virtues, in female form. This tradition was essentially that of the educated elite, which in Ireland before the nineteenth century was largely Protestant. From the seventeenth century onwards, a female personification of Ireland, often called by the Latin name Hibernia, appeared on coins and medals, and in books and cartoons. As Irish Protestants began to resent England's failure to address their political and economic grievances, allegorical female figures began to be used by critics of the government. A good example is Jonathan Swift's pamphlet *The Story of the Injured Lady*, written around the time of the Union of England and Scotland in 1707, in which the injured lady (Ireland) complains that she has been betrayed by a man (England) who has chosen another (Scotland) over her, having previously professed love to both. As if this is not bad enough, the man has also been guilty of 'Oppressions' against the Lady, who now wants only to be free of his persecutions so that she can manage her own fortune. In the 1770s and 1780s, Hibernia appeared on the flags and other paraphernalia of the Volunteers, as did the female personification of Liberty. The depiction of Liberty as a woman was another borrowing from classical tradition, separate from but easily conflated with the image of the nation as a woman. In the iconography of the Volunteers and the United Irishmen, a Liberty/Hibernia figure was shown with spear and liberty cap, and the classical influence is apparent in the fact that, unlike later depictions of Ireland as woman, she sometimes appeared naked to the waist.[46]

By the nineteenth century these three traditions of imagining Ireland as a woman had made such female personifications widely accepted as national symbols. Erin or Hibernia appears commonly on banners and in nationalist imagery generally throughout the nineteenth century, but her pose is usually passive, even submissive. Where she appears together with the great Irish political leaders, her position is subordinate to theirs: in Dublin's O'Connell monument, Erin tramples her broken fetters while pointing up to O'Connell, and in a banner from 1885 she kneels before Parnell and takes his hand as if pledging her fealty to Ireland's uncrowned king.[47] More commonly she appears alone, usually seated, and surrounded by the other emblems of Irish nationality. She often has a sorrowful or wistful expression, and it is easy to imagine that she is waiting for a hero to deliver her from bondage. The image of 'Erin wronged' encouraged a chivalric response from Irish nationalists, who were as much in the thrall of Victorian gender stereotypes as their British counterparts. Defence of an idealised and feminised Ireland could merge with defence of virtuous Irish womanhood, as in this passage from Edward Hayes's introduction to the anthology *Ballads of Ireland* (1855):

> Woman has ever been honoured in Ireland with especial reverence...
> [T]he Irishwoman's virtue and beauty have commanded universal respect,
> and made her a national deity almost to be worshipped. This national
> chivalry imparted to the poet's allegory an insinuating and enduring power
> over the heart which no appeal to the passions could possess. Ireland was
> no longer an abstraction, but a familiar being; and still more an afflicted
> woman, a forlorn mother, a fallen Queen, mourning over her sorrows, and
> calling upon her sons to avenge her wrongs and restore her to the dignity
> from which she had fallen.[48]

British and Irish nationalist cartoonists both made use of this sorrowful figure, but they had very different ideas about the nature of Erin's saviour, and of the forces which oppressed her. In British cartoons, she is saved from Fenianism or other forms of lawlessness by John Bull, St George or Britannia (who, though also a woman, is armed and ready for battle). In such representations, beautiful Hibernia represents the soul of Ireland, which remains pure despite the fact that the forces besetting her are themselves Irish. This image could be turned around by Irish cartoonists, so that Erin, under attack by Britain, finds an Irish defender, and the ready reversibility of the image was strikingly displayed in two cartoons published in 1885. A cartoon published in *Punch* showed a sleeping Erin threatened by a vampire representing the National League, but within weeks an Irish newspaper had Erin defending herself with a sword and shield labelled 'National League' against the vampire of 'British Rule'.[49]

This last image is a reminder that figures of Erin were by no means all passive, and a more active Erin, holding a sword or a flag, appeared on some monuments built for the centenary of the 1798 rebellion. Erin's passivity could be seen, not as an innate characteristic, but as a product of British domination and Irish acquiescence. This was clearly illustrated in a Gaelic League poster from 1920, which contrasted two female figures: Éire standing proud, erect, dressed in 'Celtic' costume, spear in hand, and looking to the west; and west Britain, wrapped in the Union Jack, crouching, with her hand outstretched and looking east across the Irish Sea.[50] Around the time of the 1798 centenary, some radical nationalists began to believe that a blood sacrifice was necessary to prevent the transformation of Éire into west Britain. At a practical level, this sacrifice would shock the Irish people out of their apathy, while at a metaphorical level it would give Éire back her youth and vitality. The play *Cathleen ni Houlihan*, written by Lady Gregory and W.B. Yeats, helped to propagate this idea, which harks back to the earlier 'Loathly Lady' tradition, but with the important difference that death replaces sex in effecting the transformation. In *Cathleen ni Houlihan*, which premiered in 1902 with the nationalist activist and noted beauty Maud Gonne in the title role, an old woman is changed into a young girl 'with the walk of a queen' by the willingness of a young man to die in the 1798 rebellion.[51] The young man was to have been married the next day, and the obvious implication is that instead his death will be a kind of marriage to Cathleen ni Houlihan.

It is difficult to measure the effect of this play on those who fought in the Easter Rising, but it was celebrated by Patrick Pearse and other prominent rebels.[52] That the leaders of the rising thought of Ireland as a woman was apparent in the Proclamation of the Republic, in which 'Ireland, through us, summons *her* children to *her* flag and strikes for *her* freedom' (though later in the proclamation the Irish republic and the Irish nation are referred to as 'it').[53] Here the personified Ireland sounds like a Delacroix-style *Liberty Leading the People at the Barricades*,[54] but the imagery of the Easter Rising differed significantly from that of the French republicans. In one of the best known commemorative pictures of the rising, the figure of Erin hovers above Volunteers in the midst of battle, and a white light seems to shine around her in a manner which suggests images of the Assumption of the Virgin Mary.[55] Dressed in virginal white, she holds a tricolour flag in one hand and with the other hand she holds a palm branch across her chest in such a way that, far from having her breasts bared like

Delacroix's Liberty, her breasts are not visible at all. Where Ireland was not, as in this picture, a passive, inspirational figure, she was a mother mourning her dead children, as in the picture entitled 'His Easter offering', which depicted 'a dead Volunteer, having given his life to the cause of Irish Independence, lying at the feet of Cathleen Ni Houlihan'.[56] Pearse, in particular, liked to imagine Ireland as a mother (in his poem 'Mise Éire', for example), and in 'A Mother Speaks', written just before his execution, he identified his own mother with the Virgin Mary.[57] The 1916 memorial in Dublin's Glasnevin cemetery, which takes the form of a *pietà* with Pearse as the dead Christ, would have pleased him greatly.

Even before the rising, at least one prominent separatist was unhappy with the cult of Cathleen ni Houlihan. Eoin MacNeill, the Chief of Staff of the Irish Volunteers who was deliberately deceived about plans for a rising, organised lectures to ensure that the Volunteers realised that Cathleen ni Houlihan was a pagan deity and that worship of her was idolatrous. In his memorandum of February 1916, arguing against a rising based on the blood sacrifice doctrine rather than on mass support for revolutionary action, MacNeill reminded his colleagues that:

> what we call our country is not a poetical abstraction, as some of us, perhaps all of us, in the exercise of our highly developed capacity for figurative thought, are sometimes apt to imagine – with the help of our patriotic literature. There is no such person as Caitlin Ni Uallachain or Roisin Dubh or the Sean-bhean Bhocht, who is calling upon us to serve her. What we call our country is the Irish nation, which is a concrete and visible reality.[58]

MacNeill's words failed to deter the devotees of Cathleen ni Houlihan, however, and it was only after the Civil War exposed the dangers of an over-developed capacity for figurative thought that others joined him in condemning the idea of Ireland as a woman calling on men to die for her.

Flags and anthems before 1916

Throughout the nineteenth century and into the early twentieth century the undisputed flag of nationalist Ireland was that which depicted a golden harp on a green background (hereafter referred to as the green harp flag). The adoption of green as the nationalist colour probably has its origins in traditional poetic descriptions of Ireland as a green land, and of its female personification as wrapped in a green cloak. This tradition within Gaelic literature may explain why as early as 1642 Owen Roe O'Neill flew a flag showing a harp on a green field. In the 1790s the colour green gained another layer of meaning through its association with the symbolism of the liberty tree, taken up by Irish republicans in imitation of their French and American counterparts. The United Irishmen and their supporters made widespread use of green uniforms, sashes, ribbons, cockades and other emblems, and the United Irishman William Drennan was probably the first person to call Ireland 'the Emerald Isle' in his revolutionary poem 'Erin' (1795).[59]

In 1798 rebels across Ireland flew the green harp flag, which at least one United Irish proclamation called the 'National Flag of the Sacred Green'. The very idea of a national, as opposed to a dynastic flag was a radical one, pioneered by the American and French revolutionaries, and the use of such language is indicative of the birth of modern nationalism in Ireland in the 1790s. By the time of O'Connell's campaigns the use of the green harp flag was commonplace and genuinely popular. When the Party Processions Act banned the carrying of flags or other symbols which might arouse political hostility, nationalists responded by parading with green branches (often stripped from the estates of wealthy landlords and thus doubly symbolic). By the 1880s green harp flags were ubiquitous at Home Rule demonstrations, and this banner was routinely referred to by nationalists as the national flag.[60] There is some evidence that the green harp flag was gaining greater acceptance in British and unionist circles by the early twentieth century, and it was sometimes made more 'loyal' by adding a crown above the harp or a Union Jack in the canton.[61] However, to hardline loyalist opinion the display of the uncrowned green harp flag remained subversive.[62]

In an effort to overcome Protestant and unionist aversion to the green harp flag, a new flag was created in 1848. From the 1830s, nationalists sometimes combined their own colour, green, with the orange of the Protestant and loyalist Orange Order, in cockades and banners. In 1848, when the republican revolution in France brought the French tricolour to prominence once again, sympathisers with the French Republic began to fly the Irish tricolour. It was in 1848 that a delegation of Young Irelanders travelled to Paris, and at a reception on their return to Dublin, Thomas Francis Meagher presented an orange, white and green tricolour, explaining its symbolism as follows: 'The white in the centre signifies a lasting truce between the "Orange" and the "Green", and I trust that beneath its folds the hands of the Irish Protestant and the Irish Catholic may be clasped in generous and heroic brotherhood.' On the same occasion, John Mitchel said that he hoped 'to see that flag one day waving, as our national banner, over a forest of Irish pikes'. Mitchel never saw that day, but some seventy years later the tricolour would be transformed into a national banner following its use in the Easter Rising. After 1848, however, the tricolour disappeared almost entirely until it was revived at the time of the 1798 centenary commemorations, when green, white and orange emblems and flags began to be used by republicans. To most Irish people before 1916, such emblems were either unknown, or were viewed as republican, not national, symbols.[63]

Nineteenth-century Ireland had no shortage of patriotic songs, of both the nationalist and the loyalist varieties,[64] and of these there were several which had some claim to the status of national anthems. In the first half of the nineteenth century 'St Patrick's Day' seems to have been widely accepted as the Irish national anthem, and because it was not considered a party tune it was recognised by viceroys and other representatives of the state. However, in the long run the use of 'St Patrick's Day' by the state probably discredited it among nationalists, and it was supplanted in nationalist affections by two new songs.[65] Thomas Davis's 'A Nation Once Again' became enormously popular in the second part of the nineteenth century, and remains so today. The hope expressed in its refrain, that 'Ireland, long a province, be a nation once again', had a useful ambiguity about it. It could be seen as an expression of the cultural nationalism of Davis and the Young Ireland group which sought to save Ireland from becoming a mere province of England by creating an awareness of Ireland's historical individuality.[66] At the same time, its call to action, if not to arms, could also be read as an endorsement of political struggle for Irish independence, or even of a military struggle like that of the ancient freemen of Greece and Rome mentioned in the song's first verse.

A song with a more explicitly militant message (though adopted by the decidedly unmilitant Irish Parliamentary Party) was 'God Save Ireland', written for the *Nation* by T.D. Sullivan in 1867. It commemorated the execution in that year of the 'Manchester Martyrs', three Fenians convicted of killing a policeman in England. The song's celebration of revolutionary nationalism was made clear in its chorus: 'Whether on the scaffold high / Or the battle-field we die, / Oh, what matter, when for Erin dear we fall!' However, it was quickly taken up by the constitutional nationalist movement and by the 1880s was commonly referred to as the Irish national anthem. The memory of the 'Manchester Martyrs' was revered by Fenians and constitutionalists alike, so 'God Save Ireland' was acceptable to all shades of nationalist opinion.[67] It was not the song's militancy which caused some constitutionalists to abandon it during the 1890s, but rather the bitter split within the Parliamentary Party which led the Parnellites to adopt 'The Boys of Wexford' while the anti-Parnellites retained 'God Save Ireland'.[68]

An anthem whose lyrics were even more stridently militarist was written around 1907 by two radical nationalists, Peadar Ó Cearnaigh (Kearney) and Patrick Heaney or Heeney. Ó Cearnaigh, the author of the song's lyrics, explained later that they wrote 'The Soldier's Song' in order to convince Irishmen that they did not have to join the British Army to be soldiers, and the song became popular among militant nationalists at a time of growing militarism on all sides in Ireland.[69] In 1912 the words were published in the Irish Republican Brotherhood's newspaper *Irish Freedom*, and it was taken up as a marching song by the Irish Volunteers after their formation in 1913, but it remained unknown to most Irish people. The lyrics of 'The Soldier's Song' spoke of Irish soldiers, 'children of a fighting race', who were 'impatient for the coming fight' against 'the Saxon foe'. It was, quite unambiguously, a war song, the song of men 'Sworn to be free' by armed struggle.[70] Less than a decade after its composition 'The Soldier's Song' would come to much greater prominence after a small group of Volunteers decided to confront the foe, not 'In valley green, on towering crag', but on the streets of Dublin.

1916 and after

Writing about the Easter Rising, which had such a profound impact on his own life, Seán O'Faoláin suggested that 'Few risings... have been conducted in any country with such a sense of the value of symbol'.[71] Whatever the truth of this statement, the leaders of the rising must surely have been among the most symbol-conscious revolutionaries in history. The rising itself was more an exercise in symbolic or 'demonstration politics' than a serious attempt to take political power; it was, as F.X. Martin points out, 'staged consciously as a drama by the principal actors'.[72] A number of key figures in the rising had shown an interest in symbols before the insurrection broke out. The O'Rahilly was something of an amateur herald, and had been involved in designing flags for the Irish Volunteers in 1914,[73] while Patrick Pearse had written about symbols in his 1913 essay 'From a Hermitage':

> Symbols are very important. The symbol of a true thing, of a beneficent thing, is worthy of all homage; the symbol of a false thing, of a cruel thing, is worthy of all reprobation... This matter of symbols came into my mind to-day as I watched a Bishop administer Confirmation. The Church to which I belong, the wise Church that has called into her service all the arts, knows better than any other institution, human or divine, the immense potency of symbols: with symbols she exorcises evil spirits, with symbols she calls into play for beneficent purposes the infinite powers of omnipotence. And those of her children who honour not her symbols she pronounces anathema. A nation should exact similar respect for its symbols. Free nations do. They salute their flags with bared heads; they hail with thundering cannon the nincompoops that happen to be their kings.

For Pearse, Ireland within the United Kingdom was a nation forced daily to confront the symbols of a false thing. Irish people could not look at a stamp or a coin without seeing the 'not very intellectual features' of King George V (or George Wettin, as Pearse called him in an effort to strip this particular symbol of its sacred aura). The King's head on a coin symbol- ised 'the foreign tyranny that holds us. A good Irishman should blush every time he sees a penny.' A free Ireland, by implication, would exact respect for its symbols from all the children of the nation, and it is little wonder that Pearse's words would be quoted after the establishment of the Irish Free State by people who wished to declare anathema those who failed to honour the new state's symbols.[74]

The intermingling of religion and nationality in Pearse's remarks on symbols was characteristic of his writing, but he was not alone in seeing the symbols of the nation as sacred. Even James Connolly, the supposed exponent of scientific socialism, wrote shortly before the rising that the green flag had been 'made sacred by all the sufferings of all the martyrs of the past'. Since, to Connolly, Ireland's national symbols were sacred, their use during the First World War to recruit Irishmen to the British Army represented a desecration. He complained that:

> For generations the shamrock was banned as a national emblem of Ireland, but in her extremity England uses the shamrock as a means for exciting in foolish Irishmen loyalty to England. For centuries the green flag of Ireland was a thing accurst and hated by the English garrison in Ireland, as it is still in their inmost hearts. But in India, in Egypt, in Flanders, in Gallipoli, the green flag is used by our rulers to encourage Irish soldiers of England to give up their lives for the power that denies their country the right of nationhood. Green flags wave over recruiting offices in Ireland and England as a bait to lure on poor fools to dishonourable deaths in England's uniform.

Despite this, Connolly still felt that it was right to fly in Dublin 'the green flag of this country as a rallying point of our forces and embodiment of all our hopes'.[75] Accordingly, he presided over an elaborate flag-raising ceremony at Liberty Hall carried out by the Irish Citizen Army on Palm Sunday 1916, and declared that he and his comrades were prepared to defend the Irish flag with their lives if necessary.[76]

As Connolly made clear, the green harp flag was still regarded as the national flag before the rising, even by the most radical nationalists. In 1915 Patrick Pearse himself had ordered each Volunteer unit to equip itself with a green harp flag, which he described as the Irish flag, and during the rising green flags were flown from a number of buildings occupied by the insurgents. It is difficult to be certain about the flags displayed in Easter week, but it seems that the Irish tricolour also flew above the rebels' headquarters in the General Post Office as well as above at least two other buildings in Dublin and one in Enniscorthy. Tricolour badges and armlets were also used by some of the rebels.[77] In addition, a green flag bearing the words 'Irish Republic' was flown on the GPO, and the fact that the objective of the rising had to be spelled out in words in this way shows clearly that the rebels could not rely on either the green flag or the tricolour to communicate their republican goal to the public.[78] After the rising was suppressed tricolours quickly became associated with the rebellion, and were increasingly displayed as signs of sympathy with the rebels and with the Sinn Féin movement. As early as June 1916, an eager University College Dublin student wrote to an imprisoned Volunteer: 'There are not half a dozen people in the College now who are not Sinn Feiners... You should see us all now sporting republican flags down Grafton Street.'[79] In the months that followed, the changing mood in the country was marked symbolically, as Ernie O'Malley recalled later: 'Without guidance or direction, moving as if to clarify itself, nebulous, forming, reforming, the strange rebirth took shape. It was manifest in flags, badges, songs, speech, all seemingly superficial signs. It was as if the inarticulate attempted to express themselves in any way or by any method; later would come organization and cool-headed reason.'[80]

By the first anniversary of the rising, displaying the tricolour had become a favourite gesture of defiance among Sinn Féin sympathisers. Easter 1917 saw tricolours flown from the GPO and Nelson's Pillar in Dublin and City Hall in Cork, while tricolour wreaths were laid on the graves of the republican dead of the rising, in Dublin's Glasnevin cemetery. The Royal Irish Constabulary Inspector-General's report for April 1917 noted that from Easter to the end of the month some 256 republican flags were displayed at about 165 locations around Ireland. These flags, placed on the roofs of buildings, on telegraph poles and high trees, were a simple but extremely effective challenge to Crown forces. The police could not allow such symbols of rebellion to be flown freely, but, as the Inspector-General reported, the flags could only be removed 'with much difficulty and in some cases at considerable personal risk'. Thus, for very little expenditure of time and energy, Sinn Féin supporters could tie up police time and make the RIC look ridiculous while adding to the impression of Sinn Féin's daring and ubiquity. The importance of the tricolour as a symbol of defiance was apparent in the Bogside area of Derry city during the War of Independence, when a series of republican flags painted on a wall were successively blotted out by soldiers of the Dorset Regiment. Eventually the muralists painted two flags intertwined and the words:

> This is the flag the Dorsets hate.
> It puts them all to shame,
> And every time they blot it out
> It blossoms forth again.

The Dorsets' patrol commander was so impressed with the artistry of this mural that he decided not to interfere with it.[81]

Crown forces were not usually so understanding, however, and although the RIC was at first reluctant to engage in large-scale arrests, the police cracked down as the increasing defiance of the state became intolerable. Tricolours were widely displayed during the 1917 by-election campaigns, but anyone flying the republican flag became liable for prosecution. There were, however, more subtle ways of displaying republican sympathies, as a wide variety of items were produced in the Sinn Féin colours. Whelan & Sons ('The Old Sinn Fein Shop') offered for sale everything from rosary beads and tiepins in the republican colours to 'Sterling Silver Brian Boru Harp Brooch, neatly enamelled in green, white and orange', and even 'Irish-made Knickers, with green, white and orange side stripes'.[82]

The tricolour was undoubtedly the most important symbol of Sinn Féin. It was displayed widely at Sinn Féin rallies, and mentioned frequently in the ballads of 1916–21.[83] Although the Sinn Féin newspaper *Nationality* informed its readers in 1917 that the tricolour was 'the flag of the Young Irelanders, adopted 70 years ago by them avowedly as a symbol of the union of Ireland against enforced union with England',[84] most people saw it as the flag of Easter week. As one ballad put it: 'the boys who gave a history to the Orange, White and Green / Are the boys who died in Dublin town in Nineteen and Sixteen'.[85] Its display in the years following the rising was a reminder of Easter 1916 and an inspiration to keep up the campaign to make the republic a reality. The War of Independence added to the tricolour's sacredness, as it was used in funerals and commemorations of the republican dead; and attempts by Crown forces to deliberately dishonour it by such methods as dragging it in the mud behind their trucks probably only increased its prestige in the eyes of Irish nationalists.[86] With the formation of Dáil Éireann and the establishment by Sinn Féin of its own state institutions the tricolour began to be not just a party flag but the flag of a state-in-waiting, though the authority of this state was far from being universally recognised by Irish people.

Rhetorically, the tricolour was placed in unambiguous opposition to the Union Jack, which was dismissed as a 'foreign rag'. A well-known postcard commemorating the Easter Rising, which is strikingly similar to a Fenian poster from fifty years before, shows a Volunteer holding aloft a tricolour while trampling on a Union Jack.[87] This rhetoric of opposition

between the tricolour and the Union Jack was part of Sinn Féin's repudiation of any middle position between complete separation and the continuation of the status quo. Thus, the *Irishman* claimed in 1918 that 'There
are no Parties. It is the Irish Nation against the British Government... Today but two flags float in the land – the Flag of an Irish Republic and the
Flag of England, and Irishmen and Irishwomen must elect under which
they will enrol and serve.' Interestingly, the Dublin-based Irish Unionist
Alliance made the same point in an appeal to British voters: 'It rests with
you, British Electors, to decide under which flag Irish Unionists are to
live. Is it to be the Union Jack or the Irish Republican banner? There is no
alternative.'[88]

The rejection of any compromise with 'the Saxon foe' was also apparent in Sinn Féin's adoption of 'The Soldier's Song' as its principal
anthem. Sheet music for the song was published for the first time in
December 1916, and this was a sign of its increasing popularity after the
Easter Rising. Peadar Ó Cearnaigh dated the popular adoption of the song
from the day it was sung by men being sent for internment in Britain for
their involvement in the rising, and it quickly became the anthem of Sinn
Féin and the Irish Volunteers.[89] 'The Soldier's Song' was sung at Sinn
Féin election rallies and celebrations of the release of prisoners, and its
lyrics were absorbed into republican rhetoric.[90] However, it seems likely
that most Irish people remained unfamiliar with the words of 'The
Soldier's Song', and even within Sinn Féin ranks knowledge of the song
may have been limited. Lady Gregory observed a republican demonstration in February 1919 and noted that there was 'very little singing' in
response to a call for the crowd to join in 'The Soldier's Song'.[91]

It seems likely that the song was known and sung mainly by young
men entranced by the martial spirit of the times. The association between
the bearing of arms and the attainment of manhood, while it was not
explicitly present in 'The Soldier's Song', was very much part of the
rhetoric of militarism, and this was surely a large part of the new
anthem's appeal to the young men among whom the Irish Republican
Army recruited.[92] Volunteers boasted of their transformation from 'free
and easy lads' into 'soldiers', and 'The Soldier's Song' could play a part
in this change of identity.[93] In 1917 Daniel Corkery described seeing a
young man singing 'The Soldier's Song' while working in a hay field,
and wrote admiringly: 'He stood... erect, a drilled figure, his rake-handle
falling into place like a gun.'[94] It is not surprising, then, to find Lady
Gregory reporting in 1920 and 1921 that the Wren Boys, groups of
masked young men who traditionally went from house to house on St
Stephen's Day, knew only a few lines about the wren, but all sang 'The
Soldier's Song'.[95]

The rise to prominence of the tricolour and 'The Soldier's Song' was

in part the product of a feeling among separatists that the existing
national symbols had been tainted by association with unionism, with the
state, and with the Irish Parliamentary Party. The harp could easily be
made into a symbol of the Union by surmounting it with a crown, the
shamrock by entwining it with the rose and the thistle. Therefore, Irish
unionists, who before partition generally saw no contradiction between
expressions of Irish identity and support for the Union, happily combined
harps, shamrocks and Celtic revival motifs with symbols of the connection with Britain in their campaign against Home Rule. The crowned
harp appeared on the badges and banners of the Royal Irish Constabulary
and the British Army's Irish regiments, and in 1900 Queen Victoria
decreed that all soldiers in the Irish regiments should wear a sprig of
shamrock each St Patrick's Day, in tribute to the bravery of Irish soldiers
during the Boer War. During the First World War, harps, shamrocks and
a wolfhound appeared in recruiting posters.[96] The wolfhound and other
emblems were less polluted by association with the state than the harp
and shamrock, but in the eyes of some Sinn Féiners such symbols were
suspect because they were identified with the Irish Parliamentary Party.
Republicans regarded the constitutional nationalist movement as more
lapdog than wolfhound, and felt the need to draw a symbolic distinction
between themselves and the Redmondites.[97]

Anger at the desecration of Irish national symbols during the First
World War, evident in James Connolly's comments of April 1916, was
expressed even more forcefully after the rising by a Sinn Féin propagan-
dist, the Reverend P. Gaynor:

> To-day our battle-cry is: 'The Irish Republic.' It used to be 'A Nation Once
> Again.' To-day we are 'Sinn Feiners.' We used to be 'Nationalists.' To-day
> our flag is the 'Green, White and Gold.' It used to be the 'immortal Green.'
> Why have we adopted a new battle-cry if our beliefs are the old unchang-
> ing beliefs? Why have we adopted a new flag if our principles are the old
> immortal principles? Because the sacred word 'Nation' has been corrupted
> to destroy the idea of nationhood; ... because British hirelings have pro-
> faned our symbols – the Shamrock, Harp and Green Flag – to destroy their
> old-time significance. Queen Victoria let her soldiers wear the Shamrock to
> destroy its national symbolism. The harp is set in the policemen's cap for a
> like object. The Green Flag is flaunted over the recruiting platform, and the
> national anthem of England is chanted beneath its shadow...
>
> But the cunning which sought to confuse our ideas by corrupting the
> word 'nation,' and to mislead our young men by profaning our national
> symbols, has over-reached itself. It has given to our lips words that cannot
> be misconstrued: 'The Irish Republic!' It has placed in our hands a flag that
> can never be associated with the Crown of England – the Republican Tri-
> colour. Therefore, to-day we speak of the 'Republic,' and 'Sinn Fein,' to
> express what Davis meant by 'nation' and 'nationalism.' To-day our flag is

the Republican Green, White and Gold – the flag of Easter Week, consecrated to Ireland in the blood of Pearse and his comrades![98]

If Sinn Féin needed symbols of its own, uncontaminated by association
with the Parliamentary Party and the British Army's recruiting effort, it
also had to establish itself as the true inheritor of the age-old tradition of
national struggle, as Gaynor attempted to do in the passage just quoted.
This need for continuity explains why the old symbols remained in use
within Sinn Féin ranks, despite the perception of some that they had
become tainted. Continuity of symbolism is apparent in the artwork of
those interned during the revolutionary period: internees carved bone
harps, painted harps and shamrocks on handkerchiefs, and drew harps,
shamrocks, round towers, Celtic crosses, wolfhounds and rising suns in
their autograph books.[99] Moreover, such symbols could easily be republi-
canised by combining them with the tricolour, or by colouring them
green, white and orange (or yellow). For example, a memorial card for a
dead Volunteer showed a harp and wolfhound below two crossed tricolours; a Sinn Féin banner depicted a round tower, Celtic cross,
wolfhound and rising sun inset on a green, white and yellow field; and
Sinn Féiners could buy harp brooches and shamrock tie pins in the republican colours. A ballad about the Easter Rising had a mother crying:

> My only son was shot in Dublin
> Fighting for his country bold.
> He fought for Ireland, Ireland only
> The Harp and Shamrock, the Green, White and Gold.[100]

Even Sinn Féin's rejection of the green flag was not absolute. A popular
ballad celebrating an IRA attack could still declare 'They fought 'neath
the green flag of Erin', and tricolours were sometimes depicted crossed
with green harp flags.[101] There was continuity, too, in the frequent description of the tricolour as 'the green, white and gold', since the green harp
flag had often been called 'the green and gold'. Moreover, it is unclear
whether those who waved the tricolour considered that it had replaced the
green flag as the national flag of Ireland, or whether they used it only as
a party flag. The tricolour was commonly referred to as the republican or
Sinn Féin flag, but some ballads referred to it as 'Ireland's flag' or 'Erin's
bright banner', and green, white and orange were sometimes described as
'the Irish colours'.[102] Thus, the tricolour's transformation into a national
flag began during the revolutionary period, but was very far from complete by 1922.

When Sinn Féin and the Irish Parliamentary Party competed in the
elections of 1917–18, Sinn Féin was careful not to disown all that the

green flag had stood for in the past, but rather to claim that the Parliamentary Party's true colours were those of the Union Jack. A satirical pro-Sinn Féin poem had Parliamentary Party leaders crying 'The Green, White and Orange, alas and alack / Has taken the place of the old Union Jack', and *Nationality* asked 'Why are the followers of Mr. John Dillon ashamed to come out in their true colours? **They** stand for all that the Union Jack symbolises. Why do they not wave that flag?' Nevertheless, Sinn Féin accused the constitutional nationalists of having sullied the green harp flag by their craven subservience to the British. Cleverly playing on the fact that red was both the colour of blood and the colour traditionally associated with the British Empire, Sinn Féin propaganda declared that the green flag had turned red in the hands of the Parliamentary Party's leaders.[103] While Sinn Féin did not explicitly repudiate the green harp flag, in practice the old national flag became the symbol of constitutional nationalism.[104] Displays of green harp flags and the absence of tricolours in particular areas were taken as signs of loyalty to the Parliamentary Party, and on at least one occasion Irish Volunteers trampled on green flags displayed by a Parliamentary Party candidate.[105]

For its part, the Parliamentary Party did not take such attacks lying down, and its candidates clearly felt that they would win votes by wrapping themselves in the green flag. The Party's rhetorical use of the flag was unashamedly conservative: it sought to associate the green harp flag with Irish national tradition, order and steady progress towards Home Rule; the tricolour with revolution, anarchy and repudiation of the national tradition. A United Irish League handbill entitled 'What is Wrong with the Green Flag?' began by listing the nationalist struggles which had taken place under the green flag, and then asked 'Why invent an absurd new-fangled flag for Ireland? Perhaps it is just as well. For a fake flag is the right flag for a fake policy.'[106] Typical of the conservative nature of the Parliamentary Party's appeal to rally round the flag was a speech by T.P. O'Donoghue, the Party's candidate in South Meath, who reminded his audience 'that he stands for no new policy and no new flag. The policy which was good enough for Parnell and Redmond is good enough for him, and the flag that signalised Ireland's nationhood for seven centuries is still the flag Mr. O'Donaghue prefers to fight under.'[107] The tricolour was represented as alien to age-old national tradition; it was the flag of discord and division, a mongrel flag.[108] According to a speaker at a Party rally for the East Tyrone by-election, 'the miserable imported tricolour stood for methods of physical force, a chimerical Republic, chaos, and the negation of civilised government and true religion, and there was no room for his friends or himself under that flag'.[109]

The Irish Parliamentary Party's appeal to tradition was not enough to prevent Sinn Féin's triumph in the 1918 election. Despite the decisive nature of Sinn Féin's victory, however, it is important to bear in mind that it won only 48 per cent of votes cast, or 65 per cent in the twenty-six counties which became the Irish Free State.[110] There remained a substantial body of Irish people who were opposed to Sinn Féin and unreconciled to the republican flag and anthem. Supporters of the Irish Parliamentary Party continued to scorn the tricolour and 'The Soldier's Song': in 1919, for example, Redmondites in Waterford declined to take part in the St Patrick's Day parade rather than walk behind a republican flag, while in 1921 members of the Ancient Order of Hibernians raided several houses in a South Armagh village in order to take back musical instruments from former AOH band members who had gone over to Sinn Féin and begun playing 'The Soldier's Song' instead of 'The Boys of Wexford'.[111] Unionists were even less likely to accept a flag and anthem associated with militant republicanism, and they regarded these 'rebel' symbols with horror.

Conclusion

While Sinn Féiners might believe that their flag 'Spoke of unity and concord / In an island without spleen',[112] by 1922 the people of Ireland were more divided than ever. Where once nationalists had been able to rally round a common set of symbols, despite their disagreements on questions of goals and tactics, now symbols had become a source of dissension within nationalist ranks. The emblems which had served nationalists so well through the nineteenth century, and had been seen as unproblematically representative of Ireland, were now viewed with suspicion by Sinn Féin ideologues who regarded them as too closely tied to the failures of constitutionalism. At the same time, the new flag and anthem adopted by Sinn Féin had not yet escaped their origins as party symbols, and to complicate matters further they were about to become the subject of a battle for possession of the Sinn Féin tradition following the Treaty split. Meanwhile, unionists in the three southern provinces, who still identified with all-Ireland symbols as well as with British symbols, were growing apart from Ulster unionists, who had begun to cultivate an Ulster identity with its own distinctive symbols. (See Chapter 4.) Above all, the gulf separating unionists and nationalists had widened. The stock of common, politically neutral symbols of Irishness had dwindled, and the symbolic universe seemed to have narrowed into a set of stark oppositions: Union Jack versus tricolour, 'God Save the King' versus 'The Soldier's Song', republic versus monarchy. It was in this political climate that the debates about official symbols with which this book is concerned began.

Chapter 2
From symbols of party to symbols of state: the flag and anthem of the Irish Free State

In 1922 the tricolour and 'The Soldier's Song' were still very new symbols, having become known to most Irish people only after 1916, so it is not surprising that their adoption as the official flag and anthem of the Irish Free State did not meet with universal approval. The symbols which had inspired Sinn Féiners during the independence struggle remained precious to both sections of Sinn Féin after the Treaty split, and when pro-Treaty Sinn Féiners took power in the Irish Free State, they naturally used the tricolour and 'The Soldier's Song' as the flag and anthem of the new state. However, the government's right to do so was contested by its anti-Treaty opponents, who claimed these symbols for republicanism. At the same time, ex-unionists and some Irish Parliamentary Party stalwarts rejected symbols which they associated with Sinn Féin and with painful memories of the revolutionary period. Some people thought that a new flag or anthem might help to unite the Irish people, but it proved impossible to find alternative symbols which were both uncontentious and inspiring. The Free State government showed no interest in such proposals, arguing that the tricolour and 'The Soldier's Song' were symbols of nation, not party. However, it recognised that the flag and anthem questions were potentially divisive, and moved cautiously, neither legislating to establish the tricolour and 'The Soldier's Song' as official state symbols nor taking very active measures to promote or enforce their use by the public. In this way the government largely avoided stirring up controversy, and in time its cautious approach paid off as dissident elements within the Free State population were integrated into the body politic and dropped their opposition to the state's flag and anthem.

Adoption of the Free State flag and anthem

Even before the Irish Free State had officially come into existence, the green, white and orange tricolour was being used by the Provisional

Government as the flag of the new state. The Provisional Government seems to have given little thought to the question of the flag, though it did authorise its Law Officer, Hugh Kennedy, to seek historical advice on the matter from Thomas Sadleir of the Office of Arms. Sadleir favoured a flag which incorporated a harp, while Kennedy himself was keen to find a design which pre-dated the Norman invasion and was thus authentically Gaelic.[1] However, the government continued using the tricolour, and the matter was not raised again until 1925, when the Minister for Industry and Commerce sought a definite decision on the flag so that he could proceed with legislation dealing with merchant shipping.[2] In response, the Secretary of the Department of External Affairs prepared a memorandum setting out the government's options. He explained that flags could be established by usage, by legislation or by a provision in the constitution. A land flag was of importance only within the state and there was no procedure for gaining international recognition of it, while a marine flag would be recognised without question by foreign states, once they had been notified of its design. However, the British government held that the British Shipping Acts applied to all ships registered in any part of the British Commonwealth, and that as a result all such ships had to fly the British red ensign. If Free State ships flew the tricolour it seemed likely that British representatives abroad would refuse to afford protection to these ships, just as they had refused protection to bearers of Free State passports.[3]

Again, the government made no formal decision on the flag question, but it clearly believed that it had no choice but to acquiesce in British government policy regarding the use of the red ensign on shipping. As for the land flag, the government considered that the tricolour had been established by usage and that no legislation was needed for this purpose, as President Cosgrave made clear in response to a parliamentary question about the national flag in 1926. The President was also asked 'What is the other colour besides green and white, because it varies, even in Government Buildings? Sometimes it is a pale, sickly yellow, and sometimes it is red.' Cosgrave informed the Dáil that the correct colours were orange, white and green.[4] These were the colours specified in the Defence Force Regulations of 1929, which, in addition, set out rules for use of the flag by the defence forces.[5] No flag code was introduced for civilians, however, until after the Second World War.[6] The final stage in the official recognition of the tricolour came in 1937, when article 7 of the new constitution specified that 'The national flag is the tricolour of green, white and orange.'[7] The red ensign continued to be flown by ships registered in the state, an anomaly which President de Valera was anxious to rectify, but the matter remained unresolved when war broke out in 1939. Since it was important to distinguish the ships of neutral Ireland from those of the

United Kingdom, an order was issued under the Emergency Powers Act requiring Irish-registered vessels to fly the tricolour, but legislation making the tricolour the official Irish merchant shipping flag was not passed until 1947.[8]

While it was clear from the start that the tricolour was the flag of the Free State, the situation with regard to the anthem was more ambiguous. In February and April 1924, Seán Lester, Director of Publicity in the Department of External Affairs, pointed out that there was no accepted national anthem. A Protestant nationalist from County Antrim, Lester was perhaps more acutely aware than most of his colleagues of the divisive potential of symbols. 'The Soldier's Song' was usually sung at national gatherings, he wrote, 'but it is felt that while it was excellent as a revolutionary song both words and music are unsuitable for a National Anthem'. He warned that the absence of an official anthem 'makes it easier for the pro-British elements to sing the British National Anthem at their functions', and suggested that a competition be held to provide new words for a national anthem to the tune of 'Let Erin Remember'. His comments were circulated to the Executive Council, which declined to make a ruling on the matter, but agreed informally to continue using 'The Soldier's Song' for the time being within the Free State. The air of 'Let Erin Remember' would be used when the state was being represented abroad, however, since it was 'more suitable from the musical point of view'.[9]

Lester raised the matter again in 1926, and this time the Executive Council considered that a uniform practice was desirable. It therefore decided that 'The Soldier's Song' alone should be used as the national anthem both inside and outside the state, and this decision made on 12 July 1926 was later considered to mark the song's formal adoption as the anthem of the Free State.[10] Shortly thereafter, the decision was made public in response to a question in the Dáil. A draft reply to this question stated that 'while no final decision has been come to, ['The Soldier's Song'] is at present accepted as the National Anthem'. However, when asked in the Dáil to 'state, at any rate as far as the Army is concerned, what is considered to be the National Anthem', the Minister for Defence answered simply ' "The Soldier's Song".'[11] A further step towards formalising the use of the song as the national anthem came in 1928, when Colonel Fritz Brase, Director of the Army School of Music, suggested that the song was too long, and that it should open with the chorus (the implication presumably being that the rest of the song could be dispensed with on many occasions). Brase's band arrangement of the song was approved by the Executive Council in March 1929, and it seems that from then on the official anthem was the chorus only of 'The Soldier's Song'.[12]

In February 1932 Brase was authorised to arrange scores for orchestral and other purposes, and in July that year, following the decision by theatres and cinemas to play the anthem at the end of all performances, the Executive Council approved the suggestion that an official abbreviated version of the anthem be prepared and published for use on such occasions.[13] However, the publication of any new arrangements was held up by a dispute over the song's copyright. Peadar Ó Cearnaigh had for some time been disgruntled about the state's failure to pay him for the use of his song as the national anthem. For its part, the government did not dispute Ó Cearnaigh's copyright in the words of the song, but it wanted proof that he also owned the rights to Heeney's music.[14] In 1932, Ó Cearnaigh joined with Michael Heeney (Patrick Heeney's brother), and lawyers acting for the two men wrote to the directors of the Army and Garda bands, and of the radio service, as well as to the managers of cinemas and theatres, threatening prosecution if they did not start paying royalties.[15] When Ó Cearnaigh and Heeney began legal proceedings against the Dublin Theatre, the government considered it 'inexpedient that an action such as this should proceed in the courts', and decided that the state should acquire copyright in the song. The settlement arrived at in October 1933 recognised Ó Cearnaigh and Patrick Heeney as the joint composers of the music of 'The Soldier's Song' and Ó Cearnaigh as sole author of the words. The copyright owners were paid £1000, and in exchange they agreed to assign their rights in 'The Soldier's Song' to the state, to drop their legal action, and to take no further proceedings in respect of copyright or royalties.[16]

Cumann na nGaedheal and the selection of the flag and anthem

There is very little evidence in the government files about the reasons for the Cumann na nGaedheal government's selection of the tricolour and 'The Soldier's Song' as the Free State flag and anthem. This in itself suggests that there was no doubt in the minds of members of the government about the appropriateness of these symbols. The tricolour and 'The Soldier's Song' were the flag and anthem to which they had rallied during the revolutionary period, so it was only natural that they should now adopt them as symbols of the state which the Sinn Féin struggle had created. The fact that the new state was not the all-Ireland republic of which they had dreamed in no way lessened the attachment of pro-Treaty Sinn Féiners to these symbols. On the contrary, it became all the more important for the government to retain symbols which reminded Free Staters of the glorious struggle and reassured them that they had not repudiated this past. The use of the tricolour and 'The Soldier's Song' was part of a more general attempt by Cumann na nGaedheal to establish symbolic continuity with the Sinn Féin tradition. While the government party ceded the name Sinn

Féin to its opponents, it took for itself the name of the organisation from which Arthur Griffith's original Sinn Féin evolved, Cumann na nGaedheal. The name of the state was another link with the independence struggle, since Saorstát (literally 'Free State') was the name used by the revolutionary Dáil as the Irish translation of 'Republic'.[17] Likewise, the Free State government claimed succession to the political institutions of the revolutionary period by referring to the leader of the government as the President (a sleight of hand justified on the grounds that he was 'President of the Executive Council', or Cabinet) and by naming the lower house of parliament Dáil Éireann. Continuity with the pre-Civil War Irish Republican Army was also asserted by the Free State army's adoption of the badge and Irish language name of the Irish Volunteers.

Such symbolic links with the revolutionary period were important to those who had been Sinn Féiners, regardless of which side of the Treaty divide they ended up on. 'Between 1916 and 1921 Irish nationality was reborn in blood and tears', maintained Cumann na nGaedheal's *United Irishman* newspaper in 1932. 'The flag and song of those who were the van-guard in the last struggle, of those who went into the valley of the shadow of death in those years, have been adopted by the State and the people.'[18] The tricolour and 'The Soldier's Song' brought back memories of a recent past seen as glorious and heroic, and these symbols had been made sacred by their association with the dead of the independence struggle. The tricolour was identified, according to a writer in the *Irish Independent*, 'with so many recent, sad yet glorious memories that it must ever be dear to the Gaelic heart. It has enfolded too many precious caskets to ever permit of its being neglected or dishonoured or not flown with a conscious pride.'[19] General Richard Mulcahy, addressing Free State troops on St Patrick's Day 1923, was sure that 'they could never forget the flag that had come out of the fires of Easter Week', the flag associated with the ideals of Pearse and his comrades.[20] The army newspaper *An tÓglach* instructed its readers that 'When the soldier salutes the flag he salutes the Dead whose blood consecrates it, and he consecrates himself to the service of the cause for which they died.'[21] Similarly, 'The Soldier's Song' was 'glorified by heroism, sanctified by martyrdom, and has finally won imperishable fame as the song of victory and freedom'; it was associated with 'glorious memories' and 'inspired us in a just fight'.[22] An article about the anthem in a book published in the early years of the Free State declared that:

> During the stormy years that Ireland has experienced since she made the song her anthem, her love for it has never cooled. When her peerless volunteers swooped down upon a section of the British garrison they returned with their booty singing the refrain, and when England's terrorism was at

its worst the soldiers of Ireland went to prison and to death with that song upon their lips and its sentiment in their hearts.[23]

As perceptive observers noted, the government's adoption of the tricolour and 'The Soldier's Song' was not only a response to the preferences of pro-Treaty Sinn Féiners, but also an attempt to deny a propaganda opportunity to republicans.[24] Diarmuid O'Hegarty, Secretary of the Executive Council, admitted as much privately in 1929, writing that 'as far as the Tri-colour and the "Soldiers' Song" are concerned – it was essential in 1922 to take these over as they would have been an incalculable asset to the Irregulars [the anti-Treaty IRA] if they had been allowed to retain possession of them'.[25] Had Cumann na nGaedheal abandoned these symbols, republicans would undoubtedly have seized on this as another sign of the government's betrayal of the ideals of Easter 1916. Instead, the ruling party's newspaper gloated in 1928, Fianna Fáil had been thwarted by the Free State government's:

> prompt flying of the Easter Week Tricolour and their cool assumption that its claim was beyond dispute. Had a small Union Jack been imposed upon our National Flag Mr de Valera would have material for another general election campaign…Each Deputy on the Fianna Fail side would probably hoist the proud, unsullied flag over his seat in the Dail. All these grand propaganda possibilities were denied the Opposition by the meanness of the Free State Government in deliberately putting the Tricolour in its proper place.[26]

The other major consideration in the government's selection of the tricolour and 'The Soldier's Song' must have been the absence of other suitable flags and anthems. The use of the Union Jack and 'God Save the King', which was common in the other dominions of the British Commonwealth, was ruled out because to Irish nationalists these were symbols of domination and oppression. Despite its long history as the flag of Irish nationalism, the green harp flag could not be adopted by either faction of Sinn Féin because it had come to be associated with the Irish Parliamentary Party after 1916. Apart from the tricolour, no other flag had achieved widespread recognition or acceptance as a national symbol of Ireland. Possible national anthems were more plentiful, but the popular anthems of the nineteenth century were also tainted by their associations. 'St Patrick's Day' had been leached of all national meaning for nationalists as a result of its use by the state under the Union, while 'A Nation Once Again' and 'God Save Ireland' were linked too closely to the Parliamentary Party. 'God Save Ireland' had also acquired factional associations during the Parnell split. Although the Free State did make some use of the old anthems in the early years of the state,[27] they constituted a potential embarrassment to a party determined to emphasise its Sinn Féin lineage. Another popular anthem, Thomas Moore's 'Let Erin Remember', which was used for a time to represent the state abroad, was perhaps less tied to the Parliamentary Party in the minds of Sinn Féiners, but a song which called on Ireland to 'remember the days of old, / Ere her faithless sons betray'd her' was a potential godsend to republican propagandists.[28]

In addition, as *Dublin Opinion* commented, many of the old songs were obsolete in an independent state:

> 'When shall the day break in Erin?' is out of date. (The Day has broken, and we await the settlement of the compensation claims.) As to 'God Save Ireland,' Ireland is already saved (vide any current Ministerial pronouncement). All the other good old stand-by's are part of the historic yesterday.[29]

Though *Dublin Opinion*'s tongue was, as ever, in its cheek, its point was nonetheless valid. From a pro-government perspective the independence achieved by the Free State meant that Thomas Davis's hope that Ireland might be 'A Nation Once Again' was now happily redundant. At the same time, the unfinished business of Northern Ireland, which prompted republicans to sing 'God save the southern part of Ireland / Three quarters of a nation once again',[30] made such songs potentially embarrassing. In this context, the fact that 'The Soldier's Song' was almost entirely about the struggle rather than the goal was a distinct advantage. Furthermore, many of the songs of the past were rather too concerned with meditating on the sorrows of Erin for a government which wanted to emphasise a positive future. As *An tÓglach* pointed out, 'The Soldier's Song' had the advantage that 'The note of defeat or sorrow is absent from it. In the songs of the past, sadness, disappointment and failure had too much prominence.'[31]

National or party symbols?

For at least the first decade of the Free State's existence, the tricolour and 'The Soldier's Song' were politically controversial symbols. Having only recently become familiar to the public, they were still not accepted by many Irish people as national, rather than party symbols. To republicans they were symbols of the republic declared in Easter 1916, the republic which Sinn Féin had fought for and the Free State government had betrayed. To ex-unionists and those nationalists who regretted the demise of the Irish Parliamentary Party, on the other hand, the Free State flag and anthem were Sinn Féin party symbols, associated in their minds with violence and extremism. The Free State government disputed the claims of all these groups, maintaining instead that the tricolour and 'The Soldier's

Song' were symbols of the Irish nation which were above politics and should be accepted by all.

The tussle for possession of the tricolour between supporters and opponents of the Treaty began during the Treaty debates, at the start of which Arthur Griffith announced that with the Treaty 'We have brought back the flag'. This provided an opening for the anti-Treaty speaker David Ceannt to assert that the tricolour which had been brought back with the Treaty would have a Union Jack in the corner 'to show the base betrayal', while Dr Ferran declared:

> They brought back the substance of the flag – not a shadow, not a symbol. They left the symbol behind in Downing Street where they had no authority to leave it. They brought back a yard of calico and a couple of packages of Diamond Dyes. That's the flag of the Irish Free State, but it does not stand for liberty.

Mary MacSwiney warned that the tricolour was a republican flag, that republicans would resent its use by the Free State as much as they would resent its use by the Black and Tans, and that republicans would use the tricolour with a black band until the republic was achieved. This point was hammered home by David Ceannt:

> That flag is Republican. That flag is sacred to me and to my family, and to every member who sacrificed anything in this glorious fight for the Republic. And any attempt that will be made to use that flag by the enemy – as far as I can go I will preserve that flag to the best of my ability, even to the cost of my life. I hope that Mr Griffith will make it clear what flag he is to use in the Free State, because he will never use the Republican flag except over the dead bodies of some of us.[32]

Ceannt's words proved sadly prophetic: before long the tricolour would indeed be draped over the dead bodies of all too many on both sides of the Civil War. For a time, too, the metaphorical struggles over the tricolour became literal as republicans snatched tricolours from the platforms at pro-Treaty demonstrations, the republican women of Cumann na mBan announcing that they would not allow the tricolour to fly over any meeting other than a republican one.[33] A popular republican song summed up the feeling on the anti-Treaty side that the tricolour was a republican flag which had been 'stolen' or 'appropriated' by the Free State:[34]

> Take it down from the mast, Irish traitors,
> 'Tis the flag we republicans claim.
> It can never be owned by Free Staters
> Who shed nothing upon it but shame...
> Take it down for its cause you have scorned

To make permanent o'er us the Crown
You who linked yourselves up with the foemen
The tricolor then to pull down.
'Tis we and no other can claim it
For to-day joined as one we stand, bold,
To fight England combined with Free Staters
In defence of the green, white and gold.[35]

Now the Sinn Féin rhetoric of implacable opposition between Union Jack and tricolour, and the Reverend P. Gaynor's claim that the tricolour 'can never be associated with the Crown of England', came back to haunt Cumann na nGaedheal. Like Sinn Féin confronting the Irish Parliamentary Party in 1918, republicans claimed that the Free State's true colours were red, white and blue. When Dáil Éireann voted for the Treaty, the uncompromising republican Liam Mellows arranged for a tricolour with a Union Jack in the corner to be raised over the GPO, and Mellows subsequently expressed his disgust at 'this chameleon Government which is red, white and blue one minute and green white and orange the next'.[36] Others also accused Free Staters of wanting to quarter in the tricolour 'The reeking flag of the English bully',[37] while a republican song mocked 'A Free State that's tied up with Red, White and Blue',[38] and a cartoon in the republican *Plain People* newspaper showed Griffith proclaiming 'we have brought back the flag' but pointing to a Union Jack.[39] Some republicans even declared that they were more opposed to the Free State's use of the tricolour than to the display of the Union Jack on Armistice Day: the 'Union Jackers', said a delegate to the Sinn Féin Ard-Fheis in 1925, were at least true to their flag.[40]

The Free State government was said to have dishonoured the tricolour; it had, according to the Sinn Féin newspaper *Irish Freedom*, brought back the flag with 'a stain on its folds – the ugly stain of treachery and betrayal'.[41] This 'stain' did not prevent republicans from continuing to claim the tricolour, but it may have been one reason why republicans created a new, 'pure' symbol, the Easter lily. The Easter lily was invented in 1926 by the republican women's organisation Cumann na mBan as an emblem of the republican dead, and it was most obviously an answer to the poppies worn to commemorate the dead of the First World War.[42] It was also, however, a sign of republican sympathies, a successor to the tricolour ribbons and rosettes which had been worn by Sinn Féiners before 1922 but which could not differentiate republicans from Free Staters. Cumann na mBan publicity material regarding the Easter lilies made the link with the flag explicit: the men of 1916 had 'raised the banner of complete separation from England, and the wisdom of their demand united all the people of Ireland. That banner has been basely lowered. In the Easter Lily it is raised again.'[43]

Republicans protested less at the use of 'The Soldier's Song' by the Free State, perhaps because when the conflict between republicans and Free Staters was at its most intense it was not clear what the official anthem of the state was. In 1924 the republican newspaper *Eire* saw the playing of 'Let Erin Remember' at an army band concert attended by the Governor General as a sign that the government had abandoned Michael Collins's strategy of using the Free State as a stepping stone to the republic: 'Thus is the Soldiers' Song officially disowned by the Free State, and a new national anthem bestowed upon us by the representative of the English King. Thus is another stepping-stone submerged.'[44] By 1929, when a controversy broke out about which anthem should be played for the Governor General when he visited Trinity College, it was clear that the government regarded 'The Soldier's Song' as the national anthem, and an angry republican wrote:

> Now the King's Governor-General has the audacity to claim 'The Soldiers Song,' trying by that means to fool the Irish people and the world into believing that we are a nation and free... Every time 'The Soldiers' Song' is played by the bands of King George's militia (dubbed the Free State Army) or in presence of King George's understudy, Governor McNeill, every Republican should regard it as an insult to the memory of those who fought and died to rid Ireland of English kings and Governor Generals.[45]

The charge that the Free State only used the tricolour and 'The Soldier's Song' in an attempt to blind the people to what republicans claimed was the continued domination of the Free State by Britain was repeated by other republicans, both moderates and extremists.[46] Characteristically, the matter was put most forcefully in the IRA mouthpiece *An Phoblacht*, which saw the tricolour and 'The Soldier's Song' as 'but part of the Free State camouflage of its Crown-colony partitioned freedom'. These symbols, it asserted, belonged to republicans: 'those who now would fain adopt these revolutionary symbols are usurpers... and all smoke-screens to cloud the issue availeth not'.[47]

An Phoblacht did not often see eye to eye with ex-unionists or nationalists who remained loyal to the tradition of the Irish Parliamentary Party, but these two groups joined republicans in arguing that the tricolour and 'The Soldier's Song' were revolutionary symbols which should be left to those who were still trying to continue the revolution. Ex-unionists and anti-Sinn Féin nationalists thought that a government which had accepted dominion status should not cling to the symbols of republicanism. In their view, the Free State flag and anthem were party symbols, and to make things worse these symbols were now claimed by two competing parties.[48] While some believed that the Free State government had chosen this flag and anthem in an effort to win over republicans, they considered this strategy a failure, and one writer complained that in attempting to conciliate its worst enemies the government was driving away those who wished to be its friends.[49] Professor M.D. O'Sullivan lamented that the government had missed an opportunity to rally the people to its support by adopting a flag and anthem agreeable to the nation. Instead, the government 'has preferred to stress the things which most people would rather forget and to perpetuate bitter memories by the adoption of emblems which a great number of the citizens can neither respect nor cherish'.[50]

As O'Sullivan suggested, ex-unionists and Redmondites saw the tricolour and 'The Soldier's Song' as divisive not only because they represented the triumph of Sinn Féin over unionism and constitutional nationalism, but also because they brought back painful memories of revolutionary violence. The Dublin correspondent of Belfast's nationalist but anti-Sinn Féin *Irish News* wrote that the tricolour was 'identified with methods and policies of which thousands of good Irishmen did not and do not approve';[51] the *Irish Times* noted that 'this flag still has painful associations for many dutiful subjects of the Saorstát';[52] and the Protestant clergyman Dudley Fletcher commented that the tricolour was inseparably associated in his mind with a Sinn Féin rebellion which he considered to have been morally wrong.[53] 'The Soldier's Song' provoked even more impassioned reactions, since both its history and its militarist lyrics revived 'memories of things that hundreds of thousands of patriotic Irishmen would fain forget'.[54] It was said to be 'a mere party ditty [which] brings back only the saddest memories of outrage, death and disaster';[55] a song 'closely associated with party feeling, rebellion and civil war'[56] or 'indissolubly associated with shocking events of the recent past which most people would like to forget';[57] 'merely a ballad which was popular during the troublesome times in Ireland, and [which] is reminiscent of a period in our recent history which many Irishmen would like to forget'.[58] A decade after the foundation of the state James Dillon, son of the Irish Parliamentary Party leader John Dillon and a future leader of Fine Gael, still felt so strongly about the matter that he told the Dáil: 'I will not stand up when you play the "Soldiers' Song," because I detest it, and it is associated, in my mind, with horrors.'[59] Dillon's comment, made in the course of a debate on the Constitution (Removal of Oath) Bill, prompted one wit to remark that 'as Mr de Valera would not say the words of the Oath while Mr Dillon would not sing the Soldiers' Song, perhaps peace might be brought to our distracted isle if Mr de Valera sang the Oath and Mr Dillon said the Soldiers' Song'.[60]

It is impossible to know how many Free State citizens disliked the tricolour and 'The Soldier's Song' on political grounds. One opponent of these symbols claimed that 'the masses of the Irish people themselves have no particular pride in either the new flag or the new anthem, but regard both as mere emblems of party'.[61] Such an assessment, however, cannot be taken as an accurate gauge of popular sentiment, and was surely more a reflection of the views of the writer's own social circle combined with some wishful thinking. It is probably safe to say that the ex-unionist segment of the population was almost universally hostile to the Free State flag and anthem, remaining loyal to the Union Jack and 'God Save the King'.[62] The number of nationalists who continued to prefer the flag and anthems associated with the Irish Parliamentary Party to the new flag and anthem may also have been large. After all, the bulk of Sinn Féin voters in 1918 had transferred their allegiance from constitutional nationalism. There were also many people who had not voted for Sinn Féin in 1918, and of these some remained loyal to the old nationalist party long after it had been eclipsed by Sinn Féin.

One such group was the Ancient Order of Hibernians, a nationalist and Catholic fraternal order which had been closely associated with the Parliamentary Party, but whose political influence outside Northern Ireland declined dramatically with the rise of Sinn Féin.[63] The Hibernians refused to abandon the green harp flag or songs such as 'God Save Ireland', 'The National Anthem of happier days'.[64] An article in the *Hibernian Journal* in 1925 insisted that the only solution to Ireland's problems was:

> to reawaken the old spirit that the criminal excesses of revolutionary methods have nearly strangled. Let us take our stand again under the old green Flag. It was good enough for our forefathers through many a generation... It has been sanctified by sacrifice and haloed by inspiring memories... It symbolised the sentiment of Ireland for the Irish; it exemplified the unity of the Fatherland.[65]

Similarly, D.F. Curran, a former Home Ruler living in England who wrote a number of letters about the flag and anthem to the *Irish Independent*, referred to the green flag as the 'real Irish flag' and regretted 'the complete betrayal of our national standard'. Curran wrote rather poignantly of having been left behind by developments within Irish nationalism, which 'took a twist in 1916 from which it has not yet recovered. When that reactionary and socialistic gallop took place I was left at the post, and there I prefer to stay. There are certain things one cannot do and retain one's national honour.'[66] In 1926 those who felt as Curran did organised themselves into the National League under the leadership of John Redmond's son William, and the *Irish Times* report on the meeting in Waterford at which the new party was launched noted that 'Neither on the platform nor in the houses along the route, which were decorated, was the flag of the

Free State to be seen.'[67] However, after some initial successes, the
National League quickly crumbled, a casualty of the domination of Free
State politics by the Treaty issue and the consequent pressure on all opponents of republicanism to vote for Cumann na nGaedheal. It is thus very
difficult to assess how widespread sentimental loyalty to the tradition and
symbols of the Irish Parliamentary Party, and opposition to the symbols
of Sinn Féin, were among nationalists.

While republicans, ex-unionists and anti-Sinn Féin nationalists were
all united in seeing the tricolour and 'The Soldier's Song' as party symbols, Free Staters vigorously denied such claims. According to Cumann
na nGaedheal, these were national symbols, accepted as such by the overwhelming majority of Irish people and by the three main political parties
in the Dáil, and therefore 'entirely removed from the atmosphere of politics'.[68] 'The tri-colour is not the flag of the Free State,' the government
party's newspaper asserted in 1923, 'neither is it the flag of the
Republicans – it is the Irish flag, floating above all other flags, uncon-
quered and unconquerable.'[69] When republicans were tearing down tricolours at pro-Treaty meetings in 1922, several letters in the *Irish
Independent* defended the government's right to fly the flag on the
grounds that no section of the nation could claim exclusive possession of
the tricolour. As one correspondent put it:

> The majority of the people have a constitutional right in this matter as in
> any other, and I am sure they would not think of adopting any flag other
> than that under which the fight was fought and won... With regard to the
> claim of the advocates of a semi-detached Republic, I have yet to learn that
> they are patenters of or hold a copyright in the colours of the rainbow. It
> will be quite time enough when they capture the rainbow to attempt to con-
> trol the colours.[70]

The republican claim to the tricolour could thus be portrayed as an unde-
mocratic interference with the people's sovereign rights; as the Defence
Minister told a heckler at an election rally, the tricolour 'did not belong to
any junta'.[71]

The argument that it was for the people to decide on their symbols also
reinforced the point that under the Treaty Irish people, for the first time,
had the power to make such decisions: the fact that they could choose
their own symbols without interference from Britain was itself a sign of
the independence achieved by the Free State. 'Who is to tell us what flag
we shall have?' asked E.J. Duggan in the Treaty debates. 'Ourselves. No
one else has the right.' The Treaty, according to Liam de Roiste, 'gives us
our flag and our men to defend it',[72] and a Free State propaganda poster
made this point visually by depicting a soldier standing beside a
tricolour.[73] The flag and anthem could also be seen as evidence that the

government was not dominated by ex-unionists and Masons, as Fianna Fáil alleged. Speaking at an election meeting in 1932, President Cosgrave asked whether the Masons were responsible for the government's Irish language policy, or for the national flag and anthem.[74] Implicit in such arguments was the assumption that the tricolour and 'The Soldier's Song' were the popular choices of the Irish nation, and that the government's adoption of these symbols was nothing more than a democratic recognition of this fact.

While in opposition, Fianna Fáil disputed the government's right to use the tricolour and 'The Soldier's Song' as symbols of the Free State. Once in office, however, de Valera's party not only continued to employ these symbols as the flag and anthem of the state, but actually entrenched their official status by acquiring copyright in 'The Soldier's Song' and by identifying the tricolour as the national flag in the 1937 constitution. Republican diehards remained emphatically opposed to the use of these symbols by any state other than an all-Ireland republic: Cumann na mBan, for example, protested in 1932 that 'the Tricolour is and always has been regarded not as the "National" but as the Republican flag' and that 'time can never reconcile Republicans to the insult offered their Flag in its display by the Free State Government'.[75] Moderate opponents of the Treaty, however, were reconciled to the state's use of these symbols under a government which they considered a more legitimate inheritor of the ideals of 1916 than its predecessor. Cumann na nGaedheal, meanwhile, expressed satisfaction at what it saw as general acceptance by ex-unionists and the remnants of the old constitutional nationalist tradition that the tricolour and 'The Soldier's Song' were not party symbols.[76] While the pro-Treaty party's newspaper probably overstated the extent of this acceptance, by the time Fianna Fáil came to power the ex-unionists and Redmondites had generally either withdrawn from political life or been integrated into a political system predicated on the legitimacy of the Sinn Féin struggle. Thus, with few remaining dissenters outside the major political parties, a consensus could emerge after 1932 that the tricolour and 'The Soldier's Song' were indeed national, not party symbols.

Proposals to replace the flag and anthem

Before this consensus emerged, however, there were some who argued that the Free State flag and anthem were obstacles to unity within the state as well as to the goal of uniting the whole of Ireland. If only the government would adopt a new flag or anthem, such critics contended, the task of achieving reconciliation and national unity would be made much easier.[77] Moreover, while objections to the tricolour were made mainly on the grounds of its associations, the words and music of 'The Soldier's Song' were also declared to be unworthy of elevation to the status of national anthem. Some wanted to revive one of the old flags or anthems, others to create entirely new symbols which would be free of potentially divisive associations. However, criticism of the state's existing symbols and proposals for the invention of new symbols raised the question of how symbols were properly chosen. In response to suggestions that the state needed a new anthem, supporters of 'The Soldier's Song' and even some of its critics declared that national anthems were adopted by the people, and that a self-conscious search for an anthem with broad appeal was unlikely to be successful. The example of the only serious attempt to run a competition for a new national anthem in this period seemed to confirm such scepticism.

The Irish Free State seems to have been remarkably free of would-be flag designers, and if the government file on 'National Flag: Miscellaneous Suggestions & Requests' is an accurate indication, few people gave the government the benefit of their thoughts on the matter.[78] There were occasional suggestions for new flags designed to facilitate Irish unity by appealing to nationalist and unionist alike, while others wondered if it might be possible to find a flag 'back beyond our "unhappy divisions"' in the time of Brian Boru or even further back in the mists of antiquity with Finn Mac Cumhaill and his sunburst standard.[79] But proposals either to create a new flag or to trawl through history in search of antique banners were less common than calls for the return of a flag featuring the harp. Support for the harp flag was not restricted to irreconcilable Redmondites: there was 'no reason for identifying it with the Parliamentary Party' thought one writer,[80] while another highlighted its republican history: 'What was good enough for Wolfe Tone and Robert Emmet is, or ought to be good, enough for us'.[81] Proponents of the adoption of a harp flag (green or otherwise) argued that, as the historic flag of Ireland, it had general appeal and 'would have a wonderful unifying effect'; it was also praised on aesthetic grounds as 'artistic', 'beautiful', more attractive and striking or more distinctive than the tricolour.[82] Such sporadic suggestions, however, failed to ignite any significant debate about the Free State flag, nor was there ever a competition to find a replacement.

The question of a possible new national anthem provoked livelier debate. One explanation for this is that, whereas the tricolour was used as the official flag of the Free State from the state's foundation, 'The Soldier's Song' was not confirmed as the national anthem until 1926, and even then the government's failure to promote it left some people unsure of its status. This meant that in the early years of the state people felt that the national anthem question was still open for discussion. There is also more to consider in a national anthem than in a flag: anthems have words and music which can be praised or damned on both political and artistic grounds. In addition, while nationalist Ireland only had one widely accepted national flag before the rise of the tricolour, it had a wealth of patriotic songs. This meant not only that there were many existing contenders for the title of national anthem, but also that some people had a vague sense that Irish genius could produce the perfect anthem if given the opportunity.

To critics of 'The Soldier's Song' it was astounding 'that with all the gold of our folk-music to draw upon, we should decide to set in the place of honour a cheapish piece of brass-work'.[83] Deputy MacDermot told the Dáil that:

> We have got a wide range of genuinely Gaelic melodies to choose from, and whether we want an air that is brisk and martial or an air that is tender and melancholy or one that is grave and majestic, we can find it. We could find a National Anthem that corresponded much more nearly to our desire to develop Gaelic civilisation in this country and one also that corresponded to the antiquity of this country and the antiquity of our struggle for self-government.[84]

One old song suggested as an alternative anthem by a number of critics of 'The Soldier's Song' was 'Let Erin Remember'. When he recommended it as a national anthem in 1924, Seán Lester thought 'Let Erin Remember' would need new lyrics 'appropriate to the new era',[85] but D.F. Curran saw the song's focus on the past as an advantage, since it 'deals with a period in our history when Ireland was indeed a great nation'.[86] Proponents of 'Let Erin Remember' saw it as non-partisan, a point reinforced in W.F. Trench's suggestion for a new second verse which included the lines 'The banners of party strife they have furled, / And no boundary shall them sever.'[87] It was also regarded as musically superior to 'The Soldier's Song', a point seemingly admitted even by the Executive Council when, for a short time, it ruled that 'the air of "Let Erin Remember" was more suitable from the musical point of view for external purposes'.[88]

For a number of Free State citizens almost anything would have been better, both musically and lyrically, than 'The Soldier's Song'. In the course of a letter to the *Star* calling for greater use of the anthem, one writer was forced to admit that 'The Anthem has been widely criticised, and on many grounds. Some say it is not, and never was, the national song of the country, while others content themselves by declaring that the words are silly and the music poor.'[89] The *Cork Examiner* was lukewarm, conceding that 'The Soldier's Song' had 'a bold air' and was 'associated with some stirring episodes in the latter-day history', but complaining that it did not compare well with the anthems of other countries.[90] Other critics were more damning about the anthem's poetic and musical qualities, one describing it as 'a rather poor piece of doggerel verse set to indifferent music'.[91] Both words and music were said to be 'rhetoric, and unimpressive rhetoric at that';[92] it was 'lugubrious and commonplace',[93] dreary,[94] 'a positive offence artistically',[95] 'a jaunty little piece of vulgarity', 'an abomination to any one who knows anything about music'.[96] 'As music, pure and simple, it is martial,' wrote one commentator, 'but lacks definite construction, and gives one a sense of winding round and round until it has to exhaust itself eventually in a diminuendo.'[97] Moreover, it 'has nothing about it of Irish music or of Irish poetic sentiment'.[98] Some claimed that the tune was not Irish at all, but came from a French hymn, and seeming confirmation of the anthem's lack of Irishness could be found in reports that it could not be played 'on the most Irish of all musical instruments, the Irish pipes'.[99] Army band director Colonel Brase reportedly hated the song, but did not make his feelings known publicly;[100] the internationally renowned Irish tenor John McCormack was less reticent, declaring that he favoured replacing 'The Soldier's Song' with a more 'tuneful' anthem.[101]

Some felt that the Free State anthem lacked more abstract qualities, most notably dignity. It failed to 'typify all that is best and noblest, all that is heroic, soulful, and dignified in the national character';[102] it was not 'distinctive, grand, stately and soul-stirring'.[103] W.F. Trench, Professor of English Literature at Trinity College Dublin, feared that if 'The Soldier's Song' continued to be the Free State national anthem 'we are liable to be regarded with scorn', since 'the music suggests a rabble rather than a nation'.[104] Concern was also expressed about the militarist and anti-English lyrics of 'The Soldier's Song', which some felt were out of place in the new era. One critic asked if it was still appropriate to be singing about fighting to be free,[105] while *Dublin Opinion* joked, 'The Wrong is Ended, but the Melody lingers on.'[106] W.F. Trench commented that 'The Soldier's Song', 'while not martial in tune, as it should be' was 'at the same time too militarist in tone, Ireland's future lying more in paths of peace'.[107] 'We cannot be always glorifying the gun and the sword', wrote another critic, who felt that 'The Soldier's Song' had served its purpose. 'When the "*bearna baoghail*" was to be manned, it nerved the youthful warrior. In times of peace it brings us only memories.'[108] The adoption of such a song in a time of conflict might be understandable, but this did not make it a suitable national anthem.[109] On the contrary, 'A war song of the moment, no matter how popular, has no lasting elements', and it was no more appropriate that 'The Soldier's Song' should be the Irish national anthem than that 'It's a Long Way to Tipperary' should be the British anthem.[110]

For supporters of 'The Soldier's Song', however, the Free State anthem brought to mind not 'Tipperary' but a more lasting war song, the 'Marseillaise'.[111] One admitted that the 'Marseillaise' and 'The Soldier's Song', as revolutionary anthems, might not be liked by all in their respective countries, but another pointed out that after the divisions produced by the revolution in France the 'Marseillaise' had eventually gained general acceptance there and that the same might happen in time with 'The Soldier's Song'.[112] Others saw the emergence of 'The Soldier's Song' from the revolutionary period as evidence that it was the authentic choice of the people. This view was put in 1933 during the Dáil debate on the government's acquisition of copyright in 'The Soldier's Song'. Dr O'Higgins told the Dáil that 'The Soldier's Song' 'happened to be the Anthem on the lips of the people when they came into their own', and had thus been adopted by the people before it was adopted by the Executive Council. Deputy Norton concurred: national anthems were 'never devised with an eye to getting perfect music or perfect words', least of all in newly independent nations, in which the national anthem inevitably emerged out of the independence struggle. 'The Soldier's Song' was the product of 'a period of trial and tribulation', when it reflected 'the hopes and aims and aspirations of our people', and it still reflected those aspirations in 1933.[113]

According to President Cosgrave, a national anthem 'springs from the people as a spontaneous and natural outpouring of national feeling',[114] and such claims could be used to obscure the government's role in promoting 'The Soldier's Song' as well as to excuse its musical and lyrical faults. 'The plain people do not judge patriotic songs by their musical merits', wrote one of the song's champions; 'the spirit which the words arouse, the faithful interpretation of the ideals of the people, and the memories which the song recalls are the essentials that make for lasting favour.'[115] Dr O'Higgins believed that 'National Anthems come about, not because of the suitability of the particular words or notes, but because they are adopted generally by the nation.' Deputy Fitzgerald-Kenney likewise maintained that 'national anthems are not written to order', but arise spontaneously, and that it was beyond the power of a parliament to tell the people what their national anthem was. 'The Soldier's Song', in his view, had been chosen by the people, and no action by the Dáil could change this.[116]

Some people, however, hoped that a new anthem *could* be written to order. In 1924 Seán Lester proposed to the Executive Council that a competition be held either to find a completely new anthem or to provide new words to the tune of 'Let Erin Remember'.[117] Lester's proposal was not taken up by the government, but shortly thereafter a competition to find a new anthem was announced by the *Dublin Evening Mail*, which offered a prize of fifty guineas to the writer of the best set of verses for an Irish national anthem (a further prize was to be offered later for the best musical setting of the chosen verses). The *Evening Mail* explained that:

> The real need in the Ireland of to-day is a national hymn or anthem for use on ceremonial or convivial occasions, and as a rallying song for Irishmen all over the world. There is no song at present which appeals generally to all classes, and there are extant too many songs and anthems which serve only as battle cries, not always designed to encourage one side, but to infuriate another. What is required is
> A NATIONAL HYMN TO THE GLORY OF IRELAND,
> which men and women of every shade of politics may use...Every civilised nation has its national song or anthem, and history teems with incidents of peoples who rose to great occasions stimulated by the soul-stirring strains of their national songs. Ireland is rich in the 'sweet minstrelsy of song', but she has NO NATIONAL ANTHEM.[118]

The newspaper's call for a new national anthem made several points which would be repeated by later commentators: that Ireland needed an anthem which would unite, not divide; that national anthems should be inspirational and stirring; and that the lack of an appropriate anthem was particularly lamentable in Ireland, which had produced so many great songs in the past.

When the competition closed in August, the *Evening Mail* reported that hundreds of entries had been received, and that the writers W.B. Yeats, James Stephens and Lennox Robinson had agreed to act as judges. In October, however, the paper published the judges' verdict that none of the entries was 'worthy of fifty guineas or of any portion of it'. They advised anthem writers to 'study a little the national songs of different countries, for most of the verses submitted to us were imitations of "God Save the King"'.[119] It is not clear whether the judges were likening the style or the sentiments of the entries to 'God Save the King', and they provided no examples to illustrate their point. As a result of the judges' decision, the editor of the *Evening Mail* was forced to reopen the competition. This time, readers would choose the winner by voting for their favourite from among a number of entries selected by the newspaper, and competitors would, it was hoped, be inspired by a series of articles on 'Songs of the Nations: A Survey of the World's National Anthems' to look beyond 'God Save the King' as a model.[120] Unfortunately, while the new procedure was at least guaranteed to produce a result, it could not guarantee a successful anthem. The verses chosen by the *Evening Mail* were distinguished only by their steadfast devotion to cliché, though they did manage to avoid rhyming the 'six essential words' which had earlier been identified by *Dublin Opinion* (the words were roll/soul, Ireland/Sire-land, arise/eyes).[121] The verse favoured by 'a clear preponderance of public opinion', which began:

> God of our Ireland, by Whose hand
> Her glory and her beauty grew,
> Just as the shamrock o'er the land
> Grows green beneath thy sparkling dew;[122]

won the competition,[123] but went on to find the obscurity it so richly deserved.

The *Dublin Evening Mail* anthem competition showed how difficult it was to produce a successful anthem on demand. It also demonstrated the problems inherent in the attempt to find lyrics which were both inspiring and politically innocuous. Commenting on the entries received for its competition, the *Evening Mail* remarked that:

> Some of the rejected entries reached a higher level of poetic expression; some took a more forcible and stimulating view of the political position of the country. Many excellent verses would have made admirable battle cries if Free Staters were marching upon Republicans, or Republicans were defending, say, the Ballast Office against tyrannical government. But none of these were exactly what Ireland needs at the moment, or for a future which everyone hopes will be less contentious than the past. Some quite reverent expressions of religious views could not have been sung unreservedly by all parties in a mixed gathering, and a very large proportion of the offered anthems failed because they were nothing more than topical songs, and celebrated a recently-won 'Freedom' with more reference to 'seven hundred years of wrong' than to the fact that 'To-day is,' and that what is needed is an anthem which may be adopted now, and will still be up-to-date a hundred years hence, when 'the dawn of Freedom' is only history, and the use we made of it is what will call for a rallying song for Irishmen.[124]

Humourists may have perceived the difficulty of finding such an uncontroversial anthem more clearly than the rather stuffy editor of the *Evening Mail*. *Dublin Opinion* mocked the newspaper's solemn quest for a new anthem, writing that:

> the Winning Effort must be something that the Editor of the *Evening Mail* could recite without blushing before a meeting of the Governors of the Bank of Ireland. Something that will define our status under the Treaty with the precision, almost, of a legal document. Something rather cold and dignified which will at least evoke a little restrained cheering and a little respectful hat raising when played at our public functions ... but something which will certainly not stir the blood to the pitch at which young fellows

neglect their employers' business and grope in the thatch for the pikes of
their Fenian ancestors. A little religious touch thrown in would be a help. It
must, of course, be undenominational and general, embracing in its appeal
all kinds of Christians.[125]

Dublin Opinion duly rolled up its sleeves and produced some verses for a
national anthem to be sung to 'A judicious mixture of "God Save the
King," and "Ireland, I Love You, Acushla Machree"'. Its proposed
anthem, which might have lacked 'soul-stirring appeal' but was at least
'perfectly safe', began:

> God Save our gracious King,
> For he's our gracious King
> Under the Treaty.[126]

The travel writer H.V. Morton, having been told that '"The Soldiers'
Song" is as dull as the "Red Flag"', was serenaded with another light-
hearted anthem during his stay in Dublin:

> God save the Free State, Tim Healy, and the King,
> The Harp and the Shamrock and the old Claddagh Ring,
> The round tower of Clonmacnoise, the pistol and the bomb,
> But when we get the Republic, boys, we'll make the old land hum.[127]

'That is the ideal National Anthem', declared the singer, 'because it has a
kind word to say for everybody.'

An anthem which set out to please everyone was likely to please no one.
In its efforts to avoid overtly political lyrics, the *Evening Mail* was left with
verses so bland as to be almost interchangeable: the six verses selected by
the newspaper for its readers to choose from all expressed a vague love of
country and called on God to bless and protect Ireland. Such undistinguished
verse had no chance of competing against the existing patriotic songs which,
whatever their poetic worth, at least carried an emotional charge arising
from their histories and associations. This was the difficulty facing those
who longed for 'a new national anthem, entirely devoid of political
antecedents and expressing the love and pride of all Irishmen in their
common country'[128] or one which 'should have no reference to incidents in
our controversial history, but should dwell rather on the beauty and charm of
our country, looking in fact not so much to the past as to the future'.[129] Such
an anthem might lack the negative associations which make for political
controversy, but it would also lack the positive associations which give
anthems their power to move and inspire. Unless its words and music were
exceptionally fine, then, it would stir 'like a spoon in cold porridge'.[130]

The idea of an open competition had presumably been killed off by the

Dublin Evening Mail fiasco, but a few people suggested that a committee might be formed to choose a new anthem or perhaps, in Frank MacDermot's proposal, to find another anthem which would not replace 'The Soldier's Song' but coexist with it.[131] However, the *Irish Statesman* rejected a suggestion that it should establish a committee to choose a new anthem, even though the editor of the *Statesman* (the poet George Russell, who wrote under the name Æ) had previously expressed his dislike of 'The Soldier's Song'. The *Statesman* doubted that national anthems could be discovered by committees or imposed by governments, since: 'The spirit is not won by thought. The spirit chooses whom it wills. If the spirit of poetry chooses any Irish poet to write a National Anthem, it will be sung spontaneously over Ireland without any Government orders at all. That is the only kind of National Anthem worth having.'[132] If 'A national anthem is an inspiration',[133] there was nothing for it but to wait for inspiration to strike, though Irish people might 'have to wait for a period removed some distance from the present strife before inspiration can come'.[134] In the meantime, citizens of the Free State would have to make do with 'The Soldier's Song'.

Religion and the flag and anthem

While the political associations of the tricolour and 'The Soldier's Song' were contentious, at least in the first decade of the Free State's existence, these symbols did not divide the Free State's people on strictly religious lines (most Protestants, being ex-unionists, would have disliked these symbols, but for political, not religious reasons). There was, seemingly, nothing in the Free State flag and anthem to offend any religious group, since they did not represent the religious sentiments of the Irish people in any obvious way (although the tricolour was supposed to symbolise the union of Catholics and Protestants). However, in light of the controversy over the absence of religious emblems from the coins (see Chapter 3), it is surprising that the secularism of the flag and anthem did not itself become an issue. Remarkably, given both the high level of religiosity within the state and the fact that many other countries had national anthems replete with religious references, the Free State's anthem included no mention of God, nor any religious reference at all. Despite the seeming anomaly of such a godly society being represented by a godless anthem, the critic of 'The Soldier's Song' who called for an anthem 'from which reference to the Deity is not absent, something with the note… of faith in our destiny, and in our glorious Christianity' was almost a lone voice.[135] I can only attribute this puzzling silence about the anthem's secular lyrics to the fact that, as I suggest below, few people actually knew the words of 'The Soldier's Song'.

There were some suggestions that the Free State flag should be sanctified by the addition of a religious symbol, but again such comments were surprisingly infrequent. As early as 1918 a Sinn Féin supporter proposed that a Celtic cross should be added to the white stripe of the tricolour because 'The flag would be terribly sacred then, and no Irishman could ever affect, then, to think little of it.'[136] Others subsequently repeated this suggestion, hoping that the addition of the cross to the flag would 'show that we are not Irish merely but Catholic as well'.[137] There were also some calls for the flag to be emblazoned with a more specifically Catholic symbol, the Sacred Heart. A letter to *Sinn Féin* in 1924 called for the Sacred Heart to be placed on the flag so that Ireland might recognise 'the King of Kings as Eternal Monarch of this ancient nation'. When this was done, 'abundant blessings shall be bestowed on all national undertakings, and the name of Ireland shall be written on the Sacred Heart, never to be effaced'.[138] This letter apparently brought many responses, both supportive and critical, but unfortunately the newspaper did not print more than a few short extracts. It was evident, however, that the proposal could be seen either as an aid to unity or as divisive, depending on whether the Sacred Heart was considered a 'symbol of Christianity in spite of all different religious and political beliefs', one to which 'all Ireland is consecrated', or an exclusively Catholic emblem, alienating to Protestants who might otherwise be loyal to the symbolism of the tricolour.[139] Another suggestion to put the Sacred Heart on the flag came just before the 1933 election in a letter to President de Valera informing him that 'our Lord appeared to a nun in America and told her His love for the Irish people and said for them to put the Image of His S. Heart on their Flag and they would have nothing to fear. Promise if you are returned with a huge majority that you will do so.'[140]

Given the absence of any widespread demand for a religious symbol to appear on the flag it is not surprising that the government declined to take up such suggestions. What is surprising is the apparent lack of public concern about the state's failure to represent religious tradition on the national flag. There may have been some reluctance to place a cross on the white stripe of the tricolour since this would have been reminiscent of the English St George's cross. The cross of St Patrick was likewise ruled out because of its use on the Union Jack, and because it was believed by many nationalists to be 'purely a fraud, a fiction of English politicians to suit their union jack'.[141] In the 1930s the Blueshirts and, for a time, Fine Gael adopted a blue flag with a red diagonal cross, described as 'the cross of St. Patrick, the national apostle of Ireland'. However, this was a party flag, to be flown in conjunction with the tricolour, and there is no evidence that it was ever intended to replace the tricolour as the national flag.[142] Perhaps the absence of widespread calls for a flag whose symbolism was obviously Christian can be attributed to a perception that the tricolour already represented the two major religious traditions of Ireland, or alternatively that it represented the Catholic tradition by incorporating the colours of the Vatican flag, a misapprehension which is discussed below.

Flags and anthems are commonly viewed as inherently sacred, and this may be another reason why there was no campaign in the Free State for a more obviously religious flag and anthem.[143] The clamour for religious symbols on the Free State coins can be seen as a product of people's anxieties about the profane and polluting qualities of money. Flags and anthems, by contrast, are usually set somewhat apart from the mundane, and people are made aware of them in the context of ritual. The very name 'national anthem' suggests a connection with religious music, and in the 1920s and 1930s the playing of national anthems was still greeted with the respectful removal of hats. National flags and anthems are frequently said to have been sanctified by martyrs, as the tricolour and 'The Soldier's Song' were, and any lack of decorum in relation to these symbols is liable to be viewed as an insult to the sacred memory of the nation's heroes. Citizens are expected to adopt a reverent attitude towards their flag and anthem, and if they do not they may be accused of 'desecration'. Thus, it may be that many citizens of the Free State felt no need to add religious emblems or lyrics to a flag and anthem which were already considered sacred.

The flag and anthem in public life

The government of the Free State never took any legislative action to officially recognise 'The Soldier's Song' as the state's anthem, nor did it legislate to make the tricolour the national flag until it was included in the 1937 constitution. The government did make clear that these were officially recognised symbols, not only by means of statements in the Dáil in 1926, but also through its own use of these symbols. Nevertheless, some people remained unsure of the status of the flag and anthem, or claimed to be so, and asked whether they had in fact been officially adopted.[144] It is difficult to know whether such queries, several of them in the ex-unionist *Irish Times*, reflected genuine uncertainty or simply the refusal of ex-unionists to accept the adoption of Sinn Féin symbols, but what is clear is that many people were unsure about the colours of the flag and the lyrics of the anthem. This uncertainty was a consequence of the failure of Free State governments, both Cumann na nGaedheal and Fianna Fáil, to actively promote the state's flag and anthem. Governments seem to have been satisfied for these symbols to play a relatively minor role in public life in the 1920s and 1930s.

Calls to establish the tricolour as the Free State flag by legislation were rejected by the government as unnecessary, despite Deputy Esmonde's concern about whether 'Irish citizens will pay proper respect to a State which refuses to legalise its national flag'.[145] The flag was considered to have been established by usage, but its usage by the government was in fact rather sparing. In 1928 the tricolour was displayed daily from military barracks, and from public buildings under Board of Works control on St Patrick's Day. By 1943 the flag flew daily from a few specific buildings, and from all government buildings with permanent flagpoles on St Patrick's Day and Easter Monday.[146] It seems, then, that most government buildings were bare of flags for most of the year. Nor was there any requirement that the flag be used in schools. In 1936 the Fianna Fáil Ard-Fheis carried a motion calling for the national flag to be flown by all schools under the control of the Department of Education. This idea was rejected by the government, and Minister for Education Tomás Ó Deirg told the party assembly that flying the flag was less important than the cultural rebuilding accomplished by schools. There had been a tremendous advance in knowledge of Irish language, history and literature among young people since independence, he argued, despite the fact that there had been no flags flying over the schools.[147]

As with the flag, the government declined to use legislation to establish 'The Soldier's Song' as the national anthem. In 1927 the army's Chief of Staff proposed to the Council of Defence, which included President Cosgrave, that the government should proclaim one national anthem and order that no other anthem might have priority over it. However, this idea was rejected by the Council, probably because such a law might cause embarrassment to the government if it was seen as restricting the right of ex-unionists to sing 'God Save the King'.[148] Instead, the government tried to lead by example. Army bands were instructed in 1926 to play the national anthem at the end of all concerts and other functions at which the band remained until the end, while that same year saw the commencement of Radio Éireann, which played the anthem at the close of broadcasting every night.[149] However, the government never published an official version of the anthem's lyrics, nor did it make clear whether the whole song or only the chorus was considered to be the national anthem. It is surprising, too, that the government made no attempt to promote an Irish language version of the anthem, despite the commitment of both major parties to the revival of Irish. Although several Irish translations of 'The Soldier's Song' had been made, none was considered suitable for official adoption.[150] Evidence that the public was ignorant of the anthem's lyrics prompted Colonel Brase to suggest in 1928 that newspapers be asked to print the words of the anthem weekly and that the song be taught in schools, but nothing came of these suggestions. Fianna Fáil's Minister for Education was also asked in the Dáil in 1933 and 1934 if he would ensure that the national anthem was taught in schools, but he declined to take such action.[151]

Had the government supported calls for the compulsory introduction of the flag and anthem into schools it might have had greater success in clearing up uncertainty about the correct colours of the flag and about the words of the anthem. In 1926, President Cosgrave had stated clearly in the Dáil what the correct colours of the officially recognised flag were, but despite this, the tricolour was often mistakenly believed to be green, white and yellow, rather than green, white and orange. A number of factors probably contributed to this confusion, including the fact that the old green harp flag had often been referred to as the 'green and gold'. It was natural, therefore, that the Sinn Féin tricolour should be referred to as the 'green, white and gold', especially as 'gold' is grander and easier to use in verse than 'orange'. There may also have been some reluctance on the part of Catholics who understood the intended symbolism of the flag to acknowledge the colour of their Orange enemies. However, it seems that many people did not know what the tricolour was meant to stand for.[152] It may have been commonly assumed that there was a connection with the yellow and white papal flag, especially after that flag was adopted by the newly sovereign Vatican State in 1929, the year of the Catholic Emancipation centenary celebrations in Ireland.[153] A memorandum from the Department of the President in 1932 pointed out that there was 'a surprising lack of uniformity in the popular interpretation' of the proper colours for the flag, especially in regard to the orange, which was often replaced by 'a pale yellow which has no historic basis, but which is probably due to the fact that the flag is sometimes incorrectly described as green, white and gold. The fact that pale yellow is one of the colours of the Papal flag is also not without its influence in this direction.' The flag would feature heavily in decorations for the Eucharistic Congress, the memorandum continued, and it was therefore important that there be no ambiguity about what was the correct flag. As a result, the Executive Council decided to inform the press about the history and correct colours of the flag.[154] Nevertheless, the popular use of green, white and yellow flags continued, leading Seán O'Casey to comment acidly that 'The orange stripe in the republican flag is weakening into the yellow of the Vatican, and the Orangemen aren't blind.'[155]

Public reaction to the playing of 'The Soldier's Song' suggests that unfamiliarity with the anthem's lyrics may have been at least as widespread as ignorance of the flag's colours. Fritz Brase of the Army School of Music noted in 1928 that during Horse Show Week a section of the crowd would sing along to 'God Save the King', but that no one joined in when the band played 'The Soldier's Song'. He attributed this not to a lack of respect on the part of most of the people, but to the fact that very few people knew the words.[156] At the opening of the Tailteann Games, shortly after the 1928 Horse Show, nationalists were apparently stung into attempting to sing the Free State anthem in response to the singing of 'God Save the King' by ex-unionists at the Horse Show. 'For the first time on such an occasion the crowd made a feeble but heroic effort to join in the refrain', reported the *Irish Independent*, indicating clearly that the crowd was unused to singing the national anthem.[157] The *Independent*'s reporter speculated that when Irish people had heard 'God Save the King' sung lustily in public a few more times they would be goaded into singing along whenever 'The Soldier's Song' was played, and by 1932 knowledge of the Free State anthem had evidently increased to the point where it could be 'sung with fervour by the entire gathering' at the opening of the Tailteann Games.[158] Nonetheless, it was still reportedly the case in the 1930s that the anthem's lyrics were very rarely used, and that the words of 'The Soldier's Song' were less well known than those of 'God Save the King'.[159]

If Free State citizens did gradually become more familiar with the national anthem it was probably due more to the efforts of private organisations than to any action taken by the government. The failure of theatres and cinemas to play the national anthem at the end of performances upset some patriots, one of whom described it as a 'gross insult to a free people'.[160] The December 1931 meeting of the national executive of Clann na nGaedheal, an organisation representing IRA veterans of the War of Independence, passed a resolution asking theatres and cinemas to play the national anthem. Members of the Clann subsequently approached entertainment houses in Dublin proposing that Easter 1932 would be an appropriate time to begin playing the anthem. Most venues agreed to the idea, their receptiveness perhaps influenced, as a member of the Clann na nGaedheal executive suggested, by the change of government.[161] With Fianna Fáil in power, theatre managers may have felt that it was advisable to display their patriotism and also that the use of 'The Soldier's Song' as the Free State anthem was now less open to challenge by republicans. Beginning on 28 March 1932, the anthem was played at the close of performances in Dublin theatres and cinemas, and it was reported that 'The innovation was cordially received in the houses, the great majority of the patrons standing to attention, although in the act of leaving. Men remained standing bareheaded.'[162] The practice was not universally applauded, however. Cumann na nGaedheal's newspaper, while advising that 'The Soldier's Song' should be duly honoured whenever it was played, found the association of the anthem with theatricals rather incongruous.[163] Fianna Fáil supporter Dorothy Macardle also protested against what she regarded as an English practice, arguing that if the anthem was not reserved for occasions of special national significance it would lose its dignity and its power to inspire, becoming hackneyed and eventually disliked.[164]

Playing the anthem in theatres and cinemas may have helped to familiarise people with the music of 'The Soldier's Song', but credit for popularising the words, and particularly the Irish language lyrics, should probably go to the Gaelic Athletic Association (GAA). In the early 1930s the fervently nationalist and Gaelic revivalist GAA began encouraging crowds at its well attended sporting events to sing the anthem in Irish by publishing Liam Ó Rinn's translation in its journal, *An Camán*, and in the programmes of matches.[165] The fact that Ó Rinn's translation subsequently outstripped not only other Irish translations but also the English original in popularity suggests that it was the GAA, more than any other organisation, which succeeded in getting Irish people to sing the anthem rather than observing a respectful silence while it was played. Today Ó Rinn's translation has become the standard version, and many people believe that the English lyrics were translated from Irish, but it seems likely that in the 1930s the song was still most often sung in English, when it was sung at all.

The efforts of Clann na nGaedheal and the GAA to make the public more familiar with the national anthem were no doubt motivated by the belief that more frequent use of the flag and anthem would promote national pride. This belief was common worldwide at the time (particularly in that alternative Irish homeland, the United States of America) and was expressed by a number of Free State citizens. A letter complaining about the absence of the tricolour from Waterford's Custom House claimed that 'Until the love and respect due to a national flag is impressed on the people we'll never know that we are living in a free country.'[166] Saluting the flag was one way of engendering 'a deep-rooted, lasting respect for the flag of our national resurgence', and the introduction of this American custom in schools or in society at large was advocated in two letters to the *Irish Press* in 1932.[167] The national anthem, too, was seen by some as an instrument to be used in building nationality. A letter to Cosgrave suggesting that a few lines of 'The Soldier's Song' should be sung at the conclusion of all theatrical events complained that 'The people at large seem very slow to realise the importance of the national individuality we have attained'.[168] Another writer thought that 'If the Anthem were played more frequently, such as at the termination of all theatrical performances, dinners and dances, perhaps it would help to educate the general public into a broader spirit of patriotism, and induce our people, no matter what their individual politics, to take a common pride in the fact that they were primarily Irishmen.'[169]

The Free State government, however, gave no indication that it attached such great importance to the flag and anthem when it came to fostering national pride and allegiance to the state. The Cumann na nGaedheal party newspaper did exhort all Free State citizens to honour the state's flag and anthem, and expressed particular regret at the failure of the Protestant and ex-unionist minority to do so.[170] The *Star* also insisted that the national flag and anthem should be used at public events whenever state dignitaries, especially the Governor General, were in attendance.[171] However, only on a few occasions was this insistence backed up by action. In 1926 the Royal Dublin Society (RDS) acceded to a government request to fly the tricolour over the Governor General's box in the grandstand during the international military jumping competition at the Dublin Horse Show, apparently after the government threatened to withdraw the Free State army team and to advise other countries not to send their teams to the competition.[172] Three years later there was a major dispute over the anthem to be played for the Governor General when he attended a sports day at Trinity College Dublin. In this case the Governor General was prepared to have no anthem played if Trinity refused to play 'The Soldier's Song' alone, but Trinity proved reluctant to omit 'God Save the King', and as a result the Governor General did not attend. The dispute was resolved in 1931, when Trinity agreed to play 'The Soldier's Song' on the Governor General's arrival and only to play 'God Save the King' at the end of the event, after the Governor General had left.[173] Another controversy in 1932 over the failure of the Irish Rugby Football Union (IRFU) to fly the tricolour at international matches in Dublin also provoked the government to seek a reversal of the IRFU policy, but only after a public campaign by Fianna Fáil's *Irish Press* and others proved embarrassing to a government campaigning for re-election. (See Chapter Six.)

The RDS, Trinity College and the IRFU were all organisations which had, to varying degrees, failed to expunge fully their former unionist ethos, and it was ex-unionist antipathy to the Free State flag and anthem which caused the government its greatest dilemma. In the wake of the Trinity College controversy there were some calls for legislation to make 'The Soldier's Song' the official national anthem, so that ex-unionists would have no excuse for omitting it, but the government took no such action.[174] Nonetheless, it was not quite true that 'Mr Cosgrave and his colleagues are no Fascists, and they do not call on the old Loyalists, or Unionists, to participate in the official pieties of the State.'[175] Certainly, Cosgrave was no Mussolini, but his party did expect ex-unionists to honour the state's flag and anthem and generally to respect the pieties of the new order. Unlike the Unionist government in Northern Ireland, which seemingly took it for granted that the political minority in the Six Counties would be 'disloyal' to the state and its symbols, the Free State government hoped that in time ex-unionists would share the same loyalties as the rest of the state's population. The *Star* expressed concern about evidence 'that important elements of the Protestant population dislike the Flag and Anthem of the Saorstát. The effect of that attitude must be to cause their children to acquire a distaste for life in the country in which that Flag is flown and in which that Anthem is sung.'[176] Any change to the flag and anthem at the behest of the ex-unionist minority risked losing the support of the nationalist majority, and was therefore out of the question. The government was left, then, with two options: it could force ex-unionists to accord respect to the flag and anthem in the hope of overcoming their dislike of these symbols through repeated exposure to them, or it could leave Protestants to their own devices while occasionally encouraging them to embrace the symbols of the majority community. Cumann na nGaedheal preferred the latter option, and so too did Fianna Fáil when it came to power. In the long run the policy seems to have worked, and already by the 1930s ex-unionist resistance to the tricolour, at least, was breaking down.[177]

The government's policy on the flag and anthem relied, as the *Cork Examiner* put it, 'on the peaceful penetration of the changed conditions' since the Treaty rather than on active promotion or enforced use of these symbols.[178] Instead of using the flag and anthem to promote loyalty to state and nation, both Cumann na nGaedheal and Fianna Fáil seem to have felt that loyalty would develop of its own accord, accompanied but not created by public use of the state's symbols. As Tomás Ó Deirg indicated when rejecting the idea of flying the tricolour over schools, the Free State government was more concerned to build a strong national identity through reviving the Irish language and teaching Irish history and literature than to encourage allegiance to the state by making frequent use of the flag and anthem. Its priority was to create a common Gaelicised national culture and a common view of national history; if this was accomplished, loyalty to the state and its symbols would naturally follow. Moreover, the government was aware that flags and anthems were still sensitive and contentious matters, particularly during the Free State's first decade. It therefore took a cautious approach, doubtless fearing that more active promotion of the flag and anthem might stir up trouble between the various political groupings within the state. Although debate about these symbols went on quietly, the government never provided a focus for such debate by introducing legislation to establish the flag or anthem, or by campaigning to have them more widely used. By declining to introduce legislation the government also avoided having to enforce the use of the flag and anthem on unwilling citizens or organisations, and on at least one occasion President Cosgrave used the lack of legislation as a justification for his government's non-intervention in a dispute about the use of the tricolour.[179]

Conclusion

Although the rapid rise to prominence of the tricolour and 'The Soldier's Song' after 1916, in tandem with the rise of Sinn Féin, had been remarkable, their status in 1922 was still highly ambiguous. They had come to public attention as symbols of Sinn Féin and its campaign for an Irish republic, and public acceptance of them as national symbols was far from assured. During the revolutionary period they had acquired strong emotional associations: associations which were very positive for Sinn Féiners, but extremely negative for unionists and constitutional nationalists. Because of their strong positive feelings about the tricolour and 'The Soldier's Song', pro-Treaty and anti-Treaty Sinn Féiners fought for possession of these symbols. For ex-unionists and anti-Sinn Féin nationalists, on the other hand, the Sinn Féin flag and anthem brought back painful memories of political defeat and revolutionary violence which left these groups alienated from the state's key symbols. However, attempting to find new symbols which were free of such emotional associations would not necessarily produce a more widely accepted flag and anthem, since it is precisely such associations which give symbols their power. Symbols without any pre-existing emotional charge might simply fail to inspire any section of the population, as in the case of the *Dublin Evening Mail* anthem competition, or alternatively the neglect of symbols people knew and loved might become a cause of outrage, as in the case of the Free State coinage designs. By choosing symbols associated with the Sinn Féin struggle, the Free State government could at least please its core supporters. At the same time, by showing restraint in its promotion of the flag and anthem, and by trying to avoid actions which might have caused a prolonged and heated conflict over their meanings, the government created the conditions in which these symbols could gradually gain greater acceptance.

In the long term, the tricolour and 'The Soldier's Song' came to be accepted almost unquestioningly as the national flag and anthem by Irish nationalists both in the Republic of Ireland and in Northern Ireland.[180] Their transformation from party symbols into national symbols was effected primarily by their selection as official symbols of the Irish Free State. Although the government did not actively promote them, the adoption of the tricolour and 'The Soldier's Song' as symbols of state ensured that they became part of everyday life. The flag appeared on government buildings, at sporting matches, on the coffins of political leaders, at official ceremonies and political rallies; the anthem was played on the radio, and at the conclusion of army band concerts, theatrical performances and public functions. Gradually, people became used to them, and as political stability increased these symbols were no longer associated with political conflict. They became taken-for-granted symbols of an established political order; they became banal. This process, which was underway by the 1930s, was made possible by the marginalisation of unionism, Redmondite nationalism and uncompromising republicanism, and by the triumph of a pragmatic Sinn Féin ethos. However, the transformation of the Sinn Féin flag and anthem into national symbols has meant that they are no longer directly associated with Sinn Féin. Today, when most people in the Republic of Ireland see the tricolour or hear 'The Soldier's Song', they are reminded not of particular political ideals or historical events, but simply of their membership of the Irish nation.

Chapter 3
'Silent ambassadors of national taste': seals, stamps, banknotes and coins of the Irish Free State

National flags and anthems are the primary symbols of modern states: they are given pride of place in state ritual, and are generally used more commonly than other symbols as a kind of visual and aural shorthand for the existence of states and nations. There are other state symbols, however, which citizens probably encounter more frequently and which are at least as important in reminding them of their nationality. All states have some kind of emblem, a coat of arms or seal, which is used on government documents as a sign of their official status. In addition, there are the symbols on coins, banknotes and stamps, which are part of everyday life. Precisely because they appear on commonly used items, people do not consciously notice these symbols most of the time, but they are aware of them nonetheless, and will certainly notice if they are changed or replaced. These symbols play an important role as marks of legitimacy: they signal that the objects in question are backed by the authority of the state, and they must therefore achieve widespread recognition if they are to function effectively.

Because the Irish Free State was a new state, the designs of its state seals, stamps, banknotes and coins were all new, and as a result the citizens of the state could not help noticing them when they were first issued. Only one set of designs, however, became the subject of extensive public discussion. While there was very little comment in the newspapers about the designs of the seals, stamps and banknotes, the symbols on the coins became the centre of a controversy over their appropriateness. This controversy revealed tensions and concerns within the Free State, particularly about the place of religion in public life and about the dignity of the nation. The debate about the coins, and the contrasting acceptance of the much more traditional image on the banknotes, also suggests a deep-rooted anxiety about money which was more likely to be assuaged by conventional motifs than by originality.

Rejection of established national emblems in the Irish Free State

It might have been expected that harps, shamrocks, wolfhounds, round towers, rising suns, Celtic crosses and female personifications of Ireland would feature heavily on the seals, stamps, banknotes and coins of the Free State. However, by the time the Free State was established, some members of the political and artistic elites had turned against these symbols. There were several reasons for this change of attitude. Firstly, these emblems had come to be seen by at least some Sinn Féiners as tainted by association with the Irish Parliamentary Party and the British state. The response to two designs for a ministerial seal, submitted by the Ministry for Economic Affairs for consideration by the Provisional Government in August 1922, suggests that some in the new administration felt that these symbols had dubious political associations. Both designs showed a symbolic female figure with harp, a rising sun behind her, surrounded by pictures of various industries. The designs were rejected by the Provisional Government, and the ministry was informed that: 'In general it is not considered desirable that symbols such as "The Maid of Erin", "The Round Tower", "The Wolf dog", "The Harp" and similar emblems which have received undue prominence in connection with political movements in the past should be embodied in an Official Seal.'[1] Secondly, some people apparently felt that these symbols were associated with a sentimental and impractical way of thinking which was of no use in meeting the challenges faced by the state. An editorial in the Cumann na nGaedheal newspaper *United Irishman* in 1923 remarked peevishly:

> The picture of the morning sun – the sun of Freedom – gleaming on the uncrowned harp and the round tower and wolf dog is a grand painting, but it is not the type that take their driving-force from such things that reduce the idle crowds at the street corners, and in the place of the grass lands and flowing herds give our country a half a million more of happy peasant homes.[2]

Similar sentiments were expressed in the government party's newspaper in 1927, in response to criticism of the proposed coinage designs. The *Freeman* argued that round towers, wolfhounds and so on had served well as emblems in the past, and still had their place, but that designs which reminded people of the state's reliance on agriculture were more appropriate to the needs of the day: 'We must learn to drop sun-burstry nonsense and cultivate the habit of facing actual facts. We do not live on Sunburstry.'[3]

Thirdly, such emblems had come to be regarded by some guardians of artistic taste as clichéd and indicative of 'a shallow, sentimental and ineffectual feeling for Ireland'.[4] W.B. Yeats wrote scornfully in his autobiography of the 'persons of authority' who, in the 1890s, 'found it hard to refuse if anybody offered for sale a pepper-pot shaped to suggest a round tower with a wolf-dog at its foot, who would have felt it inappropriate to publish an Irish book that had not harp and shamrock and green cover'.[5] Time had 'decried' these symbols and 'proved them synthetic', wrote Seán O'Faoláin in 1938, although he admitted that they were 'not yet killed in popular Irish thought or commercial design'.[6] If the old emblems retained some popular appeal, however, their very ubiquity may finally have produced a reaction against them among the 'persons of authority' to whom Yeats referred. Evidence of this change can be seen in the fact that the Royal Society of Antiquaries of Ireland, representing the very sorts of people whose researches had helped to popularise these symbols in the nineteenth century, rejected them in 1926 as 'hackneyed' and unsuitable for use on the Free State coinage.

There was also a more specific reason why some people turned against the female personification of Ireland. A number of writers, tired of bloodshed and particularly distressed by the Civil War, came to see the image of Ireland as a woman calling on men to die for her as repellent and dangerous. When, near the end of his life, Yeats asked himself 'Did that play of mine send out / Certain men the English shot?', he was thinking of *Cathleen ni Houlihan*.[7] Seán O'Casey had a character in his play *The Shadow of a Gunman* (1923) complaining that 'Kathleen ni Houlihan is very different now to the woman who used to play the harp an' sing "Weep on, weep on, your hour is past", for she's a ragin' divil now, an' if you only look crooked at her you're sure of a punch in th' eye'.[8] The Free State government had reason to be cautious about using the imagery which had inspired people to fight for Ireland in the past, since it still faced armed opposition from the votaries of Cathleen ni Houlihan. Assertive figures of Erin might also have been an unwelcome reminder of real life republican women such as Constance Markievicz, Hannah Sheehy-Skeffington, Mary MacSwiney and Maud Gonne MacBride, who were among the government's most implacable opponents.

It is difficult to assess the extent to which distaste for the old Irish national symbols among sections of the elite was out of step with popular sentiment, but these symbols clearly retained some popular currency. They were used, for example, on the masthead of the *Kerryman* newspaper, and appear to this day on the banners of the Ancient Order of Hibernians.[9] Wolfhounds accompanied actors in 'Celtic' costumes during the opening pageants of the Tailteann Games (a sort of Irish race Olympics) in 1928 and 1932, and a fake round tower formed part of the decorations in Dublin for the 1932 Eucharistic Congress.[10] Many of the designs sent in by members of the public when the government invited suggestions for the first series of Free State stamps and coins also incorporated the old symbols, although the response of the public to these calls for suggestions was so poor that it hardly constituted an overwhelming endorsement of the nineteenth-century array of symbols.

In any case, the government did not completely reject these symbols, though it used them sparingly and they were not depicted together as a set in official iconography. The wolfhound appeared on one of the coins, Celtic crosses were used on stamps, small shamrocks also decorated several stamps, and Ireland was personified as a woman on the banknotes and the 1937 commemorative stamp. The round tower did not appear on any official symbols, although it was proposed that, as a 'distinctively Irish mark', it should be used as a government sponsored trademark for goods made in the Gaeltacht (Irish-speaking areas).[11] Of all the old emblems, the harp was the one used most widely by the state, appearing on the coins and banknotes, on all postal stationery and on the 'official paid' stamp,[12] as well as on the 1937 and 1939 commemorative stamps and at the head of official stationery. The use of the harp as one of the main emblems of the state was established by its selection as the principal feature of the state seals.

State seals

In December 1922 the Free State government decided that a common design should be used for all ministerial seals, and it was suggested that the seal of the Provisional Government (consisting of a shield bearing the arms of the four provinces of Ireland encircled by a Gaelic letter 'E') could be adapted for this purpose. However, the design of the Provisional Government seal was rejected on the advice of the historian George Sigerson, who argued that 'its tinctures cannot be discerned, and represent divisions of a country not a United Nation. It is unknown abroad.' Instead, Sigerson suggested the harp, which 'is of ancient and exalted fame' and 'is well-known to other nations and welcomed in all our provinces'. He mentioned its use in the eighteenth century by the Volunteers, the United Irishmen, and Ireland's last independent parliament, and argued that it was 'in no sense a party or sectional symbol but one which represents the entire Nation'.[13]

The government approved the adoption of the harp as the main emblem in official seals at the end of 1922, and the following year it approved a design based on the Brian Boru harp, which had been enthusiastically championed by the Attorney-General, Hugh Kennedy.[14] Kennedy favoured the Brian Boru harp, which was 'at any rate pure Gaelic in inspiration', over a heraldic harp bearing an animal's head, despite the advice of one scholar who felt that heraldry should not be abandoned and that 'The unheraldic invention, the device of the emu, the maple leaf, the Southern Cross, or the kangaroo may be left to promoted penal settlements.'[15] The final design of the Great Seal had the Brian Boru harp in the centre, enclosed within a border copied from the decoration on the Ardagh Chalice, and Kennedy declared that these two national treasures 'represent the close of the great artistic period in Ireland, namely the twelvth [sic] century'.[16] On either side of the harp were the words 'Saorstát Éireann'. Once the design had been decided upon, Kennedy urged that it 'be proceeded with at once as I think it will be good propaganda to have such a seal adopted'. In January 1924 the government authorised the ordering of a Great Seal of the agreed design, and decided that departmental seals would also use the harp as a centerpiece, with the name of the department to be written in Irish.[17]

Kennedy wrote a lengthy justification of the government's choice of design for the Free State seal in an article in the *Irish Sketch and Lady of the House*. In his view there were three things about the harp that made it an appropriate national symbol: its distinctiveness, its dignity and its antiquity. He acknowledged that some national symbols had become associated with Ireland through 'tawdry sentiment and sickly verse', but clearly he did not believe that the harp fell into this category. The harp 'has been and is the National device', he claimed, and it was recognised everywhere as such. The government chose to disregard 'the curious and quite artificial science of Heraldry' which 'had no historical root in this country', and therefore rejected 'Maid of Erin' or animal-headed harps in favour of the Brian Boru harp 'which, in antiquity, in history, and in strength and loveliness stands on a plane by itself'. In conclusion, he explicitly linked the harp to the government's project of Gaelic revivalism. The message of the seal, he pronounced, was:

> that though the State be young, the Nation is old: that it is worth while to pick up the threads of our own arts and culture, and, jumping the years between, to restore continuity of inspiration and, progressing from what was perfection or very near perfection in its own day, to cultivate and labour for perfection without losing individuality in the arts and crafts to our hands in our day and time.[18]

Although the design of the state seal was given greater publicity by its publication in daily newspapers in May 1925,[19] there was very little public response. Only the *Irish Statesman*, which was always interested in aesthetic questions, thought the design worthy of extended comment. It saw the design of the seal, which had 'no artistic merit of any kind', as further evidence of the need for the government to seek expert advice on 'matters involving an aesthetic judgement'. Displaying the kind of artistic elitism which would so outrage some critics of the Free State coinage designs, the *Statesman* continued:

> No doubt when the responsible official saw the harp and the interlacings he felt a proper offering had been made to the national deities... What patriot could assail a seal on which there was a harp bound round with Celtic interlacings, just the kind of thing which was on the Book of Kells? It must be good and beautiful because the same interlacings were everywhere – on patriotic Christmas cards, illuminated addresses and the decorations of extra-patriotic publichouses. Such designs could not be seen everywhere without being good. Alas, it is only commonplace. Why let uneducated officials potter about with art as if it did not require special and expert knowledge, just as much as the Shannon scheme? We appeal to the Government to suppress the artistic amateurs among their employees, and to try to get competent advice on such matters from a committee of artists who have real repute.[20]

Although the government ignored the *Irish Statesman*'s criticism of the seal design, it did subsequently appoint artistic committees to choose designs for the coins, banknotes and stamps. The design of official seals was not reconsidered until the time of the constitutional changes in 1937, when the name of the state on the seals was changed to 'Éire', but the harp was retained as the central symbol.[21] The decision to retain the harp on official seals is hardly surprising, since by this time it was well established as the emblem of the state and had been used since 1930 as the crest for official stationery.[22] The stationery crest was also re-examined in 1937 at the request of President de Valera, who wondered whether the harp 'could not be replaced by something more symbolic, such as a female figure representing Ireland'. An opinion on the matter was sought from Thomas Sadleir of the Office of Arms, who claimed that the figure of Hibernia had originally been created in imitation of Britannia. It was a dignified design and in no sense a party badge, but it was 'not of native growth'. If reproduced on a small scale it would be difficult to distinguish from Britannia and 'would almost certainly be criticized as a servile imitation of Britannia'. The harp, on the other hand, 'seems deservedly popular': it was an emblem of Ireland which pre-dated the arrival of 'the Saxon' and it was associated with no faction or creed. It had been used by the Free State for a number of years, and it would therefore be 'impolitic' to change it unless a markedly superior design could be found. After reading Sadleir's comments, the President agreed that the harp should be retained as the stationery crest.[23]

Stamps

In January 1922, the newly formed Provisional Government approved proposals to overprint the existing United Kingdom stamps and to advertise for designs for new stamps. Accordingly, the old stamps bearing the King's head were overprinted, first with 'Rialtas Sealadach na hÉireann' (Provisional Government of Ireland) and then with 'Saorstát Éireann' (Irish Free State). The new stamps, however, were to bear the name 'Éire', the Irish language name for Ireland.[24] On 1 February 1922 the Postmaster General of the Provisional Government invited the public to submit designs for the definitive series of stamps which would replace the low-denomination overprints.[25] The designs were to be 'symbolical in character' and 'no representations of a personal nature' were allowed (presumably meaning that individual persons were not to be depicted on the stamps).[26] Of the 129 designs which were received, 85 have survived. Most were very conventional: there was a profusion of Celtic interlacing, shamrocks, rising suns, harps, round towers, Celtic crosses, wolfhounds and female personifications of Ireland.[27] Four designs were chosen, apparently by the postmaster General, and approved by the government.[28]

The first design, issued on 6 December 1922, depicted a map of Ireland (without any indication of the border between the Free State and Northern Ireland) enclosed within an arch, with Celtic interlaced ornamentation.[29] This was followed on 16 March 1923 by a design based on the Cross of Cong, a medieval processional cross housed in the National Museum of Ireland. The cross design was almost identical to that of a Sinn Féin propaganda stamp from 1907, and was submitted by the same artist who had designed the Sinn Féin stamp. The third design, released on 20 April 1923, was an illustration of *an claidheamh soluis*, the sword of light, accompanied by Celtic interlacing. The sword of light was a symbol of Ireland associated in oral tradition with the warrior Cúchulainn, and *An Claidheamh Soluis* had been the title of the Gaelic League journal before the war. The League's founder, Douglas Hyde, used the image of the sword of light as a metaphor for the revival of Irish language and nationality, and it was described in the *Irish Times* as 'an ancient Gaelic device symbolising Education and Progress'.[30] The final design in the first definitive series was issued on 7 September 1923 and showed the arms of the four provinces of Ireland against a background of shamrocks.[31]

Overprinted UK stamps continued to be used for the higher denominations until 1937. In 1924 the Executive Council considered a design for the 10s. stamp which depicted Arthur Griffith and Michael Collins. Griffith and Collins were considered by the ruling party to be the 'founding fathers' of the Free State, and were commemorated in official ceremonies each year while Cumann na nGaedheal was in power. The Griffith-Collins design was sent back twice for revision because the portraits were considered unsatisfactory, and eventually the idea was abandoned altogether, seemingly because of the difficulty with obtaining satisfactory portraits.[32] However, the government may also have changed its mind about the advisability of depicting figures so closely associated with the still recent controversies over the Sinn Féin split and the Civil War. Whatever the reasons for rejecting the Griffith-Collins design, it would be another ten years before the government approved a proposal to find a design for the high value stamps. In 1935 the Executive Council agreed to the suggestion that artists be invited to submit designs on the theme of '"Renaissance" as symbolised by heroic figures from Irish mythology and history'.[33] The winning design by R.J. King represented the Christian renaissance of Ireland. It showed St Patrick, attended by acolytes bearing crosses, invoking God's blessing on the paschal fire at his feet, and the picture was framed in 'that masterpiece of 11th century Irish Christian craftsmanship', the bell shrine of St Patrick.[34] This design, issued on 8 September 1937, appeared on all three high value definitives. At last the state had a complete set of definitives, and had finally abolished the King's head in time for the coming into force of the new constitution which cut the state's formal ties with the monarchy.

The nine commemorative stamps issued by the state up to 1939 are listed below:[35]

Subject	Image	Date of Issue
Catholic Emancipation Centenary	Daniel O'Connell	22 June 1929
Shannon hydroelectric scheme	Barrage on the Shannon River	15 October 1930
Royal Dublin Society bicentenary	Reaper carrying a scythe	12 June 1931
Eucharistic Congress, Dublin	Chalice set in the centre of the Cross of Cong	12 May 1932
Holy Year 1933–34	Two angels kneeling on either side of a cross	18 September 1933
Gaelic Athletic Association 50th anniversary	Hurler in action	27 July 1934
New constitution	See below	29 December 1937
Centenary of Father Mathew's temperance movement	Father Theobald Mathew	31 July 1938
Constitution of the USA, 150th anniversary	American eagle and shield flanked by George Washington and Irish harp	1 March 1939

Most or all of the Irish stamps produced between 1922 and 1939 had a number of features in common. All were produced by typography, a process which continued to be used in Ireland long after it had been replaced by other methods elsewhere. Typography tends to produce coarse lines and is thus best suited to simple outlines. Of all Ireland's stamp designers in the period to 1939, it was R.J. King who worked most effectively within the limitations imposed by this printing process, producing designs which seem to have been partially inspired by the simplicity of art deco.[36] The fact that King designed all four stamps produced between 1933 and 1937, while George Atkinson was responsible for the design of three stamps (1931, 1932 and 1939), also helped to give some stylistic coherence to Irish stamps in the 1930s. Another common element in the stamps produced in the period was the use of the Irish language. The name of the country was given in Irish; the value of the stamp was given either in Irish or in numerals only; and where there were inscriptions, they were in Irish in all but two cases (the exceptions were the Eucharistic Congress and Holy Year stamps, on which the inscriptions were in Latin). Finally, there was some commonality in the use of colour. Most notably, there was a tendency to use the unofficial national colour, green, for the standard letter rate (2p) stamp, as well as on the lowest value definitive and the cheapest of the larger (St Patrick) definitives.[37] There was, in addition, much use of blue, which also has some claims to being an Irish national colour.

The designs of the first set of definitive stamps seem to have been chosen by the postmaster general, and it is not clear how the Catholic Emancipation commemorative design was chosen, but all other stamps, with the exception of the Father Mathew commemoratives, were chosen by committees. These committees consisted of people with artistic expertise together with representatives of the Department of Posts and Telegraphs and the Stamping Department. After the rather poor results of the open competition for the 1922 definitive series, the selection committees favoured issuing invitations to compete to selected artists. They also pushed for prizes to be awarded which would make it worthwhile for the best Irish artists to compete. Officials, however, were reluctant to spend money on stamps. In 1933 a memorandum from the Department of Finance on the proposal to issue a new set of definitives argued that the only justification for a new issue was that the existing one had been in use for ten years, and that this was an inadequate reason in times of financial stringency. This was apparently enough to deter the Executive Council from proceeding with the idea. The following year another memorandum pointed out that there had been a commemorative issue every year since 1929, and questioned the value of issuing commemoratives so 'frequently'.[38] As a result of such attitudes, it was not until 1937 that the prize for artists whose designs were chosen for stamps was increased from £25 to £50.

The tendency to view stamps as a financial drain rather than a potential benefit to the state helps to explain the small number of stamps issued up to 1939. It should be borne in mind that, while the idea of commemorative stamps had been around since the late nineteenth century, it caught on slowly, and the United Kingdom did not issue its first commemorative until 1924. Nevertheless, the idea took off internationally after the First World War, and commemorative stamps became important instruments of propaganda in the United States and the Soviet Union.[39] The Free State government showed little interest in using stamps either to promote the state abroad or to mould public opinion within the state, and the initiative for four of the commemoratives came not from within the government or bureaucracy but from outside bodies.[40] The government was sufficiently concerned, however, to ensure that the Executive Council approved all stamp issues since otherwise, as Attorney General Hugh Kennedy pointed out in 1923, the minister in charge of the postal service might promote views which were not those of the government as a whole.[41]

While the Free State government did not take a great interest in stamps as message carriers, this is not to say that the Free State stamps had no political significance. Stamps can be an important source of information about the dominant ideology of the state issuing them,[42] although it is easier to discern patterns in a large body of stamps than to interpret individual stamps. Since the independent Irish state issued only fourteen stamp designs up to 1939, these stamps can reveal only a limited amount about the official ideology of the state, but broadly speaking, the stamps were in harmony with the prevailing nationalist, Catholic and Gaelic ethos. The first series of definitives issued by the state is particularly interesting in this respect, as they were issued during the Civil War and therefore can be seen as part of the Free State government's propaganda struggle with republicans for ownership of the nationalist tradition.[43] Two of them depicted symbols of a united Ireland (the map of Ireland and the arms of the four provinces), suggesting that pro-Treaty Sinn Féin was just as opposed to partition as its opponents; the sword of light was a Gaelic revivalist symbol and also referred to the title of the Gaelic League journal which had been edited for several years by Patrick Pearse; and the Cross of Cong stamp not only depicted a traditional national symbol but was in addition a copy of an earlier Sinn Féin propaganda stamp. These four stamps were part of the government's efforts to establish its Sinn Féin credentials in the face of republican claims that it had betrayed the separatist tradition.

The Gaelic revivalist aspirations of the Free State government were represented on the stamps not only by the depiction of *an claidheamh soluis* but also by the GAA commemorative and, most importantly, by the use of the Irish language. Nationalism was represented most clearly by the symbols of an unpartitioned Ireland on the definitives, by the picture of nationalist leader Daniel O'Connell, and by the commemorative for the strongly nationalist GAA. There was also a certain nationalist assertiveness in the representation of the Shannon scheme, the showpiece of the government's electrification programme.[44] Symbols of industrial progress would later be common on the stamps of newly independent and Third World states,[45] but the Free State had few industrial achievements to boast of, and balanced this symbol of an electrified future with an image of continuity with the agricultural past: the scythe-carrying reaper on the Royal Dublin Society stamp. The RDS stamp was also notable because it commemorated an organisation which had been unionist in ethos before independence, although its 'Royal' title was obscured somewhat by translation into Irish.

Religion was also represented on a number of the stamps. Three stamps featured crosses, two commemorated religious celebrations, one showed a saint and one depicted a Catholic priest. In addition, one stamp marked the anniversary of an event (Catholic emancipation) which, while it was political rather than strictly religious in nature, was commemorated in 1929 with much Catholic triumphalism.[46] The Department of Posts and Telegraphs was initially wary when the idea of issuing a stamp for the Eucharistic Congress, an exclusively Catholic festival, was suggested. The Department believed that 'sectarian and denominational matters should be avoided as far as possible', and that members of other religious groups might object to such a stamp. On the other hand, the Congress was an event 'of international importance and Ireland was selected as the venue because of the fact that the large majority of the population professes the Catholic religion'.[47] Reservations about issuing a stamp for the Eucharistic Congress were overcome, and this stamp was followed by a more blatantly sectarian commemorative, the Holy Year stamp, celebrating an event which was purely Catholic in nature, with no direct national significance.[48]

The most symbolically complex stamp, and the one in which nationalist, Gaelic and religious themes were brought together, was the 1937 constitution commemorative. It showed Ireland as a young woman, seated and resting one arm on a harp, beside a lectern decorated with the arms of the four provinces of Ireland. The lectern supported a book, whose open pages bore the first words of the new constitution: 'I nAinm na Tríonóide Ró-Naomhtha' ('In the name of the Most Holy Trinity'). This stamp suggested continuity with the past by its use of the Irish language and of traditional national symbols (the harp and the female personification of Ireland); it represented the aspiration to a united Ireland, articulated in articles 2 and 3 of the constitution, by placing the constitution above the arms of the four provinces; and it emphasised the religious basis of the state by quoting the constitution's invocation of the Christian Trinity.

There seems to have been little public discussion of the Free State stamps. There were occasional comments that the 'map of Ireland' stamp was deceptive and merely a token gesture by a government which had no real strategy for ending partition.[49] Aesthetic objections were also raised, particularly to the first set of definitive stamps. The artistic quality of the stamps was felt by some to be particularly important because stamps, unlike other official symbols, were sent all over the world. In 1923, the *Irish Independent* expressed the hope that the poor design of the first set of stamps would not be repeated, and that in future the government would offer prizes high enough to attract accomplished artists. Anticipating Yeats's description of official designs as 'the silent ambassadors of national taste', the newspaper observed that 'These things go all over the world, and we do not wish them to seem the ambassadors of our bad taste.'[50] The announcement that a Free State coinage was to be created also sparked criticism of the stamps from those who wanted an artistic committee to select the coinage designs. Speaking in support of an artistic committee on coinage design, Yeats told the Senate that a famous decorative artist had described the Free State stamps as 'at once the humblest and ugliest in the world'.[51] The *Irish Statesman* hoped that the coins would 'redeem the aesthetic reputation we lost by our stamps', and found the 'melancholy symbol of an empty Ireland with nothing on the map' depressing, but almost worse was the sword of light stamp: 'that clenched fist inside an egg holding a sword never used by man or angel with a shocked dragon writhing outside the egg'.[52] Once the new coins were in circulation, the *Star* thought it was time to improve the design of the stamps, which compared unfavourably with the coinage: 'After all, the coins circulate only at home, but our postage stamps go to all parts of the world, and few would say that they are likely to impress foreigners by the beauty or significance of their design.'[53]

Legal tender notes

In March 1926 the government appointed a commission into banking and note issue which decided that the Free State should establish a new currency unit, the 'Saorstát Pound', which should be exchangeable at par with the UK pound. Following the Banking Commission's final report, a Currency Commission was established, one of whose roles was to oversee the issuing of banknotes. Towards the end of 1927 an advisory committee on note design was set up, consisting of Thomas Bodkin, Dermod

O'Brien and Lucius O'Callaghan (all of whom had been on the coinage design committee).[54] The committee advised on the design of consolidated banknotes as well as legal tender notes, but only the latter class of notes, the ones which became most familiar to the general public, are considered here.[55] In November 1927, Joseph Brennan, chairman of the Currency Commission, wrote to Bodkin to say that 'there is a special value from a protective point of view in having an engraving of human features on the notes'. Brennan thought there was little chance of getting agreement for the use of a picture of an actual person, living or dead, so he asked Bodkin if he knew of any suitable paintings or drawings such as a figure representing Erin.[56]

Apparently Bodkin could not think of any existing picture which would be appropriate, but he approached Hazel Lavery, wife of the Belfast-born artist Sir John Lavery, about the idea of using her portrait on the notes. Lady Lavery was a prominent London society hostess with many influential friends in both Britain and Ireland. In 1921, she and her husband had facilitated the Treaty negotiations in London by hosting social events which allowed Michael Collins and the other Sinn Féin representatives to meet British politicians in a neutral and informal setting.[57] In December 1927, when he raised the idea of Lady Lavery's image appearing on the banknotes, Bodkin also sought and received her assistance in promoting his unsuccessful candidacy for the position of Irish Free State High Commissioner to London.[58] He may, therefore, have been trying to return the favour.

On 21 December he wrote to Lady Lavery saying that he had suggested using her portrait to the design committee and that, after much argument, the committee came round to the idea. They were concerned, however, 'that every jealous woman who fancies her looks will ask, "Why was Lady Lavery put up on the notes instead of myself?"', and that reproducing an existing picture from a gallery collection 'would seem to be advertising that Gallery unduly'. The committee therefore agreed to ask Sir John 'to paint a picture of a beautiful Irish type for the purpose of reproduction on the Notes', understanding that he would select '*the model who most appeals to him*'.[59] Lady Lavery replied with rather false modesty: 'I really feel you are too kind and generous when you suggest that my humble head should figure on the notes, and you know I said from the first that I thought it wildly improbable, unlikely, impracticable, unpopular, impossible, that any committee would fall in with such a suggestion.'[60] Sir John was initially hesitant about the idea, and suggested that an open competition be held.[61]

At the end of December, Brennan invited Sir John Lavery to paint for the banknotes 'a portrait of a beautiful female head treated in some emblematic fashion which might perhaps have some Irish association'.[62] Sir John accepted, and began reworking a 1909 portrait of Hazel, turning her into a figure of Erin.[63] Dressed in a shawl, resting one arm on a harp and supporting her chin with her hand, she looked somewhat wistful, but not sorrowful. Behind her was a lake and some hills, suggesting perhaps that she represented the spirit of the land. The committee on note design was 'greatly taken with the picture itself' and felt that Lavery had succeeded 'in getting into it just the atmosphere that we desire',[64] so the design was proceeded with and the legal tender notes issued to the public on 10 September 1928.

The notes as finally issued included two representations of Erin, since the watermark was based on a head of Erin by the nineteenth-century Irish sculptor John Hogan. Lavery's picture appeared on all the legal tender notes, but the full picture appeared only on the £10 notes and above, the lower denominations showing only the head and shoulders of the 'emblematic female figure'. On the reverse of the notes were designs based on sculpted heads representing Irish rivers, created in the eighteenth century by Edward Smyth for the façade of Dublin's Custom House. A different head was shown on each of the seven denominations.[65] Two of the rivers represented (the Lagan and the Bann) flow entirely within Northern Ireland, an anti-partitionist gesture which was not too subtle to escape notice in Belfast, where it was received 'with mixed feelings' according to the *Irish Times* correspondent there.[66] Particularly observant Orangemen might also have noticed that the date of the Battle of the Boyne (1690) which appeared on the head representing the River Boyne on the Custom House, was omitted on the banknote version of this head.[67] The inscriptions on the notes were fully bilingual, unlike the Irish-only inscriptions on the coins and stamps. The only change made to them in the following decade came in 1938, when 'Ireland' and 'Éire' were substituted for 'Irish Free State' and 'Saorstát Éireann', in accordance with the changes to the name of the state in the 1937 constitution.[68]

According to Brennan, the depiction of a symbolic female figure on the notes was prompted by practical considerations: human features were difficult to forge convincingly, but portraits of actual people were likely to be too controversial. There is no reason to doubt this explanation, and it is certainly true that portraits are commonly used on banknotes as a protection against counterfeiting, but there may also have been other considerations. For one thing, there was a well established, international tradition of using female figures on banknotes.[69] In addition, while an assertive female image might have been considered dangerous, the picture of Ireland as woman on the banknotes was reassuringly conservative. The demure, passive figure of Erin was in line with prevailing gender ideology in the Free State,[70] and the picture was also highly conventional in its imagery. By the time the image for the banknotes was selected, criticism of the departure from traditional national symbols in the proposed coinage designs had already started, and the committee may have thought it advisable to choose a more conventional design for the notes.

There may also have been some significance in the committee's selection of Lavery to paint the picture on the notes, in the knowledge that he would use his wife as the model. Following the creation of the Free State, there was speculation that Sir John Lavery would be appointed Governor General.[71] He was not offered the Governor Generalship, but the banknote commission may have been a less high-profile recognition of the Laverys' role in the Treaty negotiations. However, it seems that the fact that the figure of Erin was modelled on Hazel Lavery was not meant to be publicised.[72] There are a number of reasons why the government may have been reluctant to acknowledge the identity of the model, including Lady Lavery's social position (a titled London society hostess may not have been considered an appropriate embodiment of modest Irish womanhood), her nationality (she was American, though of Irish ancestry), and her rumoured romantic attachments to Michael Collins and Kevin O'Higgins.[73] Perhaps, too, it was felt that if the figure on the notes came to be associated with a particular woman it would not be seen as representing the Irish nation.[74]

When the banknotes were released the secret of Sir John Lavery's model for the female figure quickly got out, but despite this there was little controversy about the notes.[75] The *Irish Times* reported on their release that the 'appearance of the new notes was the subject of favourable comment' in Dublin, and after they had been in circulation for several months Joseph Brennan assured Sir John Lavery that there had been 'only a negligible amount of adverse criticism'.[76] There was remarkably little discussion of the notes in the newspapers, especially considering the debate about the new coins that raged several months after the banknotes were released. The Gaelic lobby criticised the use of English on the notes,[77] but no one seems to have objected to the picture of the female figure. An article in the *Leader* praised the banknotes as expressions of 'Christian idealism':

> There is poor Erin looking out at you with a look of Catholic modesty and chastity centuries old...What I admire still more is the idealism of those notes, for what is the little Irish maid but idealism personified...These notes undoubtedly recommend our Irish taste, our Irish Catholic intelligence.[78]

However, the writer went on to warn that when the new coins were issued with their materialistic designs it would seem that idealism was dead. The public reaction to the release of the coins was to contrast strikingly with the general indifference which greeted the designs of the seals, stamps and banknotes.

Selection of the coinage designs

The process which led to the issuing of a Free State coinage started towards the end of 1923, when the Minister for Finance, Ernest Blythe, began informal consultations on the advisability of creating a separate coinage.[79] A number of arguments were put forward in favour of such a move, among them the assertion that the issuing of a separate coinage was in itself symbolic of the Free State's independence. A draft memorandum in June 1924 claimed that the introduction of a separate coinage would be welcomed by well-wishers of the Free State 'as bringing home vividly to the ordinary citizen the wide extent in one important respect of the independence ascured [sic] by the Treaty. The public effect might thus be valuable by tending to discomfit further the opponents of the Treaty settlement.'[80] By late 1925, coinage legislation was being prepared, and officials had started to turn their minds to the question of design. Joseph Brennan, the Secretary of the Department of Finance, was already suggesting that a harp like that on the state seals could appear on one side of the coins, and had also sought suggestions from George Atkinson, Principal of the Metropolitan School of Art. Atkinson, in turn, asked whether portraits of individuals (for example, Arthur Griffith or Michael Collins) were admissible as designs for the coins. Brennan sought the views of the Minister on this question, advising him that 'So far as British opinion is a relevant factor I imagine that while it would not very much mind the elimination of the King in favour of some impersonal design it might look otherwise on the replacement of the royal by another effigy.' Blythe decided that portraits would not be admissible.[81]

Blythe introduced the Coinage Bill into Dáil Éireann on 19 January 1926, and while moving the second reading he told the Dáil that the bill's purpose was 'to establish a separate and distinctive token coinage for the Saorstát. It is the natural and logical consequence of the setting up of the Saorstát that we should have here a coinage distinctively our own, bearing the devices of this country.'[82] Both the *Irish Times* and, more surprisingly, the pro-government *Irish Independent*, expressed apprehension about the government's decision. The *Irish Independent* said that there had been no public demand for a new coinage, and was worried that the coinage could affect relations with Northern Ireland as well as inconveniencing travellers to Britain.[83] The *Irish Times* was also concerned that the issuing of a Free State coinage might be an obstacle to Irish unity: 'A Free State *pingin* [penny], stamped with a Celtic device, will be as innocuous as a Free State postage stamp of the same value; but nothing will convince the people of Northern Ireland that a separate coinage is not meant to provide a stepping-stone not only to an independent currency, but also to an independent Republic.'[84] The following day, the *Irish Times* quoted the reactions of the three principal Belfast unionist papers to the Coinage Bill. Their comments lent credence to the concerns of the *Irish Times*, the *Belfast Telegraph* declaring plainly that 'This latest scheme affords another vindication of Ulster's attitude towards the Free State, and we do hope that those who are continually crying out that Ulster should go into the Dublin Parliament will now give that sentiment a rest.'[85] Blythe, however, was unmoved by newspaper comments, saying that if there was not a newspaper demand for a new coinage there was a popular demand. He had met many people who were anxious for the Free State to have its own coinage, he said, and this demand was inherent in the historical background of the state: 'There was always a vehement demand which embraced all this and a great deal more.'[86]

On 4 February Blythe told the Dáil that he intended to appoint 'a committee of prominent artists' to advise him on the design of the coins.[87] This announcement was welcomed by Senator W.B. Yeats, who in his Senate speech on the Coinage Bill described stamps and coins as 'the silent ambassadors of national taste', and in May 1926 Yeats was asked to chair the committee on coinage design.[88] Another appointee to the committee, Thomas Bodkin, was a Governor of the National Gallery of Ireland and soon to become its Director. Anne Kelly has written of Bodkin that 'His greatest loyalties were to the Catholic Church and to Ireland, but his Ireland was one which would not have been recognised outside the better off Dublin world of good taste and refinement, and his Catholicism did not mean he approved of the Academy of Christian Art.'[89] Bodkin's alienation from much popular sentiment in Ireland, a characteristic which he shared with Yeats, helps to explain some of the passion with which the committee's designs were attacked. Men like Yeats and Bodkin were regarded by their critics, with some justification, as elitists who wished to impose their own ideas of good taste on the Irish people. Both Yeats and Bodkin had displayed an interest in official design soon after the Free State was created. Yeats had tried to persuade the government to appoint an artistic committee to advise it on the design of stamps, seals, and other artistic questions, while Bodkin had given a lecture in February 1922 about the idea of a Ministry of Fine Art to advise on official designs.[90] In the course of this lecture, Bodkin said that 'The coin was the most important symbol of the State. If its design be good and properly minted, the prestige of the State was greatly increased.' The other members of the committee were Dermod O'Brien, President of the Royal Hibernian Academy; Lucius O'Callaghan, Director of the National Gallery (he resigned from this position in February 1927 and was replaced by Bodkin); and Barry Egan, head of a Cork firm of goldsmiths and jewellers, who was to become a member of Dáil Éireann while serving on the committee.[91]

The function of the committee was to advise the Minister for Finance, 'firstly, as to the steps which should be taken with a view to getting designs submitted, and, secondly, as to which of the designs that may be submitted are the most suitable for adoption'. At the committee's first meeting in June 1926, Joseph Brennan told them that the Minister had made three provisional decisions about coinage design: that a harp should be shown on one side of the majority of the coins, if not all; that the inscriptions should be in Irish only; and that no effigies of modern persons should be included in the designs. However, these decisions were not to be regarded as final or binding.[92] The committee then began seeking suggestions for the designs, writing to three major learned societies: the Royal Hibernian Academy (representing artists), the Royal Irish Academy (representing scholars), and the Royal Society of Antiquaries of Ireland (representing mostly amateur historians and archaeologists). The most important response came in the letter from the Royal Society of Antiquaries, whose committee formed to consider the matter was: 'strongly of opinion that hackneyed symbolism, (round towers, shamrocks, wolf-dogs, sunbursts) should be entirely avoided: even the shamrock, as a symbol, has no dignity of age behind it, being not much more than a hundred years old. They also consider that obscure allusiveness such as the "sword of light" is undesirable.'[93] This opinion would be used by the committee on coinage design to justify their own decision not to use traditional national symbols (other than the harp and wolfhound) on the coins.

In July 1926 the committee placed advertisements in Free State newspapers seeking suggestions for coinage designs from the public, but the response was extremely disappointing. Few suggestions were received, and those which were sent in were mostly unimaginative: harps, round towers, wolfhounds, rising suns, shamrocks, female personifications of Ireland, Celtic crosses, maps of Ireland, the arms of the four provinces, St Patrick, the head of the President.[94] A few suggested animals other than the wolfhound, including one correspondent who waxed lyrical about the Kerry cow, which seemed to him 'typically Irish in its smallness, its beauty, its generosity and its health. Let other states have buffaloes and eagles, but let us have our Kerry cow'.[95] However, another letter-writer felt that animals 'tend to be wooden and common-place'. This same correspondent was in favour of the round tower ('hackneyed perhaps but distinctly belonging to this Country'), but also suggested, perhaps uniquely among all those who contributed suggestions between 1926 and 1928, a symbol of modern industry: 'A Power or Turbine House artistically emblematic of the coming Power unit Electricity.'[96]

There was little discussion of coinage designs in the newspapers at this stage. The satirical magazine *Dublin Opinion* got in early with its

suggestions, including the principal industry of the four provinces (showing a man leaning against a post) and the arms of the four provinces (guns
and bombs).[97] The *Irish Statesman* suggested various symbols: the salmon
of wisdom and the swans of Lir from Irish mythology; the wolfhound, harp,
and figure of Erin, but not the round tower, whose shape was not appropriate for a coin; and the bull and the horse, which were 'not at all unfitting for
an agricultural country'.[98] A contrary view was put by Tomás Ó Duibhir,
who wrote to the *Irish Independent* that although 'this is at present a
predominantly agricultural country', he did not see 'the utility or beauty of
adopting a bullock or an ear of corn'. He feared for the worst, since Yeats's
'antagonism to the designs on our admirable postage stamps will not tend
to reassure many who possess the Gaelic sympathy and tradition'.[99] For its
part, the *Catholic Bulletin* needed only to point out that Yeats was a member
of the coinage committee to damn the entire enterprise. Yeats was well
known to readers of the *Catholic Bulletin* as 'the author of that foul swan
song' (a reference to his supposedly immoral poem 'Leda and the Swan')
and no good could come of anything in which he was involved.[100] The
Bulletin also noted that, while the committee had consulted various bodies
with 'Royal' titles, it had not sought suggestions from any of the Catholic
organisations. However, the *Bulletin*'s staunch republicanism led it to
conclude that perhaps the government was only being honest since 'a religious symbol on a Free State coin would be a mockery'.[101]

Uninspired by the suggestions the committee received from the public,
Yeats turned also to his friends for advice. Lady Gregory gave a 'delight-
ed' Yeats a copy of *Coins of the Ancients*,[102] thus pointing him in the direction of ancient Greek and Roman models. At the committee's third meeting Yeats mentioned that the artist Sir William Orpen had suggested that
the series of coins should 'tell one story', and that Senator and poet Oliver
St John Gogarty had suggested a Sicilian coin with a horse's head on it as
a model. Using these suggestions as a starting point, Yeats proposed that
the designs should portray the products of the country, each denomination
showing a different product. The committee endorsed this idea, and by the
time they presented their interim report to the Minister for Finance on 6
August 1926 they had narrowed the theme down to animal products.[103] In
the interim report, the committee outlined their decision to have designs
representing the natural products of the country, with 'the more noble or
dignified types' assigned to the higher denominations and 'the more humble types to the lower'. They then listed their specific recommendations,
along with their reasons for choosing these particular animals.

- Half-crown: a horse. The horse had been used successfully on ancient
  Greek and Carthaginian coins, and 'the fame of the Irish horse' made
  further justification unnecessary.

- Florin: a salmon. The salmon was an important natural product and appeared in Irish mythology as the salmon of wisdom.
- Shilling: a bull. The bull had also been used successfully on ancient Greek coins, and 'the excellence of Irish cattle, their importance in the trade of the country' made it an appropriate symbol.
- Sixpence: a wolfhound. This was the committee's nod in the direction of popular sentiment; they noted that the wolfhound had been suggested by members of the public, and that since they had rejected other popular symbols they decided the wolfhound should be included. While they admitted that 'its inclusion strains to some extent the idea underlying the series and though it cannot be regarded as a natural product of the country', it was 'so peculiarly identified with Ireland it merits a place as a type'.
- Threepence: a hare. Once again, the hare had been used on ancient Greek coins, and it was 'likely to recommend itself to the public because of its association with sport'. Furthermore, 'If the hound and the hare are approved of as types for the two nickel coins, this group will possess a certain unity.'[104]
- Penny: a hen, possibly with chickens. This would represent a staple industry which the government was trying to foster. It might be criticised as being too 'homely', but its homeliness could be an advantage 'since it will make an immediate appeal to farmers and especially to their wives and daughters to whom the care of poultry is a particular concern'.
- Halfpenny: a pig. The committee admitted to being hesitant at first about recommending the pig, 'because of the ridicule with which it is associated in connection with this country'. However, they concluded that as 'a valuable product of the country' it could not be excluded and that 'the objections to it are unworthy of serious consideration'.
- Farthing: a woodcock. Like the hare, the woodcock 'makes a special appeal to sportsmen'.

In addition to pointing out the appropriateness of these designs as symbols, the committee emphasised their suitability from an artistic point of view, and concluded that they would make a series 'at once beautiful, intelligible and appropriate'. They also defended their neglect of 'the obvious popular symbols associated with this country', claiming that they were supported in this 'by the more intelligent public opinion', including that of the Royal Society of Antiquaries of Ireland. However, they did recommend that the harp should appear on the obverse of all the coins.[105]

In a memorandum to the Minister regarding the committee's interim report, J.J. McElligott, Assistant Secretary of the Department of Finance, said that for the most part the committee's recommendations were reasonable. He noted without comment that no figures from history or heroic legend had been chosen, and suggested that the committee should at least move away from the category of animal products to the extent of including some cereal product, such as a sheaf of wheat. He had reservations about various of the animals, but his most serious objection was to the pig, which he felt should not be accepted, adding 'it might even offend the Jews!'[106] The Minister recommended the committee's suggestions to the Executive Council, which gave authority for the preparation of designs on the lines recommended. However, Blythe suggested to the committee that the ram might be included in the list of symbols to be sent to artists as an alternative to the pig, and he also took up McElligott's suggestion of depicting non-animal products.[107] The coinage committee accepted the Minister's suggestion about the ram, though they still felt that the pig was more likely to produce a fine design. They stuck by their decision to exclude products other than animals, however, on the grounds that including them would break the series of animals, and that the only plant product which could be successfully reproduced was a wheat-ear or wheat-sheaf, which had already been adopted by a number of other European countries.[108]

Having decided on the symbols to be shown on the coins, the committee sought designs from artists. Seven artists, three of whom were Irish, accepted the invitation and took part in the competition. They were supplied with a list of the symbols and inscriptions required, along with some supporting material to aid inspiration and accuracy. In February 1927 the committee considered the designs received from the artists. They examined each denomination separately rather than looking for the best set of designs submitted by one artist, and they were not told which artist had produced each set. Despite this, the committee selected the designs submitted by the English artist Percy Metcalfe for each of the denominations, and for the harp. Of the two alternative designs which he had submitted for the halfpenny (ram and pig) they recommended the pig. Metcalfe's designs were 'incomparably superior' to the others, the committee wrote in their report to the Minister, and were 'certain to provide a coinage of unusual interest and beauty'. Accordingly, they recommended that Metcalfe be commissioned to execute the designs for the whole series of coins.[109] There followed a lengthy process of revision of the designs of the horse, bull, pig and wolfhound on the basis of expert opinion from the Department of Lands and Agriculture and the Wolf-Hound Club. Yeats particularly regretted the changes made to the pig and piglets, which were slimmed down on agricultural advice, and while he admitted that 'the state of the market for pig's cheeks' made the jowly pig of the original design impossible, he felt that the resulting animals were 'better merchandise but less living'.[110]

Eventually the experts were satisfied, and in April 1928 the committee inspected a complete set of trial pieces of Metcalfe's designs which they recommended to the Minister for Finance for acceptance. The coins were produced by the Royal Mint in London, and went on display in the Dublin Metropolitan School of Art on 30 November 1928. Opening the exhibition of the new coins Blythe, Minister for Finance, once again emphasised that the issuing of a Free State coinage was a demonstration of the state's independence. He did not think that there had been a real Irish coinage before, since the Irish coinage of the past had been issued under foreign authority, but 'Now we have a coinage issued under the authority of a Parliament democratically elected by the people. The possession of a distinctive coinage is one of the indications of sovereignty.' The procedure adopted for choosing the designs of the new coins, he thought, had 'resulted in a coinage more interesting and beautiful than any token coinage in the world'. The coins began to be issued to the public on 12 December 1928.[111]

The coinage debate

At the opening of the exhibition of the coins, Thomas Bodkin gave a speech in which he tried to outline the thinking behind the committee's choice of symbols. While he perhaps hoped that his somewhat flippant tone would disarm potential critics, his rather tactless comments on the reasons for the committee's avoidance of religious symbols probably helped to stir up controversy instead.[112] Bodkin explained that the Minister had saved the committee much trouble by deciding that effigies of modern persons should not be used, though he neglected to say that the Minister's decision had not been binding. It would have been very difficult, he said, to have selected eight figures from among the patriots of recent times, and then to have allocated them to the various denominations, thereby running the risk of outraging public opinion by elevating one hero over another. Selecting ancient heroes was also a problem, because there were no portraits of such figures as Brian Boru or St Patrick which dated from their lifetimes, and had they been depicted on the coins there would have been controversy about the historical validity of these images. As for the committee's avoidance of traditional Irish emblems, Bodkin offered no explanation of his own, but he mentioned the Society of Antiquaries' view on the use of 'hackneyed symbols'. Most controversial of all, he explained why he personally considered that religious symbols were not appropriate as designs for coins:

> It seemed to me that the placing of religious symbols or the effigies of saints upon our coins would give rise to an unavoidable and most

> reprehensible irreverence. I saw, in my mind's eye, a peasant at the fair
> being paid for a bonham with the image of St Patrick and, impelled by the
> habit of centuries, to spit upon that image for luck before he rammed it in
> his trouser pocket. I saw two loafers at the bar of a public house tossing as
> to which of them should pay for drinks, according as to whether the image
> of St Bridget or St Columbcille came uppermost.[113]

He also claimed that had religious symbols appeared on the coins many
people would have drilled holes in them and used them as medals, and
would thus have become liable for prosecution for defacing the
coinage. As to the reasons for choosing to depict animals on the coins,
Bodkin said that the committee had been inspired by the coins of antiquity, and that since coins are tokens of a people's wealth it was entirely
appropriate to show on them the source of that wealth. To the committee's critics he pointed out that the public had been apathetic when
suggestions for designs were sought, and he asked anyone who wished
to criticise the committee's choice to 'consider whether he is justified
in doing so by virtue of having offered us valuable advice which we
rejected'.[114]

This last comment of Bodkin's indicates that he was expecting criticism of the symbols chosen for the coins, and in fact by the time the
designs were officially released to the public they had already been the
subject of controversy due to unauthorised disclosures of the committee's choice of symbols. In December 1926 the short-lived newspaper
Irish Truth had accurately listed the symbols chosen, and predicted that
they 'will not merely be unpopular, but will be met with positive derision'.[115] However, it was not until Percy Metcalfe revealed the symbols
to an *Irish Independent* interviewer in July 1927 that the first round of
criticism began.[116] This revelation provoked some negative comment in
the newspapers, and the Minister for Finance was asked in the Dáil:

> whether the design of a pig and her litter and other farmyard animals is cal-
> culated to inspire the public as to the standard of Gaelic culture that
> National Ireland is striving for to-day; whether something more in keeping
> with the Christian glories of Ireland should not be substituted for a series of
> designs which are regarded by many people as a travesty on our country.[117]

Blythe defended the designs, claiming that they were 'not intended to
be symbolical', by which he presumably meant that they were not
meant to symbolise ideals.[118] By this stage work on Metcalfe's designs
was already too far advanced to change the symbols, even if the
government had been inclined to do so, but these first rumblings of
discontent may have alerted Bodkin to the storm to come and to the
need to defend the committee's selection.

The debate over the coinage designs took the form of editorials and letters to the editors in the Free State's newspapers. There were editorials not only in the Dublin newspapers but also in a number of local newspapers, and there was comment in various newspapers representing particular religious and political interests. There was a flood of letters to the editor of the *Irish Independent*, a Dublin daily, and editorial notes in that newspaper indicated that it was only publishing a selection of the letters received.[119] There was probably more negative than positive comment about the coins in the newspapers, and it was the critics of the coinage designs who started the debate, but the vehemence of the attack on the designs quickly provoked a spirited defence. The coins were condemned by their detractors for promoting paganism because they bore no religious symbols; for repudiating the national tradition by neglecting conventional national emblems; for stereotyping Ireland as an agricultural nation; and for putting forward the pig, long associated with the Irish in caricature, as an appropriate symbol of the Irish nation. In reply, defenders of the coins praised their beauty and originality; declared that they were entirely appropriate for a nation whose economy relied so heavily on agriculture; and accused those who wanted religious symbols on the coinage of trying to associate God and Mammon.

A pagan coinage?

Although Bodkin clearly expected criticism, he claimed that the committee had not expected that so much of it would be 'directed to our failure to identify God and Mammon'.[120] The absence of religious emblems from the coins was a major issue for critics of the designs, who declared that Ireland was a Christian nation, and that this fact should be represented on the coins. According to the Cathedral Chapter of Tuam and the St Brendan Feis Committee, the coinage designs were unsuitable for a great Christian nation. They should give expression to 'the ideals which kept the national and Christian spirit alive in this land through the centuries' and to 'the exalted mission of our old and great nation'.[121] Ireland's mission to the world was also in the minds of some critics who mentioned the Irish role in evangelising Europe during the Dark Ages, and lamented that 'the Gaelic mind' had now seemingly forgotten such lofty ideals.[122] Instead, the coins were 'disfigured by grotesque representations of beasts and birds, which brings us back from Christendom to the age of blank materialism'.[123] The *Standard* ('An Organ of Irish Catholic Opinion') saw the issue in terms of a conflict between materialism and idealism, and warned that: 'It would be foolish, as well as impious to forget the sources of the spiritual strength that sustained the nation in its adversities. Even for material

success the nation will need to draw on the springs of courage, perse-
verance, honesty, domestic content and clean living which were found in
the old idealism.'[124]

For a number of critics, this abandonment of idealism was no acci-
dent, but was part of a larger conspiracy to remove religion from public
life. They professed to see the coinage designs as signs of the 'steady
Protestantising of Irish mentality, resultant in the suppression of all
outward sign of belief in God';[125] as a victory for 'those who spare no
effort to paganise this country of ours';[126] as falling in with 'that ignoring of God which is the way of the new paganism';[127] as evidence that
'every department of State is being secularised, and that God is being
shut out from our counsels';[128] as 'a crafty step in favour of paganism';[129]
and as a 'turning down of God'.[130] The reference to 'Protestantising' indicated what some imagined to be the source of this supposed secular
trend. The *Catholic Bulletin* accused Yeats, backed by the Royal Society
of Antiquaries, of 'foisting upon Ireland a Godless coinage', and for the
Catholic Bulletin Yeats stood as a cipher for Protestant Ireland.[131] The
Freemasons, those other *bêtes noires* of the *Catholic Bulletin*, were
referred to by a correspondent who asked Bodkin why he did not simply
emboss the Masonic square and compass symbol on the coins,[132] and by
a priest who wrote:

> If these pagan symbols once get a hold, then is the thin edge of the wedge
> of Freemasonry sunk into the very life of our Catholicity, for the sole object
> of having these pagan symbols instead of religious emblems on our coins
> is to wipe out all traces of religion from our minds, to forget the 'land of
> saints,' and beget a land of devil-worshippers, where evil may reign
> supreme.[133]

An equally bleak future for Catholicism in a Freemason dominated
Ireland was forecast in another letter:

> Faith and Fatherland are once more to be relegated to oblivion to please a
> small minority. The Dail is practically pagan; the blessing of God is never
> invoked, beginning or ending its sittings. Is this another 'sop to Cerberus'
> (Freemasonry) which is getting such a firm footing in the Free State? A
> pagan Parliament, a pagan coinage – we are getting along ... The next thing
> will be a raid on sacred emblems – Crucifixes and holy water, scapulars and
> medals, will be by law forbidden. Then, of course, the Mass and the priests
> will be attacked in turn. Catholic churches, monasteries and convents will
> be seized as Government property, and an oath of conformity will be
> passed. The reign of Calles may be nearer to us in Ireland than most of us
> imagine.[134]

The terms 'pagan' and 'paganism' were popular with critics of the coinage designs.[135] These terms seem to have been used in political debate in Ireland since the late nineteenth century, particularly with reference to the allegedly immoral, materialistic and irreligious popular culture of Britain, which was seen as a threat to holy Ireland.[136] A few critics of the coins, perhaps influenced by a tradition within Christianity which associated animals with evil and demonic forces,[137] were more literal in their accusations of paganism, suggesting that the coins presaged a reversion to pagan animal worship. A columnist in the *Drogheda Argus* claimed that many people saw in the coins an indication of a drift 'back to an age when people worshipped beasts and birds', and alluding to the fact that Metcalfe had also designed the Iraqi currency, asked 'whether the designs appropriate for the heathens in Irak should be fit symbols for the coins to be circulated in a Christian and civilized and cultured country like Ireland'.[138] However, for most, paganism was just a more pejorative term for secularism and materialism: 'The coins are called pagan in the sense that there is a total absence of a sign that they symbolise the sovereignty of a Christian nation', one critic explained.[139]

Those who took this view were contemptuous of the argument put by defenders of the coinage designs that it was not appropriate to put religious emblems on coins because this would result in the profaning of holy symbols. Money was not inherently evil, and as Beatrice Burke argued, 'if Christian men pondered the Christian emblems on their coins before taking action, the result would be more likely to promote the welfare and benefit of their fellow-men'.[140] 'It is strange', thought the *Nation*, 'that Catholics should be so squeamish and puritanical about putting an Irish saint's image on a thing of common use. According to all Catholic tradition that is where the saints belong.'[141] The *Standard* agreed:

> If a religious symbol is not to be stamped on a coin because of the possibility of profanity, then there should be no crucifix in a public place, no calling on God to witness in a court of law. For an unbeliever may be guilty of a profanity towards the crucifix, and a perjurer may insult God by calling on Him to witness to a falsehood.[142]

In the *Standard*'s view, religion should manifest itself in social life and in official recognition of God's sovereign dominion.[143] Margaret Gibbons also thought that nations, like individuals, were under obligation to acknowledge God: 'A coin of the realm is an official national token. To send it out into the markets of the world minus any reference to the Ruler and Dispenser of nations – in Whom, surely, we all believe – is an offence against that honour which is His rightful due.'[144] In neglecting to honour God on the coins, the Free State was said to be departing from the norm in the Christian and civilised world, and critics gave examples of other countries which put religious images or slogans on their coins and stamps.[145]

Both Yeats and Bodkin challenged the claim that the Free State was unusual or even unique among Christian states in not having religious emblems on its coinage. 'I wish they would tell us what coinage seems to them most charged with piety', grumbled Yeats.[146] Some defenders of the coins argued that there was nothing irreligious about the animal symbols, pointing out that animals played an important role in Biblical stories, and were part of God's creation.[147] A correspondent who wrote under the name 'Pelican' asked whether those who described the coinage designs as pagan 'wish us to believe that the humbler animals owe their existence to the creative act of some pagan deity', while Bodkin believed that 'those who venture to assert that animals are particularly pagan tremble on the border of Manichaeism'.[148] To the liberal *Irish Statesman*, the accusations of paganism were another example of the ridiculousness of the illiberal forces in Ireland:

> One would imagine that while man was created by God the animal world was created by the devil, so angry are the critics... We rather think St. Francis would have liked these coins. What has happened to the animal creation since he spoke of his affection for his little brothers the birds?... Who would have thought that that poor little hare on the threepenny bit was a form of the devil, or that little woodcock was a demon. Oh, shade of St Francis![149]

Others argued that the absence of religious symbols from the coins was a virtue, and several quoted the Biblical verse about rendering unto Caesar what is Caesar's and unto God what is God's.[150] One writer was pleased:

> that the leading nation of Europe has had the decency to refrain from making sanctimonious use of the name of God. For a State which keeps up a standing army to put the name of God on its coins would be blasphemous effrontery, just as it would be blasphemous effrontery for a burglar to inscribe the name of God on his jemmy.[151]

The Reverend P.V. Higgins agreed with some critics of the coinage that 'the State as well as the individual should acknowledge its Creator', but he drew a distinction between the State's religious and its civic acts. The issuing of a coinage was a purely civic act, like carrying out a legal hanging, and it was as reasonable to expect a religious coinage as to expect that the hangman should be clothed in sacred vestments.[152] 'For religion's own sake let religion be kept far away from the coinage', Higgins pleaded. 'If Ireland has no other way of proving her religion than by turning her coins into medals, God help her.'[153]

The accusation that the coinage designs represented the triumph of materialism over idealism could be thrown back in the critics' faces by stressing the incompatibility of God and Mammon. It is best not to associate sacred images with 'the fair, the market and the racecourse', reasoned the *Enniscorthy Echo.* 'It is not for Catholic Ireland to suggest or countenance an unnatural union between the Temple and the traffic of the money changers.'[154] '[I]t is not by identifying sacred personages and things with the cult of Mammon that we may best express our Christian feelings,' wrote 'Pelican', who rejoiced that the coins would give no comfort to those who wished to believe that religious sentiment inspired their cupidity.[155] The *Dundalk Democrat* advised that 'We do not – or at least we should not – worship money. To many a devout mind it might even appear to be an irreverence to vulgarise and debase symbols of religion by using them to distinguish pence from ha'pence.'[156] M.J. Kennedy, a Fianna Fáil politician who appears to have been a proponent of social credit theories, was clearly worried that the Irish were in danger of worshipping money. He believed that religious symbols could be used to hide the truth about the workings of 'finance' from the public, and so was thankful to the designers of the coinage for 'separating Christian emblems from a system that has become a burden and not a blessing to mankind'.[157]

Other issues in the coinage debate

Critics of the coinage designs were not impressed by the committee's decision to look to classical rather than native models. While some saw the animal symbols of pagan Greece and Rome as inherently inappropriate for Christian Ireland,[158] others argued that ancient pagan art, unlike the designs on the Free State coins, was at least beautiful, and used animals to symbolise ideals rather than economic resources.[159] In any case, classicism had little appeal to those who wanted symbols rooted in Irish traditions.[160] A number of critics were angered by the absence of traditional emblems such as the shamrock, round tower and sunburst; treasures from the Celtic past such as the Ardagh Chalice and the Tara Brooch; or historical figures such as St Patrick and Daniel O'Connell.[161] Even 'Beppo', the scourge of the Freemasons, suggested a round tower as a suitable symbol, apparently unaware that round towers had been claimed by Irish Masons as a symbol of their Craft.[162] The popularity of such symbols was linked to the belief that Ireland was an ancient nation with a glorious history and civilisation, and the views of the Royal Society of Antiquaries of Ireland were given short shrift: 'The round tower and Celtic cross may be hackneyed, but still they are symbols of Ireland's Golden Age.'[163] Familiarity with these symbols had 'endeared them to Irish sentiment as emblems of the nation's hopes and memories', and they typified 'all that is noble and elevated' in Ireland.[164] One critic was sure: 'that the average Irish artist, who is possessed of a Christian outlook, often dreams for days and nights on the possibilities of such glorious themes that ancient Erin visualises for him, and he does not forget those personalities who made such great sacrifices in our own days.'[165] Others, however, saw artistic ideas, or at least the ideas of the 'so-called artists' on the 'high art' coinage design committee, as the problem; in pursuit of art, they had turned their backs on sentiment.[166] They had forgotten the heroes of the past, 'those who made our history, the great-hearted and noble ones who greatly lived and greatly died', thus signalling that Ireland was 'to be thrown to the dogs of disillusionment'.[167] This was scarcely surprising to some commentators who noted snidely that a majority of the members of the coinage committee were 'outside the Irish tradition' and were 'not gentlemen who have been prominently associated with the national aspirations of the Irish race'.[168] The coinage designs, and Bodkin's defence of them, were examples of 'the un-Irish snob mind' and 'the usual superiority complex of all our aesthetes'.[169] In a thinly veiled reference to the Protestant and ex-unionist minority, Archdeacon J. Fallon wrote that symbols of Ireland's glorious past had been ignored 'for fear of wounding the tender susceptibilities of a self-constituted superior caste who have neither sympathy nor respect for ourselves or our ideals'.[170]

The accusation that the committee had rejected Ireland's national ideals was as much a matter of what was on the coins as of what was not on them. 'This collection of animals may typify Ireland in the minds of some foreigners who look on our country as a mere farmyard,' sniffed the St Brendan Feis Committee, 'but we regard such designs as a travesty on our land'.[171] The *Leader*, an independent Irish-Ireland newspaper, also bridled at the apparent suggestion that Ireland's mission was to be a farmyard, with coins catering for 'the aesthetic tastes of Bookies, Anglers and Beefeaters', and others joined it in regretting the impression being given to the world that Ireland could do nothing but raise livestock.[172] The *Leader* had long argued that the development of self-respect through a return to Gaelic culture must go hand in hand with the development of Irish industry, and now it saw in the coinage signs that the pro-British element in the Free State wanted to keep Ireland dependent on Britain by confining its economic role to agricultural production.[173] Arthur Griffith, founder of Sinn Féin and one of the founders of the Free State, had also seen industrialisation as crucial if Ireland was to be economically self-reliant, and Marie Lynch pointed out that the coinage designs were a betrayal of Griffith's vision. They proclaimed Ireland's economic weakness, its dependence on agricultural exports to just one market and its failure to develop local industry.[174]

On the other hand, some felt the emphasis was too much on the economic: 'The hen and the bull are associated with eggs and beef and money-making, and we do not wish to be represented before the world as a nation of money-grubbers.'[175] The designs stood for nothing more uplifting than 'the material idea of eggs and bacon',[176] they expressed 'only the sordid ideals of commerce, wealth and food',[177] and while they might be appropriate as medals at agricultural shows, they failed to display 'the traditions and imagination of the Celtic races'.[178] 'Ireland, in virtue of the high place she occupied, and does occupy, in spirituality, art, and culture', was worthy of something more refined than these purely materialist emblems.[179] The *Nation* worried that such agricultural symbols conveyed the impression 'that the Irish are a practical, material, unimaginative, humdrum kind of race, delighting in their unrelenting daily toil and demanding no escape even in imagination from it'.[180] *Irish Truth* declared itself thankful that the committee did not go further down the utilitarian path; otherwise the coins might have been bordered with interlacing lines of sausages or alternating egg and butter pats, while the salmon might have been depicted in the form best known to the public: 'in three portions decked out with a skewered ticket bearing the legend "3s. 6d. per pound"'.[181]

Many critics of the coinage designs were concerned about Ireland's dignity, which they felt had been slighted by the coinage design committee's choice of symbols. The sensitivities of many Irish people, determined that their country should achieve an honoured place in the world after centuries of domination by its more powerful neighbour, were apparent in the words and phrases used in attacking the coinage designs: 'an ecstasy of national self-abasement';[182] 'a totally inadequate conception of the dignity of the Irish Free State';[183] 'derision';[184] 'impaired the ideals and prestige of Ireland';[185] 'insult';[186] 'make us the laughing stock of Europe';[187] 'travesty on our land';[188] 'self-respect';[189] 'degrading';[190] 'crude, stage-Irishmen's ideas';[191] 'not dignified';[192] 'mockery';[193] 'outrage on the national taste';[194] 'unseemly and belittling';[195] 'humiliating'.[196] The feeling that the national dignity had been affronted was most obvious in the great offence which was taken by some people at the depiction of a pig and piglets on one of the coins. Pigs had commonly been used in the past by British cartoonists and commentators to represent Irish people as brutish and dirty.[197] Such caricatures relied on the negative associations of pigs in Western culture, which have been well summarised by Paul Shepard: 'From the corpse- and shit-eating brute, sunk in mud, to the menacing boar and the slob of a sow, through all the images of greed and intractable pigheadedness, pigs have come to represent the degraded status connoting "animal" or "flesh" or "body"'.[198]

Little wonder, then, that some Irish people were shocked to see the

Free State government seemingly approving of the pig, with all it con-
noted, as a national symbol. 'If the Government Party wish to save their
bacon, / They will forthwith get rid of the pig', advised an anonymous
critic who went on to ask 'Why not put a Black and Tan, Hamar
Greenwood on the coins? It would give less offence.'[199] 'Do we want our
grandfathers pig-in-the-kitchen for ever thrown in our faces?' cried the
Leader, perhaps reflecting the embarrassment of some middle class city-
dwellers about their peasant ancestry.[200] Another critic wrote indignantly:
'One could easily imagine that an Englishman's first thought would be to
give a permanent domicile to "Paddy and the Pig," but to find Irishmen
so devoid of all national feeling as to accept so calmly such degrading
designs is amazing!'[201] Others were equally astounded that Irish people
should consider the pig a suitable image with which to represent the
nation: 'The pig is associated with the mire and wallowing in the mire,
and our greatest enemies could not offer us a bigger insult than to represent this as one of our grand ideals.'[202] The *Catholic Bulletin*, however,
was not surprised by what it saw as a studied insult, and came up with this
ingenious explanation: 'Perhaps the absence of the King's head on the
coins had to be balanced in some way, consequently the pig's cheek! If the
King of England was to be slighted in the Free State coinage, the offence
would be mitigated by an obvious insult to the religion and patriotism of
Ireland.'[203]

The attempt by critics of the coins to claim for themselves the mantle
of defenders of national dignity did not go unchallenged by supporters of
the designs. The *Irish Statesman* considered that it was not the coins, but
the objections to them, that would make Ireland the object of ridicule:

> Our literature is to be censored in this spirit – our coinage is denounced as
> devastating in its fell purpose. What next will happen to proclaim to the
> world the supreme delicacy of the Irish soul? Will the Department of
> Agriculture be attacked because it sanctions very loose relations between
> bulls and cows? One bull, one cow! Will that be the next slogan? These
> fanatics are going to make Ireland the jest of the planet.[204]

The Irish correspondent of the Commonwealth journal, the *Round
Table*, also saw a connection with the censorship debate, and suggested
tongue-in-cheek that, since the coins had offended 'some of our sensitive moralists', they should be called in 'as subversive of public
morality' as soon as the Censorship Bill was passed.[205] Both the *Irish
Statesman* and the *Round Table*'s Irish correspondent considered that
the coins were unsurpassed in beauty by any of the other coinages of
Europe, and so could be a source of national pride.[206] They were joined
in this view by the *Church of Ireland Gazette*, which believed that the

coins would 'challenge comparison with those of any other country', and the *Irish Times*, which found them beautiful and entirely suitable for a nation which derived its wealth from agriculture.[207]

Those who liked the designs saw nothing undignified in having animals on the coins; on the contrary, they considered it quite appropriate that the coins should depict creatures which were Ireland's principal source of wealth and which were themselves bought and sold with money. 'We don't think there is any insult to Irish pride or sentiment in having on these coins such figures as hounds and horses, bulls or pigs or chickens', said the *Dundalk Democrat*. 'These are matters of everyday commerce in Ireland – and a very good thing it would be if Ireland had more of them.'[208] The *Enniscorthy Echo* thought likewise: 'So much of our national wealth depends upon our lifestock [sic] that it is only giving our horses, cattle and poultry their due to have them represented.'[209] 'Three-fourths of the country's wealth is based on agricultural produce and the designs on the coins bring home that fact' wrote the *Freeman* approvingly, though it also hoped that industrial development would soon lead to a more balanced economy which could be represented by the addition of symbols of industry to the coins.[210] A Mayo small farmer wrote to the *Irish Independent* with thoughts not so much of the national wealth as of his own livelihood. Animals were his daily bread, he pointed out, and he liked to see them on the coinage, 'for they are surely my friends. Idealists may say I am materialistic, but as long as I have bacon and eggs for breakfast they can have their ideas.' Even the much-maligned pig had a place in his heart and in his stomach: 'Surely this interesting and useful little animal has been and is the poor man's friend, if he really ever has had one. The pig is on our breakfast table, at dinner, too, and in our pockets in the shape of good banknotes. He saved many from starvation, multitudes from the roadside.'[211] Other defenders of the coins played the Gaelic card, reminding their opponents that animals figured prominently in Irish mythology and in the lives of 'Our Gaelic ancestors [who] loved nature, wild and tame'.[212]

Silences and key concerns in the coinage debate

In all the debate about the coinage designs there were several matters about which there was a significant and perhaps surprising silence. There was little mention of the fact that the coins were designed by an Englishman and minted in Britain, although the veteran republican activist Maud Gonne MacBride expressed mock surprise at the criticism of the coins which were 'so entirely suitable – designed by an Englishman, minted in England, representative of English values, paid for by the Irish people'. She noted sarcastically that Metcalfe had 'pushed

English politeness to unwonted lengths by not including a jackass in his farmyard collection'.[213] Another matter which went largely unremarked was the absence of the King's head from the coins. Despite the fact that the Free State was still a dominion, the government's unstated policy of removing all signs of the connection with Britain from public life was apparently uncontroversial among nationalists. (See Chapter 6.) More surprisingly, the organ of the ex-unionist community, the *Irish Times*, published only one letter complaining about the removal of the King's likeness from the coins.[214] Perhaps, like the *Irish Times*'s editorial writer, its readers could not bring themselves to accept that a separate coinage was necessary in the first place. The *Irish Times* editorial on the coinage designs was positive, but not enthusiastic, and was prefaced with the words 'If a sweeping change in the whole character of the Free State's coinage was necessary... '[215] There can be little doubt that ex-unionists would have preferred the King to be represented on the coins, and it was reported in the first month of the coins' release, while both the old and the new coins were in circulation, that shopkeepers were having trouble with 'admirers of the old regime', described as 'mainly elderly ladies', who were refusing to accept the new coins as change, insisting that they would only take those which bore the King's head.[216]

Commentators on the coinage designs also showed a complete lack of interest in what people in Northern Ireland might think about them, despite the fact that the coins were repeatedly said to represent 'Ireland' rather than the Irish Free State. With a few exceptions, those who wanted religious symbols on the coins referred to Ireland as a Christian rather than a Catholic nation, and some Protestants joined in the call for a recognition of religion on the coinage.[217] It was the insistence that Ireland be represented as a distinct nation, completely separate from Britain in its politics and culture, which was more likely to alienate Protestants and unionists, particularly in Northern Ireland. The release of the coinage designs provoked no discussion in the Belfast unionist newspapers, but the failure to put the King's head on the Free State coins was added to the list of actions which showed the Free State government's determination to assert the maximum degree of independence from Britain. Such actions were regularly cited as reasons why 'loyal Ulster' could never consent to join a united Ireland, and unionists made it clear that they would never swap their King's head for a horse. (See Chapter 6.)

If certain topics were largely ignored by defenders and critics of the coins alike, it was because participants on both sides shared particular concerns, on which the debate focused. Two main concerns emerged: the place of religion in public life, and the achievement of national dignity and self-respect. Both of these concerns were products of the political context into which the coinage designs were released. As the divorce and censorship debates revealed, many Catholics expected the Free State's laws to be consistent with Catholic teaching, believing that religion was not simply a matter of private conscience.[218] Despite the evidence that the trend in the Free State was actually towards a greater identification of church and state, vigilant Catholics detected a move towards secularism,[219] and saw evidence of this trend in the coinage designs. They believed that a Christian nation should acknowledge God on its coinage, and that the failure to do so was a deliberate rejection of God which reflected ill on the people. On the other hand, some defenders of the coinage designs thought it was all to the good that God was not identified with money and the evils which could be associated with it. They were adamant that God, Caesar and Mammon should be kept apart, but they too wanted the state to bear in mind Christian principles, reminding 'Catholic Ireland' that it should not countenance a union of the temple and the money-changers.

As for the obsession with national dignity, it was a product of political and cultural insecurity.[220] If critics of the coins recalled Ireland's glorious past, and were affronted by designs which, in their view, portrayed Ireland as a mere farmyard and a nation of pigs, it was not from a sense of cultural self-confidence. On the contrary, they feared that, as one writer in the coinage debate put it, 'in this age of enlightenment, Gaelic revivals and Irish-Ireland ideals, we are noticeably inconsistent, and not so bravely Christian and unconquerably Celtic and national as we pretend to be'.[221] Those who felt this way wanted coins which would reassure them by displaying to the world Ireland's idealism and the grandeur of Irish civilisation. The coins' defenders were less obsessed with national dignity, but they did want coins in whose beauty they could take pride, and which would stand comparison with the coins of other countries. The *Irish Statesman*'s concern with Ireland's aesthetic reputation paralleled its opponents' preoccupation with Ireland's moral reputation; if critics believed that the coins would make Ireland 'the laughing stock of Europe', the *Statesman* believed the campaign against the coins would make it 'the jest of the planet'.[222]

Like the *Irish Statesman*, Yeats was concerned above all that the coins should be beautiful, though he was an unlikely champion of the idea that a nation could take pride in the beauty of its coins. He had, after all, famously expressed disdain for money, as well as for the kind of religiosity which was so evident during the coinage debate, in his poem 'September, 1913':

> What need you, being come to sense,
> But fumble in a greasy till
> And add the halfpence to the pence

And prayer to shivering prayer, until
You have dried the marrow from the bone;
For men were born to pray and save.[223]

One of the main divisions in the coinage debate could be described as being between those who wanted to pray as they saved, and those who wanted to keep their praying and their saving separate. But there was some common ground between the two groups: both agreed that religious principles should inform public life, just as people on both sides of the coinage debate shared a concern with Ireland's standing in the eyes of the world. As they argued over the contents of the greasy till, Irish people were fumbling with the question of how best to represent the nation, and in the process revealing their insecurities and their aspirations. It must have been little comfort to Yeats to realise that all the participants in the debate at least agreed with him about one thing: that the design of coins was no small matter, and that such designs were indeed the silent ambassadors, not only of national taste, but also of the nation's morality, economics and politics.

Conclusion

The debate about the Free State coinage designs shows clearly that symbols are important to people, that debates about symbols provide an opportunity to argue about the nation which those symbols are meant to represent, and that symbols are open to a wide variety of interpretations. The committee on coinage design no doubt hoped to avoid political controversy by putting animals on the coins. They probably imagined that choosing the more obvious political and religious symbols would accentuate the divisions which dominated Irish political life (Catholic/Protestant, nationalist/unionist, republican/Free Stater), but they found, perhaps to their surprise, that passing over these symbols was itself considered by many to be a political act. Far from being inoffensive or neutral, the animal symbols on the coins were considered by their critics to be positively harmful to religion and national prestige. Supporters of the coins also saw political significance in their designs: the coins could play a beneficial role by enhancing the state's aesthetic reputation internationally, promoting agriculture and separating religion from finance. One thing which emerges clearly from the coinage debate is that there is no such thing as an inherently innocuous symbol: in the right context, any symbol can become a focus for debate.

This raises the question of why the meaning of the symbols on the coins was hotly contested, while the designs of the seals, stamps and banknotes created little controversy or indeed comment of any kind. State seals are part of the paraphernalia of government and are not used by ordinary citizens, so it is not surprising that there was little public interest in the seal. Stamps are used by the general public, but they are not part of everyday life to the same extent that money is. Even banknotes would not have been used as commonly as coins in the 1920s; coins were the medium of exchange in day-to-day commerce, from buying a loaf of bread to paying a tram fare. Money is also something people worry about: they worry about not having enough of it, but they may also feel that they should not be too attached to it. In the English-speaking world there is a taboo on discussing how much money people earn, yet most people are very concerned about how their own incomes compare with those of their fellows. As Virginia Hewitt points out, such ambivalent attitudes towards money run deep:

> Both in use and as a concept, money arouses complex feelings, which are not necessarily all positive. From biblical times we have been taught that man cannot serve God and Mammon, that the love of money leads to evil. Obviously this does not mean that money in itself is bad, but it does point up an unease, and uncertainty as to what attitude we should properly take. People are often reluctant to admit, even to themselves, how much they care about money, but negotiating its use and distribution can reveal strong feelings and cause deep disagreement.[224]

In the Irish Free State, these feelings came out not in an argument about the use and distribution of money but in a debate about its design. Underlying the contention about the appropriateness of putting religious symbols on the coins was a difference of opinion about money itself, and about whether it was right to associate religion and commerce. It is hard to imagine a debate of similar passion about whether or not it is appropriate to place religious symbols on stamps, for example.

Hewitt goes on to say that good images on notes and coins alone will not eliminate the negative connotations of money, 'but inappropriate ones will almost certainly aggravate them'.[225] What is good and what is inappropriate is not self-evident, however: it is a matter of expectations.[226] Conventional designs, employing symbols which are perceived to have some basis in tradition, are more likely to reassure people and overcome their ambivalence towards money than symbols which challenge people's preconceptions. The need for reassurance was felt particularly strongly in the Free State, which had emerged out of great political turmoil and many of whose people still lacked confidence in their country's capacity to live up to their aspirations. In the conservative and insecure political climate of the Irish Free State's first decade, even such a cautious innovation as using animals as symbols on coins could seem threatening. The picture of

Erin on the banknotes, by contrast, was highly conventional and thus comforting. The banknotes depicted a national symbol with a long history, one with which all Irish people were familiar and which had appeared countless times in popular artwork. No doubt it could be interpreted in as many different ways as the designs on the coins, but the conventionality of the design meant that people could accept it without giving much thought to what it represented. It seems that, when it came to avoiding controversy, 'hackneyed symbols' had their uses.

Chapter 4
True to the red, white and blue: official symbols of Northern Ireland

As a devolved government within the United Kingdom, the Northern Ireland government did not have the same powers to decide on official symbols as did the Irish Free State government. It could not issue its own currency or stamps, and the national anthem and flag of the United Kingdom were already in existence. It could, however, choose symbols to represent its own administration, and it could also have encouraged the use of a local or 'provincial' flag and anthem.[1] There was nothing contradictory about using local symbols while remaining loyal to the United Kingdom state: both Wales and Scotland, which did not have governments of their own, had symbols representative of Welsh and Scottish identity which were not seen as in any way subversive of British patriotism. The Northern Ireland government, however, displayed a reluctance to use symbols to promote a provincial identity. Instead, it emphasised Northern Ireland's continuing connection with Britain and the British Empire, as symbolised by the Union flag (commonly known as the Union Jack). The Union Jack was the most important unionist symbol, one which linked Northern Ireland to the wider British world, while at the same time it had particular local meanings. It was used in unionist rhetoric to evade the question of where unionists' loyalties lay, and also to distinguish the loyal from the disloyal. Display of the flag was an important expression of unionist identity, and a way of claiming public space for loyalism. Some unionists called on the government to take a more active role in ensuring that visual evidence of Northern Ireland's loyalty could be seen throughout the province. They wanted the Union Jack to be flown from all buildings which received government funds, regardless of whether or not these buildings were directly under government control. The government, however, rejected such proposals, arguing that there was no point in trying to compel the loyalty of those who did not want to fly the Union Jack.

Ulster unionists and their symbols

There were four main sources of symbols on which the Northern Ireland government could draw: Irish national symbols, Ulster Protestant symbols, non-sectarian Ulster symbols, and United Kingdom or imperial symbols. Although it might seem obvious that the Unionist government would not want to use Irish national symbols, it is important not to assume that this was the case on the basis of the present-day insistence of many unionists that they are not Irish. As late as 1968, 20 per cent of Northern Ireland Protestants surveyed described their own national identity as 'Irish',[2] and before partition unionists commonly referred to themselves as Irish. They saw no opposition between the categories 'British' and 'Irish', and instead distinguished between the 'loyal Irish' (unionists) and the 'disloyal Irish' (nationalists).[3] For this reason, unionists were quite happy to use harps, shamrocks, Celtic revival motifs and Irish language slogans alongside Ulster and British symbols in their propaganda materials.[4] A good example of this is the badge of the 1892 Ulster Unionist Convention, which included a crowned harp, shamrocks, a Union Jack and the red hand of Ulster.[5] However, by 1912 it had become clear to most Ulster unionists that the best they could hope for was the exclusion of all or part of Ulster from Irish Home Rule, and as support for complete independence grew among nationalists after 1916 it became even more important for Ulster unionists to distance Ulster from the rest of Ireland and to demonstrate its special attachment to the British connection. In the face of an assertive, separatist Irish nationalism, it became more difficult to maintain that unionism and Irishness were compatible, so it is not surprising that the Northern Ireland government turned to Ulster and British rather than Irish national symbols for official emblems of the new state. However, the government did make an exception in the case of the Royal Ulster Constabulary, which retained the Royal Irish Constabulary badge, featuring harp and shamrock wreath (together with the Crown).[6]

Ulster Protestant symbols can be further subdivided into three types: esoteric Orange Order symbols, Biblical symbols, and symbols from Ulster Protestant history.[7] The Orange Order employs a variety of esoteric symbols, mostly adopted from Freemasonry.[8] Although these symbols are public in the sense of being freely displayed in the regalia of parading Orangemen and on arches constructed across streets in Protestant areas, knowledge of their significance is largely restricted to members of these organisations.[9] This means that, despite the strong popular base the Orange Order maintained for most of the twentieth century (a 1968 survey estimated that 32 per cent of Protestant men in Northern Ireland were members),[10] knowledge of the secret meanings of these symbols was denied to most Ulster Protestants. Furthermore, they have no specific associations with Ulster, except in so far as the Orange Order itself is considered part of Ulster Protestant culture. The biblical symbols employed in Orange symbolism present similar problems. Although most Protestants earlier this century would have been familiar with Bible stories, it is unlikely that the connection between the emblems used in Orange symbolism and the stories they represent would be apparent to the uninitiated. They also have no obvious association with Ulster, though Anthony Buckley argues persuasively that they suggest the identification of Ulster Protestants with the Israelites confronting alien peoples in the chosen land of Canaan.[11] In addition, the use of biblical symbols by the Northern Ireland government might have been seen as inappropriate by some Protestants who were opposed to the identification of church and state. Symbols from Ulster Protestant history, on the other hand, had an obvious connection with the province and, though they were used by the Orange Order, knowledge of the stories connected with them was widespread in the Protestant community. The most common of these symbols was the image of King William III on horseback,[12] but other emblems, most notably those associated with the Siege of Derry, would also have been widely known. Had the government wished to represent Northern Ireland as a Protestant state, it would probably have drawn on these images from Ulster Protestant history.

The principal non-sectarian Ulster symbols are the red hand device, and the arms and flag of the province, on which the red hand appears. The arms and flag of Ulster consist of the red hand on a white shield, superimposed on the centre of a red cross on a yellow field. The red hand first appeared on the seal of the O'Neills, the kings of Tír Eoghain, in the fourteenth century, while the red cross on yellow is the coat of arms of the Norman de Burgh family, who were made earls of Ulster. Thus, the provincial arms combine the devices of the most important families in both the Gaelic and the Norman-Irish aristocracy of Ulster. The red hand may have been intended to represent the hand of God, and disembodied hands representing God's authority appeared also in Orange symbolism.[13] The rediscovery of the red hand as an Ulster symbol occurred in the late nineteenth century, when the struggle against Home Rule led to the beginning of provincial consciousness among Ulster unionists. It may have come to the attention of unionist political leaders through its use on the cover of the *Ulster Journal of Archaeology* from the 1850s, and by the beginning of the twentieth century it was being used as the trademark of the large Ulster linen manufacturing firm, Barbour's, while red hand badges were being mass-produced by Belfast metalworkers.[14] Its use became widespread during the crisis over the third Home Rule Bill from 1912, when an Ulster symbol was needed for the campaign to have Ulster excluded from Home Rule. As Alvin Jackson has argued, the 1912–14 period saw Ulster unionist image-makers employing the latest technology and the techniques of mass-marketing to get their message across, and the red hand featured on many of the postcards, stamps and badges produced as part of this campaign. It appeared at the head of 'Ulster's Solemn League and Covenant', a pledge to resist Home Rule signed by well over 200,000 Ulster Protestant men, and was used as the emblem of the Ulster Volunteer Force, the armed body formed in preparation for such resistance.[15] In addition to its provincial and religious associations, the popularity of the red hand may be explained in part by the fact that the upraised hand suggests both the swearing of an oath (which has an obvious connection with the Solemn League and Covenant) and the sign for 'Stop' (reflecting both the immediate campaign to prevent the imposition of Home Rule and the more general tendency of Ulster Protestants to see themselves 'as an embattled and enduring people... [facing] an endless repetition of repelled assaults').[16] Despite the appropriation of the red hand by unionists in the 1912–14 period, it also appeared as a symbol of Ulster in nationalist and labour iconography.[17]

The main symbols of the United Kingdom and of the British Empire are the emblems of the monarchy, the anthem 'God Save the King/Queen', and the Union Jack. The monarchy itself is the primary symbol of the United Kingdom, as the very name of the state suggests. By focusing on the monarchy, the ambiguities of nationality in the multinational UK state can be avoided, something which is particularly important for Ulster unionists, whose sense of nationality is notoriously problematic. As Richard Rose explains, 'The Crown is an idea, not a territory. The Crown is without an identifying place name; it is a Crown of indefinite domain.'[18] The fact that the monarch was head of state throughout the Empire was very important to Ulster unionists, who were able 'to avoid the implications of nationality altogether by identifying with a community, the Empire, to which no actual nation-state corresponded'.[19] The self-proclaimed 'loyalty' of many unionists was not to that troublesome concept, the nation, and certainly not to the government of the day, but to the Crown, though the loyalty of Orangemen even to the monarchy depended upon its remaining Protestant.[20] The main emblems of the monarchy are the royal arms and standard, and the crown. Use of the royal standard has come by convention to be restricted to the monarch personally, but the royal arms are widely used by UK government departments, and were available for use by the Northern Ireland government.[21] The royal arms were used to some extent by unionists in the campaign against Home Rule,[22] but the monarchy was more commonly symbolised in unionist imagery by a crown. Crowns appear frequently in Orange symbolism, representing not only the Order's support for the earthly Protestant monarchy but also Christ's kingdom and a heavenly crown.[23]

The United Kingdom was a constitutional monarchy, and therefore the monarch was supposed to represent the people. However, as the state democratised additional symbols were required, and in particular the need for a national flag and anthem which ordinary British subjects could use to display their loyalty was increasingly felt. The current lyrics of 'God Save the King' were first sung in 1745 as an ode to the monarch, but by the early nineteenth century it was regularly referred to as the *national* anthem.[24] Its popularity seems to have increased greatly from around 1890, and David Cannadine points out that 'there were more histories and choral settings of the national anthem in the decades 1890–1910 than in any period before or since'.[25] Cannadine attributes this to the revitalisation of royal ritual coinciding with the English musical renaissance in this period, but it was also a result of the growing need for popular national symbols which allowed the increasingly enfranchised masses to express their patriotism, together with the requirement for symbols which could unite all the diverse peoples of the Empire. The Union Jack came to play a similar role in the same period. Like the national anthem, the Union Jack was initially associated with the Crown, but it took on a life of its own from the late nineteenth century. The present design of the Union Jack was created at the time of the Union of Ireland and Britain in 1801 by adding the cross of St Patrick, representing Ireland, to the crosses of SS George and Andrew, representing England and Scotland.[26] Although it is used as the flag of the United Kingdom, it has no official or legal standing as such, and is strictly speaking a royal flag, flown by private citizens by verbal license of the Crown. As a result, there has been some confusion about the right of British subjects to fly the Union Jack, and even the Colonial Secretary's statement to the House of Lords in 1908 that the Union Jack was the national flag and could be flown by all the King's subjects failed to dispel this uncertainty completely.[27]

The Union Jack's transformation into a popular national symbol owed much to the efforts of an Irish peer, Lord Meath, who began campaigning in the 1890s for greater public use of the flag. On returning from the United States, where he had presumably been impressed the prolific display of the US flag, Meath was struck 'by the popular ignorance in regard to the national flag' in the UK. He campaigned successfully to get the flag flown from the Houses of Parliament, and was also a vociferous advocate of introducing the Union Jack into schools.[28] As part of his crusade to promote British patriotism, Meath also came up with the idea of Empire Day, an Empire-wide imperial holiday in which the Union Jack was to play a prominent part. Although Empire Day was not officially endorsed by the British government until 1916, two decades after Meath first proposed it, the day became one of the most important occasions for patriotic display in the United Kingdom and throughout the Empire. A particular effort was made on Empire Day to teach children to honour the flag: many schools flew the Union Jack from their flagpoles on the day, and pupils saluted the flag, sang songs about it, and formed living Union Jacks.[29] The Union Jack was given a central place in the celebrations because it was a symbol which linked all the people of the Empire, and one reason for increasing popular use of the Union Jack was the growth of imperialism and the perceived need for common imperial symbols. As one imperial patriot wrote in 1900, 'There are occasions – and they are likely to come with increasing frequency – when the Empire thinks, acts, and moves as a whole; when all Britons, no matter where, bow together in common grief, rise together in common anger, shout together in common joy. Surely there ought to be a common flag for use on such occasions.'[30] By the early twentieth century it was generally agreed that this common imperial flag should be the Union Jack; as *The Encyclopaedia Britannica* put it, the Union Jack was the 'national flag of the British Empire'.[31]

The Union Jack's status as an imperial symbol was particularly appealing to unionists in Ireland, who were keen to display their loyalty to the Empire. Like other British subjects, Ulster unionists made little use of the Union Jack before the last decade of the nineteenth century, but they took it up with a vengeance from the time of the 1892 Ulster Unionist Convention onwards. Union Jacks were used in anti-Home Rule propaganda, often together with the red hand, and in April 1912 Ulster unionists unfurled what they claimed was the largest Union Jack ever made, to be used in unionist demonstrations.[32] By giving such a prominent place to the Union Jack, unionists were showing their determination to remain part of the United Kingdom and the Empire, but in the process the Union Jack also became a symbol of a localised Ulster unionist identity. As an editorial in the unionist *Belfast Newsletter* on Empire Day 1904 declared proudly: 'The Union Jack is *our* birthright; it is *our* very own. Kings may die, Governments may change, dynasties pass away, but the flag remains. Loyalty to the flag means loyalty to *ourselves*.'[33] In selecting official symbols of Northern Ireland after 1921, the government had to choose between symbols which represented Northern Ireland's connection with Britain and Empire and those which symbolised the Ulster unionist community itself. The Union Jack was such a powerful symbol for unionists because, more than any other, it represented both Ulster and Empire.

Choosing symbols of Northern Ireland

The main official symbol chosen by the Northern Ireland government was the coat of arms of Northern Ireland. The arms were considered to be a matter for the Northern Ireland government, unlike the Great Seal of Northern Ireland, which was regarded as 'an Imperial affair' and designed by British officials. Northern Ireland Prime Minister Craig, consulted about the design of the Seal, remarked that 'if it is necessary for Ulster to have a separate Seal from the United Kingdom he thinks it should be made clear that it is the Seal for Northern Ireland', and was concerned that the inclusion of a four-leafed shamrock was more appropriate for an all-Ireland seal. The Imperial Secretary in Belfast tactfully remarked that 'Craig's view was, no doubt, affected by his influenza', and the design was adopted despite Craig's reservations.[34] The seal depicted King George V mounted on a horse, superimposed on a shamrock; the design also included a small rose and thistle, and was surmounted by a crown.

Consultations about the arms of Northern Ireland began in early January 1924, when Neville Wilkinson, the Ulster King of Arms, advised the Duke of Abercorn, Governor of Northern Ireland, that there should be no problem with registering the Ulster arms as the arms of Northern Ireland. Subsequently, however, John Anderson from the British Home Office met Wilkinson and discussed with him 'the political considerations' relating to the question of the arms. Anderson went away from the meeting hopeful that Wilkinson would produce a design 'which will be acceptable to Northern Ireland without needlessly offending sentiment elsewhere'. Probably as a result of his meeting with Anderson, Wilkinson told Abercorn in a later discussion that, because three of the counties of Ulster lay outside Northern Ireland, the College of Arms could not sanction the use by Northern Ireland of the Ulster arms unless some arrangement could be reached with the Free State. The Governor thought such an arrangement inadvisable, and instead suggested that the arms of Ulster might be modified by placing the red cross on a white ground, thus turning it into the cross of St George, 'typifying that Northern Ireland was a portion of the United Kingdom'. Abercorn also insisted on the inclusion of the Imperial crown in the design, despite Wilkinson's objection that the Crown covered Ireland as a whole. The Governor explained to Prime Minister Craig that 'while the inhabitants of the Free State had never shown any particular enthusiasm in regard to this matter, I felt sure the people of Northern Ireland would welcome and approve' of the inclusion of the crown.[35]

The arms of Northern Ireland were granted on 2 August 1924, and supporters to these arms were granted on 17 August 1925. The final design produced by Wilkinson showed a red cross on a white background, with a red hand inside a white, six-pointed star superimposed on the centre of the cross, and surmounted by a crown.[36] It thus suggested the old arms of Ulster, while also including elements (the cross of St George and the crown) which emphasised Northern Ireland's links with Britain. Wilkinson later described the significance of this design in the following terms:

The ancient badge of Ulster, the bloody right hand of the O'Neill, is charged upon a white star or estoile, the North Star, which has six points to represent the Six Counties. This central design is ensigned by the Imperial Crown to show both loyalty to the Throne and partnership in the Commonwealth of British Nations. The field bearing the Cross on which the design rests is a token of trust in the support of those who fight under the symbol of Saint George. The Supporters represent the Lion chosen as the emblem of Great Britain, who bears the Royal Badge of Ireland [a gold harp on a blue ground, surmounted by a crown]; while the Irish Elk displays the red cross on a gold ground which were the ancient Arms of Ulster.[37]

Neither the Governor nor the Prime Minister particularly admired the design of the supporters, and Craig had earlier suggested that the supporters be replaced by such emblems as the *Mountjoy* or the Derry cannon, symbols of the Siege of Derry.[38] Nothing came of his suggestion, however, presumably because such symbols from Ulster Protestant history were seen as too nakedly sectarian. Likewise, a suggestion mentioned by the Governor's private secretary, that 'something incorporating the industrial life of Northern Ireland be added to the Arms', was not taken up, despite the fact that unionists liked to contrast Northern Ireland's industrial strength with the industrial backwardness of the Free State.[39]

The Cabinet decided that the Ministry of Home Affairs should deal with all questions relating to the arms of Northern Ireland, including applications by non-government bodies to use the arms.[40] The policy adopted by the Ministry was to approve the use of the arms by organisations 'which are "national" in their character', and it refused an application to use the arms as a trademark, since this might give the impression that the business was connected with the Northern Ireland government.[41] Cabinet also decided to use the royal arms rather than the arms of Northern Ireland on official notepaper, emphasising that the royal arms 'should be used wherever possible'.[42] In 1928, in response to an inquiry from the British Home Office, Cabinet considered its policy on which arms to use on public buildings. In a memorandum prepared for Cabinet, the Prime Minister argued that since special arms had been granted to Northern Ireland which incorporated a royal crown, 'there need be no feeling that the use of the Arms of Northern Ireland as against the Royal Arms is in any degree derogatory either to the Sovereign or to Ulster'. He proposed that the royal arms should be displayed on buildings wholly or mainly used for the administration of 'Imperial Services' (such as Government House, courts, post offices, Customs and Excise) and the arms of Northern Ireland on buildings used wholly or mainly for the administration of purely local services. However, after Craig circulated this memorandum, the Minister of Labour drew his attention to 'a new aspect of the question', the nature of which was unspecified. The Minister 'instanced the case of the recent flag trouble in South Africa', which had been resolved the previous year after much acrimony between Afrikaner and British South Africans. As a result, Cabinet decided to use the royal arms on all government buildings in Northern Ireland, though should any local authority wish to use the Northern Ireland arms the Prime Minister did not think there would be any objection.[43] In 1930, Cabinet approved the use of the red hand on its own as a 'national emblem' for Northern Ireland (equivalent to the rose and thistle of England and Scotland) to be used, for example, in Empire Marketing Board posters.[44]

The arms of Northern Ireland were incorporated into the Governor's flag, but this flag was personal to the Governor of Northern Ireland, and not to be used by anyone else.[45] The Northern Ireland government did, however, consider the possibility of creating a flag for Northern Ireland which could be used more widely. In early 1924 the Minister of Agriculture and Commerce raised the question of a flag for use on the Northern Ireland pavilion at the British Empire Exhibition at Wembley. He suggested that the red ensign be used, as in the overseas dominions, with an insert containing the red hand. The Minister of Labour pointed out that Northern Ireland's position was different from that of an overseas dominion and said 'that we should emphasise our union in the United Kingdom by flying the Union Jack without any special symbol'. The Minister of Agriculture and Commerce countered that Scotland and Wales both displayed special flags, though they were also part of the Union. Cabinet agreed that while the Union Jack should be displayed in the most prominent position, a red ensign bearing the red hand should also be displayed.[46] However, the discovery that a royal warrant would be needed for any Northern Ireland flag delayed action on the matter.[47] The question was raised again later in the year at the instigation of Oscar Henderson, the Governor's private secretary, who noted that the Governor received 'frequent requests from persons and societies in Northern Ireland as to whether there is a flag symbolical of Ulster sentiment and authorised for use as the Northern Ireland flag', and that there had also been correspondence in the press on the matter.[48] The Secretary to the Cabinet then circulated a memorandum asking the Cabinet to consider 'whether a special flag should be registered for general use in Northern Ireland or whether the Union Jack alone should be regarded as the flag of Ulster'. Cabinet decided that 'there should be no change in the Ulster Flag which should remain Union Jack as at present'.[49]

The fact that the Governor had received so many inquiries about an 'Ulster' flag suggests that there was some popular sentiment in favour of such a banner, and there is also evidence that, in the absence of an official flag, people improvised their own. In 1926 an official in the Ministry of Home Affairs reported having recently seen 'the Ulster Arms superimposed on the Union Jack; a Blue Ensign and a Red Ensign with the Arms; and a plain blue flag with the Arms of Ulster surrounded by six stars',[50] while the *Irish News* claimed in 1932 that a Union Jack charged with a shield bearing the arms of Ulster was often flown from Belfast City Hall and that many Belfast merchants flew 'a blue ensign charged with the Arms of Northern Ireland surrounded by six stars'.[51] Given these signs of support for a Northern Ireland flag, it is all the more remarkable that the government dismissed the idea. This was, however, consistent with the government's determination to emphasise that Northern Ireland was part of the United Kingdom, a determination apparent in its decision to include the crown and cross of St George in the arms, and to use the royal rather than the Northern Ireland arms on official paper and on government buildings. Similarly, there is no evidence that the government even considered promoting a Northern Ireland anthem which might have been played together with 'God Save the King'.

It would be easy to explain the government's policy in terms of Jennifer Todd's distinction between the Ulster loyalist and Ulster British traditions in unionist political culture, with Ulster loyalists having as their primary imagined community the Ulster Protestant people themselves, and Ulster British identifying primarily with the imagined community of Greater Britain.[52] It could be argued that the government was dominated by Ulster British, and was therefore more concerned to symbolise Northern Ireland's links with Britain than were the Ulster loyalists among the unionist rank and file, who wanted a Northern Ireland flag. However, while this division is useful in analysing Ulster unionist political culture generally, it is not particularly helpful in examining government decision-making. The government's primary concern was to keep unionists united behind the Unionist party, that coalition of interests which cut across class and ideology, and thereby to preserve both the Union and the party's own political power. In doing so, it is not surprising that the government emphasised those symbols which were honoured by all unionists: the Union Jack and the emblems of the monarchy, to which Ulster loyalists were just as fervently committed as Ulster British.[53] The reference in the *Irish News* to Belfast merchants displaying a Northern Ireland flag may hint at another reason why the government felt no need to create a provincial flag. The smaller businesses represented by the Ulster Industries Development Association, which were engaged mainly in production for the local market, had an obvious interest in promoting provincial loyalty. They ran a 'Buy Ulster Goods' campaign which employed the red hand device and they may also have used flags as part of this campaign. The government, however, was more attentive to the interests of the large linen and shipbuilding firms which were fully integrated not only into the UK economy, but into the world market, and had no need for such parochialism.[54] The concerns of the smaller businesses were largely ignored within the Cabinet, so the government would have felt little pressure from the business sector for the promotion of an 'Ulster' identity.

The government's policy should also be seen in the context of the division within the Cabinet between 'populists' and 'anti-populists'.[55] The dominant populist faction centred on Prime Minister Sir James Craig, Minister of Labour John Andrews, and Minister of Home Affairs R. Dawson Bates. The populists were more 'Ulster'-centred in their thinking than the anti-populists, yet paradoxically, the anti-populists 'had a more exalted conception of the Northern Ireland parliament and state' than the populists, who stressed Northern Ireland's subordinate status. This in turn relates to their differing views of Northern Ireland's financial relationship with the UK government: the anti-populists emphasised that with autonomy went the necessity for financial restraint, while the populists, concerned above all to keep their supporters within Northern Ireland happy, pushed successfully for substantial British government spending on Northern Ireland to ensure parity with the rest of the United Kingdom. Thus, the populists, although probably more Ulster loyalist in identification, had very good reason to symbolically emphasise Northern Ireland's links with Britain.

The importance of the Union Jack to Ulster unionists

The key symbol for unionists, and the one behind which they could all unite, was the Union Jack. The Union Jack played a much more important role in Ulster unionist rhetoric than did the tricolour in the rhetoric of nationalists, whether in the Free State or in Northern Ireland. No election address by a Unionist politician, no speech by an Orangeman on 12 July or similar occasions, was complete without some reference to the Union Jack. The pattern was set during the first election for the Northern Ireland parliament in 1921, when Unionist party leader Sir James Craig called on unionists to 'Rally round me that I may shatter our enemies and their hopes of a republic flag. The union jack must sweep the polls.'[56] Thereafter, declarations that 'We will keep the Union Jack flying in Ulster' or 'We will never see the flag of Empire replaced by the tricolour of an Irish republic' were routine. Clearly, such statements reflected continuing apprehensiveness on the part of unionists about the security of Northern Ireland's position within the United Kingdom, but this does not explain why their concern was so commonly expressed in these terms. It is the fact that the Union Jack was simultaneously the flag of Ulster unionism, of the United Kingdom, and of the Empire that made it so useful rhetorically. By talking about flags, unionists could sidestep questions of nationality and of where, precisely, their loyalties lay. The statement 'We want Northern Ireland to remain under the Union Jack' suggests a range of distinct but related meanings: 'We want to keep Ulster Protestant/British/part of the United Kingdom/part of the British Empire.'

The emphasis on loyalty to the Union Jack was also useful when it came to distinguishing unionists from nationalists. The unionist writer Ronald McNeill put it this way: 'In the mind of the average Ulster Unionist the particular point of contrast between himself and the Nationalist of which he is more forcibly conscious than of any other, and in which all other distinguishing traits are merged, is that he is loyal to the British Crown and the British Flag, whereas the other man is loyal to neither.'[57] That disapproval of the nationalist attitude towards the Union Jack was shared by Orangemen and liberal unionists alike is apparent in two letters received by the liberal unionist Hugh Montgomery in 1935. The County Grand Master of the Orange Order in Tyrone asked Montgomery not to assume that he disliked Roman Catholics because of their religion:

> I call anyone who refuses to acknowledge the King and Constitution a rebel and can never understand why they insist on living under a rule which they openly detest and insult on every occasion. It is indeed surprising to hear of Roman Catholics joining your Boy Scouts and saluting the flag. In all my experience they would not dream of doing so and the Union Jack dare not be seen in any Roman Catholic locality.[58]

A more liberal correspondent, who admitted to Montgomery that Catholics had been driven into permanent disloyalty by the treatment they had received since 1922, nevertheless also condemned 'the open and profound expression of disloyalty shown by so many Roman Catholics on every occasion which we hold dear, such as Armistice Day or the late Royal Wedding, and the attitude towards flying the Union Jack, tragic (if it were not so childish)'.[59] Unionists insisted that the Union Jack, like 'God Save the King', was not a party symbol, and professed to be unable to understand nationalist aversion to this flag and anthem. Ronald McNeill argued that:

> If the National Anthem has become a 'party tune' in Ireland, it is not because the loyalist sings it, but because the disloyalist shuns it; and its avoidance at gatherings both political and social where Nationalists predominate, naturally makes those who value loyalty the more punctilious in its use. If there is a profuse display of the Union Jack, it is because it is in Ulster not merely 'bunting' for decorative purposes as in England, but the symbol of a cherished faith.[60]

If the Union Jack symbolised a 'cherished faith', unionist rhetoric about the flag was usually vague about the tenets of that faith. Apart from loyalty to King and Empire, the flag was most often said to stand for civil and religious liberty,[61] a theme taken up by the Reverend J.E. Doyle in his sermon for the Relief of Derry service in 1933:

> Our grand old flag, the Union Jack, baptised with the tears of millions of mothers and dipped in the altar fragrant with sacrifice, is the emblem of liberty and British rule. That flag is a living thing, pulsing with the throbbing ardours of humanity and glowing with the fervour of immortal hopes. It is a flame springing up to consume injustice and hate, and make liberty and love prevail. It is a voice that speaks with the eloquence of graves where sleep those who died to make it mean purity and righteousness. He who looks on that flag with ransomed eyes beholds within its folds prayers of the just and upright; the fierce splendours of the ocean that was the cradle of Lord Nelson and the valour and faith of Ulster's brave sons who died shouting 'No Surrender' on the battlefields of France and Flanders. We can see the full glory of that flag reflected within the Six Counties of Ulster. Wherever it floats there is civil and religious liberty; and wherever it leads we will follow, for we know that the hand which bears it onward is the unseen Hand of God and we can never retreat. For such a flag true men will always gladly die; for such a flag good men will always nobly live.[62]

However, even as Doyle proclaimed that the flag stood for civil and religious liberty, his language carried sectarian implications which would not have been lost on his audience. The message of the Union Jack was only apparent to those with 'ransomed' eyes; that is, those who had been ransomed by Christ's sacrifice. To evangelical Protestants this term could only apply to those who had accepted that sacrifice into their hearts, and could never refer to Catholics.[63] While all unionists agreed that the liberty of which the flag was an emblem was available to all British subjects without distinction, Orangemen maintained that the Union Jack stood for a liberty which depended on the defence of Protestantism. In 1932, when some unionists criticised the absence of Union Jacks from the streets of Dublin during the Eucharistic Congress, the Reverend C.W. Maguire told an Orange service that this absence was just as well, for the Union Jack:

> stood for conceptions of life and religion and liberty which simply had no place in the Roman Catholic scheme of things. He was not claiming the Union Jack as an exclusively Protestant flag. All creeds and classes received a square deal under it. He was claiming that it stood for what Britain at her best had stood for these past 400 years. He claimed that it was the Reformation blood in her veins that had made Britain what she had been these past 400 years ... The Union Jack was never dearer to them because

of the way it had been banned in Dublin. (Applause.)...Communism and
Romanism did not readily flourish under its folds.[64]

In this view, to have flown the Union Jack in the midst of popery would
have been to pollute it. When, at another Orange rally, Alderman W.J.
Bradley's reference to the failure to fly the Union Jack for the Eucharistic
Congress was greeted with cries of 'Shame', he retorted: 'It was no
shame. It was no atmosphere for that flag to fly in.'[65]

It was not only in rhetoric that the Union Jack was used to highlight
unionist loyalty and nationalist disloyalty: actually displaying the flag
was also very important to unionists. In contemporary Northern Ireland
symbolic display is crucial to unionist identity, as Michael Ignatieff
observed when he visited the province: 'The sashes, the bonfires, the
burning Popes and Tricolours, the Lambeg drums, the marching bands,
the Red Hand flags, the songs: in all my journeys, I've never come across
a form of nationalism so intensely ritualized...Here Britishness is ritualized because it is up against its antithesis and nemesis: Irish
Republicanism.'[66] In Britain itself the vagueness of the concept of
Britishness, with its shifting social and territorial boundaries, was not,
until recently, a problem, because the concept was rarely challenged. It is,
as Ignatieff points out, the confrontation with a substantial community
which repudiates Britishness and identifies instead with the Irish nation,
which necessitates the active expression of Britishness in Northern
Ireland. Nationalists also create and reinforce identity partly through
symbolic display, and if nationalist displays have, in the past, been more
restrained than those of their unionist counterparts this has been partly
due to unionist dominance of the public sphere.[67] But even in Northern
Ireland today, nationalists appear to be less concerned about using their
symbols than unionists, despite the fact that nationalist symbols can now
be displayed much more freely than in the past.[68] Nationalists may fly the
tricolour as an expression of pride or defiance, but they do not need to do
so to feel that they are Irish: Irishness is for them a given, a natural state
of affairs which requires no demonstration or justification. Unionists, on
the other hand, do not believe, as nationalists do, in a nation with clear
and natural boundaries, and most of them lack a political vocabulary
which could adequately explain their position within the United
Kingdom.[69] As a result, Ulster unionists have employed symbolic display
as the primary expression of their identity and loyalty.

The display of Union Jacks and of red, white and blue bunting, and the
painting of kerbstones and lamp-posts red, white and blue, is also used to
mark out territory, to declare that a particular area is Protestant and loyalist. Today these displays are often left in place all year, but in the past they
generally only appeared around the Twelfth of July and remained for a

week or so.[70] This practice could be seen as a way of warning off members of the other community,[71] but Neil Jarman notes that contemporary residents of Belfast do not need such markers to tell them where they can or cannot go. These displays occur not on territorial boundaries, but within an established territory: 'By the time one is aware of the physical signs of allegiance, one has already crossed the boundaries.'[72] Their main function, then, is to build solidarity and communal identity: the activity of painting and putting up flags and bunting draws the Protestant community in each locality together,[73] and the end result provides reassurance that the local area is still predominantly 'loyal'. Moreover, all the local displays together proclaim the loyalty of Northern Ireland as a whole.

The use of the Union Jack and the colours red, white and blue in this way was already an established tradition when Northern Ireland was created. At the time of the royal visit to open the Northern Ireland parliament in 1921, Lady Craig, wife of the Northern Ireland Prime Minister, was heartened by such displays of loyalty, which she saw as a repudiation of the betrayal of Ulster by some English politicians:

> the King and Queen have the most wonderful reception, the decorations everywhere are extremely well done and even the little side streets that they will never be within miles of are draped with bunting and flags, and the pavement and lampposts painted red white and blue, really most touching, as a sign of their loyalty. Imagine radicals in England thinking they would ever succeed in driving people like that out of the British empire, or wanting to![74]

Sir James Craig himself was aware of the value of such province-wide displays as demonstrations of Northern Ireland's loyalty, and on Empire Day in 1922 he called on 'every person who has the Union Jack or the Red, White, and Blue, [to] bring it out and fly it from their windows, and let them show that, even after all the attacks made on us, the blood of Ulster is the same as ever it was, and that the flag of Great Britain and of the Empire is the flag of Ulster'.[75]

However, for many unionists such individual displays of loyalty, though very important, were insufficient. A speaker at an Orange rally in 1933 told his audience:

> The other day I was travelling from Cookstown to Antrim, and at practically every cross-roads I noticed there was a flag-pole with a Union Jack at the top fluttering in the breeze, and I could not help thinking that here was a part of the country where they showed they valued freedom and intended to remain part and parcel of the Great British Empire. (Cheers.) I hope the day is not far distant when we will see the Union Jack flying from the top of every Government building and every school in the North of Ireland. (Applause.)[76]

Those who took this view believed that the government had a duty to claim public space for loyalism by requiring the Union Jack to be flown from public buildings. The Northern Ireland government followed the practice of the rest of the United Kingdom by flying the Union Jack from buildings under its control on a number of days associated with the monarchy, on the day of the nation's patron saint (St Patrick's Day), on Empire Day, and on Armistice Day. In addition, the practice of flying the flag on New Year's Day, Easter Sunday and Christmas Day was inherited from the pre-partition Irish administration.[77] Some unionists, however, wanted to see the Union Jack flown 'on schools and all *public* buildings constantly'.[78] The category of 'public' buildings was wider than just those controlled by the Northern Ireland government: it could include all buildings which received government grants.

Elementary schools were funded by the government, but were under the control of local boards. There were two elementary school systems in Northern Ireland: a fully government funded public system whose pupils were almost entirely Protestant, and a partially government funded Catholic system.[79] The Departmental Committee on the Educational Services in Northern Ireland, under the chairmanship of Sir Robert Lynn, recommended in its final report in 1923 that the Ministry of Education should encourage all state-aided schools to fly the Union Jack on all suitable occasions. This did not go far enough for two committee members, who proposed in a reservation to the main text that 'not only should the flag be flown over every State-aided school but even the youngest children should be assembled at very frequent intervals and taught to salute the flag, thus inculcating loyalty in the children'.[80] The government, however, followed the more cautious recommendations of the Lynn committee's majority, preferring encouragement to coercion. In 1928 the Unionist MP Rowley Elliott asked the Parliamentary Secretary of the Ministry of Education in the House of Commons whether the government intended to instruct school boards and school managers to have the Union Jack flown over all school buildings which received financial assistance from the government. Elliott was informed that the Minister of Education did not propose to do so, 'but he is very willing that the managers, in whom the local control of the schools is vested, should have the flag flown on school buildings on suitable occasions'.[81] The result of this policy was almost certainly that public (that is, Protestant) schools flew the Union Jack, while Catholic schools did not.

It is not clear how widespread the display of the Union Jack on public schools was, but in 1927 the Director of Education for Belfast County Borough sought and received approval from the Ministry of Education for the purchase of one Union Jack flag, to be used for instruction in citizenship, for each of the new public elementary schools in Belfast.[82] In 1931, when the Belfast County Borough Education Committee sought recognition of the flag as 'a necessary part of the school equipment', a Ministry of Education official noted that private individuals had presented flags 'to the more important schools in Belfast', but that this left many schools without a flag. The official commented that 'While a flag can hardly be regarded as a necessary part of the school equipment its provision might be justified as an adjunct in the teaching of loyalty as a desirable feature of the education of the children of Northern Ireland.'[83] The provision of flags for all Belfast public schools had to wait until 1932, however, when the Director of Education sought approval for expenditure on flags and flagpoles so that all schools under the Belfast education committee's control could fly the Union Jack on the occasion of the visit by the Prince of Wales. With the royal visit coming up, and with the sensitivity of unionist opinion about perceived slights to the flag still fresh in their minds after a controversy over the flying of the Union Jack from Newry Town Hall, it is not surprising that Ministry officials decided to approve this expenditure.[84] Subsequently, the Dungannon, Larne, County Armagh and County Tyrone committees also decided to fly the Union Jack from all schools under their control, and other committees may have done so as well without informing the government.[85]

This situation did not satisfy Rowley Elliott, who in 1930 still wished 'to see the Union Jack over every school in Northern Ireland, and inside the school I should like to see the children being taught what the National Flag stands for, to respect the flag, and to salute it, as is done in the United States of America with the American flag'.[86] The idea of requiring all schools to fly the Union Jack, and of using the schools to promote respect for the flag, was raised again after the Newry flag dispute in 1932. A letter from 'Loyalist' in the *Belfast Telegraph* argued that all schools which received any government funding should be compelled to fly the Union Jack and to spend at least an hour a week 'teaching the children the history of the flag of their country and what their forefathers suffered so that we might have liberty and protection. All classes have that who live under it no matter what they may say to the contrary.'[87] This view was supported by another writer, who alleged that 'in many parts of the United Kingdom' there were schools teaching hatred of all the flag stood for, 'viz., our God, our King, and our country. Surely our schools could devote a little time each week to frustrate this and other offensive teachings by inculcating something about this, our flag, that has braved a thousand years the battle and the breeze.'[88] A third letter called for the introduction of saluting the flag in schools, as in the United States, in order to produce 'a loyal and patriotic body of citizens'.[89]

These ideas were also taken up in a 1932 resolution of the Dungannon Regional Education Committee, which requested that the Ministry of

Education make an order directing that the Union Jack be displayed on all schools funded, wholly or partially, by the government, and that 'the pupils of such schools be taught to honour that flag and be instructed on a specified day in each month on Imperial, National, and Civic duties, Responsibilities and Privileges'.[90] A Ministry of Education official wrote that he did not think the ministry had the power to carry out this resolution, and that even if it did have the power it would not be advisable to take action which 'would simply invite trouble'. No good would come of such a move, since 'Loyalty under compulsion would be of a purely formal type.' The Minister of Education agreed that no action should be taken regarding the resolution.[91] The government was aware that any policy which required the flying of the Union Jack at Catholic schools would meet with strong nationalist resistance, as Nationalist MP J.J. McCarroll made clear when responding to Rowley Elliott's call for the teaching of respect for the flag in schools. McCarroll accused the Unionists of making the Union Jack a party flag and declared that 'if I speak the Catholic mind and the National mind there is not a child that will ever enter a school in which it is compelled to salute that flag, so long as you maintain it as a party flag and a partisan flag. It is a substitute for the Orange flag.'[92]

The Newry Town Hall flag incident

The government's policy in relation to flags on schools was that loyalty could not be compelled, and that any attempt to force local bodies to appear loyal by making them fly the Union Jack would be counterproductive. The same approach was adopted by the government in relation to another type of building supported by government funds but not directly under the government's control: the town hall. The question of whether the government could force 'disloyal' bodies to fly the flag became the subject of public debate in 1932, when a controversy developed about the removal of the Union Jack from Newry Town Hall. Along with a number of other local authorities which had pledged their allegiance to Dáil Éireann and refused to recognise the Northern Ireland parliament, the Newry council had been dissolved in 1922, and its functions taken over by a government appointed commissioner.[93] In 1923 Newry nationalists decided to contest the municipal elections, and, after they took the oath of allegiance under protest, a nationalist majority sat on the Newry Urban Council.[94] During the period when the commissioner was carrying out the council's functions, he had given permission for the Union Jack to be flown from the Town Hall. Despite the council's nationalist majority, this flag was subsequently 'renewed' periodically by private citizens (described by Newry's nationalist newspaper, the *Frontier Sentinel*, as local Orangemen and members of the Ulster Special Constabulary).[95]

The hoisting of the Union Jack over the Town Hall in 1932 was probably a response to Catholic preparations for the Eucharistic Congress. The council had given permission for a Eucharistic Congress flag to be flown from the Town Hall (though apparently this opportunity was not in fact taken up by the church authorities who had requested it)[96] and the streets were extensively decorated for the Congress. The sudden appearance of Union Jacks not only on the Town Hall but also on the city's lamp-posts was seen by the *Frontier Sentinel* as a Protestant answer to the Eucharistic Congress decorations and a calculated affront to the Catholic community.[97] As the *Sentinel* explained: 'It was only when other Union Jacks were hoisted at different centres along the route of a procession of the Blessed Sacrament, as a studied and deliberate insult to beliefs that Catholics cherish most dearly, that the fulness of the "No Popery" malice behind the flag on the Town Hall was indisputably seen.'[98]

With communal tensions high as a result not only of preparations for the Eucharistic Congress but also of Fianna Fáil's recent election victory in the Free State, a Labour member of the Newry Urban Council, Myles Connell, moved that the Union Jack be taken down from the Town Hall. Connell told the council at a meeting in June that in the past fortnight a group of people had forced their way into the Town Hall and put up a Union Jack with the intention of 'insulting a certain section of the community'. Alluding to his military service, Connell said that no one had made greater sacrifices for that flag than he had, but that he resented seeing the Union Jack used to insult his fellow Catholics. He also pointed out that the council had given no permission for the flying of any flag on the Town Hall, apart from the Eucharistic Congress flag. Another Labour councillor agreed with Connell that the flag 'had been erected in a provocative spirit to create ill-feeling amongst a certain section of the people', and as an example of its sectarian nature mentioned that the Union Jack had been lowered to half mast when a special constable died, but had been flown at full mast when Cardinal O'Donnell's funeral passed through Newry a few days later. A Unionist councillor, however, rejected the charge that any insult to Catholics had been intended, and pointed to the friendly reception given to the request for the hoisting of the Eucharistic Congress flag as evidence of Unionist goodwill. The Unionists on the council could not see how the Union Jack could give offence to anyone, since it was an emblem of liberty and fair play (an assertion disputed by Connell). It was, said one Unionist, 'the flag of the Empire, of which they formed a part, and he could not see how it could give any offence unless those offended were particularly narrow-minded'.

When Connell refused to withdraw his motion, the Unionists walked out of the meeting. Connell was then persuaded to withdraw the motion after receiving assurances from the council chairman that negotiations were proceeding with the government on the matter, and that the chairman would report the result to the council at a future meeting.[99]

While the council waited for the chairman's report, events connected with the Eucharistic Congress kept the Union Jack in the news and heightened sectarian tensions. An article on the Congress in the *Belfast Newsletter*, headed 'All Flags Except Union Jack', noted that, while the flags of other countries were flying in Dublin, 'the Union Jack plays no part in the scheme of decoration'.[100] The *Newsletter* pointed to the failure to fly the Union Jack in Dublin as another example of the Free State government's hatred of Britain,[101] and a speaker at an Orange meeting on 12 July asked:

> If the great Congress just over in Dublin was purely religious why was there a political element brought into it? Why was the flag of every other nation floated over the city and the Union Jack hauled down...? Surely that was an insult to the Roman Catholic pilgrims from all parts of the Empire, who, while loyal to their Church, were also loyal to their flag. If the people of the Free State acted in this way it was a matter for them and England, but it was the duty of the people of Ulster, and especially of the members of the Orange Order, to see that the Union Jack – and no other hostile flag – floated over the Six Counties. (Cheers.)[102]

A speaker at a Royal Black Institution rally contrasted the intolerance shown in the Free State towards the Union Jack with the tolerance in Northern Ireland of the Eucharistic Congress flag, and the *Belfast Newsletter* was angry that the Newry council took advantage of this tolerance by allowing the Congress flag to be flown from the Town Hall while refusing to fly the Union Jack.[103] The *Frontier Sentinel*, on the other hand, was incensed at the proliferation of Union Jacks in the Newry district since the opening of the Eucharistic Congress, commenting that 'So much have these flags been identified with anti-Catholic feeling, that they are now unanimously regarded as "No Popery" flags.'[104] In various parts of Northern Ireland the weeks around the Congress were the occasion for angry confrontations. It was reported that a woman in a nationalist quarter of Strabane, which was decorated for Congress week, had been forced by a hostile crowd to remove a Union Jack from her window, while in another border town, Newtownbutler, the erection of a string of Union Jacks alongside Eucharistic Congress bunting brought rival parties onto the streets.[105] More serious disturbances took place after the Congress, when trains and buses carrying Catholics back from Dublin were attacked in several towns by Protestant mobs.[106] The nationalist *Irish News* observed bitterly that:

if Dublin did not see the Union Jack during the Eucharistic Congress, Belfast and parts of the North certainly did. It was seen heading the rabble which attacked the Northern pilgrims to the Congress. It was introduced as the emblem of mobs whose deeds shocked the civilised world. All the neglect the Union Jack has received in Dublin cannot bring it into the contempt which has been flung upon it by the desperadoes in the North, who waved it over their deeds of bigotry.[107]

Thus, by the time the Newry Urban Council reconsidered the flag question in September the political atmosphere had, if anything, worsened. The council chairman reported that he had been to see Major Harris, Secretary of the Ministry of Home Affairs, who told the chairman that the council had authority to do what it liked in regard to such matters. The chairman had asked Harris whether the council's property would be protected if the flag was taken down, and Harris had assured him that it would. Despite this confirmation of the legality of removing the flag altogether, the chairman proposed to the council that in the interests of preserving social peace the Union Jack should be flown on the Town Hall on the same specified days as on government buildings. The Unionist councillors, however, rejected this suggestion, since, as one of them explained, if there was an objection to flying the flag permanently there would be an objection to flying it on particular days. 'It will never be said of a Unionist that he took part in anything tending to the lowering of the Union Jack under whose folds we are protected', he declared. It was the emblem of the Empire of which Northern Ireland formed part, and he could not understand how anyone taking advantage of that association with the Empire could take exception to it. The Unionists then left the meeting. Mr Connell said he was sorry that the chairman's offer had been refused, and that it was not a question of a particular flag, but of whether flags should be put up without the council's authority. The discussion concluded with the passing of Connell's resolution: 'That the flag be taken down, and that no flags or decorations be permitted on the Town Hall without the approval of the Urban Council.'[108] The flag was taken down secretly and quietly in the early morning a week later.[109]

The *Frontier Sentinel* felt that its campaign against the Union Jack had been vindicated. In June the *Sentinel* had published strongly worded editorials opposing the flying of the Union Jack on the Town Hall:

Whatever the Union Jack may mean in England or Canada or Australia, in the area controlled by the Belfast Government it means 'No Popery.' An Orange flag would convey the same meaning, but, then, an Orange flag could not be used with such perfect legal safety and prosecutions might ensue; so when Catholics are struck in the teeth with a Union Jack the insulting party can always plead that there can be no grounds whatever for offence since the flag of Empire, absolutely detached from religious and party issues, is the flag of freedom and equality. (Moryah!)...

It will be noticed that when public feeling is referred to by Unionist members of the Urban Council they mean non-Catholic feeling. The feelings of Catholics do not count. They are nobodies and made for suffering. At one period of our history, 'Union Jack' laws did not suppose them to exist at all; now they are not supposed to have any feelings...So long as Newry Catholics take insults meekly, so long will they be more systematically insulted.[110]

If 'the anti-Catholics of Newry' wished to fly the Union Jack, they were free to do so all year on the Orange Hall, but not on the Town Hall, which 'must cease to be a medium for wounding the religious feelings of the overwhelming majority of the ratepayers'.[111] Indeed, so overwhelming was the Catholic majority in Newry that the *Sentinel* had no qualms about calling the Town Hall 'the Assembly Place of the Catholic people'.[112] Following the council's decision to remove the Union Jack, the *Sentinel* rejoiced, claiming that the flag had been flown over the Town Hall as a taunt and an emblem of the defeat of those who had opposed partition. Furthermore, the people who had attacked Catholics and nationalists had often done so while waving Union Jacks, 'thus trying to forestall the law by showing that they were "loyal" and their victims "disloyal"'. Only a few months before:

> pious and unoffending pilgrims proceeding to worship God were barbarously attacked by hooligan bands of Lord Craigavon's followers, carrying Union Jacks, and the same emblems were floated on arches and from the buildings of bigots as a deliberate insult to the religious convictions of the vast majority of the Irish people. Intolerance had now shot its bolt. It stood revealed in its true colours. The religious and political significance of the Union Jack was exposed by its own idolatrous worshippers, and the end of its message of hatred and scorn on the Town Hall of Newry approached.[113]

Unionists, naturally, took a rather different view of the council's decision. The *Irish Times* reported that threats had been made as to what would happen if the flag was taken down, and that police were watching the Town Hall.[114] The reporter perhaps had in mind the resolution of the Newry District of the Royal Black Institution that if the 'dastardly act' of removing the Union Jack took place 'we will resist same by every means in our power, and we are determined to keep this flag, symbolic of liberty, justice and peace, flying on the Town Hall in the same spirit as the men of Derry kept the crimson Standard flying on the walls of that maiden city years ago'.[115] In the event, unionists did not take matters into their own hands, but some called instead on the government to require the flying of the Union Jack from all buildings which received government funds.[116]

The Unionist MP Major McCormick told the House of Commons that he had received many strong resolutions regarding the Newry flag incident, and he read out one resolution from the members of the Newry B Special Constabulary protesting against the government's acquiescence in the removal of the Union Jack from Newry Town Hall. Because the B Specials were only part-time police, they were able to make their frankly political protest 'as citizens'. Calling for the removal of Major Harris from office, they labelled his meeting with the Newry council chairman 'a slur and an insult to the loyalists of the town of Newry, and a grave weakening of Ulster's position in general'. Harris should, according to the Specials, have informed the Newry Urban Council 'that the Government would take a very serious view of any rebel demand for the hauling down of the flag which is Ulster's foundation'. The reference to the Union Jack as Ulster's foundation, and to its removal as a serious weakening of Ulster's position, revealed clearly both the insecurity of unionists in a majority nationalist border town and the importance which unionists attached to displaying the flag as a sign of unionist supremacy. The resolution pledged the B-men to 'bind ourselves together to resist by all means in our power all attempts by Government officials or other persons to thwart the political wishes of the loyalists of Ulster', that is, the wishes of 'the ordinary Ulsterman' who knew how to deal with rebel demands.[117] The Newry B Specials ended by affirming their confidence in the government, but their faith was not shared by the proposer of a protest motion from the Sons of Ulster Drumming Club, who 'declared that if the Government of Northern Ireland was going to play the part of cowards Protestants would have to unite and clear them out'.[118]

The views of some 'ordinary Ulstermen' who wrote to the *Northern Whig* showed that unionists were not of one mind on the flag question, though unfortunately the paper received many more letters on the subject than it was able to print, and the editor called a halt to the correspondence after only a week.[119] A letter from 'British Ulster' called for legislation to make the flying of the Union Jack on all buildings 'under Government control' compulsory. In contrast to the *Frontier Sentinel*, which believed that the Town Hall belonged to Catholics because they made up the bulk of Newry's population, 'British Ulster' thought it belonged to Protestants, who paid 80 per cent of the rates (a claim repeated in the Commons by Major McCormick).[120] The incident had, according to this correspondent, humiliated unionists, since it was now evident that 'it is possible in this loyal British province for persons who hate our flag and the British connection to insult, disgrace, and drag in the mud all that we Protestants stand for, and be assured of Government protection in doing so'.[121] Others also called for legislation to protect 'the emblem of our common freedom', or even to 'make the degradation of our country's flag a treasonable and punishable offence', while one writer thought that the Newry council should be disbanded, since 'To remove the flag, which is not only the emblem of the nation's faith, but of personal freedom, is maladministration of the worst type.'[122] The regular columnist 'An Old Fogey' also thought legislation requiring the display of the Union Jack on all buildings under government authority was needed. In light of the 'studied insults' to the Union Jack in the Free State, it was essential that 'not even the semblance of a slight' should be allowed in Northern Ireland.[123] On the other hand, two writers considered the Newry council's action justified, since the flag on the Town Hall had been flown without authority. One pointed out that the Union Jack was not a party flag, and that Protestants and Catholics had fought side by side under it, while the other asked 'why bring religion into the matter at all?' Many Catholics preferred to be under the Union Jack, and even more would feel this way if the flag were hoisted less on 'so-called religious festivals' and more on Empire festivals.[124] This secular view of the flag did not appeal to some of a more Orange hue, however. 'The Union Jack is the emblem of the British Empire, the Mother Country of which has done most to spread the glorious Gospel of free salvation through our Lord Jesus Christ among the nations of the world, and thereby pierced the awful gloom of superstition and ignorance which for centuries held mankind in bondage', explained one correspondent. 'The Union Jack stands for freedom, security, and faith through knowledge, which, summed up in one word, is Protestantism.'[125] Another argued that the British Empire, with the Union Jack as its emblem, was made possible by Protestantism, and that Catholics would always place the interests of the Vatican first rather than those of the Empire. The very people who insulted the Union Jack 'would to-day be in slavery, ignorance, and poverty' were it not for the presence of that flag.[126]

Some Unionist MPs shared the concern of sections of the unionist rank and file about the government's failure to prevent the removal of the Union Jack from Newry Town Hall. Major McCormick took a particular interest in the Newry flag issue because, as the government appointed commissioner in Newry in 1922, it was he who had first authorised the raising of the Union Jack over the Town Hall. In his view, the Ministry of Home Affairs should have told the Newry Urban Council that the removal of the Union Jack would be looked on as an unfriendly act. He recognised that the government could not prevent the Newry council from taking down the flag, but he wanted to see the introduction of legislation making it compulsory for all bodies which received government grants to fly the Union Jack. It was, he said, the duty of the citizens of any country to uphold their national flag.[127] Rowley Elliott likewise thought that all who enjoyed the benefits of British citizenship should be taught that 'with British money must go the British flag, and those who despise that flag should no longer be allowed to receive the benefits that are attached to it'. He repeated his earlier calls for the flag to be flown from all buildings supported from government funds, including schools.[128] However, another Unionist MP, Edward Murphy, drew a distinction between schools and town halls. Recognising the *de facto* segregation of schools, he said of them that 'Nobody wants to see the Union Jack flying in places where it will be exposed to insult.' The town hall, on the other hand, belonged to the whole community; but rather than arguing that it should, therefore, be free of symbols to which a substantial section of the population objected, he maintained that the government should order councils to fly the Union Jack from town halls.[129] Once again, it was clear that unionists considered the Union Jack to be politically neutral, and believed it was only nationalists who politicised it.

The Independent Unionists John Nixon and Thomas Henderson were well aware that the Union Jack was exploited as a political symbol by the Ulster Unionist Party. As Henderson told the Commons:

> You never go to any ceremony where there is one of the right hon. Gentlemen opposite where you do not see the Union Jack spread on the table, and before they finish their speeches they refer to the glorious flag, the Union Jack...*You* have always taken advantage of it, and *you* are responsible for making political capital out of it.[130]

Nixon and Henderson, however, simply wanted to make political capital of their own, by showing that their attachment to the flag was heartfelt, not cynical. Henderson continued the statement quoted above by claiming: '*We* love the Union Jack because it is the symbol of our country'.[131] They saw the Newry flag incident as an opportunity to embarrass the government by making it appear disloyal, and Nixon therefore moved a motion regretting 'the action of the Government in consenting to the removal of the Union Jack from the Newry Town Hall and other places' (the 'other places' were not specified). As far as he was concerned, the issue was a simple one:

> The Union Jack is either the flag of the country, or it is not. Fortunately it is the flag of the country, and I hope that it is going to remain the flag of the country, notwithstanding the weakness of this Lundy [traitorous] Government...The Ministry could have told the Newry Urban Council that if they removed the Union Jack – the emblem of our unity with Great Britain; the flag we are proud to serve under; the flag we are proud to live under; the flag that hon. Members wave when they want votes – they would be again suppressed and a Commissioner sent down to hoist it. If the Ministry had taken up that attitude the flag would still be there...I submit further, that every public building, just the same as in any other country in

the world that is under public control, should fly the Union Jack, and if people were more accustomed to their own flag, the flag they get protection
under, there would be less exception taken to it.[132]

If Nixon was sincere in his claim that familiarisation with the flag would
lead to greater acceptance of it, this marked a fundamental difference
between his view and that of the government. It suggests that, for him,
requiring the flying of the Union Jack from public buildings was not simply about claiming public space for loyalism, but that he hoped to see
such symbols used to turn the disloyal into loyalists. Whether or not this
was Nixon's view, it was an idea utterly rejected by the government. Sir
Dawson Bates, the Minister of Home Affairs, explained to the Commons
that the government's policy was to fly the Union Jack on national holidays from all buildings used and occupied by the government. However,
to suggest the withholding of grants to local authorities which did not fly
the Union Jack savoured of 'paying a man to appear to be loyal' (as
George Hanna, Parliamentary Secretary to the Ministry of Home Affairs
put it, 'the flag would lose its symbolism of freedom, and become a sort
of official receipt for financial assistance').[133] It was, Bates said, a privilege and not a penalty to fly the Union Jack. He could not understand the
suggestion 'that the Government should compel disloyal people to fly the
emblem of our country. After all you cannot make a disloyal man loyal by
force any more than you can put intelligence into certain individuals'
heads.' Furthermore, while he hoped that the discussion of this subject
would ensure that those loyal local authorities which were not presently
flying the flag would begin to do so, it would be an insult to such loyal
authorities to pass legislation compelling them to fly the flag. He also
referred to the question of using the flag in schools, and said that while
much could be done by masters and parents to teach children what the flag
stood for, he did not think the flag should be placed in a position in which
it could be reviled (meaning, presumably, in Catholic schools).[134] In his
speech to the Commons, George Hanna emphasised that the government
had no power to prevent the Newry Urban Council from taking down the
flag. He claimed that, if the parliament gave the government the power to
take such action, the government would use it,[135] but this was a transpar-
ent attempt to avoid the issue, since the government clearly had the numbers to get such legislation passed if it had wanted to do so. It was lack of
political will, not lack of power, which held the government back.
Legislation requiring the flying of the Union Jack on buildings supported
by government funds, far from helping to combat disloyalty, would have
invited nationalist unrest, which might in turn have led to unwelcome
inquiries by the UK government.
     The government's position was supported by some unionists, includ-

ing R.N. McNeill, an Independent Unionist whose views were more moderate than those of Nixon and Henderson. McNeill endorsed the view that forcing the Union Jack on people who did not want it would simply bring the flag into disrepute.[136] The *Northern Whig* agreed that 'Forced loyalty is valueless, and the outward proclamation of a loyalty that is non-existent is the sheerest hypocrisy.'[137] Similarly, the *Londonderry Sentinel* supported the government's stance, since 'Loyalty is an instinct with Ulster Protestants', while disloyalty was too 'ingrained' in 'the minority' for there to be any hope of teaching them respect for the flag.[138] As for those unionists who were not satisfied with the government's stand, the government hoped to placate them by increasing the display of the Union Jack from buildings under its control. In August, after the flag question had arisen but before the Newry council had made its decision, Cabinet decided to add police barracks and labour exchanges to the list of buildings on which the Union Jack would be flown on approved days (the *Frontier Sentinel* thought the labour exchange the most appropriate building on which to fly the Union Jack since, it claimed, partition had destroyed Newry's industries).[139] Then, immediately after the removal of the flag from Newry Town Hall, Prime Minister Craig received a deputation of loyalists. As a result of this meeting he promised to consider adding 12 July, the date of the Orange Order's most important annual parades, to the list of days on which the flag would be flown on government buildings. The government must have felt it had little choice but to accede to this request as a gesture towards hardline loyalist opinion, and it was approved by Cabinet in April 1933.[140]

Thus, one result of the Newry flag incident was that the Union Jack began to be flown from government buildings on a blatantly sectarian holiday, which can only have served to reinforce nationalist and Catholic hostility towards the flag. The government must have been aware that flying the Union Jack from government buildings on the Twelfth would further entrench the impression that it was a sectarian and party flag. In fact, George Hanna told the Commons, in relation to the case of a police constable who was cautioned for flying the Union Jack from his house on 12 July, that the constable's action had robbed the flag 'of its great national significance and symbolism and... left the constable open to the charge of pure political partisanship'.[141] The same charge could surely be levelled at the government, but unlike the constable, the government was motivated purely by pragmatism. Although its commitment to the Union Jack was undoubtedly real, the government was concerned neither to claim public space for unionism, nor to encourage the acceptance by Catholics of the Union Jack and the state for which it stood. Rather, it sought to keep its supporters happy by flying the flag from buildings under its direct control while preserving public order by declining to impose the flag on 'disloyal' bodies.

Conclusion

The main concern of the Unionist government of Northern Ireland when deciding which symbols should be adopted by the new state was to leave no room for uncertainty about Northern Ireland's position as an integral part of the United Kingdom. This concern was evident in Craig's reservations about the Northern Ireland seal, in the inclusion of the crown and St George's Cross in the Northern Ireland arms, in the government's use of the royal arms in preference to the Northern Ireland arms, and above all in the decision to use the Union Jack alone as the flag of Northern Ireland. There is little evidence of dissent from this policy of emphasising Northern Ireland's position within the UK rather than using symbols as a focus for a local, 'Ulster' identity. However, some unionists felt that the government had not gone far enough in using its powers to assert Northern Ireland's loyalty to the British Empire. They expected, now that unionists had their own government, that the power of the state would be used to extend the display of the Union Jack. Wherever they went in Northern Ireland they wanted to be reassured by the familiar sight of the Union Jack that the province's position within the Union was secure. Conversely, any admission that the Union Jack could not fly in some areas, or on some buildings, seemed like a dangerous concession to the enemies of the state.

The Union Jack was important to unionists because it was a symbol which united the disparate strands within unionism. While some unionists saw the flag as a symbol of Protestantism, others regarded it as an emblem of the common British citizenship of all Northern Ireland's people, Catholic and Protestant. In a classic case of solidarity without consensus, it was precisely this lack of agreement about the meaning of the Union Jack that made it so useful. Liberals and Orangemen, Ulster loyalists and Ulster British, all joined in professing and displaying their loyalty to the red, white and blue. Furthermore, all unionists agreed that the Union Jack was not a party symbol, and that there could be no legitimate reason for refusing to fly it. To most Catholics and nationalists, however, it *was* a Unionist party symbol, and to many it was also a sectarian symbol, a substitute Orange banner. The Northern Ireland government and some of its supporters, while deploring the attitude of nationalists towards the flag, thought attempts either to force or to encourage the disloyal to use the Union Jack were pointless and misguided. No amount of persuasion or coercion would make the disloyal turn loyal, and so long as unionists kept displaying their determination to remain within the United Kingdom, the nationalist minority could be ignored. The safest policy to adopt in relation to the minority was to avoid provoking it and to ensure that nationalists, for their part, did not engage in symbolic displays which provoked the unionist majority. The policies of the governments in both parts of Ireland towards the use of symbols by the minority communities in each state is the subject of the next chapter.

Chapter 5
Disloyal displays?: minority national symbols in Northern Ireland and the Irish Free State

Following partition, the governments of both parts of Ireland faced the question of how to deal with the significant minority populations within the borders of the two states. In 1926, 33.5 per cent of Northern Ireland's population was Catholic, while the non-Catholic minority in the Irish Free State stood at 7.4 per cent.[1] In both states, membership of religious minorities equated almost exactly with membership of political minorities: Catholics in Northern Ireland were overwhelmingly nationalist, hoping for a united and independent Ireland, while Protestants in the Irish Free State were almost all former supporters of the Unionist party who, while they did not seriously expect the Free State to rejoin the United Kingdom, remained loyal to King and Empire and hoped that in time their fellow citizens would share this loyalty. Thus, both parts of the island contained minorities which felt some degree of identification with states other than the ones in which they lived.

One way in which these alternative identities and loyalties were expressed was through the use of national symbols. The use of the Irish tricolour by nationalists in Northern Ireland, and of the Union Jack and 'God Save the King' by ex-unionists in the Free State, caused headaches for each government. In both cases, the use of these symbols was commonly considered by the majority to be offensive and disloyal. Unionists in Northern Ireland saw the tricolour as a symbol both of a subversive movement which sought the downfall of Northern Ireland, and of a neighbouring state which entertained irredentist hopes with regard to the Six Counties. Similarly, nationalists in the Free State regarded the Union Jack and 'God Save the King' as symbols of a unionist minority which had for many years thwarted the national desire for independence, and also as emblems of the state which had until recently held their nation in captivity.

While the Belfast and Dublin governments shared their supporters' hostile attitude towards the use of minority symbols, and engaged in harsh rhetoric on the subject of minority disloyalty, the primary concern of both governments was the maintenance of public order. A policy of banning minority national symbols would probably have fuelled minority discontent, thus increasing political instability, and furthermore, because these minority symbols were also the symbols of neighbouring states, such a ban might have invited unwelcome outside attention. On the other hand, governments had to bear in mind the strong antipathy of the majority of the electorate towards the public use of these symbols, and the fact that more extreme republicans in the Free State and loyalists in Northern Ireland were prepared to use intimidation to prevent such displays. Therefore, the governments of both states settled on a policy which steered a middle course between prohibition and complete toleration. Such action as each government took against minority symbols was primarily directed towards preserving the peace, and there was no attempt in either state to ban these symbols outright.

The Irish tricolour and 'The Soldier's Song' in Northern Ireland

Use of anthems and flags by nationalists in Northern Ireland

Not surprisingly, given the very different political situations in the two Irish states, nationalist politics in Northern Ireland differed significantly from that in the Irish Free State. Whereas in the Free State the rise of Sinn Féin had completely eclipsed the Home Rule tradition of the Irish Parliamentary Party and the Ancient Order of Hibernians (AOH), in Northern Ireland people who had opposed the rise of Sinn Féin remained influential, if not dominant, within the nationalist movement. Joseph Devlin, the acknowledged leader of nationalists in Northern Ireland until his death in 1934, had been a senior member of the old Irish Party, was lifetime president of the AOH, and had been responsible for turning the Hibernians into a political machine which worked for the cause of Home Rule. However, the nationalist movement over which he presided after partition was a loose coalition which included pro-Treaty Sinn Féiners and even supporters of Fianna Fáil. This disparate grouping, united in their opposition to partition and to the Unionist government, was riven by conflicts over tactics, and particularly over the question of whether or not to participate in the Northern Ireland parliament.[2]

The Devlinite influence meant that use of the tricolour and 'The Soldier's Song' in Northern Ireland was largely restricted to republicans. In the 1920s, writers in the *Irish News*, Northern Ireland's main nationalist newspaper, saw the Free State's adoption of the Sinn Féin flag and anthem as divisive, as did the *Hibernian Journal*, which expressed the undiminished loyalty of the AOH leadership to the green flag and the old national songs.[3] Reports of Hibernian and nationalist rallies in Northern Ireland record the singing of 'A Nation Once Again' and 'God Save Ireland' rather than 'The Soldier's Song', and during the 1933 election for the Northern Ireland parliament, when constitutional nationalists were challenged by republican militants, constitutionalists sang the old anthems while republicans sang 'The Soldier's Song'.[4] Even among republicans it is quite likely that 'The Soldier's Song' was little known. It was reported (albeit by a unionist newspaper) that when the chairman of a republican election meeting in Derry in 1933 asked for 'The Soldier's Song' to be sung 'it was evident that very few of the audience knew the "anthem," as the singing was confined principally to the members of the platform party'.[5] As in the Free State, it was probably the Gaelic Athletic Association (GAA) which was most responsible for increasing familiarity with 'The Soldier's Song'. Yet even within the GAA there were differences of opinion as to its appropriateness, and the Derry GAA board split in 1934 as a result of its chairman's opposition to playing 'The Soldier's Song', which he saw as 'likely to raise trouble' in Northern Ireland.[6]

While constitutional nationalists in Northern Ireland went on singing the old songs, they do not seem to have continued using the green flag to any great extent, even though no restrictions were placed on the use of this flag in Northern Ireland. The Hibernians and the Irish National Foresters made some use of the green flag, and it is significant that during polling in Derry in 1933 the electoral agents for the nationalist candidate wore green and gold emblems (the colours of the old harp flag) while the republicans wore tricolour ribbons, but on the whole it is striking that reports of nationalist meetings do not record the presence of any flags at all.[7] This can be attributed partly to a feeling that nationalists had to be cautious about displaying their symbols in a Unionist-controlled state, but it may also be that nationalists avoided using flags because they were divided on the question of whether the green flag or the tricolour was the Irish national flag. Even when Devlin died, the *Irish News* report on his funeral made no mention of any flags being flown or placed over his coffin, nor were there any flags in the accompanying photographs.[8] That the death of such a prominent nationalist politician was apparently unmarked by any display of national flags seems astonishing, but it is probably a reflection of uncertainty within nationalist ranks about which flag to use. Devlin himself had spent most of his career campaigning under the green flag, and was no doubt reluctant to adopt the tricolour which had been the flag of his Sinn Féin opponents in 1918, yet he appeared standing in front of a tricolour in a 1928 portrait by Sir John Lavery.[9]

Ambivalence towards the alternative Irish national flags, giving way to acceptance of the tricolour, can be traced in successive statements by the nationalist MP J.J. McCarroll. In 1930, McCarroll told the Northern Ireland parliament that 'I do not know what the National flag of Ireland is at the moment, constituted as the country is'. However, when challenged during the 1933 election campaign by republicans who asked why he did not display the tricolour, he suggested that the tricolour could unite nationalists, if only republicans would stop using it divisively. By 1934, he had evidently come round to supporting the tricolour, calling it 'the National flag...the flag for all Ireland'.[10] McCarroll's path from uncertainty to acceptance of the tricolour must have been typical of nationalists in Northern Ireland, since it is clear that in the long term the tricolour supplanted the green flag in the Six Counties as it had in the Free State. This may be explained in part by the continued use of the tricolour as the flag of the state with which Northern nationalists wished to unite and of all-Ireland organisations like the GAA. But it may also be partly attributable to restrictions on display of the tricolour, which had the effect of turning such displays into acts of defiance in Northern Ireland, as they had been throughout Ireland in the 1916–21 period.

Restrictions on display of the tricolour before 1933

Although the tricolour had been devised as a national symbol which was supposed to represent unity between Irish Catholics and Protestants, it was never likely to gain widespread acceptance among Protestants. For one thing, liberal Protestants who opposed Orangeism were unlikely to feel that the orange stripe represented them, while Orangemen would scarcely have been placated by the appropriation of their colour. The *Orange Standard* (the newspaper of the Orange Order in England) protested angrily in 1920 that: 'One of the most dastardly things about the Sinn Fein movement is the Orange on its flag. Orange Ireland repudiates the traitorous movement; why seek to make Ulster appear as adopting Sinn Feinism by putting Orange on the flag?'[11] The *Orange Standard*'s complaint highlights the main reason why Protestants were never likely to adopt the tricolour as a symbol of Irish nationality. Protestants were overwhelmingly unionist in their politics, and because the tricolour came to prominence with the post-1916 rise of Sinn Féin, Protestant acceptance of this flag was limited to those few unusual individuals who supported Sinn Féin's separatist programme. For unionists, the tricolour was a rebel flag, associated with those who sought by force to end Ireland's (later Northern Ireland's) union with Britain.

Despite unionist hatred of the tricolour, display of this flag was never strictly illegal in Northern Ireland. However, the Civil Authorities (Special Powers) Act gave police the power to take action against such displays. When the Special Powers Act was passed in 1922, one MP noted that the whole Act could be summed up in one sentence: 'The Home Secretary shall have the power to do whatever he likes, or let somebody else do whatever he likes for him.'[12] The Act gave the Minister for Home Affairs (and, in effect, the police) the power 'to take all such steps and issue all such orders as may be necessary for preserving the peace and maintaining order'. It was renewed annually until 1928, when it was renewed for five years, and it was made permanent in 1933.[13] As Laura Donohue shows, the use of the Special Powers Act changed over time: 'from measures aimed at returning civil order, the government increasingly turned to regulations designed to prohibit the expression of republican ideals'.[14] The Special Powers Act was undoubtedly used to stifle nationalist (and especially republican) expression, and was not used in an even-handed way to prevent provocative displays by unionists. While the Special Powers Act could also be used to prevent the display of the Union Jack when it was felt that this was in the best interests of preserving the peace, it is clear that the police and unionist authorities were much more likely to see nationalist displays as a threat to public order than unionist displays, since unionists regarded their own symbols as politically neutral.[15] However, the case of the restrictions placed on display of the tricolour suggests that the practical application of the Act was guided by a pragmatic concern with maintaining public order and placating unionist public opinion, rather than by an ideological drive to banish all signs of Irish nationalism from Northern Ireland.

The fact that the police could make arbitrary decisions to prohibit displays of the tricolour on the grounds that they might endanger the peace must have acted as a deterrent to such displays. In 1924, for example, policemen saw a tricolour flying from a window of a house occupied by two priests. One of the priests was asked if he knew that it was an offence to display the 'Sinn Fein' flag, and he replied that he thought it was no harm because it was St Patrick's Day. The priest refused to hand over the flag, and a search of the house failed to locate it, so the police removed the flagstaff and cord. The policemen's superiors considered this action justified because display of the flag in a 'mixed area' was prejudicial to the peace.[16]

Tricolours could be removed even when they were clearly intended to represent the Irish Free State. In 1926 police removed a Free State flag which was flying in Warrenpoint together with other national flags in honour of Cardinal O'Donnell,[17] and the following year the removal of a tricolour from Belfast City Hall was reported in the Free State press. In Empire Week 1927 the tricolour was flown from Belfast City Hall alongside the Union Jack and other flags representing the Empire, a gesture which the Northern Ireland commentator for the *Irish Times* saw as 'prophetic of those happier relations between the two States which all patriotic men desire'.[18] The *Irish Independent* reported that the display had been the subject of favourable comment in Belfast, and that one businessman had remarked: 'That shows our tolerance. You will not see our flag displayed in Dublin at official functions like these.' Unfortunately, the atmosphere of tolerance was short-lived. Only a few hours after Empire Week was officially declared open, the tricolour was removed by a City Hall employee and replaced by a Union Jack, to wild cheers from those watching below.[19] It seems that the tricolour was taken down due to pressure from what the nationalist Alderman Jamison called 'a small "soviet" of irresponsible people'. Jamison believed that the inclusion of the Free State flag in the decorations as a gesture of goodwill to the neighbouring dominion had given pleasure to 99 per cent of the population, but that 'a small percentage of the people were led to believe that this was the political flag of the old Republican Party' rather than the official flag of a dominion of the British Empire.[20] Although the *Irish Times* correspondent claimed that the incident had 'aroused a wave of sympathy with the Free State, and indignation was freely expressed on all sides at the removal of the flags', expressions of indignation were not to be found in the unionist press, which did not even report on the matter.[21] For the *Irish News*, however, the removal of the tricolour was another sign of the Orange Order's domination of Northern Ireland politics:

> They have decreed that Catholics shall be excluded, and the Government have accepted their dictum as easily and as openly as they have accepted it with regard to the Free State flag. This is a matter of no particular consequence. People will laugh at it in the Free State. But it signifies much to us – for we see in it the old hereditary enmity to the Catholic community.[22]

This incident highlighted the ambiguous position of the tricolour in Northern Ireland. On the one hand, it could be seen as the flag of Irish republicanism, which was out to undermine the constitutional position of Northern Ireland within the United Kingdom, but on the other hand it was the flag of a dominion within the British Commonwealth. There was also an ambiguity in the attitude of nationalist leaders, who did not necessarily identify with the tricolour, but who nevertheless saw any attack on this flag as an attack on the Catholic community. It was presumably for this reason, as well as because of their concern for civil rights, that nationalist politicians defended the right of people in Northern Ireland to display tricolours or tricoloured emblems. In doing so, they placed particular emphasis on the tricolour's status as the flag of the Free State. After a number of men were arrested for wearing tricoloured Easter lilies following Easter Sunday commemorations in Belfast in 1928, Cahir Healy asked Dawson Bates whether it was illegal to wear the emblem of the Free State in Northern Ireland. Bates replied that it was not an offence to do so, but that when such emblems identified the wearer with the republican movement or other illegal organisations, 'and where such display is likely to be prejudicial to the maintenance of the peace and preservation of order, it is the duty of the Government to prevent such display', even if the emblems in question were also those of a neighbouring state.[23] This answer did not satisfy the nationalist MPs, who wore Easter lilies themselves in the House of Commons the following day 'to vindicate the rights of the citizens to wear whatever badges they like'.[24] Healy spoke again, accusing the government of showing partisanship by targeting nationalist emblems while ignoring much more provocative displays by unionists, and he commended the attitude of the Free State government which, he said, allowed Orangemen and ex-unionists to display their emblems freely.[25] In response, the Attorney General merely repeated the government's position that it was not the display of particular emblems *per se*, but their display in circumstances which might lead to breaches of the peace, which was at issue.[26] The unionist *Belfast Newsletter*, meanwhile, cast doubt on the genuineness of the nationalists' concern with civil liberties, asking:

> Why are the Nationalists concerned about the arrest of Republicans who act in a provocative manner? If there is really no difference between them and the Republicans they should say so; but if they are Constitutionalists and desire the preservation of peace in Northern Ireland they should support the Government. Such questions as those of Mr Devlin and Mr Healy will strengthen the opinion that, whatever may be the differences among the Nationalists, they are all enemies of our State.[27]

Background to the 1933 'ban' on the tricolour

The question of whether the tricolour was a 'rebel' flag or the flag of a British dominion arose again in 1933, when, for the first time, the government introduced a regulation referring specifically to the tricolour. This decision occurred in the context of rising tensions both between the Northern Ireland government and its counterpart in the Free State, and between Protestants and Catholics in Northern Ireland. The election of a Fianna Fáil government in the Free State, its moves to dismantle the Free State's remaining ties with Britain, and its instigation of an 'economic war' with the United Kingdom were all viewed with alarm by unionists in Northern Ireland, who saw these developments as conclusive proof of Free State perfidy. At the same time, the Unionist government felt threatened from the left by the bugbear of socialism which, particularly at a time of economic depression, had the potential to separate the Protestant working class from the Unionist leadership, while from the 'right' the government was assailed by the Ulster Protestant League.[28] The result was a more determined banging of the Orange drum by the government, and a series of sectarian statements by its members, including Prime Minister Craig's declaration at a 1932 Orange rally that, although it was his duty to be fair to all in Northern Ireland, 'ours is a Protestant Government. I am an Orangeman, and I am going to have no dictation from anybody who is an enemy of His Majesty the King.'[29]

These developments formed the general background to the government's decision to 'ban' the tricolour in 1933, but there were also more specific events which made the tricolour a focus of attention, particularly in the border city of Derry (or Londonderry, the official name of the city at that time and the one preferred by many unionists). Derry had a nationalist majority but, thanks to gerrymandering, Unionists controlled local politics and were determined to defend their position as their forefathers had during the Williamite wars. At Easter 1933 a number of tricolours were flown in different parts of Northern Ireland, and in Belfast a bomb (which failed to explode) was thrown at police while they were removing a tricolour.[30] Then in July tricolours were included in the decorations for the opening of the Craigavon Bridge in Derry, but were taken down after a large crowd of loyalists gathered and demanded the flags' removal. The *Londonderry Sentinel* approved of the crowd's action, since it could see no distinction between the use of the tricolour as a republican symbol and its use as the flag of the Free State. The *Sentinel* remarked that 'this same tricolour was the rebel flag of Sinn Fein and the Irish Republican Army and... is the flag of a country whose Government has systematically banned and insulted the Union Jack'.[31] Perhaps in response to this incident, Assumption or 'Lady Day' (15 August), which was both a Catholic religious feast and an occasion for nationalist political demonstrations, was marked by extensive displays of the tricolour in Derry.[32]

In October the response of police to a display of tricolours at a hurling match outside Derry demonstrated the pragmatic attitude of the police towards such displays. A police sergeant who was present at the match asked that tricolours be removed from the goalposts, but was told that they were displayed in accordance with the decision of the GAA congress in April 1933 that 'the national flag' should be flown at all matches, and furthermore that the flags could not be removed without removing the goalposts. The police therefore decided to leave the flags in place, as there was a large crowd in attendance and it was felt that removal of the flags might lead to a breach of the peace. A police report on the incident noted that police in Derry had been told that it was not illegal to display the tricolour, so they should not interfere with such displays unless they were likely to lead to a breach of the peace.[33] The failure of the police to act in this case concerned Joseph Cunningham, who asked a question about the incident in the Senate. Cunningham saw the flying of the tricolour in Northern Ireland as an act of provocation by the Free State, whose politicians 'have longing eyes on the North of Ireland'. He did not think 'they should be allowed to fly this flag of theirs as they care or think fit', since the people of Northern Ireland had no desire to join up with the Free State. He also expressed surprise at the failure of the police to remove the tricolour, alleging that in Belfast police were quick to remove Union Jacks displayed in places where they might give offence to nationalists.[34] In reply, the Leader of the House reiterated the government's view that the primary consideration of the police was the maintenance of law and order, and that flags should only be removed when they were likely to endanger the peace.[35]

Further provocation, from the point of view of the unionists of Derry, came during the election campaign in November. The nationalist MP for Foyle faced a serious challenge from a republican candidate, some of whose supporters carried tricolours during parades and election rallies. On one occasion police intervened to prevent tricolours being carried through, or near, unionist areas of Derry, but otherwise they do not seem to have stopped republicans from displaying their flags.[36] An outraged 'Orange Unionist' wrote to the *Londonderry Sentinel* expressing his hope that when the Unionist member for Derry City, Edward Murphy, was re-elected, he would 'make it his business to see the tricolour thrown out of our peaceful and loyal Ulster', and this hope was well placed.[37] Murphy wrote to the Minister of Home Affairs during the election campaign to tell him that many unionists were unhappy about the display in Northern Ireland of the tricolour, which was 'not flown as a Dominion flag but as a rebel flag',[38] and he made the same point in an election speech, promising that, if returned, he would put an end to the display of the rebel flag in Northern Ireland.[39] Once he had been re-elected, Murphy repeated his pledge, saying that the time had come 'to put an end to the flying in Loyalist Ulster of that emblem of disloyalty. (Loud cheers.)' Murphy, who had moved to Northern Ireland from Dublin, continued: 'No one who has had the long experience I have had in Southern Ireland can associate that flag with anything but disloyalty, revolution, and murder... That flag is flown not as a Dominion flag but as a rebel flag.'[40]

The 1933 regulation regarding the tricolour

The government's decision to introduce a new regulation under the Special Powers Act specifically relating to the tricolour was presumably aimed at addressing the concerns of Murphy and his constituents. The regulation, issued on 14 December 1933, prohibited the display of any flag or other emblem consisting of three stripes of green, white and yellow, where such emblems purported to represent the Irish Republican Army, or an Irish Republic, or any organisation declared to be unlawful, and authorised police to seize emblems displayed contrary to the regulation.[41] The official announcement of the new regulation stated that it had been 'made for the further preservation of the peace and the maintenance of order',[42] thus indicating that the new regulation was in line with the government's established policy on the use of the Special Powers Act. A question immediately arose, however, as to whether the new regulation constituted an outright ban on the tricolour, and whether it applied to the use of the tricolour in Northern Ireland as a symbol of the Irish Free State.

The Bangor branch of the North Down Unionist Association expressed satisfaction that 'the tricolour symbol of treachery, rebellion, and murder is to be completely banned from exhibition in public and private anywhere in Northern Ireland',[43] and they were not alone in assuming that the flag had been banned outright. Most unionists probably saw the distinction between the use of the tricolour as a republican symbol and its use as the flag of a dominion as a false one: all nationalists, whether constitutionalists or republican militants, whether in Northern Ireland or in the Free State, were united in their aim of undermining Northern Ireland's position within the United Kingdom. The tricolour, therefore, was not the flag of a loyal British dominion but a rebel flag, 'the emblem of a subversive movement intended to destroy Northern Ireland as a self-governing entity'.[44] It had been carried through the streets of Derry, according to the *Londonderry Sentinel*, 'because it typified all that was antagonistic to Britain and British instincts and interests, and those who bore it through the streets would be the first to tear it in shreds if it were only regarded as the flag of a British Dominion'.[45] The *Belfast Newsletter* concurred, pointing out that the Union Jack had been 'virtually proscribed' in the Free State, which was now, 'to all intents and purposes, an independent Republic. Those who honour the tricolour do not do so because they regard it as a Dominion flag – they honour it solely because it is to them the sign and symbol of anti-British feeling and of militant Republicanism.'[46]

The representatives of nationalism in the press and in the parliament disagreed strongly with this point of view. Tongue in cheek, they pointed out that the government had not in fact banned the Irish Free State tricolour, which was green, white and orange (not green, white and yellow);[47] surely, one letter-writer observed sarcastically, the government 'would never do such a childish, stupid, and silly thing' as prohibiting the flag of the Free State.[48] Some suggested that the government was afraid of the tricolour's symbolism, and wished to distract attention from the orange in the flag 'lest its Orange supporters should ask questions and begin to learn'.[49] The main argument put by nationalists, however, was that, despite the government's seeming misapprehension as to the flag's colours, the tricolour which the government wished to eliminate from Northern Ireland was an official symbol of the Irish Free State, a neighbouring and friendly dominion within the British Commonwealth. This flag, they claimed, was recognised throughout the Commonwealth and beyond; it could fly in London, but not in Londonderry.[50] Even members of the Northern Ireland government had recognised the tricolour when visiting the Free State.[51] Despite the election of a Fianna Fáil government, the Free State remained a dominion, and the possibility of its becoming a republic was purely hypothetical.[52] In any case, it was the Northern Ireland government's responsibility to protect the flags of other states, whether inside or outside the Commonwealth, and as a subordinate government within the United Kingdom it had no power to ban them.[53]

The 'ban' on the tricolour apparently caused some resentment among political circles in the Free State itself, with the *Irish Independent* calling it a violation of the Treaty.[54] A leading supporter of Fine Gael declared that the tricolour was the officially recognised flag of the Free State, that it did not represent the IRA, and that any attempt to prohibit it was 'an act of impertinence'.[55] Responding to the latter statement, the Northern Ireland Attorney General, Mr Babington, was defiant. In the past twelve years, he said, the Northern Ireland government had not taken any drastic action against the display of various flags because it had been hoping for a change of heart in the Free State. No such change had come about, however, and Northern Ireland's constitutional status had not been recognised by the Free State. Probably thinking of Éamon de Valera's recent election as an abstentionist MP for South Down, Babington claimed that Free State politicians were still trying to interfere in Northern Ireland affairs and to bring Northern Ireland into an all-Ireland republic.[56] Despite Babington's apparent unconcern about how the regulation restricting display of the tricolour would be viewed in the Free State, however, the Northern Ireland government did have to be careful about banning the flag of a dominion, as a writer in the nationalist *Derry Journal* noted before the new regulation was introduced. Under the Statute of Westminster, the *Journal* columnist argued, the Free State had equal status with Britain, and its flag had the right to fly anywhere in the Commonwealth. As a result, the Northern Ireland government 'was forced to **appear** brave to [the loyalists of] Shankill and Wapping Lane' while 'taking care not to get a rap over the knuckles from Westminster'.[57]

The new regulation did not mean that the government had abandoned its policy of caution. In fact, the regulation's description of the tricolour as green, white, and *yellow* rather than green, white and *orange* may have been an attempt to avoid the impression that it was intended as an insult to the Free State. In response to a nationalist MP's question about the status of the tricolour when used within Northern Ireland as the flag of the Free State, the Parliamentary Secretary to the Ministry of Home Affairs explained that the regulation would not apply 'where the recognised flag of the Irish Free State is genuinely displayed as the flag of that State', so long as it was not displayed in circumstances which contravened the regulation (that is, where the flag could be considered to represent the IRA or an Irish Republic) or which might lead to a breach of the peace.[58] However, Cahir Healy pointed out that in the past the tricolour had been flown under perfectly lawful conditions, but had been removed due to mob agitation, and the *Derry Journal* saw no reason to believe that in future the mob would not continue to have its way, regardless of whether the tricolour was displayed as the flag of the Free State or not.[59]

In practice, it was by no means easy to tell whether the tricolour was being used to represent the Free State or an Irish Republic, as the Minister of Home Affairs confessed to Cabinet. He explained that the onus of proof that the flag was flown as an emblem of the IRA rather than of the Free State rested on the prosecution.[60] More specific guidelines about how police were to deal with displays of the tricolour were issued by the Inspector-General of the RUC in February 1934. The Inspector General's circular pointed out that under the new regulation it was not an offence to display the tricolour genuinely as the flag of the Irish Free State. Where the tricolour was not displayed as the Free State flag, police should in the first instance try to get those responsible for it to remove the flag, and failing this, should institute a prosecution, rather than attempting to remove the flag themselves. It was undesirable, the circular continued, 'that the police should be drawn into situations involving climbing or cutting down poles or trees for the purpose of removing flags, or proceeding in strong parties to remove flags in places where no question of a breach of the peace arises; neither is it necessary to enter private houses or meetings not open to the general public, solely for the purpose of searching for flags'. However, where police had reason to believe that the display of the tricolour would lead to a breach of the peace, those responsible should be asked to remove the flag, even if it was being displayed as the Free State flag. If they refused to do so the police should remove the flag and institute a prosecution where possible.[61] Another directive issued by the Minister of Home Affairs in the same month instructed police to remove the tricolour when deliberately displayed at election meetings as a symbol of the Irish Free State.[62]

Two incidents in 1934 showed that the primary concern of the police when it came to enforcing the regulation was still to preserve the peace. In the first incident, tricolours were carried in Derry by people returning from a political meeting in Donegal addressed by de Valera. The main procession was headed by a single tricolour, which police did not interfere with because it 'was not considered likely to lead to a breach of the peace', but a later group waved tricolours, sang, and used 'expressions of a party nature'. Five members of the latter contingent were charged by police, and a senior police official commented that the display of tricolours 'in parts of Londonderry is calculated to lead to breaches of the peace, and it is believed that the pending prosecutions will go far to prevent a repetition of the occurrence'.[63] Later in 1934 a tricolour was displayed at a Gaelic football match at Coalisland, County Tyrone, ostensibly in honour of the visiting team from County Louth in the Free State. Police asked that the flag be removed, but GAA officials told them that it would not be wise to remove it at that point. The police took no further steps to have it removed, since they felt that its display was not likely to lead to a breach of the peace, but it was removed later in the day, presumably after the match was over. The circumstances of the incident were reported to the Law Department for instructions, but a senior RUC official doubted that the display of the tricolour was in breach of the regulation in this instance.[64] However, the Attorney General subsequently directed that 'the responsible persons' should be prosecuted.[65]

In neither of these cases is there any suggestion in the police reports that police considered whether or not the tricolour was being used to represent the IRA or an Irish Republic; instead, their decisions seem to have been based entirely on the old criterion of whether display of the tricolour would lead to a breach of the peace. This did not satisfy some unionists, who wanted to see a complete ban on the tricolour in Northern Ireland. After the incident mentioned above, when tricolours were carried through the streets of Derry in 1934, the *Derry Standard* editorialised on behalf of the 'loyal citizens of Londonderry who believed that they had seen the last of the Sinn Fein tricolour in the Maiden City'. The 'Sinn Fein flag flaunters' who had 'defied the law of the country by displaying before the loyalists of the city an emblem which they knew would give offence ... **must be taught to realise that they live here under the flag of the Empire and not of Sinn Fein**' the *Standard* thundered. The incident, it warned, lent credence to the fears of the Protestant League, and although republicans worked in secret to subvert Northern Ireland, they were 'sufficiently aggressive, nevertheless, to come into the open with their objectionable flags'. This editorial was enclosed by Edward Murphy in a letter to Dawson Bates in which Murphy informed the Minister of Home Affairs that he would be asking a question in parliament about the incident. 'I don't want to cause trouble', Murphy told Bates, 'but am sure that some diplomatic assurance from you would help in Derry where this Protestant League may be a source of dissension if they think the Sinn Feiners are "getting away with it." '[66] An assurance 'that the police will continue to take all the necessary steps to prevent a recurrence of any such incidents' was duly given by Bates in the House of Commons.[67] Following the Coalisland incident, Mr Elliott sought a pledge that 'steps will be taken at any such gatherings in future to ensure that the law in this matter will be complied with, [and] that sufficient force is present to prevent a recurrence of this disloyal action', but on this occasion no such assurance was forthcoming from Bates.[68]

The use of discretionary powers by police, rather than an outright ban on the tricolour, clearly suited the Northern Ireland government. As in the case of the Union Jack, the government's aim seems to have been to keep its supporters happy by talking tough and taking limited steps to address loyalist concerns, while avoiding legislative action which might have endangered the peace. 'Rebels' could not be seen to display their flag with impunity, but a policy of removing tricolours every time they were displayed would almost certainly have led to clashes between police and nationalists. Furthermore, a complete ban on the flag of another state, particularly a dominion of the British Commonwealth, risked provoking an intervention by the UK government. The 1933 regulation exemplified two unfortunate characteristics of Craig's prime ministership which, according to Patrick Buckland, became more pronounced during the 1930s: the politics of gestures rather than solutions, and the attempt 'to shift attention from bread-and-butter issues by appeals to Protestantism and loyalty'.[69] If the government's approach was a pragmatic one, it also displayed the limited vision of a Unionist administration more concerned to contain the tensions which were manifested in conflict over flags than to seek ways of easing those tensions.

Government policy towards 'The Soldier's Song'

It was not until 1935 that the Northern Ireland government considered banning 'The Soldier's Song', perhaps because the Free State anthem was not widely used by nationalists in Northern Ireland. In November 1935, the Secretary of the Ministry of Home Affairs informed the RUC Inspector-General that the Minister of Home Affairs considered the playing or singing of 'The Soldier's Song' at republican election meetings to be 'so likely to lead to disturbance that he desires that it should not in any circumstances be allowed to take place'.[70] The Inspector-General's reply pointed out that playing or singing 'The Soldier's Song' was not in itself an offence, so police could only take action where performance of the song seemed likely to endanger the peace. In predominantly nationalist areas it seemed unlikely that the song would lead to a breach of the peace, but any action taken against it might precipitate disorder.[71] Despite the Inspector-General's warning, a regulation under the Special Powers Act was drafted, making it an offence to sing or play 'The Soldier's Song'. The Secretary of the Ministry of Home Affairs advised his minister that it would be best to specifically prohibit 'The Soldier's Song' rather than making a general order prohibiting songs likely to provoke disorder (as was initially proposed) because 'If you produced a Regulation in general terms the other side would immediately press for having Orders made prohibiting "Dolly's Brae" etc, and although they will probably do the same in regard to this Regulation the point is not quite so obvious as if we did the thing in the form originally intended.'[72] In December the draft regulation was submitted to the Attorney General, who disapproved of the regulation, saying that it was a mistake to promulgate it until the government was forced to do so, and the proposed regulation was evidently dropped after this.[73]

In 1938, however, the Minister again instructed that 'The Soldier's Song' should not be allowed to be played or sung at election meetings, and a draft regulation making it an offence under the Special Powers Act to play or sing the anthem was submitted to the Inspector-General of the RUC for comment in May 1938. The Inspector-General replied that the singing or playing of 'The Soldier's Song' in public was uncommon in Catholic areas and almost unknown in Protestant areas. It occurred mainly on occasions when political or sectarian feeling was running high, such as soccer matches between Celtic and Lindfield when both sides were singing 'party' songs,[74] or at events confined to the Catholic community, such as GAA matches. In such cases, the Inspector-General continued, it would be practically impossible for the police to interfere except in a very strong force, and the result of police intervention would be to create a disturbance rather than to prevent one. Police already had ample powers to deal with conduct likely to lead to a breach of the peace, and the proposed regulation would be almost impossible to enforce. Either large contingents of police would have to attend nationalist meetings to deal with any possible breach of the regulation, or alternatively police would have to avoid such meetings so that they were not seen to be impotent in the face of such breaches. The regulation would have the effect of encouraging use of the song 'simply for the purpose of defying the police and would lead to complaints from the Protestant side that the Regulation was not being enforced when to do so would only aggravate what probably was already a difficult situation'. In conclusion, the Inspector-General stated his strong opposition to the proposed regulation, arguing that it would simply lessen respect for the police, who would be unable to properly enforce the regulation, with the result that the police would face organised defiance on every possible occasion.[75] Although the regulation was subsequently redrafted so as to make it an offence to sing or play 'The Soldier's Song' 'in such a manner as is likely to cause a breach of the peace or to give offence to any of His Majesty's liege subjects', this did not overcome the Inspector-General's objections, and the matter was then dropped once again. The situation remained as it had been before: individuals could be, and indeed were, prosecuted for performing 'The Soldier's Song' in a manner likely to lead to a breach of the peace, but no specific ban on 'The Soldier's Song' was ever imposed.[76] Once again, pragmatism won the day, and the need to preserve the peace was considered more important than the desire of many unionists to see a ban on 'offensive' expressions of republican sentiment.

The Union Jack and 'God Save the King' in the Irish Free State

Unionists in Northern Ireland who wished to ban the tricolour sometimes justified their position by pointing to the ban on the Union Jack which they claimed operated in the Free State.[77] When nationalists complained that the Northern Ireland government had banned the flag of a friendly dominion, the *Belfast Newsletter* wrote:

> If Constitutional Nationalists are so eager to see displays of flags of friendly States within the Commonwealth of Nations, they might, with advantage, make representations to the authorities of the State which they regard as their spiritual home. There the Union Jack is under a strict ban, and not merely the Union Jack but the official flags of all the other dominions – for no other reason than that these flags proclaim the States they represent to be within the Empire.[78]

Nationalist MP Cahir Healy, by contrast, saw the Free State as a bastion of liberalism compared to Northern Ireland, pointing out that ex-unionists in the Free State were free to carry Union Jacks on Armistice Day, while in Northern Ireland the Free State flag could not be displayed alongside other flags in Empire Week.[79]

Nationalists and imperial symbols

The actual situation with regard to the use of imperial symbols in the Free State was rather more complicated than was allowed for by either side of the debate in Northern Ireland. There can be little doubt that the great bulk of the Free State population had no desire to see either the Union Jack or 'God Save the King' in use, and that many people in the state were actively hostile to these symbols. Both had long been seen by nationalists as Unionist party symbols and as emblems of British domination. In 1907 the French writer L. Paul-Dubois commented that Irish unionists had 'converted the English national anthem, *God Save the King*, into a party song, which forms an appropriate pendant to *To Hell with the Pope*, and means *Down with Ireland*',[80] while James Joyce recalled that he had never heard this anthem performed 'without a storm of hisses, shouts and shushes that made the solemn and majestic music absolutely inaudible'.[81] As for the Union Jack, its very design was objectionable to nationalists, since to them the combination of the crosses of St Patrick, St George and St Andrew symbolised the forced Union of Ireland and Britain which meant the humiliation and subjection of Ireland.[82] Fianna Fáil supporter Dorothy Macardle declared that she had no objection to the flying in Ireland of the English flag (St George's cross), and during the Eucharistic Congress in 1932 English, Scottish and Welsh flags flew in Dublin, but the flag of the hated Union was quite a different matter.[83] It was sometimes claimed that the demise of the United Kingdom of Great Britain and Ireland meant that the Union Jack was now obsolete, but this did not lessen nationalist hatred of it.[84]

For nationalists the Union Jack and 'God Save the King' evoked no pleasant memories or associations. Instead, they were associated with a history of British domination of Ireland, and with unionism and Protestant Ascendancy. The Irish were very forgiving, wrote one correspondent to the *Irish Independent*, but they could not forget in a few years all they had suffered under the Union Jack.[85] Another wrote that the Union Jack 'does not possess, for us, very happy memories, being associated with a particularly bad type of tyranny for over seven centuries of blood and tears . . . The scars inflicted by the lion's paw have not yet, unfortunately, quite healed.'[86] Similarly, 'God Save the King' was 'inseparably associated, in this country, with evil memories of British domination and misgovernment'.[87] More recently, these symbols had been associated with oppression suffered at the hands of Crown forces during the War of Independence, including incidents in which suspects were forced to sing 'God Save the King' or to salute the Union Jack.[88] In this period the Union Jack became a symbol of 'military oppression and of coercion by lawless and violent methods', wrote Denis Gwynn, while Lady Gregory recognised that to most Catholics this flag meant 'the Black and Tans and the dominance they [Catholics] have been fighting against'.[89] For republicans, moreover, the war was not yet at an end, since they claimed that the Treaty had been signed under duress of Lloyd George's threat of 'immediate and terrible war', a threat which had not been withdrawn, and 'no country allows the flag of a self-declared enemy to be flown in its territory'.[90]

If the Union Jack and 'God Save the King' were seen to stand for both a general history and specific instances of British subjugation, they were also considered by nationalists to be emblems of a Protestant and unionist minority which was hostile to the majority of Ireland's people. According to Fianna Fáil's *Nation* newspaper, these 'symbols

1. Monument to Stephen O'Donohoe, Glasnevin cemetery, Dublin, with a typical set of traditional national symbols: harp, wolfhound, rising sun, shamrocks, and ruined round tower. (Photo by Ewan Morris.)

Ingenious candidate goes the whole hog in appealing to the sentiments of the people.

2. Cartoon from *Dublin Opinion*, August 1923, suggesting that the traditional national symbols might not have lost their popular appeal.

THE SOLDIER'S SONG.

We'll sing a song, a soldier's song, with cheering, rousing
chorus,
As round our blazing fires we throng, the starry heavens
o'er us;
      Impatient for the coming fight,
      And as we wait the morning's light,
      Here in the silence of the night,
           We'll chant the soldier's song.

Chorus—
Soldiers are we, whose lives are pledged to Ireland;
    Some have come from the lands beyond the wave
Sworn to be free. No more our ancient sireland
    Shall shelter the despot or the slave.
      To-night we man the Bearna Baoghal
      In Erin's cause, come woe or weal,
      'Mid cannons' roar and rifles' peal
          We'll chant the soldier's song.

In valley green, on towering crag, our fathers fought
before us,
And conquered 'neath the same old flag that's proudly
floating o'er us.
      We're children of a fighting race
      That never yet has known disgrace,
      And as we march the foe to face
          We'll chant the soldier's song.

Sons of the Gael, men of the Pale, the long watched day
is breaking,
The serried hosts of Innisfail shall set the tyrant quak-
ing.
      Our camp fires now are burning low;
      See in the East a silvery glow;
      Out yonder waits the Saxon foe.
          Then chant the soldier's song.

3. Lyrics of 'The Soldier's Song' as published in *Irish Freedom*, September 1912.

4. Great Seal of the Irish Free State. (Courtesy of Department of the Taoiseach.).

5. Stamps of the Irish Free State/Éire, 1922–1939: definitive series and commemorative issues. (Courtesy of An Post.)

6. £50 Irish Free State banknote: front (showing Lady Lavery portrait) and reverse (showing sculpted riverine head). (Courtesy of Central Bank of Ireland.)

7. Irish Free state coins. (Courtesy of Department for Finance and Central Bank of Ireland.)

8. 1892 Ulster Unionist Convention badge, combining Irish national symbols (harp and shamrocks), Ulster symbols (red hand), and British or imperial symbols (crown and Union Jack).

9. Anti-Home Rule postcard with red hand suggesting the taking of a pledge.

10. Great Seal of Northern Ireland: King George V superimposed on a shamrock, with shamrocks, rose and thistle. (Courtesy of Public Record Office, London)

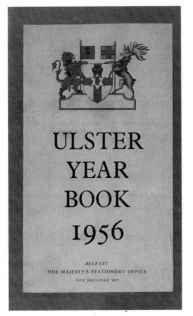

11. Northern Ireland coat of arms (reproduced on the cover of the *Ulster Year Book 1956*).

12. Unveiling of Longford War Memorial, 27 August 1925: an example of the use of the Union Jack in the Free State in connection with commemoration of the First World War (courtesy of British Pathé Library).

13. Green pillar-box in Dublin displays its imperial origins with crown, royal monogram, and red paint showing through. (Photo by Ewan Morris.)

14. Two murals showing the importance of flags and other symbols as markers of identity in Northern Ireland. Loyalist mural (top) combining Ulster symbols (red hand and Northern Ireland flag) with symbols of the Union (Union Jack and rose, shamrock and thistle). Republican mural (bottom) featuring tricolour, starry plough flag of socialist republicanism, and map of united Ireland. (Photos by Bill Rolston.)

15. Crest of the Royal Ulster Constabulary (left) featuring harp and shamrocks surmounted by crown. Crest of the Police Service of Northern Ireland (right), approved December 2001, featuring sunburst representing a new beginning for the police service; cross of St Patrick placing the emblem within the context of Northern Ireland; harp and shamrock representing Irish national identity; crown representing British identity; scales representing justice and equality; torch representing truth and enlightenment; olive branch representing peace and stability. (Courtesy of the Police Service of Northern Ireland.)

16. Cartoon by Martyn Turner, June 2000, at the height of the controversy about the flying of the Union Jack in Northern Ireland. (Courtesy of Martyn Turner.)

of oppression and slavery... were used in the past by the garrison to show their domination and our subjection, and were deliberately flaunted to hurt and to wound the pride and the national spirit of our people'.[91] Letters to Cumann na nGaedheal's *Star* agreed: 'God Save the King' was said to be a party song, 'associated with a very small party indeed who were hostile to the national aspirations of the people', while the Union Jack was 'the flag of the party in the country who despised Irish things and Irish customs and who, for their own interests stood by that union which the mass of the people hated'.[92] Even the politically moderate Free State correspondent for the Commonwealth journal *Round Table* saw the singing of 'God Save the King' in Ireland as 'not so much a prayer for the King as an expression of the old Unionist ascendancy spirit'.[93] Others were harsher still in their judgements, echoing the observation made by Paul-Dubois earlier in the century: to the *Leader*, 'God Save the King' meant 'God Damn Ireland', while for the magazine of the Passionist fathers it stood for 'To Hell with the Pope'.[94]

Ex-unionist use of imperial symbols

Because most of the Free State's people were nationalists of one sort or another who were at best indifferent to, and more commonly antagonistic towards the Union Jack and 'God Save the King', these symbols largely disappeared from public life after 1922. Although the other dominions of the British Commonwealth used these symbols together with local flags and anthems, the Free State government did not consider the use of both local and imperial symbols to be appropriate in an Irish context, a policy which seems to have had popular support. (See Chapter 6.) It was only members of the small, mostly Protestant, ex-unionist minority who continued to fly the imperial flag and sing the imperial anthem in the Free State, and who felt keenly the abandonment by the new state of the symbols of the old order.

The disappearance of the Union Jack and 'God Save the King' was most complete outside Dublin, and by 1928 'God Save the King' fell 'somewhat unfamiliarly on ears now grown almost unaccustomed to it', according to a report on 'Armistice Day in the Country' in the *Church of Ireland Gazette*.[95] Church of Ireland and other Protestant churches may have been among the only places where 'God Save the King' could still be heard in rural Ireland, since it was still listed in the Church of Ireland hymnal as the national anthem. 'God Save the King' could also be heard outside Dublin at some private gatherings, as became apparent in 1930, when Mallow Urban District Council in County Cork was informed by one of its members that at the conclusion of the Duhallow Hunt Ball, held in the Town Hall, the 'English National Anthem' had been played and the Irish anthem omitted. The councillor who raised the matter stated that 'playing the national anthem of any other country without playing the Irish one offered a direct insult to every Irishman' and proposed a motion requiring that any function held in the Town Hall conclude with the Irish national anthem. The motion was passed, but was rescinded the following month, after the chairman of the council noted the extensive press coverage the decision had received, reminded the other council members of the economic importance of hunting to the district, and alerted them to the danger of 'gratuitously insulting the feelings of our neighbours who do not see eye to eye with us in all things'.[96]

While there were only small pockets of ex-unionists scattered throughout the countryside, there was a relatively large ex-unionist population in Dublin, so it is not surprising that most of the controversy over the use of the Union Jack and 'God Save the King' was centred on the Free State's capital. Protestants and ex-unionists in Dublin had their own clubs where they could display their imperial allegiances, and owned businesses in the city centre which displayed Union Jacks on Armistice Day and other occasions.[97] Protestant schools in Dublin likewise continued using imperial symbols for some time.[98] Ex-unionists also controlled one of Dublin's two universities, Trinity College, which occupied an imposing position in the centre of the city and therefore attracted considerable ire from nationalists who saw it as a citadel of imperialism. Trinity flew the Union Jack (as well as the tricolour) until 1935 and played 'God Save the King' at the conclusion of Commencements as late as 1939.[99] Trinity's steadfast loyalty to King and Empire became a political issue in 1929, when Governor General James McNeill, backed by the government, insisted that he be received with 'The Soldier's Song', and not with 'God Save the King', when he attended the Trinity College races. Trinity refused to accede to this request, the Provost explaining that 'God Save the King' was regarded by the college as 'at once an expression of its traditional loyalty to the Throne, and an act of courtesy and respect to the King's Representative', and as a result the Governor-General did not attend the races.[100]

There were two annual events in Dublin at which ex-unionists were able to express symbolically their support for continuing the link between Ireland and Empire: the Dublin Horse Show and Armistice Day ceremonies. When the first military jumping competition was held as part of the Horse Show in 1926, the *Irish Times* celebrated it as 'the beginning of the end of old animosities'. The paper claimed that when the band heralded the British and Irish teams with their respective national anthems, 'thousands of Irish hearts throbbed to a dear and long unfamiliar music, and greeted with a new respect a music which till then had the most painful associations for them'.[101] The *Irish Independent* also saw it as a highly significant occasion, but for rather different reasons: the *Independent* emphasised that for the first time the British anthem was 'acknowledged publicly by such an immense crowd in Ireland as that of a foreign nation, and respectfully saluted as such'.[102]

For a section of the crowd, however, there was nothing foreign about the 'dear and long unfamiliar music' of 'God Save the King'. The *Irish Times*, whose unionist sympathies were apparent in the fact that it continued to refer to 'God Save the King' as the national anthem long after the Free State achieved independence, reported what was to become an annual occurrence: 'The outstanding memory of the occasion, perhaps, was the distinct demonstration in favour of the English team. That was most noticeable on the grand stand of the enclosure, when the National Anthem was taken up vocally by a large section on both occasions when it was played.'[103] Two years later, the *Irish Times* claimed that the British team in the military jumping competition was greeted with 'tumultuous' cheering, and that thousands of people stood to attention and sang 'God Save the King'.[104] This annual display infuriated nationalist observers, attracting hostile comment in newspapers representing a variety of positions on the nationalist political spectrum.[105] When it appeared that the British team would not make it to the military jumping competition in 1930, the Secretary of the Department of External Affairs privately welcomed this 'opportunity for putting an end to the disgraceful scenes of pro-Britishism which are created year after year at Ballsbridge by the disloyal element in our population'.[106]

Whether the anthem was sung by thousands or, as the *Star* claimed in 1929, by 'a few sour-faced females and their friends',[107] both nationalist and ex-unionist sources agreed that the singing of 'God Save the King' was loud and fervent. While references in nationalist party newspapers to 'frenzied' singing and to the 'almost hysterical acclamation' of the British team were undoubtedly meant to disparage this 'regrettable and ill-mannered political outburst by the remnants of the former Ascendancy',[108] it is quite plausible that there was indeed an element of hysteria in the reaction of some ex-unionists to the playing of the old anthem. For most of the year the disapproval of their fellow citizens inhibited ex-unionists from singing 'God Save the King' publicly, so the opportunity to do so once a year must have been a tremendous emotional release. What had once been a commonplace experience, though always a contentious and politically charged one, had, because of its rarity, increased enormously in emotional intensity. For those few minutes, ex-unionists once again had the confidence and the numbers to declare their imperial loyalties publicly, and could feel connected both to their own past and to the wider imperial community.

Armistice Day, the annual commemoration of the dead of the First World War, provided ex-unionists with another opportunity not only to

sing 'God Save the King' but also to display the Union Jack. The commemoration would probably have been controversial even without such
displays, since the memory of the First World War in Ireland was a fraught
one,[109] but the principal objection of nationalists seems to have been to the
contamination of the day by what they called 'Union Jackery'.
Nationalists accused ex-unionists of exploiting the dead by turning a
solemn commemoration into an occasion for 'imperialistic displays', and
the day became marked by violence between republicans and people
wearing poppies (which were seen by extreme republicans as tainted by
association with imperial symbols) or waving Union Jacks.[110] Ex-unionists replied that the imperial flag and anthem were not used as party symbols on Armistice Day, since Irishmen of all parties and creeds had fought
and died together under the Union Jack, while 'God Save the King' 'may
not be the National Anthem any longer; but it is the only one our soldiers
knew, and this is their day'.[111]

   Neither the display of the Union Jack nor the singing of 'God Save the
King' was an official part of the Armistice Day commemorations organised by the ex-servicemen's association, the British Legion. However,
Union Jacks appeared on the regimental colours carried in Armistice Day
parades, and they were also waved by onlookers as well as being flown
by some businesses in the city centre. The singing of 'God Save the King'
was, according to reports in the *Irish Times* each year, a spontaneous gesture which followed the two minutes' silence. A few individuals would
start singing the anthem, which would gradually be taken up by the whole
crowd and 'sung with all the old fervour and all the old lustiness' before
the crowd broke into loud cheers.[112] The lustiness of the singing and the
cheers were no doubt partly a way of releasing the emotion built up during the silence, but as with the singing of 'God Save the King' at the
Horse Show, they must also have been, for ex-unionists in the crowd, a
release from another silence: silence about loyalty to King and Empire.

The question of ex-unionist loyalty

The imperial loyalty of ex-unionists, and the expression of this loyalty
through the display of the Union Jack and the singing of 'God Save the
King', drew very hostile comments in nationalist newspapers. The *Cork
Examiner* found the playing of 'God Save the King' 'on every
conceivable occasion' by 'certain circles' in Dublin 'undoubtedly aggravating, and meant to be so'.[113] In similar vein, Diarmuid O'Hegarty,
Secretary of the Executive Council, wrote that a minority within the state
took every opportunity of using the Union Jack and 'God Save the King'
'for provocative purposes'.[114] Such displays were seen not merely as

provocative, but as disloyal and anti-Irish. The *Leader* saw the waving of the Union Jack as 'a gesture of bitter hostility to the Saorstát' and the singing of 'God Save the King' as an expression of hatred of Irish nationality.[115] The National Association of the Old IRA was not alone in asserting that 'In Ireland, above all places, there can be no room for dual allegiance',[116] and various commentators assumed that those who honoured symbols of the imperial connection must, *ipso facto*, be disloyal to Ireland.

A writer in the Cumann na nGaedheal newspaper the *Freeman* acknowledged the existence of 'an element whose first loyalty is not to Ireland, and who consider themselves first and before all Britons', glorying in the Union Jack for 'reasons that make it repugnant to the national sense'.[117] A letter in the *Irish Independent* warned that 'our kindness is being mistaken for servitude, and in no other country would such conduct be tolerated towards its dearly-cherished national sentiments'.[118] Some felt that the 'disloyalty' of the minority should be tolerated no longer, particularly after the Trinity College anthem controversy, in the wake of which the *Limerick Leader* insisted that if the 'garrison' was not loyal to Ireland they should be compelled 'to give full allegiance to the country that is supporting them'. In the *Limerick Leader*'s view, ex-unionists had been treated with 'more than fair play', but had responded to kindness with ingratitude and appeared determined to work in opposition to the best interests of the state.[119] Belfast's *Irish News*, seemingly oblivious to the implications of its argument for the nationalist minority in Northern Ireland, told those at Trinity College who insisted on playing 'God Save the King' for the Governor General that if they did not regard themselves as Free State citizens they should get out,[120] while the republican newspaper *Honesty* advised those who sang 'God Save the King' in place of 'The Soldier's Song' to 'clear out of this country to the land of their love and not remain here like a poisoned bullet in the body of the Irish body-politic'.[121]

Others agreed with *Honesty* that displays of imperial loyalty by ex-unionists marked them as something alien embedded within the body politic. Fianna Fáil's *Nation* newspaper, alleging that ex-unionists would soon force their 'slaves' in the Free State government to honour the Union Jack and 'God Save the King', called ex-unionists 'a foreign band' and 'a cancer in the body politic'.[122] Both *Honesty* and the *Nation* accused 'the garrison' of being neither British nor Irish.[123] 'They live and thrive in our midst,' snarled the *Nation*, 'and yet they hate and detest us; their highest wish, if their mean hearts had the courage to express it, is to see this country again enslaved and pauperised.'[124] Fianna Fáil TD Seán Lemass charged Trinity College with being the headquarters of 'the alien section in our midst' which flaunted the Union Jack to insult the Irish people.[125]

Trinity's attachment to 'God Save the King' marked it as anti-Irish in the eyes of the *Leader*; to the *Nation* it was 'the citadel of the new pale', while Cumann na nGaedheal's *Star* believed that by flying the Union Jack and playing 'God Save the King' on the slightest pretext Trinity showed that it still regarded itself as 'a little bit of England set in the middle of Ireland's capital'.[126]

Naturally, ex-unionists rejected the charge of disloyalty. During the Trinity anthem controversy, the Reverend A.A. Luce defended the members of the Trinity Week committee, writing: 'One and all they are loyal to Ireland, and one and all they turn down the policy of "little Ireland." That is why they refuse to ban the National Anthem or break the imperial connexion for which that Anthem stands.'[127] Luce could see no reason why 'God Save the King' and 'The Soldier's Song' should be placed in permanent antagonism. Imperially-minded citizens of the Free State, he claimed, were quite willing to accept both a dominion and an imperial anthem, but they could not accept 'sudden and arbitrary attempts to ban the old and impose the new'.[128] The ex-unionist position was elaborated in editorials in the *Irish Times*, which consistently made the case that loyalty to the Free State and loyalty to Empire not only could, but should, coexist. It expressed a hope that in time the Union Jack and the tricolour would be flown together, and argued that in each dominion the Union Jack complemented, but did not overshadow, the dominion's national flag.[129] Ironically, nationalists in Northern Ireland and ex-unionists in the Free State both stressed the Free State's dominion status: while nationalists in Northern Ireland argued that the flag of a dominion should be free to fly anywhere in the Empire, ex-unionists in the Free State insisted that the flag of Empire should be free to fly in any dominion.

For ex-unionists, unlike for most nationalists, Empire was not a dirty word. They called the Union Jack 'the flag of an empire that stands for freedom' and 'the flag under which more good was done than any other'.[130] The *Irish Times* considered that participation in the Empire provided the Free State with opportunities it would not other-wise enjoy, and when the Governor General refused to be received with 'God Save the King' at Trinity College the *Irish Times* saw this rejec-tion of 'the Empire's National Anthem' as confirmation of a dangerous development in government policy. The Free State, lamented the *Irish Times*, 'is to be in the British Empire, but not of it; she is to reap all the benefits of the imperial connection, but is to abjure its loyalties'.[131] To Empire loyalists, the attachment of Trinity College to 'God Save the King' was entirely consistent with the constitution, under which the Free State was part of the British Commonwealth of Nations, headed by King George V.[132]

Most ex-unionists denied that the flag and anthem of the Empire were party or divisive symbols; on the contrary, they saw them as more inclusive than the tricolour or 'The Soldier's Song' because they represented more than just the Free State. In particular, the symbolic acknowledgement of the Free State's position within the Empire could help to bring about a united Ireland, since people in Northern Ireland 'would never join with anyone who refused to recognise the Union Jack or the King'.[133] There was no doubt also a strong element of nostalgia for the pre-1922 world in the attachment of ex-unionists to the Union Jack and 'God Save the King'. One correspondent to the *Church of Ireland Gazette* claimed that the Irish people 'would thank God if they could put the clock back and find the country in the position it was in when, without a shadow of doubt, there was only one National Anthem, *viz.*, "God Save the King"'.[134] The *Nation* was probably correct when it alleged that ex-unionists longed for a return to the old order; but what Fianna Fáil called enslavement, ex-unionists called freedom within the great British Empire.

There were, however, some members of the minority community in the Free State who felt that ex-unionists had to be sensitive to the feelings of their fellow citizens. At the time of the Trinity anthem dispute, Cyril Jackson, an ex-unionist resident in London, and Edward Culverwell from Trinity College both acknowledged that 'God Save the King' had become a party anthem in Ireland, one which, as Culverwell put it, 'expressed, in words not free from offence, the sentiments of those who fought on the losing side in the struggle which ended in the establishment of the Free State'.[135] Given this history, and also bearing in mind the 'menace of the Republican Party', Culverwell felt that the government had been right to insist that 'God Save the King' was an inappropriate anthem with which to receive the Governor-General, and that it had adopted the course of action most likely to preserve the Free State's position within the British Commonwealth. The singing of 'God Save the King' at Armistice Day ceremonies also disturbed two writers to the *Irish Times* who, while they did not object to the anthem personally, recognised that in the Free State the singing of this anthem produced division on a day which should be one of reconciliation and unity.[136] Another sign of unease among some ex-unionists about the use made of 'God Save the King' in the Free State was a debate about national anthems in the pages of the *Church of Ireland Gazette* during 1929, prompted by a letter complaining that by continuing to treat 'God Save the King' as the national anthem, the Church of Ireland was adding to 'the existing impression that we are the Church of England in Ireland'.[137]

Responses of the political parties to the use of imperial symbols

While some ex-unionists evidently understood the ill will that use of the symbols of the old order could engender, most probably shared the resentment expressed in a letter to the *Irish Times*, which complained that 'The Irish Free State is the only part of the British Empire where one may not fly the Union Jack without fear of molestation'.[138] Such molestation as occurred, however, was neither instigated nor condoned by the Cumann na nGaedheal government. Both the government party and the Fianna Fáil opposition entertained hopes that pro-British displays would simply disappear in time, with 'the healthy advance of national ideas' and 'the revival of national feeling and pride', though both parties also felt that the advance of Irish nationality was being held back by divisions among the 'pro-Irish forces', divisions for which each party blamed the other.[139] In the short term, however, divisions between the parties were only increased by their differing responses to the question of direct action against 'pro-British' displays.

It was the climate of intimidation created by private citizens, rather than by government policy, which led ex-unionists in the Free State and unionists in Northern Ireland to form the impression that the Union Jack was under a ban in the Free State. The IRA newspaper *An Phoblacht* declared in 1926 that 'Wherever the Union Jack appears in an unfree Ireland it should be torn down, or shot down, or burnt down. Wherever the British National Anthem is played there should be the maximum of turmoil.'[140] More extreme republicans continued both to preach and to practise this doctrine throughout the 1920s and 1930s. The singing of 'God Save the King' in the centre of Dublin on Armistice Day was countered by republicans singing 'The Soldier's Song',[141] while displays of Union Jacks were met with more drastic action. Union Jacks were routinely snatched from onlookers on Armistice Day, and imperial flags (including an Australian flag in one instance) were sometimes forcibly removed from premises where they were displayed on Armistice Day or other occasions.[142] Some of these raids for Union Jacks led to prosecutions, and in one case the prosecution led in turn to the murder of a man named Armstrong who gave evidence against the raiders.[143]

Clearly the Cumann na nGaedheal government did not support such direct action against displays of the Union Jack, since it was responsible for prosecuting those who engaged in it. This was despite the fact that the pro-Treaty party was just as opposed as republicans to 'provocative' displays by ex-unionists, agreeing that the Union Jack and 'God Save the King' were still used by a section of the ex-unionist community as anti-Irish symbols.[144] The *Star* blamed Trinity students for Armistice Day rioting, since it was their 'anti-national' displays which stirred up antagonism and on occasion led to the maiming and even murder of Dublin citizens.[145] President Cosgrave, Diarmuid O'Hegarty (Secretary of the Executive Council) and Police Commissioner Eoin O'Duffy all referred to the murder of Armstrong as an example of what happened when such displays occurred.[146] Moreover, those ex-unionists who remained loyal to British symbols were accused not only of provoking republicans, but of being like them, since both groups represented a threat to the stability and the very existence of the state. 'Bitter enmity to the State and all its institutions is the bond between both minorities of extremists in this country' concluded the *Star* after the Trinity College anthem dispute, while Cosgrave wrote in a letter sent to British critics of his government's position on the anthem that 'If this State is to be saved for the Commonwealth we must safeguard the lives of the citizens of this State from extremists on the one side and the life of the nation itself from extremists on the other.'[147]

Although Cumann na nGaedheal sometimes found it necessary to launch scathing attacks on the ex-unionists, its newspapers also stressed that most ex-unionists had accepted the new order and were 'better Free Staters than they ever were Unionists'.[148] The party actually enjoyed quite good relations with the ex-unionist community, and while it could not afford to be seen to be dominated by the old Ascendancy (a common Fianna Fáil accusation), neither was it wise for it to alienate this small but economically influential section of the Free State population. For their part, ex-unionists might not have been enamoured of the Cumann na nGaedheal government, but they were more inclined to support it than to support an opposition sworn to sever the Free State's connection with the Crown.[149] It would have been foolish, therefore, for Cumann na nGaedheal to have offended the ex-unionists by banning the symbols they loved. Such a ban would also doubtless have angered the British government, and seriously damaged British-Irish relations. While Cumann na nGaedheal did not accept the argument that it was incumbent upon the Free State, as a dominion, to fly the Union Jack, the party did believe that the Treaty had established a relationship of equality between the United Kingdom and the Free State, so that in time displays of pro-British sentiment should excite no more hostility than displays of pro-French sentiment.[150]

There was, therefore, no attempt by the Cumann na nGaedheal government to compel ex-unionists to abandon the Union Jack or 'God Save the King'. The *Irish Times* claimed that after the Bank of Ireland displayed the Union Jack on its building on College Green in Dublin it had been approached by a member of the government who had put some pressure on the bank authorities not to repeat the display, reminding them that the government was an important customer of the bank's and that the bank was associated with the government in the public mind.[151] However, even if the report was correct, this request by the government seems to have been uncharacteristic, and in any case scarcely qualifies as coercion. Likewise, the government's stance in the Trinity College anthem controversy constituted a rather heavy-handed attempt to promote a change of attitude at Trinity, but stopped well short of forcing the college to give up 'God Save the King'.

A more forceful approach to the use of unofficial national symbols had in fact been considered at a 1927 meeting of the Council of Defence, of which President Cosgrave was a member, following the circulation to council members of a note by the Chief of Staff of the Defence Forces. His note was prompted by 'many unpleasant incidents' which took place during Horse Show Week in Dublin, when the British national anthem was played at the conclusion of a number of dances, and he asserted that such incidents, at a time when many foreign visitors were in town, harmed the prestige of the Free State. Accordingly, he considered it imperative that the government 'proclaim one National Anthem and order that at all functions in this State no other Anthem may have priority to it'.[152] However, the Council of Defence decided that 'it would be useless to make a law in this particular without attaching a penalty for the breaking of it, and that to enforce a penalty would involve difficulties. It was further agreed that it would be preferable to allow public opinion to develop with regard to the question.'[153] This seems to have been the policy pursued consistently by the Cumann na nGaedheal government in relation to both the anthem and the flag, and as a result Diarmuid O'Hegarty could truthfully write that 'we have never endeavoured to prevent anybody from flying the Union Jack or from singing "God Save the King"'.[154]

Before it took office in 1932, Fianna Fáil castigated the government for its toleration of the Union Jack and 'God Save the King'. It was as vehement as more extreme republicans in attacking the use of imperial symbols and in defending those who sought to prevent the flying of the Union Jack. Senior Fianna Fáil politicians denounced Armistice Day displays of the Union Jack at public rallies in 1927 and 1930, in the latter year sharing the platform with IRA men like Frank Ryan, who told the crowd that 'Police or no Police, Union Jacks would not float tomorrow. There was a limit to patience, and that they would meet baton with baton, and bayonet with bayonet.'[155] Fianna Fáil's pronouncements were less inflammatory than those of Ryan and his comrades, but in 1927 a succession of the party's leading lights passionately condemned the 'flaunting' of the British flag in Dublin, and de Valera defended those who removed Union Jacks:

> When Nationalist sentiment was outraged; when the flag of the foreigner was flaunted in their faces, young men of spirit would be driven to defend

National principles, and make it clear that the flag was there against their will. The result would be, as in the past, that young men would be arrested and put into prison, and the attitude of this country would be misrepresented abroad.[156]

In closing the meeting, the chairman pointed out that George Gilmore was in prison for tearing down and burning a Union Jack, and that 'If the national will had been properly awake that man would have been honoured as a true citizen. Thank God, they had hundreds of George Gilmores to follow him.'[157] The Fianna Fáil party organ blamed those who engaged in provocative displays for the ensuing raids on their premises, warning that 'No man has a right to use even his private property for the purpose of insulting his fellow citizens', and maintained that the display of the Union Jack and the singing of 'God Save the King' should be prohibited as they led to disturbances of the peace.[158]

In office, however, Fianna Fáil adopted a more moderate policy towards the use of imperial symbols than the party's rhetoric while in opposition might have suggested. With regard to the singing of 'God Save the King', Fianna Fáil continued Cumann na nGaedheal's policy of non-interference. The continuity of policy on this matter was apparent as late as 1943, when, in response to a resolution of the Fianna Fáil Ard-Fheis that 'The Soldier's Song' should be officially recognised as the national anthem, the Department of the Taoiseach's advice to de Valera was modelled on the 1927 decision of the Council of Defence: 'if a law were to be made on this matter a penalty for the breaking of the law must be attached. To enforce such a penalty would involve difficulties and even the procuring of evidence with the hope of securing a conviction would in a large number of cases be an arduous and expensive task.'[159] While Fianna Fáil was probably less concerned than Cumann na nGaedheal about the reactions of ex-unionists and the British government to action taken against the singing of 'God Save the King', it still had to consider the implications of trying to enforce a policy of coercion. Preventing people from singing 'God Save the King', or forcing them to give priority to 'The Soldier's Song', was not as easy as confiscating Union Jacks: it would have required either the use of police to break up meetings at which the imperial anthem was sung, with the attendant risk of provoking public disorder, or the prosecution of individuals who sang the anthem, a costly and time-consuming process.

Fianna Fáil was, however, more active on the question of the display of Union Jacks on Armistice Day. A 1932 memorandum from Eoin O'Duffy, Commissioner of the Free State police force, set out his concerns about the drain on police resources which the maintenance of order around Armistice Day entailed. The commemoration in previous years

'was in its essence an imperialistic display', he argued, and among other
things he pointed to the display of Union Jacks in parades and along the
parade routes, the use of Union Jack emblems in connection with poppy
sales, and the singing of 'God Save the King' in the city centre as being
aspects of the commemoration which were considered provocative by
many citizens. He therefore recommended that, if parades and poppy
sales were to be allowed at all, Union Jacks should not be carried in
Armistice Day processions, nor displayed going to or returning from such
processions, 'on the grounds that such display is likely to lead to a breach
of the peace'. Likewise, poppy-sellers should not be allowed to use Union
Jacks as badges or wrappers for their collection boxes. The government
accepted these recommendations.[160]

Despite such efforts to avert disorder, and despite assurances from the
British Legion that they would instruct poppy-sellers not to wear flags or
bunting which might cause trouble, the *Irish Times* recorded that 1932
saw 'the stormiest Armistice night known'.[161] The violence of the
Armistice Day clashes in 1932 can probably be attributed to an increased
confidence among extreme republicans following the election victory of
Fianna Fáil and the new government's decision to lift the ban on the IRA.
However, their confidence would be short-lived. As Fianna Fáil set about
severing the remaining links with Britain one by one, the non-constitu-
tional republican movement tore itself to pieces in ideological conflicts
and declined almost into insignificance. The increasing marginalisation of
radical republicanism, reflected in dwindling numbers at the annual anti-
imperialist rallies around Armistice Day, is undoubtedly one reason why,
from 1933 onwards, conflict over Armistice Day died down.

The other major reason why Armistice Day conflict subsided is that the
government took a determined stand against displays of the Union Jack on
the day. In 1933 the police commissioner, fearful of even greater disorder
than in the previous year, recommended that Armistice Day parades and
public ceremonies should not be allowed, but the Secretary of the
Department of Justice did not support this recommendation, commenting
that 'this Department is slow to arrive at a decision which might give offence
to the large body of ex-Servicemen in this country'. The government
decided to allow the parades and ceremonies subject to a number of conditions, including that no Union Jacks should be displayed, and this continued
to be government policy thereafter.[162] The British Legion cooperated with
the government, instructing its members not to carry Union Jacks in the
procession, and Legion officials even said it was unfortunate that the crowd
at Phoenix Park continued to sing 'God Save the King'.[163]

In the following years, police were instructed to take action to prevent
the display of Union Jacks on Armistice Day, and officials took note of
instances when Union Jacks were displayed, even if only in the corner of

regimental banners.[164] When such banners were displayed in 1936, the British Legion was to be informed that 'if any such flag is flown the Government will not allow public parades in future'.[165] The government's approach to Armistice Day displays from 1933 onwards met with success: 1933 was reported to be the most peaceful Armistice Day since 1918,[166] and for the most part peace continued to prevail on Armistice Day for the remainder of the decade. Even republican diehard Frank Ryan declared himself satisfied in 1935 that no imperialist emblems had been displayed on the day, and he therefore called on republicans not to snatch poppies.[167]

Undoubtedly the Fianna Fáil government, like its Cumann na nGaedheal predecessor, was deeply unsympathetic to the motives of ex-unionists who displayed the Union Jack and sang 'God Save the King'. Nevertheless, its policy in relation to imperial symbols was a pragmatic one. 'God Save the King' and the Union Jack were disappearing from the Free State due to a combination of IRA intimidation and the continuing decline in numbers of the Protestant and ex-unionist minority, so a general ban on these symbols was unnecessary as well as impractical. When a Fianna Fáil cumann complained to President de Valera in 1934 about the carrying of a Union Jack by a pilgrimage of Irish ex-service-men to Lourdes, it was decided that no action could be taken on the matter, and a public servant noted that 'The use of the British flag would cease in time. It was a phenomenon inseparable from our past history.'[168] This relaxed attitude, which presents such a striking contrast to the rhetoric of Fianna Fáil before it took office, was replaced by a more coer-cive approach only in relation to Armistice Day. This was the one day on which Union Jacks might still be widely displayed, and as a result, it had become a security headache for police and the government. In the case of Armistice Day, therefore, security considerations prompted the government to ban displays of the Union Jack. Perhaps, too, Fianna Fáil, like the Unionist government in Northern Ireland, wanted to placate its more radical supporters[169] by being seen to take action against 'offensive' displays while avoiding the complications which a more draconian approach would have entailed.

Conclusion

Despite their rhetorical bluster against 'disloyal' minorities, both major parties in the Free State and the ruling party in Northern Ireland were more concerned to preserve public order than to prevent the use of minor-ity national symbols. Any attempt at complete suppression of minority symbols risked tying up vast amounts of police time and provoking the minority into open confrontation with the state. At the same time, if there were no restrictions on the use of minority symbols, members of the majority community might take matters into their own hands, causing public disturbances of the sort seen on Armistice Day in the Free State's first decade. A pragmatic policy of limited toleration of minority symbols proved to be an effective means of forestalling such outbreaks of public disorder in both states. However, while no ban on minority national symbols was in place in either state, perceptions that such bans existed are understandable. In addition to the deterrent effect of government restrictions, however selectively applied, a climate of intimidation was created by the actions of republican and loyalist ultras. When republicans in the Free State could snatch Union Jacks or even take them at gunpoint, and loyalists in Northern Ireland could force the removal of tricolours from public places, it is not surprising that members of the minority communities became somewhat circumspect in their use of these symbols. Moreover, the overt intimidation carried out by more militant sections of the majority communities was backed up by a widely shared hostility towards minority symbols.

In both parts of Ireland symbols acted as barriers between the majority and minority communities. Ex-unionists in the Free State and nationalists in Northern Ireland saw the official flags and anthems of the states in which they lived as party symbols. Likewise, use of the tricolour in Northern Ireland, and of the Union Jack and 'God Save the King' in the Free State, was seen by the majority in each state as a sign of disloyalty and antipathy towards the interests of the state. These conflicts over symbols were a product of the very different meanings and associations of these symbols for nationalists and unionists. Constitutional nationalists in Northern Ireland emphasised that the tricolour was the flag of a friendly dominion, but unionists considered it a rebel flag and the emblem of a movement whose aim was to force Northern Ireland into an Irish republic. In the Free State, where ex-unionists described the Union Jack and 'God Save the King' as symbols of the state's voluntary and beneficial association with the British Empire, nationalists loathed what they regarded as symbols of British and unionist domination. Such divergent views, and the attachment of nationalists and unionists to different symbols, highlighted the differences between the two communities within each state. Differences over symbols also acted as an obstacle to unity between the two states, as the next chapter shows.

Chapter 6
Pillar boxes and partition: symbols, sovereignty and Irish unity

In 1924 Lord Carson, the veteran Dublin Unionist politician and leader of the Ulster Unionist resistance to Home Rule, spoke in the House of Lords about the political situation in the Irish Free State and its implications for Irish unity. The Free State, he said, was already a republic; it had made this clear by repudiating the Union Jack and refusing to acknowledge the King. To Carson these symbolic changes had great meaning, and though he knew that some might dismiss such matters as mere sentiment, he felt that 'there is a great deal in sentiment regarding the country you live in and the Flag you live under'. As one who was familiar with unionist sentiment in Northern Ireland, he informed the Lords that:

> The North is not prepared to go from under the Flag. The North is not prepared to wipe out the King's name from every document used in connection with carrying on the Government...Ever since the Treaty, North and South have gone farther and farther apart, instead of coming nearer and nearer to one another...Heaven knows I wish there was unity, but there never will be unity in Ireland between North and South until the South gives up the *rôle* of being an enemy of this country [Britain], prepared at every opportunity to insult its King, and in every way to degrade him.[1]

Carson had recognised two important points about partitioned Ireland: firstly, that the Free State government was using symbols to create the impression that the southern state was already a *de facto* republic; and secondly, that this policy had disastrous implications for the prospects of union between the Free State and Northern Ireland.

In the other dominions within the British Commonwealth of Nations, official symbols of state represented imperial loyalty as well as local patriotism. In these dominions, people of British birth or ancestry made up a substantial proportion of the population, and such people generally saw no contradiction between their loyalties to nation and Empire. Irish nationalists, by contrast, regarded themselves as members of a nation quite separate from Britain; indeed, most nationalists posited an opposition between Irishness and Britishness. As a result, the approach of the other dominions was unacceptable to most people in the Free State, and instead, the Free State government used symbols to make the state as distinct as possible from Britain. However, nationalists also longed for unification of the Free State and Northern Ireland, where the majority of people were devoted to the very symbols of Britishness which the Free State was busily repudiating. Unionists in Northern Ireland repeatedly railed against the Free State's refusal to accord official recognition to British symbols, and declared that they could never become part of such a disloyal state.

With a few exceptions, nationalists in the Free State proved reluctant to acknowledge the devotion of unionists to symbols of Northern Ireland's connection with Britain and Empire, or to face up to the fact that the Free State's symbols acted as obstacles to a united Ireland. They refused to compromise the symbolic assertion of the Free State's independence in the interests of reconciliation with unionists, and this privileging of sovereignty over unity was apparent not only in government policies but also in sport. Pressure was put on several all-Ireland sporting bodies to fly the tricolour, despite the fact that these organisations represented unionists as well as nationalists. Such reluctance to compromise on the part of nationalists did nothing to persuade unionists that they could enter a united Ireland without abandoning their British heritage. Because of their own deep-rooted attachment to particular traditions and a particular view of history, nationalists were glad to see British symbols disappearing from the Free State; yet they failed to perceive that unionists were just as strongly attached to their own traditions and history, and that every move to differentiate the Free State from Britain made a united Ireland seem less attractive to unionists.

The use of symbols to display the Free State's distinct nationality began from the moment the Provisional Government took over the administration of the nascent Irish Free State at the beginning of 1922. It was vital, particularly in light of the conflict with opponents of the Treaty, that the government symbolically mark the state's hard-won sovereignty. Accordingly, less than three months after running down the Union Jack and raising the tricolour over Dublin Castle, the government brought visual evidence of the change of regime into suburban streets and country lanes when it ordered that the red British pillar boxes be painted green.[2] In the years that followed, it continued using symbols to demonstrate the Free State's independence, and to distinguish it from Britain.

The very act of creating official symbols was an assertion of sovereignty, as the Cumann na nGaedheal party newspaper the *Freeman* eagerly pointed out on the release of the legal tender banknotes: 'Gradually but surely, the Saorstat is acquiring the visible manifestations of a distinctive, sovereign State. Peacefully, almost prosaically, it is asserting dominion in all that appertains to its national existence.'[3] These symbols could be effective propaganda against the republican accusation that the Free State was not truly independent, and representatives of the government did not fail to make the link between symbolism and sovereignty explicit on occasion. In 1922 the Postmaster General, J.J. Walsh, wrote that the postage stamp:

> has come to be one of the symbols of nationhood; and for Ireland it is the label which its own people have looked for and hoped for so long, while to the people scattered in different parts of the world, where Irish letters go, it reminds them of our own Government, under our own emblems, which have at last secured an international recognition.[4]

Similarly, Chief Justice Hugh Kennedy wrote rather quaintly of the Free State's Great Seal as part of the paraphernalia which allowed 'this Cinderella of the world politic become *débutante*' to 'maintain her proper position in the Society of her Sister Nations'.[5] To Minister for Finance Ernest Blythe, opening an exhibition of the new coinage in 1928, it was of great significance that 'Now we have a coinage issued under the authority of a Parliament democratically elected by the people. The possession of a distinctive coinage is one of the indications of sovereignty.'[6]

Official symbols in the other dominions

The mere creation of official symbols was not enough to demonstrate that the Free State had completely broken free from Britain, however: the nature of those symbols was equally important. After all, the other dominions had their own symbols, but these symbols represented the dominions' imperial ties as well as their individual national identities. The Free State alone excluded all signs of membership of the British Commonwealth of Nations from its official symbols. In order to see how anomalous the symbolic assertion of independence by the Free State government was within the Commonwealth, it is worth briefly reviewing the situation in the other dominions. The four dominions which had developed from settler colonies (the Commonwealth of Australia, the Dominions of Canada and New Zealand, and the Union of South Africa)[7] varied in the degree to which their governments sought to express distinctive national identities, but in all of them symbols of the imperial connection had an important place in public life.[8]

The coexistence of national and imperial symbols was most apparent on the coins of the settler dominions, which in the inter-war years bore the King's head on the obverse and local symbols on the reverse. In New

Zealand, demand for symbols of a distinctive dominion identity was apparently so lacking that no separate New Zealand coinage was issued until 1933. In South Africa, by contrast, it was probably the difficulty of finding symbols on which British and Afrikaner South Africans could agree which led to the delay in issuing a separate coinage until 1923, and to the use of emblems on the reverse which were rather abstract and less distinctively national than those of the other dominions.[9] Australian banknotes also combined imperial symbols (the crown or the monarch's head) with national ones (the Australian coat of arms), and the £1 note in the series issued from 1923 actually depicted Britain's claim on Australia, with a picture of Captain Cook raising the Union Jack at Botany Bay.[10] The coats of arms of the settler dominions were largely made up of local emblems, but New Zealand's and Canada's were surmounted by crowns, and Canada's included symbols of both the British and French elements of the population in addition to the distinctively Canadian symbol of the maple leaf. The designs of all the settler dominions' coats of arms followed the conventions of British heraldry and were granted by royal warrant.[11]

On stamps both national and imperial images appeared, but the two were kept separate to some extent, since none of the dominions adopted the United Kingdom's practice of including the monarch's head on every stamp.[12] All of the settler dominions issued stamps showing the King's head in addition to those showing purely local devices, but even so, the issuing of stamps from which the King's head was absent could be controversial. The first stamp issued by the Commonwealth of Australia, which appeared in 1913 under a Labor government, showed a kangaroo against an outline map of Australia, but when a Liberal government came to power several months later it accelerated production of its preferred design, which featured George V.[13] In South Africa, Empire loyalists were outraged at the appearance in 1926 of stamps which did not show the King's head, seeing this as one of a number of changes which weakened South Africa's links with Britain and seemed to signal the beginning of an Afrikanerisation policy by the new National Party government.[14] Indeed, the designs on the South African stamps issued by the National government, and by the United government that succeeded it, contrasted strongly with the designs on the coins issued under the previous government. The images on the stamps were much more distinctively South African than those on the coins, and included a number with particular appeal to Afrikaner nationalists: the 1926 series included the ship of Jan van Riebeeck, who established the first Dutch base in South Africa, and ox wagons suggestive of the nineteenth century Voortrekkers who travelled to the interior of South Africa to escape from British rule, while a number of stamps in the 1930s explicitly commemorated the Voortrekkers.

Use of anthems and flags representing each dominion coexisted with the widespread use of 'God Save the King' and the Union Jack in the settler dominions. These dominions were extremely slow to officially adopt national anthems, but all had songs which could be used to represent dominion patriotism, usually in conjunction with 'God Save the King'. In South Africa a song associated with Afrikaner nationalism, 'Die Stem van Suid Afrika' ('The Voice of South Africa') was given some official recognition in the 1930s, when it began to be played by the South African Broadcasting Corporation in addition to 'God Save the King', and its status was confirmed when both anthems were played at the opening of parliament in 1938.[15] The South African government probably moved cautiously in seeking acceptance of a national anthem because of the tremendous difficulties which had been encountered in trying to find a flag for the dominion. In other dominions, too, flags proved to be the most contentious national symbols of all during the 1920s.

Surprisingly, given New Zealand's reputation as the most imperially minded dominion, its parliament became the first to pass legislation giving official recognition to the dominion's flag in 1900.[16] Australia and Canada were much more tardy in legislating to officially adopt national flags, not doing so until 1953 and 1965 respectively. Canada, however, had had a distinctive merchant flag (the arms of Canada on the British red ensign) since shortly after confederation. This flag had been authorised by the Admiralty in 1892, and from 1924 it was used by Canadian delegations abroad. In 1925 a committee was set up to consider the question of a national flag for use on land within Canada, but this was cancelled following a storm of protest from Empire loyalists. The result was that the Union Jack remained the flag which was generally used for official purposes on land, though the Canadian red ensign was still used in some contexts.[17] In Australia both a merchant flag and a flag for the Commonwealth received royal approval in 1902 and were gazetted the following year. The Australian flag's design was based on the blue ensign and therefore included the Union Jack, but after the First World War use of this flag alone, unaccompanied by the Union Jack, came to be seen by loyalists as a sign of disloyalty to Britain. Nevertheless, the Australian blue ensign continued to be flown from Commonwealth government buildings.[18]

The New Zealand, Canadian and Australian flags were created by adding a dominion symbol (the Southern Cross in the Australian and New Zealand cases, the arms of the dominion in the case of Canada) to the blue or red ensigns. As a result, all bore the Union Jack in the canton, the place of honour. For a time, South Africa also had such a flag: a red ensign emblazoned with the arms of South Africa was created for the opening of the first parliament of the Union of South

Africa, but it was never officially adopted by the parliament and remained unknown to most South Africans. When the Afrikaner nationalist National Party formed a government in 1924, it moved quickly to find a flag which could unite Afrikaners and British South Africans, but this proved extremely difficult to achieve.[19] As in Ireland, imperial loyalists would not countenance a flag from which the Union Jack was excluded, and were generally opposed to the use of any flag other than the Union Jack itself, while nationalists could not accept any flag which included the Union Jack. For Afrikaner nationalists the Union Jack was not only a foreign emblem, but one which had within living memory been the flag of their enemies. N.J. van der Merwe spoke of his reaction to seeing the Union Jack in terms reminiscent of those Irish nationalists who associated the imperial flag with the depredations of the Black and Tans:

> Whenever I see the Union Jack...it reminds me of many occasions when I saw it in the Boer War, and I do not want to see it...Can I possibly get away from the fact that indelibly impressed itself on my mind when I saw the Union Jack waving victoriously over the sobbing of women and children?...How on earth can I love a flag...if there is something in that flag that reminds me of the bitter experiences of the past?[20]

Because it saw existing flags as too divisive, the National government wanted a 'clean flag', one which excluded both the Union Jack and other flags from the past (most notably the flags of the old Boer republics). The South African Party opposition, however, insisted that the new flag must feature the Union Jack. Several years of bitter debate followed as a variety of flag designs were considered and rejected. By September 1927 the flag question was completely dominating campaigning by both the major parties, and a flag-related riot at the end of that month led to fears of widespread civil disorder. Such fears probably prompted the talks between the leaders of the two parties which at last produced a compromise. A new flag was created based on the old Dutch flag from the time of the first Dutch settlement of South Africa, with three tiny flags superimposed upon it: the Union Jack and the flags of the two former Boer republics. In addition, the Union Jack was officially recognised as a symbol of South Africa's membership of the Commonwealth, and was to be flown together with the national flag over the Houses of Parliament, the principal government buildings in the provincial capitals, and other specified places. The result was that display of the Union Jack came to be restricted almost entirely to the cities, disappearing from the rural areas where Afrikaners made up most of the white population.

Symbols and dominion status in the Irish Free State

It is clear that the Free State government's approach to questions of state symbolism departed radically from the precedent set by the other dominions. The settler dominions all included the king's head on their coins and some of their stamps; their coats of arms were within the British heraldic tradition; their flags included the Union Jack (even if, in the South African case, it only took up a small part of the flag's surface); and they made extensive use of the Union Jack and 'God Save the King' in addition to the local flag and anthem. Of the settler dominions, South Africa, with its strong Afrikaner nationalist tradition, was most like the Irish Free State on matters of official symbolism: the government made some attempt to promote a national anthem in addition to 'God Save the King'; the name of the state was given in both the major languages of white South Africans on coins and stamps; and from 1928 the Union Jack was both marginalised on the national flag and effectively banished from most of the country. Nevertheless, the Irish Free State was the only dominion to completely remove the king's head from stamps, coins and banknotes; to choose a non-heraldic state seal rather than a coat of arms; to use a non-English language alone on its stamps, coins and state seal; to have a national flag which bore no trace of the Union Jack; and to make no official use whatsoever of the Union Jack and 'God Save the King'.

From the start, the Free State government was at pains to distinguish itself as much as possible from Britain. A pro-Free State letter to the *Irish Independent* in 1922 anticipated the government's approach:

> How can people speak as if the Treaty only gave us a restricted measure of Dominion Home Rule? Has Canada a flag of her own without any Union Jack in the corner? Has she an official language which is not English? Has she stamps, coins, and banknotes of her own not imprinted in English, and without King George's head? How any foreigner entering the Free State in a few years' time could possibly mistake it for a mere portion of the British Empire passes my humble understanding.[21]

For the members of the Free State government, the removal of every sign of the link with Britain was no doubt motivated in large part by their own genuine desire for the fullest possible expression of Irish national individuality. They were, after all, former Sinn Féiners, committed separatists who had accepted dominion status only under duress. The elimination of British symbols was made not merely desirable but imperative, however, by the republican challenge to the Free State's legitimacy.

In attempting to counter the republican emphasis on the symbolism of the monarchy, the government followed the advice of George Gavan Duffy and 'relegate[d] the King of England to the exterior darkness'.[22] In

1913, Patrick Pearse had written that the King's features on a coin or stamp symbolised 'the foreign tyranny that holds us. A good Irishman should blush every time he sees a penny.'[23] Ten years later, the new government was determined that the Irish should blush no more: the King's head did not appear on the stamps, coins, banknotes or seal; no crown appeared above the harp on the seal or the coins; there was no reference to the king in the national anthem, nor any official use of the anthem in conjunction with 'God Save the King'. Whereas in the other dominions emblems of the monarchy represented the links between each dominion and the rest of the British Commonwealth, in the Free State they suggested an unwanted ambiguity about the extent of the state's independence. Such was the importance of the monarch as symbol of the United Kingdom that UK stamps did not even identify their country of origin by name: the monarch's portrait alone identified them.[24] Because the monarch was the key symbol of the United Kingdom, from which the Free State had so recently seceded, the use of royal imagery would not only have provided propaganda opportunities to Irish republicans but might also have created confusion abroad about the political status of the Free State.

Although it declined to use emblems of the monarchy in the official symbols of the Free State, the Cumann na nGaedheal government did accept the King, at least in theory, as nominal head of state and as a symbol of the Free State's link with the Commonwealth. When it came to the Union Jack and 'God Save the King' there was no such acceptance. During the Treaty debates, the republican hardliner Mary MacSwiney had predicted that the creation of a Governor Generalship for a notionally self-governing Irish state would mean that 'you will have the Union Jack and "God Save the King" for the first time with the consent of the people of Ireland'.[25] No doubt the Free State government took great satisfaction in proving MacSwiney wrong on this, as on other points. The Union Jack and 'God Save the King' were to Irish nationalists of all persuasions hated symbols of unionism and British domination, and there is no evidence that the Free State government even considered giving them official recognition.[26] Likewise, there was no question of putting the Union Jack in a corner of the Free State flag, since it would have been seen by most nationalists not as a recognition of the Free State's membership of the Commonwealth but as an admission of continued subordination to Britain.

Although the Cumann na nGaedheal government declined to follow dominion precedent on matters of symbolism, it was able to reconcile its stance with its own interpretation of dominion status, a status which was in any case evolving in the decade leading up to the Statute of Westminster, which in 1931 confirmed the autonomy of the dominions.[27] On occasion the Cumann na nGaedheal newspaper represented the Free

State as being in the mainstream of dominion practice, claiming that coins without the King's head were in circulation in New Zealand and other colonies which could not be suspected of anti-British feeling,[28] or that in Canada, as in the Free State, there was widespread recognition of the need for a dominion flag and anthem.[29] At other times, however, the government party's newspaper argued that the Free State was ahead of the other dominions in giving expression to a distinct national identity. In the government's view, the Free State's position was not the same as that of the other dominions, where a substantial part of the population was of British settler origin. As External Affairs Minister Desmond FitzGerald noted in 1926, Ireland was 'an ancient kingdom with a great past, [which therefore] could not acquiesce in a state of things which could be tolerated, temporarily at least, by direct offspring of Great Britain'.[30] Nowhere was this view more evident than on questions of symbolism. The resolution of the South African flag dispute allowed the *Freeman* to boast that 'The Free State has in many respects moved in advance of the other States of the British Commonwealth... We in the Irish Free State have a flag which is purely an Irish flag and it is the sole State flag.'[31] According to the *Freeman*, the Free State's claim to a distinctive flag was stronger than that of South African nationalists because 'Ireland is a mother nation; not a dominion.'[32]

The government's use of national symbols was a reflection of what the Free State correspondent for the Commonwealth journal, the *Round Table*, called 'the policy of maximum separation within the terms of the Treaty of 1921'.[33] Dominion status, in the government's view, involved no overarching Commonwealth loyalty, nor even loyalty to the King, who was simply the symbol of the free association of separate nations in the British Commonwealth. This view became clear when the government considered the question of which anthem it was proper to play for the Governor General. In 1928 Governor General James McNeill was received with 'God Save the King' at Trinity College Dublin, and a few months later the organisers of a dance refused to play 'The Soldier's Song' on the Governor General's arrival. Following these incidents, McNeill sought a decision from the government as to which anthem should be played for him. He was informed by the Executive Council that 'the National Anthem for all purposes is "The Soldier's Song"'. Accordingly, when he was invited to the Trinity College races in 1929, McNeill insisted that he must be received with 'The Soldier's Song' or no anthem at all. The Trinity authorities refused to play 'The Soldier's Song' without also playing 'God Save the King', and so McNeill, on the government's advice, declined the invitation to attend.[34]

The government's line on this matter was that since the King was the Free State's head of state, and the Governor General was his representative, it was appropriate to play for him only the state's own national anthem. 'God Save the King' might be regarded as the national anthem in the other dominions, but it was not so regarded in the Irish Free State.[35] British officials were not persuaded by this argument, insisting that 'God Save the King' was not the British national anthem but a tribute of respect to the Crown, and pointing out that in the other dominions 'God Save the King' was used together with the dominion anthems.[36] In reply to these and other criticisms, President Cosgrave justified the government's stance in a letter apparently drafted in the Department of External Affairs.[37] He explained that the Free State's acceptance of membership of the Commonwealth was predicated on the understanding that, while cooperating for the common good, the member states would preserve their individual national identities. One important expression of national identity was the national anthem, and it was for the people of the nation to choose their anthem. It would have been inappropriate for the Free State government to have chosen an anthem, 'God Save the King', which had long been associated with opposition to the realisation of Irish aspirations and ideals. Instead, it did the King the highest possible honour by playing for his representative the Free State's own national anthem. Cosgrave's government did not accept that 'God Save the King' (which Cosgrave called 'the National Anthem of England') was the anthem of the Commonwealth, nor did it think that such an anthem would be an appropriate expression of the Commonwealth ideal of 'diversity of national character in unity of purpose'.[38] A similar argument in relation to the Union Jack was put in the *Freeman* in 1928 by the Earl of Longford, a supporter of the Free State government. Longford maintained that the Union Jack was not the flag of the Commonwealth but only of the United Kingdom and of the settler dominions: 'Ireland, a free and ancient nation, owes this flag no allegiance, and its origin is singularly hateful for us to think of.'[39]

It was not only the absence of any symbolic acknowledgment of the Free State's connection with Britain which highlighted the state's independence. Equally important was the contrast between the Free State's symbols and those of the United Kingdom. The tricolour contrasted strongly with the Union Jack both in colour and in design. Furthermore, it linked the Free State symbolically to the many republics which had tricolour flags, and more particularly to Britain's long-time enemy, France, and its more recent enemy, Germany. 'The Soldier's Song' was also more in keeping with the celebration of revolutionary warfare in the anthems of the French and American republics than with anything in the British tradition. Musically, 'The Soldier's Song' was closer to a military march than to a hymn like 'God Save the King'. Moreover, its lyrics, with their reference to 'the Saxon foe', were explicitly anti-English. In the case of the seal, the contrast with the British tradition took the form of a conscious abandonment of heraldry and the selection of a harp and a border design thought to be thoroughly Gaelic in design. The Gaelic element was also present in the use of the Irish language and 'Gaelic' script. Irish language and lettering alone were used on the seal, coins, and most of the stamps. They served both as markers of nationality and as tokens of the government's commitment to making Irish the primary language of the state. A further contrast with British symbols was apparent in the design of Irish stamps, which 'differed radically from British graphic design', partly as a result of the continued use of typography after the UK had abandoned this printing method.[40]

There was little dissent from the Free State government's policy of using official symbols to mark a distinct Irish identity, an identity which had no place for Britishness. Certainly, ex-unionists were disappointed at the government's failure to acknowledge symbolically the state's membership of the Commonwealth.[41] A few pro-Treaty nationalists also criticised the government for lacking the honesty to symbolise the Free State's links with Crown and Commonwealth. D.F. Curran, a former supporter of the Irish Parliamentary Party, wrote to the *Irish Independent* that, until Ireland became completely independent, the Free State's dominion status should be symbolised by the inclusion of a Union Jack in the flag. 'I am quite aware', he wrote, 'that this suggestion will be received with anything but favour by certain sections, but it is surely about time to have done with cant and humbug. To claim the advantages of connection with the British Empire, and yet to refuse to acknowledge it in our flag, is, to put it plainly, dishonest.'[42] Anti-Treaty nationalists were much more inclined to accuse the government of dishonesty. It was, after all, the government's intention to create the impression that the Free State had already achieved all that Sinn Féin had been fighting for before 1922. As W.F. Trench, Professor of English Literature at Trinity College, recognised: 'Alone among the nations constituting the British Commonwealth of Nations, Saorstát Éireann claims the right to a National Anthem of its own, and the universal recognition of that right is the tacit recognition of Saorstát Éireann's having won what for practical purposes is the equivalent of a republican form of government.'[43] The attempt 'to represent our Irish Constitution as if it were *virtually* that of a Republic', so distressing to ex-unionists, was also galling to republicans.[44]

To opponents of the Treaty, the official symbols of the Free State masked the reality of Ireland's continued subordination to Britain. William Magennis, who left Cumann na nGaedheal to join the small, moderate anti-Treaty party Clann Éireann, wrote in 1929 that:

> [Cosgrave] and his colleagues have issued a token coinage with queer field and farmyard figures of beasts and birds replacing the king's head; they

float the tri-colour, a type of flag which everywhere the world over indicates an independent Republic; they encourage Army Bands to play 'The
Soldiers' Song' by way of a national anthem. All that is simply designed to
create a false impression and thereby to delude simple minds into a belief
that our twenty-six counties dependency is what it is not.[45]

This was the policy which Fianna Fáil's *Nation* newspaper called 'using
the symbols the people love, to keep the people in a subjection they
loathe'.[46] Like the ex-unionists, but for very different reasons, the *Nation*
deplored Cumann na nGaedheal's attempt to disguise the Free State's
political status. At the time of the Trinity College anthem dispute, it
accused Cosgrave of hypocrisy in 'pretending not to want "God Save the
King" played' for the Governor General. 'Let Mr. Cosgrave stand by his
Free State with all that it connotes' urged the *Nation*; 'let him honestly
and courageously tell his people that as the King is the head of the Free
State with a Governor General as his deputy, "God Save the King" is
bound to be played at all official ceremonies.'[47] The IRA newspaper *An
Phoblacht* saw the anthem question in a similar light, sneering that: 'The
King's Representative and the King's Ministers have no case for objecting in their partitioned colony to their master's voice. It is by King
George's bounty they move and have their being: they can do naught
without his Royal sanction, their puppet Parliament and Senate are called
into being by his royal breath and have no life apart.'[48]

   The problem of reconciling the Free State's dominion status with the
assertion of a distinct national identity separate from Britain ceased to be
an issue once Fianna Fáil came to power in 1932. Fianna Fáil was dedi-
cated to dismantling the Treaty settlement, and in government it set about
removing the state's remaining symbolic ties to Britain, principally by
doing away with the Oath of Allegiance and the Governor Generalship.
However, perceptive observers could see that Cumann na nGaedheal had
not only made things easier for Fianna Fáil by helping to expand and
define the powers of the dominions, but had also paved the way for
removing those formal ties to the monarchy and the Commonwealth
which, indirectly, linked the Free State to Britain. A Free State citizen
writing in the *Round Table* observed in 1934 that 'an emphasis on distinct
nationality dominated from the beginning the whole policy of the new
Free State government'. This policy found expression in the adoption of
the tricolour and 'The Soldier's Song' as the national flag and anthem, and
the removal of the king's head from stamps and coins, actions which,
though 'small in themselves, were deeply significant'.[49] Three years later
the *Round Table*'s correspondent pointed out that Fianna Fáil's new constitution was simply a logical development of Cumann na nGaedheal policy, despite the Treatyites' claims to the contrary: 'It cannot be forgotten

that they themselves removed the King's head from our stamps and coinage, discouraged the playing of "God Save the King", and removed practically all reference to the King from official documents. Mr. de Valera's performance naturally followed their overture.'[50] This continuity, and the symbolic separatism pursued by both parties in the Free State, was readily perceived by unionists in Northern Ireland. Unionists had not enjoyed Cosgrave's overture, and they detected no change in the music once the maestro de Valera took the stage. They preferred instead to stick to their own tunes.

Unionists in Northern Ireland and the official symbols of the Irish Free State

Unionists in Northern Ireland were not slow to see the significance of the Free State government's selection of official symbols. In 1924 the *Northern Whig* commented that:

> The Free State is supposed to occupy the same position in the Empire as Canada or Australia, but a colonial coming to the South of Ireland would have great difficulty in discovering the nexus between the Free State and the rest of the Empire. The flag which is flown and loved by the Colonies is anathema to the Free State. The King, who is the living symbol of the Empire, finds no place in the Free State Parliament, in the Free State courts, or in the Free State administration.[51]

In the same year, a County Armagh resident made a similar point in a letter to the *Irish Times*, and spelled out the consequences of the Free State's symbolic separatism for the nationalist aspiration to Irish unity:

> The Free State is British only in name. She flies a Godless flag from which every Christian emblem has been expelled. She has expunged the King's name and likeness from her courts, her stamps and the commissions of her officers. This is the real obstacle to union. Ulster will never go under the tricolour. If the Free State really wants Ulster to come in of her own free will, the Free State's first step to that end must be to hoist the Union Jack. All the other dependencies of the Empire are content with the flag which, all the world over, stands for liberty, justice and truth. This is the case in a nutshell, and all the pious aspirations of lovers of peace, who are content to dream pretty dreams thereof, but will take no real and practical steps thereto, will not bring union any nearer.[52]

Condemnation of the Free State's symbolic repudiation of its connection with Britain became commonplace at Orange rallies, and such signs of disloyalty to King and Empire in the Free State were advanced as conclusive proof that union between the two parts of Ireland was impossible. The Trinity College national anthem dispute in 1929 was seen by union- ists as indicative of a trend in Free State politics which confirmed them in their belief that they should stay out of the independent Irish state. Speaking at the laying of a foundation stone for an Orange Hall, Northern Ireland's Minister of Labour told his audience that the incident 'had shown clearly how different were the views of those in the Free State and Northern Ireland; and the Ulster people should be thankful for their Parliament, which owed its existence to the Orange Order'.[53] The *Belfast Telegraph* saw in the incident evidence of the futility of 'the pious plati- tudes that emanate so frequently from Dublin as to the union of North and South',[54] while the *Belfast Newsletter* stated that 'Those who talk of a united Ireland should have sufficient intelligence to see that the loyal North can never unite with the disloyal South. For this reason, even if there were no others, partition must be permanent.'[55] The Free State's refusal to recognise 'God Save the King' as its national anthem was but one of a number of actions seen by unionists as acts of disloyalty to the King. Since unionists set such great store by their own loyalty, it is little wonder that Northern Ireland government ministers such as Sir Edward Archdale hastened to assure their followers that:

> there was not the slightest chance of a United Ireland when they saw the Free State Government going to remove Queen Victoria's statue in Dublin; removing the King's head from the postage stamps and coinage, and doing everything they could to show that King George had no sovereignty in Ireland. At present the Free State government gave them no encouragement for a United Ireland. (Hear, hear.) Until the Free State flew the Union Jack, they in Ulster would remain apart. (Hear, hear.)[56]

The objections of unionists were not only to the Free State's failure to acknowledge its connection with Britain; they also objected strongly to the particular flag and anthem adopted by the Free State government. They saw the tricolour and 'The Soldier's Song' as Sinn Féin party sym- bols, associating them with republicanism and with the violence of the revolutionary period. As the previous chapter showed, unionists hated the tricolour, and they regarded 'The Soldier's Song' with equal loathing. The mere fact that the Free State had an anthem of its own was provocative enough to some unionists, who claimed that there could be no anthem in the British Empire other than 'God Save the King'.[57] But to replace the imperial anthem with a song whose militarist lyrics and reference to 'the Saxon foe' evoked painful memories of revolutionary violence was noth- ing short of an outrage to unionist opinion. Unionists pointed out that 'The Soldier's Song' was 'replete with anti-British sentiment'[58] and 'insulting to the Anglo-Saxon race';[59] they called it 'a rebel song – a song breathing in its every line hatred of England',[60] a tune 'used by the Republicans when they were murdering policemen',[61] 'a song made infamous by rebel use during one of the most disgraceful periods in the history of Ireland',[62] 'the ditty associated with the Rebellion and the murders of servants of the British Crown'.[63] A columnist in the *Northern Whig* summed up unionist objections to the Free State anthem following the Trinity College anthem dispute:

> Both the verse and tune of 'The Soldier's Song' are reminiscent of a period that everybody would like to forget as soon as possible. They were evolved at a time when murder ran amok through the land pretending that it was war. The words speak the sentiment, not of a people rejoicing in newly-granted legislative freedom, but of revolutionaries aching to demolish 'the Saxon foe.'... A ditty with such an origin and history and expressive of such sentiments is a challenge to everyone in Ireland who has all through the Irish embroglio [sic] been loyal to King and Empire.[64]

If President Cosgrave would repudiate this Sinn Féin legacy, the writer continued, 'he would be doing good service to the cause of friendly feeling in both Northern and Southern Ireland'.[65] In the absence of any such repudiation, however, the strong suspicion remained in Northern Ireland that Cosgrave's government was simply pursuing the old republican aims by different means.

Thus, when Fianna Fáil came to power in 1932, it did not strike unionists as marking a radical shift in Free State politics, but rather as the continuation of a trend begun by Cumann na nGaedheal, which would inevitably culminate in the declaration of a republic in the twenty-six county state. Edward Murphy, MP, told an Orange rally in 1932 that:

> No attempt was now made to conceal the fact that a completely independent Republic was the objective towards which Mr De Valera, at the bidding of the I.R.A., was rapidly advancing. Everything which was said by Unionists in the past as to the Nationalist movement in Ireland had been verified by events. Full Dominion status, the elimination of the King's name from the Courts of Justice and the King's head from the coinage and the stamps, the substitution of the Tricolour and the 'Soldiers' Song' for the Union Jack and the National Anthem, and the steps taken to render appeals to his Majesty's Privy Council impossible. These startling changes had only whetted the appetite of the extremists who appear to be satisfied that their ideal, an independent, self-contained Republic, would soon be realised.[66]

Unionists saw no distinction between Fianna Fáil and the pro-Treaty party, except perhaps that, as Murphy suggested, Fianna Fáil was open about its republican and anti-British agenda. William Grant, MP, told another Orange meeting in 1932 that the election result had revealed the true position in the Free State. The pro-Treaty section of Sinn Féin, he said, had accepted dominion status only as a stepping stone, and he reminded his audience that 'Once in power, the Cosgrave Party proceeded to relegate King George into outer darkness, to issue their own coinage, to make Gaelic a compulsory language, to substitute the rebel Soldier's Song for the National Anthem, and to wipe out everything of a British nature.'[67]

Unionists saw this policy of 'driving out everything British from the Free State "bag and baggage"' as an attack not only upon the neighbouring island but also upon their own traditions.[68] British symbols were not alien to unionists, as they were to nationalists; rather, they were cherished symbols of unionists' own identity. Orange Grand Master Sir Joseph Davison explained that Ulster loyalists would have nothing to do:

> with those who insult and refuse to recognise our beloved King – or those who have torn down and trampled the cherished flag of Empire, 'the dear old Union Jack.' We live under the protecting folds of that flag, which in Ireland has often been described as 'the hated flag of Great Britain,' but we love and respect what is to us the flag of freedom. (Cheers.)[69]

Because unionists claimed these symbols as their own, outrage at the Free State's lack of respect for British symbols could be combined with contempt for the weakness of British governments, as in this speech by Sir William Allen, MP: 'The British Crown is buried in the mud and filth of the Liffey. The old Flag of the Union is torn to shreds, trampled underfoot and spat upon. The oath of allegiance is gone . . . And the British government of 1920–21 is responsible for it all. ("Shame.")'[70] A unionist writer informed *Irish Times* readers in 1934 that, just as unionists did not regard the Empire as 'England's Empire' but as 'Our Empire', so also:

> the Union Jack is not regarded in Ulster as 'England's' flag, but as 'our flag'. When insult is offered to that flag Ulstermen resent it as an attack upon 'their flag.' Is it not formed by the symbol of Christianity – the cross? The cross of St. Patrick linked with those of the patron saints of Scotland and England. Why should anyone call it 'England's flag'? So it is with the King. There were 'Kings of England' once, just as there were Kings of Scotland and Ireland. Now there is a King over all, the symbol of the unity of the Commonwealth. The King to Ulster is 'Our King' and not merely 'England's King.' When the toast of 'The King' is not honoured Ulstermen regard it as a personal affront to 'their sovereign.'[71]

This emotional identification with the symbols of the United Kingdom and of the British Empire, however, was not only incomprehensible to Irish nationalists, but stood in direct contradiction to nationalist stereotypes about unionists. Nationalists did not believe that unionists' desire to remain within the United Kingdom had any basis in sentiment, and consequently they chose to ignore unionist concerns about the Free State's rejection of British symbols.

Nationalists in the Irish Free State and unionist concerns

In her study of the responses of nationalists to partition in the independent Irish state, Clare O'Halloran has seen their approach to the question of Irish unification as characterised by 'the primacy of rhetoric and the rejection of compromise'.[72] By this she means that Irish nationalists outside Northern Ireland continued to express an unwavering commitment to a united Ireland, but were completely unwilling to contemplate the modification or abandonment of those policies pursued by governments in the Irish Free State and Republic which alienated unionists. In addition to their concerns about the Free State's rejection of British symbols, unionists objected to such aspects of Free State life as the compulsory teaching of the Irish language in schools, the influence of the Catholic church over government, and Fianna Fáil's autarkic economic policies.[73] However, both governments and private commentators rejected the idea that nationalists should make compromises in the interests of encouraging unification. Indeed, they claimed that unionists would lose all respect for nationalists if nationalists abandoned their own goals in order to court unionist opinion. So divorced were some nationalists from the reality of unionist sentiment that the *Irish Tribune* could find in Irish-Ireland policies a positive asset in the quest for union with Northern Ireland: 'By becoming more and more Irish we become more and more ourselves: we deepen in personality: our attractive power is heightened.'[74] The element of fantasy and wish-fulfilment in much nationalist rhetoric about partition was a way of coping with the uncomfortable reality that there was little they could do to unite the two parts of Ireland, short of asking to rejoin the United Kingdom. Even if they had pursued a more conciliatory policy it is highly likely that unionists would still have chosen not to bring Northern Ireland into the independent Irish state. The failure to compromise, however, undoubtedly removed any remaining possibility of agreement on a united and independent Ireland, and impeded the development of friendly relations between the two parts of the island.

Both the primacy of rhetoric and the rejection of compromise were very apparent in the approach of governments and nationalists in general in the Free State to questions of national symbolism. The state's symbols were themselves part of the anti-partitionist rhetoric. The tricolour, for example, had been created as a symbol of the union of Catholic and Protestant in a common allegiance to Ireland, and since in post-partition Ireland Protestants were concentrated mainly in Northern Ireland, the Free State flag could be described as 'a visible sign of our hope of a United Ireland'.[75] The national anthem of the Free State also called for unity between the descendants of the Gaels and of the more recent settlers ('Sons of the Gael, men of the Pale'), and spoke of soldiers 'whose lives are pledged to *Ireland*', despite the fact that, as the republican *Catholic Bulletin* snidely remarked, 'Juridically, there is no such place as Ireland, and therefore the words have no sense.'[76] The anti-partitionist message on the banknotes was rather subtle: they featured a female personification of Ireland which suggested the organic unity of the nation, and also included on the reverse riverine heads representing two rivers which flowed entirely within Northern Ireland. The stamps made a much more obvious claim to Irish unity, which was clear from the very first issues. Unlike the coins, seal and banknotes, which bore the name 'Saorstát Éireann' (Irish Free State), the stamps declared their country of origin to be 'Éire' (Ireland). The arms of the four provinces of Ireland, which appeared on one of the 1922 definitives and on the 1937 constitution commemorative, were also suggestive of a united Ireland. The simplest and most effective anti-partitionist symbol of all was that which appeared on the very first stamp issued by the Free State: the map of the whole island of Ireland, with no indication of the border between the two states.

Such symbols, however, were surely more provocative than enticing to unionists, since they seemed to declare that Northern Ireland would be part of the independent Irish state whether unionists liked it or not. When it came to symbolic gestures which might have accommodated unionists' loyalties and sense of identity, Free State governments were not prepared to compromise their use of symbols to assert the state's complete inde- pendence from Britain. Although there were some within the Free State who called for changes to the Free State's symbols in order to conciliate unionists in Northern Ireland, such voices came from outside the nation- alist mainstream, generally from the ex-unionist community and some anti-Sinn Féin nationalists. The *Irish Times* warned when the decision to issue a Free State coinage was announced that 'The accentuation of dif- ferences [between the Free State and Northern Ireland], more especially in bagatelles such as pillar-boxes and halfpence, is doing incalculable harm to the cause of Irish unity; for in politics, as in many of the deeper things of life, the greatest mischief often springs from the most trifling causes.'[77] In an editorial on 'Irish Unity' in 1934, the same newspaper lamented that no one was prepared to make sacrifices to achieve a united Ireland; that while the Northern Ireland government was moving to iden- tify itself ever more closely with Britain, de Valera's government was try- ing 'to abolish every trace of the British connection'.[78] A few brave peo- ple suggested that placing the Union Jack on the Free State flag would be a significant step towards a united Ireland.[79] Others worried that 'The Soldier's Song' would be an obstacle to unity, and called for a more neu- tral anthem on which all Irish people could agree.[80] An article on the anthem in the *Irish Independent* reminded readers that 'we have a hinter- land that must be included. War songs of a party can never be adopted by another party. They will only estrange one from the other the more.'[81]

Such occasional calls, however, failed to persuade the Free State government to change its symbols. The *Manchester Guardian*'s Irish correspondent pointed out at the time of the Trinity College national anthem dispute that unionists in Northern Ireland could never accept incorporation into a polity in which attachment to Britain and loyalty to Empire were regarded as heresy. The *Guardian* writer therefore concluded that 'the decision taken in regard to the National Anthem, taken in conjunction with the Irish language policy, proves that the Cabinet has made up its mind to leave Ulster entirely out of account, trusting that internal forces in the Six Counties will ultimately give the Catholics there also the upper hand'.[82] This analysis seems to be correct, at least in relation to the question of Free State symbols. When these symbols were being selected there is no indication that the Cumann na nGaedheal government gave any thought to how unionists might react to them, nor did either this government or its successor consider changing the Free State's symbols in response to unionist objections. There was one notable exception to this statement, but it was an exception that proved the rule.

In 1926 Kevin O'Higgins, the Free State's Vice-President, tried to resurrect Arthur Griffith's original Sinn Féin policy of a dual monarchy. Under this plan there would be a united Ireland, and Britain and Ireland would be recognised as independent kingdoms with a common King.[83] While in London for the 1926 Imperial Conference, O'Higgins outlined his idea to L.S. Amery, the Secretary of State for the Dominions. Amery gave him a sympathetic hearing, but, as a British Unionist who had been centrally involved in the campaign against Irish independence, he was well aware of the importance which Ulster unionists attached to symbols. He therefore told O'Higgins that the plan would have a much greater chance of success if the Free State government could accept the King's head on stamps and coins and was prepared to use the Union Jack in some way. O'Higgins replied that he could see no difficulty about the King's head[84] and no sentiment about dropping the tricolour, but that 'there would be grave difficulty about a flag containing the Union Jack'. O'Higgins suggested a flag with a harp and crown on a blue background, which Amery thought might be acceptable if the Union Jack was also used on occasions which had an imperial connection.[85] O'Higgins was one of the most dynamic and influential members of the Free State government, and had he lived it is possible that he might have persuaded his Cabinet colleagues to support the plan. He might even have won the support of a majority of Free State citizens, though there would undoubtedly have been strong republican opposition to the notion of a dual monarchy. As it turned out, however, when O'Higgins was assassinated in 1927 his plan died with him. The fact that no one took up O'Higgins's proposal, and that no other Free State minister came up with any similar suggestion involving the achievement of a united Ireland through symbolic compromise, is evidence of the lack of interest in conciliating unionists on the part of the Free State government.

Within the Free State parliament, only one politician, Frank MacDermot, spoke out consistently during the 1930s about the need for compromise in the interests of Irish unity. MacDermot, however, was an outsider: a veteran of service in the British Army during the First World War, he entered the Dáil in 1932 as a member of the small pro-Commonwealth National Centre Party, which was amalgamated into Fine Gael in 1933. He resigned from Fine Gael in 1935, became an independent, then resigned from the Dáil in protest against the 1937 constitution but remained in the parliament as a senator, in which position he showed his independence by opposing Irish neutrality during the Second World War.[86] MacDermot was committed to achieving a united Ireland (he stood as a nationalist candidate in West Belfast in 1929) but he believed that it could only be achieved through compromise. He has been described by John Bowman as the 'most persistent contemporary critic of the contradictions in de Valera's policy' on Northern Ireland, and during the debate about the new constitution in 1937 he spoke out about the need to offer Northern Ireland 'an Ireland in which a place can be found for their traditions and aspirations as well as for ours'.[87] In a 1939 Senate debate on partition, instigated by MacDermot, he showed his willingness to apply this principle to the question of national symbols. Northern Protestants, he argued, would not easily be persuaded to lose interest in the flag and anthem of the United Kingdom, and if there was to be a united Ireland nationalists would have to consider whether there should be no national anthem but 'The Soldier's Song' and no national flag but the tricolour, or whether a Commonwealth flag and anthem could be used alongside the Irish symbols.[88]

The complete lack of sympathy for MacDermot's views among his parliamentary colleagues is symptomatic of the extent of nationalist consensus about partition. Nationalists found it easy to dismiss the idea of making gestures which would appeal to unionist sentiment, partly because they saw partition as an issue between Britain and Ireland rather than between nationalists and unionists within Ireland, but also because they believed unionist sentiment to be essentially superficial. Clare O'Halloran has identified the stereotype of the 'hard-headed unionist' as one of the key images of Ulster unionists employed in nationalist analyses of Northern Ireland.[89] According to this stereotype, unionists lack idealism and are attached to Crown and Empire for purely economic reasons. Seán O'Faoláin, for example, wrote of 'Orangeism' (which, like most nationalists, he equated with unionism) that:

as long as Big Business in the North of Ireland is making money out of Imperial connections and Imperial preferences, it will hide its resolve to go on making money out of these connections under the poor, tattered, soiled piece of cloth which calls itself The Flag. If – most unlikely of historical eventualities – the British Empire were to crash financially, I am confident that Orangeism would vanish with it. I can say this, too, quite dispassionately, and objectively, for the South – it has stuck to its ideals through centuries of poverty and slavery. Orangeism has never yet been associated with anything that did not pay.[90]

That even such a trenchant critic of many of the conventional pieties of Irish nationalism as O'Faoláin could dismiss unionist sentiment and attachment to symbols such as the Union Jack so easily is indicative of the power of the stereotype of the hard-headed unionist.[91] This stereotype was useful to nationalists because it allowed them to believe that unionists, lacking the idealism of their nationalist compatriots, were not concerned with issues of symbolism and sentiment, but could be won over simply by the development of a prosperous society in the Free State.[92] This was a comforting thought, since it required of nationalists nothing but the continued pursuit of their own economic goals, and for this reason it was only rare individuals such as MacDermot who challenged the nationalist consensus by suggesting that unionist sentiment be taken into account.[93] So pervasive was the stereotype that the Irish correspondent for the *Round Table* was forced to acknowledge it even while contesting it: 'Strange as it may appear, the North is more sentimental than the South. Its hard-headed people are deeply attached to the Crown and the Union Jack. That attachment is as real as the attachment of their Southern fellow countrymen to the Soldiers' Song and the tricolour. It cannot be destroyed overnight by political legerdemain.'[94] If nationalists in the Free State were unable to make unionist sentiment vanish by political sleight of hand, however, they did manage the lesser conjuring trick of making this sentiment, and the problems it created for the goal of a united Ireland, disappear from nationalist consciousness. Nowhere was this clearer than in debates about the flags to be used by all-Ireland sporting bodies.

Flags and all-Ireland sporting bodies

One important area in which nationalists failed to consider the attachment of unionists to their own symbols was sport. The politics of sport in Ireland is extremely complicated and different sports have been affected by Ireland's political divisions in different ways.[95] Some sports (those associated with the Gaelic Athletic Association) are played only by nationalists, while others (cricket, for example) are largely restricted to unionists. Soccer or association football is played both by Protestants/unionists and by Catholics/nationalists, but this has not made it a unifying game. On the contrary, Irish soccer split into two rival leagues in 1921 (partly as a result of an incident in which officials of the Belfast-based Irish Football Association ordered the removal of an Irish tricolour at a France-Ireland match in Paris) and the game has been a focus for sectarian tensions within Northern Ireland itself.[96] A number of other sports, however, continued to be organised on an all-Ireland basis after partition, and some of these organisations brought nationalists and unionists together in the one body. Sport, therefore, provides an interesting test case of willingness to compromise on matters of symbolism in the interests of Irish unity. In particular, the question of which flag should be used by all-Ireland sporting bodies was a fraught one in partitioned Ireland.

One all-Ireland sporting body which had no hesitation about using the tricolour as the national flag at its matches was the Gaelic Athletic Association (GAA). The GAA is well known for its strong nationalist stance, and both Gaelic revivalists and physical force republicans played prominent roles in the organisation in its formative years. Because of the association's politics, and its long-standing bans on the playing by GAA members of 'foreign' (i.e. non-Gaelic) games and on participation in Gaelic games by members of Crown security forces, unionists have shunned the GAA.[97] As a result, there has never been any question about the use by the GAA of Irish nationalist symbols. At the association's annual congress in 1933, a motion was passed calling for 'the National Flag' (admittedly an ambiguous phrase, but one which to GAA members could only have meant the tricolour) to be displayed at all matches.[98] Since the GAA was a thirty-two county organisation, this policy applied to Northern Ireland, and it could lead to conflict with the Northern Ireland police on occasion. (See Chapter 5.) However, a Royal Ulster Constabulary report noted that GAA authorities in Belfast took the view that the tricolour should not be displayed when it might lead to a breach of the peace, and that no team would be compelled to display the flag.[99]

Although the GAA did not go out of its way to display the tricolour provocatively in Northern Ireland, it clearly gave no thought to the possibility of using another flag in order to appeal to unionists. Other sporting organisations, however, were troubled by the question of which flag to use, since they wished to avoid stirring up trouble between nationalists and unionists within their ranks and also wanted to remain on good terms with both the Northern Ireland and Free State governments. A common solution adopted by all-Ireland sporting bodies was to use the official flags of neither state, but to create instead a neutral flag for the organisation itself, which incorporated some sort of all-Ireland symbolism. The

Royal Dublin Society (RDS) already had its own flag, and from 1920 this banner was flown in front of the buildings where the Dublin Horse Show was held.[100] Other organisations adopted a flag composed of the arms of the four provinces as their banner, and flew it at sporting events held under their auspices.[101]

Such solutions, however, failed to avert controversy in the Free State. In 1926, Senator Oliver St John Gogarty complained about the absence of the tricolour from the Fitzwilliam Lawn Tennis Club in Dublin during an international lawn tennis tournament, and about the Royal Dublin Society's failure to display the tricolour at the Dublin Horse Show. Suggesting that the tennis club was probably following the example of the RDS, he lambasted both bodies for their 'studious insolence' and accused them of being out of sympathy with the sentiments of their members. By ignoring national sentiment, he alleged, such organisations were helping the cause of those narrow-minded people who wished to ban 'foreign games' (a reference to the GAA).[102] The Fitzwilliam Tennis Club defended itself by pointing out that the Irish team in the international tennis competition represented all Ireland, and that the use of the tricolour would present difficulties for players from Northern Ireland.[103] Gogarty, however, was unsympathetic to such arguments, and speaking in the Senate he made it clear that the assertion of Irish nationality was more important to him than the continued participation of people from Northern Ireland in the Horse Show. He also displayed a readiness, shared by many nationalists, to dismiss the people of Northern Ireland as un-Irish when it suited him to do so. Referring to a recent conversation with 'an eminent lawyer', who told him that flying the tricolour at the Horse Show might prevent people coming from Belfast, Gogarty asked: 'Are we, alone among the European nations, to deny our nationality and become non-entities in order to take the chance of a few people coming down from that suburb of Glasgow, Belfast, to the Horse Show?'[104]

Perhaps as a result of Gogarty's stirring, the government put pressure on the RDS, and the tricolour appeared for the first time at the 1926 Horse Show.[105] The government probably shared the view expressed by one of its supporters, the Earl of Longford, who wrote that the display of unofficial emblems in place of the national flag was 'deplorable, as it puts the country in a very humiliating position in the eyes of the world, even if it is done with an idea of conciliating the Orange North. Other countries have lost integral parts of their territory before now, but did not on that account repudiate their national flag.'[106] However, while the Cumann na nGaedheal newspaper was critical of sporting bodies which failed to fly the tricolour, particularly at events attended by the Governor General,[107] the government generally preferred persuasion to pressure. There was only one other occasion on which the Free State government took a more active role in a controversy over the failure of an all-Ireland sporting organisation to display the tricolour at international matches. This was just before the 1932 election, when the government reluctantly responded to a campaign to make the Irish Rugby Football Union (IRFU) fly the tricolour at international matches in Dublin.

Rugby union is a game followed in both parts of Ireland, and while Protestants and unionists have traditionally been disproportionately involved in the game, it also has a substantial following among (mostly middle class) Catholics and nationalists.[108] The IRFU remained an all-Ireland association after partition, and people in both Irish states took pride in a rugby team which continued to represent the whole island. In order to ensure that this situation was not disturbed, the IRFU made every effort to maintain its political neutrality. Unfortunately, in a deeply divided society even the most strenuous efforts at neutrality inevitably seem like partiality to some, as the IRFU discovered in 1932. The IRFU decided at its annual council meeting in 1925 to adopt as its banner the flag of the four provinces, and to fly this flag alone at all international matches played in Ireland.[109] The failure to display the tricolour at rugby matches at Lansdowne Road in Dublin was the subject of some criticism in Cumann na nGaedheal newspapers,[110] but it was not until it was taken up by the pro-Fianna Fáil *Irish Press* in 1932 that it became a major issue.

The matter was initially raised at the beginning of January by the rugby club of University College Galway, whose protest against the absence of the tricolour from international matches in Dublin was quickly backed by the Connacht branch of the IRFU.[111] The IRFU council declined to respond publicly, but in a letter to the Connacht branch, leaked to the *Irish Press*, it stated its intention not to depart from its existing policy.[112] The *Irish Press* gave extensive coverage to the issue, publishing a number of letters to the editor on the subject and seeking the views of prominent figures in Irish rugby. The *Press*'s own rugby writer, 'Rugger', devoted several columns to campaigning for the tricolour to be flown at international matches in Dublin. 'Rugger' saw the failure to fly the tricolour as an offence against national dignity, and sought to refute the argument that the Free State flag could not be flown because the Irish team represented all Ireland. He claimed that the Union Jack was flown at international matches in Belfast, and that in any case flying the flag had nothing to do with the team, but was a mark of respect to the country in which the match was played.[113] Although the IRFU denied that any national flag was flown at home internationals, whether played in Dublin or in Belfast, it seems that the Union Jack flew over the war memorial at the rugby stadium in Belfast.[114] Thus, to nationalists the IRFU appeared to be operating a double standard.

However, the option of seeking the removal of the Union Jack during international matches in Belfast was not canvassed in the debate, and the question of whether or not flying the tricolour at Lansdowne Road was consistent with the Irish rugby team's representation of all Ireland was also largely ignored. Instead, nationalist rugby supporters in the Free State used the issue as an opportunity to display rugby's nationalist credentials and to attack what they saw as the IRFU's domination by a small union-ist clique. Nationalist rugby supporters were particularly sensitive to the charge that rugby was 'anti-Irish' because of the GAA's position that rugby was a foreign game which should not be played at all by true Irishmen. Thus, Dr Morris, Vice-President of the Connacht branch of the IRFU, declared that 'The majority of Rugby enthusiasts are not anti-Irish', while Father Cogavin, president of a rugby club in County Galway, told a meeting of Connacht clubs that:

> He would be slow to ask any Irish boys to take up a game if the attitude of the Union towards it was that it was an English game and that they were simply trying to make them so many parasites of England. They played the game on the understanding that they were not sacrificing their nationality, but now they were told they must hide the national flag.[115]

If nationalist rugby supporters were keen to defend their game against accu-sations of anti-Irishness, they were also quick to accuse the IRFU council of anti-national prejudice. It was claimed that the IRFU council had not adjusted itself to the changed situation in Ireland, nor had its members been 'scraped of the barnacles of prejudice against our flag and all that it stands for'.[116] The council was said to be still dominated by the mentality which had approved the flying of the Union Jack under the old regime, and Father Cogavin felt that the rugby authorities should be made to realise that they lived in Ireland not Britain.[117] One correspondent asked what nationality the IRFU claimed to be, adding that if they claimed to be British they should be forced to take out Free State citizenship, while another wrote that the very names of the IRFU council members 'give us the impression that noth-ing to the Gaelic or Celtic interest inspired their action'.[118]

The tricolour, insisted a letter in the *Irish Press*, was the national flag, and must be honoured by all claiming Irish nationality, regardless of politics or creed.[119] Those who held this view had probably not even con-sidered the feelings of unionists in Northern Ireland, and were more con-cerned with the internal politics of the Free State. As 'Rugger' put it, 'Rugbyites' in the Free State were 'determined that *within this area at any rate*, no body of men will be allowed to escape paying it [the tricolour] due respect and honour, much less insult it'.[120] Such sentiments were another example of the kind of hostility to ex-unionists within the Free State, and anger at ex-unionists' neglect of the Free State's symbols, discussed in the previous chapter. In this context, the demand that the tricolour be flown at Lansdowne Road was not considered political. Thus, when a letter to the editor pointed out that the tricolour only represented the Free State, while the Irish rugby team represented all Ireland, and asked if the *Irish Press* was making a political issue of sport, the sports editor replied that the *Press* did not tolerate politics in sport.[121]

The only rugby club to speak up in support of the IRFU position was the University College Dublin club which, while it acknowledged 'that some members of the I.R.F.U. are anti-national in outlook' and deplored the fact that Belfast had breached the compromise agreement by flying the Union Jack, nevertheless felt that the flag compromise had been necessary in the interests of unity. The IRFU's policy could not be considered an affront to national dignity while Ireland remained divided, it argued. At the same time, it suggested a new arrangement whereby the IRFU flag would be flown from the official mast while the tricolour would be flown above the Governor General's box in Dublin and the Union Jack above the war memorial in Belfast.[122] The UCD club was not making the running on the flag issue, however, and it was the Connacht branch of the IRFU which forced the government's hand by sending a deputation to meet President Cosgrave, who was now in the midst of an election campaign. A meeting of Connacht clubs had passed a resolution accusing the IRFU of disloyalty to the state and calling for a plebiscite of all affiliated rugby clubs in the Irish Free State on the flag question.[123] The fact that they were oblivious to the views of clubs in Northern Ireland was also apparent in a letter to Cosgrave from Connacht branch Vice-President Dr Morris, who wished to draw the President's attention to the position taken by all the Connacht clubs, and by clubs in Munster and Leinster, but who made no mention of Ulster.[124]

In his meeting with the Connacht deputation, President Cosgrave tried every argument he could muster to put them off the idea of government intervention. He told them that if the government stepped in on this issue it would also have to interfere with a number of other activities, and that furthermore 'the flag as adopted is really not legalised'. Dr Morris, however, was (in the words of the official who reported the meeting) 'very sticky', and he finally suggested that if the Governor General attended the match the national flag should be flown above his box, adding that the government should instruct the King's representative not to attend if this was not done. The President replied that the government would be stretching its authority if it tried to influence the Governor General's attendance at sport (a highly disingenuous statement in light of the government's instructions to the Governor General not to attend the Trinity College sports at the time of the anthem dispute in 1929). Cosgrave went on to say that he had been informed that some players (from Northern Ireland, presumably) would walk off if the tricolour were hoisted, but Morris was undeterred by this, pointing out that the British flag was flown at matches in Belfast and declaring that 'they intended to fight the insult to the Flag at Lansdowne Road'. Morris wanted the issue resolved within a week, but the President told him that this was impossible and that 'they are raising a matter which would cause trouble during the period of the General Election'. After the meeting the President gave no indication to his aides that he wanted anything done about the matter.[125]

Cosgrave clearly hoped that the rugby flag question would go away, but it probably became apparent that inaction on the part of his government was a potential electoral liability. The Connacht deputation released to the *Irish Press* the statement they had submitted to Cosgrave calling on him 'as the guardian of the honour of the State, to protect from this insult the National emblem', and at least one Fianna Fáil candidate referred to the issue at an election meeting.[126] As a result, the Minister for External Affairs met with the IRFU council and told them that, while he understood that the union was not an exclusively Irish Free State body, he could see no reason why they could not follow the international practice of flying the flag of the country in which international matches were played. He informed them that, in his opinion, the tricolour should be flown from the principal flagstaff at Lansdowne Road – a position which the IRFU accepted and implemented shortly thereafter at the Ireland-England international.[127] This solution to the rugby flag problem was a triumph for a kind of pragmatic partitionism; an acceptance that 'They can fly their flag in their part of Ireland, and we will fly our flag in our part.' From 1932 onwards, the IRFU's policy was that the national flag and anthem of the host state alone should be used at matches within Ireland, but that no anthem or flag, apart from the IRFU banner, should be used for the Irish team at away matches. This seems to have been acceptable both to unionists and to nationalists, and the IRFU did not split over the issue.[128]

A dispute over flags in athletics proved rather more intractable. In 1922 the National Athletics and Cycling Association of Ireland (NACA) was formed as the governing body for athletics throughout Ireland, and this association was recognised in 1924 by the International Amateur Athletics Federation (IAAF). However, in 1925 a group of Northern Ireland clubs broke away and formed the North of Ireland Amateur Athletics Association (AAA), which was subsequently recognised by the English AAA.[129] This led to conflict between the two associations, with the NACA claiming to be the sole representative body for all Ireland and the AAA asserting an exclusive claim to represent Northern Ireland athletes. By 1932 the matter had been brought to the attention of the IAAF, but the international federation had not yet brought down its ruling. If, as seemed likely, the IAAF ruled that the NACA could not represent Northern Ireland, the NACA would have no alternative but to accept this decision if it wished to remain affiliated with the international body. A withdrawal of IAAF recognition would lead to a ban on participation by NACA athletes in international competitions, including the Olympic Games.[130] With this threat in mind, an attempt was made to maintain unity in Irish athletics by creating an overarching authority for national and international events. The new organisation, to be called the Irish Amateur Athletics Union (IAAU), was to be a federation between the two autonomous Irish athletics bodies. It was during negotiations to establish this union that the flag question emerged as a major point of contention.

By February 1932 discussion between the NACA and the Northern Ireland section of the AAA had progressed to the point where the issue of the flag to be used at national and international competitions was the only unresolved question. Accordingly, a conference between representatives of the two bodies was held to discuss the flag issue, and an agreement was reached to adopt as the IAAU flag the arms of the four provinces on a field of St Patrick's blue. General Eoin O'Duffy, President of the NACA, stressed after the meeting that the tricolour would still be flown at meetings held in the Free State, while the Northern Ireland association would be free to fly what flag it liked at events held under its auspices, but that the IAAU flag would also be flown at all events held in either part of Ireland. Presumably (though this was not spelled out) the IAAU flag alone would be flown at international events apart from the Olympic Games. The question of the flag to be used at the Olympics was left to the Irish Olympic Council, since athletics was but one of a number of sports represented on that council.[131]

At a special congress of the NACA held in April 1932 to consider the proposed resolution of the flag question, O'Duffy told the delegates that if they approved the flag settlement then all the terms of the union would have been approved. He explained that he had been unable to convince the Northern Ireland AAA to fly the tricolour, pointing out that 'The Governments had failed to do this, and, being unable to work miracles, he, too, had failed.' In the debate that followed, some delegates expressed opposition to a settlement which they saw as compromising national dignity. Dr Seán Lavan of the Connacht Council preferred a partitionist solution rather than a settlement which 'would give the Northern Ireland body a chance to compete under what they regarded as a foreign flag. He would rather have the twenty-six counties cut off in loyalty to a thing that the majority of the people were loyal to than go selling a thing that was hard won.' Dr E.N.M. O'Sullivan was equally vehement in his opposition, but he was determined to maintain the NACA's position as the athletics body for all Ireland, with the tricolour as its flag, even if this meant that NACA athletes would be barred from international competition and that many athletes in Northern Ireland would remain in the British association. They should not imitate the evasions of the rugby union, which had been forced to accept the national flag, O'Sullivan told the conference.

> It is our duty as a national body to recognise the national flag and a compromise flag is only worthy of an organisation that is prepared to compromise itself... We must maintain national prestige at home, even if it is denied to us abroad. By all means give the athletes of Ulster the freedom of action they might require to make athletics a success in that area, but if they are not prepared to take their proper place in the national body, with a respect for national traditions and outlook, then let us not compromise our national status to please people who have no sincere interest in the furtherance of athletics, and no respect for or pride in the national flag.[132]

Delegates from Ulster saw things rather differently. Mr Fay of County Cavan said he could see no loss of national dignity in accepting the settlement, and maintained that 'At present if the tricolour was used in Northern Ireland the person so doing would be finished.' Mr Briggs of County Down agreed that the tricolour caused dissension in Northern Ireland, and that for a successful settlement both the tricolour and the Union Jack would have to be replaced by a flag acceptable to all parties, while Mr Ferguson of the NACA's Ulster Council said that the association should not be concerned with politics but should be aiming to preserve the unity of Irish athletics. Ferguson continued: 'They had an Orange streak in the Free State flag as a sop to Ulster. Ulstermen wanted no sops. They wanted a flag thoroughly representative of Ireland.' In conclusion, O'Duffy pleaded with delegates to accept compromise, telling them that 'he wanted the Tricolour as the all Ireland flag, but he was not blind to the fact that that under present conditions it would not be possible to have the Tricolour flown at games in Portadown'. Eventually, a resolution was passed by forty-one votes to six approving the proposed resolution of the flag question, but with the significant amendment that the flag to be used in all international competitions should be the tricolour.[133]

In June, Mr Ferguson, Secretary of the Ulster Council of the NACA, tried to have this decision reconsidered, claiming that the IAAU's four provinces flag would be more representative of all Ireland than the tricolour, which was not accepted as an all-Ireland flag by the Ulster Council. The NACA's Central Council, however, decided that no useful purpose would be served by calling yet another congress to reconsider the flag question.[134] At a meeting of the Ulster Council in November, Ferguson moved a motion objecting to the use of the tricolour for international competitions and calling for a settlement on the basis of the agreement reached with the Northern Ireland AAA in February. Ferguson argued that, while they did not want to bring politics into sport, the tricolour was undeniably seen in Northern Ireland as representing a particular political party. William Anderson said that the tricolour was the flag of the Free State and was not accepted in Northern Ireland as the flag of the whole island, though Anderson also claimed that Northern Ireland people were satisfied with the use of the tricolour at the Olympic Games. Others disagreed: Mr M'Cann told the meeting that he knew from experience that the tricolour was honoured in every parish of Northern Ireland, while Mr Fearon observed that since the twenty-six counties were in a majority both geographically and in number of athletes 'he did not see how they could get away from the Tricolour'. Ferguson's motion was defeated, and General O'Duffy expressed satisfaction with the Ulster Council's decision, declaring that 'on those comparatively rare occasions when Ireland is represented on the international athletic field we consider that any athlete who may be selected from the North...should not object to the flag recognised by the majority of his fellow Irish athletes being displayed'.[135]

The flag debate became redundant when, in 1934, the IAAF ruled against the NACA's claim to represent all Ireland, although in 1936 an official of the Irish Olympic Council was still hoping vainly that the split with the Northern Ireland AAA could be ended by adopting the flag of the four provinces for international competition. The NACA refused to accept the IAAF ruling and was first suspended, then expelled, from the IAAF, with the result that Irish teams were excluded from international competitions, including the 1936 Olympic Games.[136] Nevertheless, the debates which took place during 1932, and the NACA's decision to insist on using the tricolour for international competition despite knowing that this would be unacceptable to the Northern Ireland AAA, provide another example of nationalists' reluctance to make symbolic compromises in the interests of Irish unity. Once again, nationalists showed a preference for the assertion of national independence, even if it was only possible within the twenty-six counties, to steps which might have helped to bring the two parts of Ireland together. By their actions nationalists in the Free State showed, in sport as in other areas, what Dr Lavan and Dr O'Sullivan acknowledged with uncharacteristic bluntness in words: that they would rather keep their state separate from Northern Ireland than compromise their ideals, and that if unionists were to come into a united Ireland they would have to accept the 'national traditions and outlook' which nationalists held dear.

Conclusion

In declining to follow dominion precedent, and instead using symbols to differentiate the Free State as much as possible from Britain, the Free State government was undoubtedly acting in accordance with the wishes of nationalists in the twenty-six counties. By making the Free State symbolically indistinguishable from a republic, Cumann na nGaedheal also sensibly deprived the republican opposition of propaganda opportunities, while preparing the way for more radical breaks with dominion status by subsequent governments. The Free State government's inability to see the contradiction between trying to make the state as independent and distinct from Britain as possible on the one hand, and aspiring to a united Ireland on the other, did not represent a unique failure of insight on the government's part. Rather, it was the product of a contradiction which lies at the heart of Irish nationalist ideology, as Clare O'Halloran has shown. The blindness to unionist sentiment which was apparent in debates about national symbols in the Free State was a necessary blindness, because unionist sentiment was fundamentally incompatible with the nationalist and Catholic tradition, at least in the form that tradition had taken by the 1920s.

As Edward Carson acknowledged in his speech to the House of Lords in 1924, sentiment is an important part of political life in all societies, and symbols are a crucial focus for political sentiment. The importance of symbols as assertions of the Free State's sovereignty and as obstacles to a united Ireland provides striking evidence that symbols are not peripheral to politics but are in fact central to it. Anyone travelling from the Free State to Northern Ireland could not help but be struck by the importance of symbols as boundary markers, and mentioning the change from green to red pillar boxes, from the tricolour to the Union Jack (or vice versa) became a cliché of Irish travel writing.[137] These symbols made travellers aware of the borders between states, but symbols also marked social boundaries. It is because symbols are such powerful and emotive markers of identity that most people in the Free State could not accept symbols of that British identity which had for so long been seen as opposed to Irish nationalism. For the same reason, the majority community in Northern Ireland was inevitably alienated from a Free State which seemed determined to banish all the symbols which were such an essential element of unionist identity. From the lowliest letter box to the most exalted emblem, symbols formed an emotional barrier between the majorities in the two parts of Ireland, a barrier as real as any border checkpoint.

Chapter 7
Symbols, conflict and conciliation: 1940 to 2000

The period since 1940 has seen little change to the official symbols of state in the two parts of Ireland. In what became the Republic of Ireland symbols largely faded from the political agenda, but conflict over symbols continued in Northern Ireland. Northern Ireland's 1954 Flags and Emblems Act became itself symbolic of a polarised society in which nationalists felt that unionist symbols were unfairly protected and nationalist symbols suppressed, while unionists were appalled that nationalists identified themselves symbolically with another state and failed to respect the official symbols of the United Kingdom. More recently, however, the renewed outbreak of violence in Northern Ireland since the late 1960s and the search for ways to end this violence have led to a reassessment of questions of symbolism in both parts of Ireland. There has been growing acceptance of the need to find ways of managing conflict over symbols, and increasing discussion of the need for new symbols which might aid reconciliation. Since the signing of the Good Friday Agreement in 1998 there have been proposals for significant symbolic changes in Northern Ireland as part of the new constitutional arrangements set out in the agreement. It remains to be seen, however, whether such changes will gain widespread acceptance, and there can be no doubt that symbols will remain highly contentious in Ireland for some time to come.

Symbols in Éire/the Republic of Ireland

By 1940 the main symbols of the independent Irish state were well established, and there were no changes to the symbols of the state when it became a republic and left the Commonwealth in 1949. The banknotes featuring the portrait of Lady Lavery were replaced with new designs over several years from 1976, while a number of Percy Metcalfe's animal designs continued to feature on the coinage of the Republic up until the introduction of the euro in 2002. In 1968 a new definitive series of postage stamps replaced the series created immediately after the foundation of the Irish Free State, and this definitive series in turn has since been replaced by others. Commemorative stamps have been issued with increasing frequency since 1940, and although nationalist anniversaries have remained a popular subject for commemoratives, a wide range of other subjects have also featured.[1]

During the 1940s a few new official symbols were created, but none of these new symbols achieved great public prominence. In 1944 Michael McDunphy, the Secretary to the President, suggested the creation of a presidential standard. He thought such a standard should be based on the tricolour, but noted that many people regretted 'the complete abandonment of the former national flag, the harp on a green, or more correctly, blue ground, and would like to see it restored in some form', an interesting comment given that the harp flag had by this stage been largely absent from national life for more than twenty years. He therefore suggested that the presidential standard could be created by superimposing a gold harp on a blue ground on the white stripe of the tricolour. The Taoiseach, Éamon de Valera, supported the idea of creating a presidential standard, but preferred that the design should be completely distinct from the national flag, and the design finally chosen and approved by the government in February 1945 was a golden harp on a blue ground. The standard was to be reserved to the President and not to be used without his or her permission, and was to be flown in conjunction with the national flag.[2]

A similar design (a gold harp with white strings, on a blue background) was adopted as the coat of arms in 1945 at the instigation of Dr Edward MacLysaght, the first head of the Genealogical Office (which replaced the Office of Arms in Dublin Castle). MacLysaght pointed out that no official coat of arms for Ireland was registered in the Office of Arms, and the government, having apparently overcome any lingering nationalist objections to what Hugh Kennedy, two decades before, had called 'the curious and quite artificial science of Heraldry', approved the registration of the coat of arms in November 1945. The arms were duly registered at the Genealogical Office as the arms of 'Ireland', although in practice ('pending the reintegration of the national territory', as the 1937 constitution had it) they were the arms of the twenty-six county state.[3] Another official symbol adopted in the 1940s also featured a harp. This was the jack of the Naval Service, adopted in 1947, which consisted of a gold harp on a green ground, the old flag of Irish nationalism thus finally gaining some form of official recognition from the independent Irish state.[4]

The tricolour, having been enshrined in the 1937 constitution as the national flag, was further entrenched after the Second World War when an official flag code was introduced. The code was a guide to the public on the correct design and proper use of the flag, but no penalties for improper use of the national flag were introduced.[5] As for the national anthem, no official changes were made to 'The Soldier's Song', but gradually the Irish translation by Liam Ó Rinn supplanted Peadar Ó Cearnaigh's English lyrics, and the song came to be known by Ó Rinn's title, 'Amhrán na bhFiann'.[6] One consequence of the popularity of Ó Rinn's translation is that the words of the anthem have acquired the appearance of a party political meaning which Ó Rinn never intended, due to his rendering of the song's opening words, 'Soldiers are we', as 'Sinne Fianna Fáil'. Ó Rinn's translation was first published in 1923, three years before the political party Fianna Fáil was founded, and while it may be that the triumph of this translation over others was due to enthusiastic promotion by Fianna Fáil supporters, it is certainly not true (as was sometimes claimed) that de Valera influenced the choice of lyrics in order to benefit his party. In any case, no Irish language version of the song has ever been officially adopted by the state. While the dominance of an Irish translation over the original English lyrics was certainly in line with the state's promotion of the Irish language, the ironic consequence of this shift has been that many of those who sing the anthem today probably have little understanding of what the words mean.[7]

By the 1940s, the symbols of the independent Irish state had gained fairly widespread acceptance within the state, and the conflicts over symbols which had marked the state's first decade were largely a thing of the past. There was a brief outbreak of symbolic conflict following the announcement of Germany's surrender in 1945, when the Union Jack was widely flown in Dublin. Some students at Trinity College sang 'God Save the King', hoisted the Union Jack and the flags of the other Allied countries, and burned the tricolour. Then, 'this being Ireland, everyone went home to tea', as the young Garret FitzGerald (a future Taoiseach) wrote at the time. Later, there were protests against the burning of the tricolour at Trinity, some protesters wearing swastika badges and giving Nazi salutes, and another future Taoiseach, Charles Haughey, set fire to a Union Jack. There was also fighting between pro- and anti-British factions, with attempts to tear red, white and blue badges off those with British sympathies, and rioting which was met with police baton charges.[8] However, while all this recalled the Armistice Day conflicts of the inter-war period, it was simply the last gasp of the old antagonism between nationalists and unionists in Dublin (and more particularly, between Trinity College and University College Dublin students), rather than the start of a new round of conflict over symbols. It was only with the renewed outbreak of violence in Northern Ireland in the late 1960s that national symbols were to become the subject of some debate once again in the Republic.

Symbols in Northern Ireland

Only one new symbol was created by the Northern Ireland government after 1940. In 1953, the government introduced a flag for Northern Ireland, which had the same design as the Northern Ireland coat of arms: a red cross on a white background, with a red hand inside a white, six-pointed star superimposed on the centre of the cross, and surmounted by a crown. The Minister of Home Affairs announced during the celebrations of the coronation of Queen Elizabeth II that 'while the Union flag was the only standard officially recognised, those who wish to have a distinctive Ulster symbol' could use the new flag, which was flown for the first time in honour of the Queen's visit to Northern Ireland in 1953.[9] It seems, then, that the Northern Ireland flag was created in order to provide unionists with a symbol of local identity which they could use in conjunction with the Union Jack at a time when they were eager to display their loyalty to the new monarch. It was not until the 1970s that the Northern Ireland flag became widely used by unionists, and by then the political context was very different.

The 1953 coronation celebrations also provided an opportunity for unionists to show their undiminished attachment to the Union Jack. However, the profuse display of Union Jacks by unionists provoked nationalist protests. In an echo of the flag controversy twenty years before, the nationalist-controlled Newry council prohibited the flying of patriotic bunting on council property, while in Cookstown, County Tyrone, nationalists tore down bunting erected by the Unionist-dominated council, which had the decorations replaced and guarded by police. When two Protestant residents of Derrymacash, near Lurgan in County Armagh, displayed Union Jacks, some ten households responded by flying tricolours, and police intervened to prevent fighting. Fearing that the conflict might escalate if they removed the tricolours while leaving the Union Jacks in place, the police resolved the situation by persuading everyone to remove their flags. In Dungiven, County Derry, a coronation day children's parade was stopped by a Catholic crowd, and only allowed to go ahead when a large Union Jack was removed from one of the floats. Such incidents outraged unionists, and were raised by Independent Unionist candidates standing against the Ulster Unionist Party in the 1953 Northern Ireland election, in which the UUP suffered a serious decline in its vote. The party's post-election analysis attributed this loss of support in part to a belief that the government was doing too much to placate nationalists, and referred specifically to incidents involving the Union Jack. As a result of the Independent Unionist campaign, the Prime Minister, Lord Brookeborough, promised unionists that 'the Union Jack will fly in any part of this country in future'.[10]

In addition to the pressure on the government to protect the display of
the Union Jack, there had for some years been a campaign by unionists,
and especially Orangemen, to have the tricolour completely banned in
Northern Ireland. There was a dramatic increase in the number of letters
and resolutions from unionist individuals and organisations calling for a
ban on the tricolour following the declaration of the Republic of Ireland
in 1948 and the passage of the Government of Ireland Act in 1949.
Apparently prompted by what they saw as a relaxation in the government's attitude towards displays of the tricolour, such messages often
threatened that loyalists would take matters into their own hands if the flying of the tricolour was not completely prohibited. The Minister of Home
Affairs responded to these letters by agreeing with their general sentiments, but pointing out the difficult position in which the government
found itself following the UK government's recognition of the Republic
of Ireland: 'This recognition covers Northern Ireland and therefore there
is difficulty in prohibiting the flying of this flag any more than the flag of
any other foreign country.'[11]

In 1954, following the Prime Minister's promise to protect display of
the Union Jack, the government decided to deal with both the Union Jack
and the tricolour issues in one piece of legislation, the Flags and Emblems
(Display) Act (Northern Ireland) 1954. Section 1 of this Act made it an
offence to interfere with the display of a Union Jack by a person on her or
his own property, while Section 2 authorised police to remove or require
the removal of any emblem whose display might lead to a breach of the
peace.[12] The Inspector-General of the RUC was unhappy with the legislation, which he considered unnecessary, and the enforcement of which he
believed would be excessively burdensome for the police.[13] Two government ministers also expressed concern that the Act revealed a government
willing to capitulate to extremist agitation, but Brookeborough insisted
that the legislation must be passed as he had made a public pledge that the
right to fly the Union Jack would be guaranteed.[14]

Announcing the new legislation, Minister of Home Affairs George
Hanna explained that he could not ban the tricolour outright as it was the
flag of another state, and therefore such a ban was a foreign policy matter reserved to Westminster.[15] However, he told the House of Commons
that, while he had no wish to interfere with the flag of any state with
which the United Kingdom was at peace, the Republic of Ireland's constitution claimed jurisdiction over Northern Ireland, so anyone supporting
that claim by displaying the tricolour was asserting the right of a foreign
country to govern Northern Ireland, an act he saw as close to treason.
With regard to the Union Jack, Hanna said it was ridiculous to see it as a
party emblem, declaring that 'in the Six Counties the flying of the Union
Jack on one's own property is an act of loyalty', the flag being a symbol

of loyalty to 'our native land . . . the Six Counties of Northern Ireland'.[16] As in the inter-war period, unionists clearly saw the Union Jack not only as a symbol of their links with Britain and the Commonwealth, but also as an emblem of their own provincial identity. Yet they also continued to assert that the flag was apolitical, even as they claimed that it represented loyalty to an entity which nationalists regarded, not as their 'native land', but as an artificial 'statelet'.

The RUC was issued with instructions about how the new Act was to be implemented, informing them that they should not in any circumstances direct or advise that the Union Jack should not be displayed on premises. It is notable, however, that Section 1 of the Act only protected the right of individuals to display the Union Jack on their own property: it did not in fact guarantee that the Union Jack could fly anywhere in Northern Ireland, as Brookeborough had promised. With regard to the tricolour, police were advised that where they believed that display of the tricolour was likely to lead to a breach of the peace, they should ask those responsible to remove the flag immediately, and if this was not done they should remove it themselves and institute proceedings against those responsible for the display.[17] There can be no doubt that, although Section 2 of the Act did not mention the tricolour, it was primarily directed against that flag. However, this section was completely redundant, as the Act gave police no new powers in relation to the tricolour, and retained the focus on preventing breaches of the peace which had characterised the government's approach to the display of the tricolour before 1954. Section 2 was included in the legislation partly so that the government could be seen to be meeting unionist demands for a ban on the tricolour, and also in order to avoid situations in which the display of the Union Jack could be countered by the display of numerous tricolours, as had happened in the Derrymacash incident.[18] As in the 1930s, the government acted to placate militant unionists, while ensuring that its legislation retained a degree of flexibility and ambiguity which would avoid controversy with the UK government and allow the preservation of public order to remain the primary goal.

Not surprisingly, the Flags and Emblems Act did nothing to decrease conflict over national symbols in Northern Ireland. Nationalists remained hostile to the Union Jack, and the government's efforts to suppress the tricolour only increased its appeal to many nationalists. In 1951 the nationalist MP J.F. Stewart told the House of Commons that the tricolour was a flag for all Ireland, adding provocatively that 'you people . . . should salute it, because the time is coming when you will do it anyway'.[19] In this context, the Flags and Emblems Act was seen by nationalists as another form of discrimination against the nationalist community, especially as it was assumed on all sides that it banned the tricolour.[20] At the same time, not all unionists were satisfied with the situation after the passing of the 1954 Act. In the late 1950s, Ulster Protestant Action held rallies demanding that the Union Jack be flown over every public building, and after one such rally in 1958 the Reverend Ian Paisley led a large crowd to a mixed Catholic/Protestant area of Belfast, where they raised the Union Jack over a children's play centre and burned a tricolour.[21] Unionists still insisted that the Union Jack was not a political emblem, however. Also in 1958, a Unionist MP, responding to nationalist complaints that the Union Jack was being used provocatively, declared that by 'displaying the Union Jack, the members of the Orange Order showed that they were positive, active adherents of the Crown and of the Protestant faith – nothing to do with politics'.[22]

Conflict over symbols continued into the 1960s, but there was a great deal of inconsistency in the application of the Flags and Emblems Act where displays of the tricolour were concerned.[23] The most famous incident involving display of a tricolour in the 1960s occurred in 1964, when a small tricolour appeared in the window of the republican election headquarters in Divis Street, in predominantly Catholic West Belfast. The police took no action at first, probably because the flag was displayed in a solidly nationalist area and therefore was unlikely to cause offence or lead to a breach of the peace. However, Ian Paisley heard about it, and threatened to lead a march to Divis Street to remove the flag if the authorities did not take action. With this threat in mind, it was decided to send the police in to remove the tricolour. The flag was removed peacefully, but was subsequently replaced, whereupon police smashed the window in order to remove it. The removal of the flag led to the worst rioting in Belfast since the 1930s, and both nationalists and liberal unionists were outraged that, by stirring up trouble over the display of a flag in an area where it could not have been considered likely to lead to a breach of the peace, Paisley had in fact caused a major breakdown in public order.[24]

By attempting to stamp out the tricolour, however inconsistently, the Northern Ireland government succeeded only in making it an important symbol of defiance within the nationalist community.[25] Republican commemorations of the fiftieth anniversary of the Easter Rising in 1966 were marked by widespread displays of the tricolour in Catholic areas of Belfast in a deliberate challenge to the Flags and Emblems Act.[26] As conflict escalated in the late 1960s, nationalists became more assertive about using their symbols, especially the tricolour, and since the 1970s they have adopted the loyalist practices of depicting their flag in murals and painting its colours on kerbstones.[27] Republicans have also used the tricolour as a way of challenging Crown forces, just as their predecessors did after the Easter Rising. In the republican stronghold of Crossmaglen, County Armagh, for example, a tricolour was repeatedly erected on the market house and regularly removed by the Army, which was even forced to use a helicopter for this purpose.[28]

The main change to the use of symbols within the unionist community in recent decades has been the growing popularity of the Northern Ireland flag since the early 1970s, when it came into widespread use by loyalists who felt that they had been betrayed by the government at Westminster.[29] The increasing use of the Northern Ireland flag has sometimes been seen as symptomatic of a growing sense of Ulster nationality and support for Ulster separatism among Protestants in Northern Ireland, especially since some unionists have expressed a preference for what they call 'the Ulster flag' over the Union Jack, or have even repudiated the Union Jack altogether.[30] Certainly, the Union Jack has been displaced somewhat from its position as the key symbol of Ulster unionism, and it would have been unthinkable before the 1970s for a Unionist politician to suggest, as Harold McCusker did after the signing of the Anglo-Irish Agreement in 1985, that he might never wave the Union Jack again.[31] There is, however, little evidence of support for an independent Northern Ireland among unionists, and since the 1970s the Union Jack has remained a popular symbol with unionists, though often displayed alongside the Northern Ireland flag. The Union Jack has continued to play an important role as a symbol which can unite the Ulster loyalist and Ulster British traditions, and display of the Union Jack is still a very important assertion of unionist identity. In 1974 a member of the loyalist Vanguard movement, having just declared his preference for the 'Ulster' flag over the Union Jack, nevertheless acknowledged the continuing importance of the Union Jack to unionists, explaining poignantly: 'We tend to identify ourselves with the flag, what other way can we?'[32]

Symbols and the search for peace in Northern Ireland since 1985

In 1985, the governments of the United Kingdom and the Republic of Ireland signed the Anglo-Irish Agreement establishing an Inter-Governmental Conference which, among other things, was to look at measures to 'recognise and accommodate the rights and identities of the two traditions in Northern Ireland, to protect human rights and prevent discrimination'. Included under this heading was the question of the use of flags and emblems.[33] One of the measures which resulted from this attempt by the two governments to find a way of ending the Northern Ireland conflict was the repeal of the Flags and Emblems Act as part of the Public Order (Northern Ireland) Order 1987.

An explanatory document produced by the Northern Ireland Office outlined the government's reasons for considering that the Flags and

Emblems Act was unnecessary. The document explained that the Act was widely, but wrongly, believed to protect any display of the Union Jack and prohibit any display of the tricolour. In fact, the document pointed out, Section 1 of the Act only made it an offence to interfere with a Union Jack displayed on private premises. However, even without the Flags and Emblems Act, display of the Union Jack in such circumstances was protected by the law and anyone interfering with such displays anywhere in the United Kingdom 'would be committing at least one of a range of offences, such as conduct likely to lead to a breach of the peace and criminal damage'. Moreover, the document continued, the Act gave no protection to the display of the Union Jack in public places, in workplaces, or by marchers.

The document went on to explain that Section 2 of the Act did not make the display of the tricolour illegal in itself, but rather authorised its removal where its display would be likely to lead to a breach of the peace. As with the provisions relating to the Union Jack, this power was redundant, as police had other public order powers which they could use to remove any flag if they believed that its display would lead to a breach of the peace. The Act was, therefore, unnecessary, while at the same time:

> it is seen by many groups as a piece of legislation which is discriminatory and offensive to certain sections of the community in Northern Ireland. Those who see it in this way believe that the effect of the Act is to protect displays of the Union flag even where these are clearly being used simply to assert domination of one section of the community over another, rather than to encourage respect for the national flag.[34]

Repealing the Act would simply bring the law on display of flags and emblems in Northern Ireland into line with the rest of the UK, while it would make no difference to the position of the Union Jack as the official flag of Northern Ireland and the UK as a whole.[35]

Many unionists were not reassured by such statements, seeing the repeal of the Flags and Emblems Act as another sign that Northern Ireland's position within the United Kingdom was not secure. The fact that this repeal was a product of the Anglo-Irish Agreement, an agreement which had been met with a massive protest campaign by unionists, only increased unionist suspicions. A pamphlet by a group of Unionist MPs fumed that 'the flying of the Union Jack would now appear to be an offence where there are enough opponents of that flag to threaten disorder'.[36] Unionists perceived clearly that changes to the law and practice in relation to the use of symbols were being made in order to accommodate nationalists, and while a minority of unionists may have hoped that such changes would allow nationalists to become reconciled to the state, many more saw such concessions as a dangerous indication that the government was willing to capitulate to nationalist demands. As a result, further proposals for change relating to the use of national symbols since 1985 have inevitably met with unionist resistance.

One area in which there has been significant change in relation to the use of national symbols in Northern Ireland has been the workplace. It was previously generally assumed that employees had to accept the dominant ethos in the workplace, whether that ethos was nationalist or unionist, and this meant accepting the symbols of the prevailing ethos. Over the past two decades, however, symbols which might seem to identify the workplace with a particular religious/political tradition, or which might cause offence to members of another tradition, have been removed from workplaces. This has come about largely as part of the attempt to counter discrimination in employment, symbols being seen as contributing to a 'chill factor' which might deter applications from members of whichever community was under-represented at a particular workplace. The Fair Employment Commission's Code of Practice specifically stated that employers should:

> promote a good and harmonious working environment and atmosphere in which no worker feels under threat or intimidated because of his or her religious beliefs or political opinion: e.g. prohibit the display of flags, emblems, posters, graffiti, or the circulation of materials, or the deliberate articulation of slogans or songs, which are likely to give offence or cause apprehension among particular groups of employees.[37]

Attempts by employers to implement such policies have sometimes met with resistance from workers, most notably in the case of the aircraft manufacturing company Short Brothers, the largest manufacturing employer in Northern Ireland, which had a predominantly Protestant workforce. The presence of bunting had been accepted at the company in the past, but in the 1980s management adopted a comprehensive equal opportunity policy, including a commitment to remove flags and emblems. The attempt to enforce this policy came at a time when unionist sensitivities had been heightened following the signing of the Anglo-Irish Agreement. On two occasions in 1986 and 1987, workers walked out of the Short Brothers plant, at least in part because of the management's insistence on removing all flags and emblems from the factory. Management, however, held firm, finding support for its position from union officials, and the workers returned to work, thereby accepting the company's policy. According to Bryson and McCartney, this dispute 'clarified the boundaries of acceptable conduct', and probably influenced the development of the Fair Employment Commission's Code of Practice.[38]

Queen's University, Belfast, is one institution which has had to address questions of the use of national symbols in the process of attempting to

create a neutral working environment, and because Queen's is an important public institution, its policies have attracted a great deal of interest
outside the university itself. In the 1990s, the university became
embroiled in a major public controversy about the playing of 'God Save
the Queen' at graduation ceremonies. 'God Save the Queen' was played
near the beginning of the graduation ceremony, just after the academic
procession, so the audience was already standing and was expected to
remain standing for the anthem. For some time there had been opposition
to this procedure from some students, and some of those attending the ceremony chose to sit down when 'God Save the Queen' was played. In early
1993, newspapers reported that the playing of the anthem at Queen's
graduation ceremonies was under review, and these news stories may
have been prompted by a report into the fair employment situation at the
university which, among many other recommendations, suggested that
the playing of 'God Save the Queen' might be in breach of the Fair
Employment Code of Practice.[39] The university set up a committee to
examine the issue of creating a neutral environment at Queen's, including
the question of the national anthem at graduation ceremonies, and at the
end of 1994 the university announced that it would be replacing 'God
Save the Queen' with the European anthem, 'Ode to Joy'.

The university came under a great deal of public pressure over this
decision, and it was reported in May 1995 that the topic of the anthem at
Queen's had featured more prominently in newspaper letter columns in
Northern Ireland over the previous six months than any other issue, including the paramilitary ceasefires and the 'Framework Document' on the
future of Northern Ireland. Many unionists were incensed at the idea that
the university would stop playing the national anthem of the state because
of what they perceived as opposition from people hostile to that state.
Belfast's Unionist Lord Mayor Reg Empey declared in 1994, while the
matter was still under consideration by the university, that: 'Removing the
national anthem means the university is bowing to republicanism and
really saying we are no longer part of the United Kingdom.' The Chairman
of the Unionist Graduates' Association also saw the anthem decision as
contributing to a 'chill factor' which had resulted in the under-representa-
tion of Protestants in the student body.[40] The university, however, stuck by
its decision to stop playing 'God Save the Queen' at graduations, although
the idea of using 'Ode to Joy' instead was also dropped and no anthem was
used. The Queen's Pro Vice Chancellor explained that by not using 'God
Save the Queen', the university was showing that it was a non-doctrinal
institution open to all, but that, having chosen not to play that anthem, it
was decided that no other anthem should be played either.[41]

While debates about national symbols have been most intense within
Northern Ireland, the outbreak of violence in the North and the search for

a resolution of the conflict there have also caused some reassessment of national symbols in the Republic of Ireland. The Northern Ireland conflict has made nationalists in the Republic more aware of features of their society which unionists might find objectionable and which might act as obstacles to reconciliation in Ireland. The violence prompted many to reconsider the Sinn Féin tradition with which the state's flag and anthem are so closely associated, and brought home to them the fact that unionists do not see the Republic's symbols as apolitical emblems of a shared Irish nationality. While there is certainly no widespread demand within the Republic for a change to the state's symbols, there has been discussion in recent years about the possibility of changing these symbols, especially the national anthem, in order to conciliate unionists and to reflect a less militant, more pluralist conception of Ireland. In 1993, for example, a Green Party TD suggested that the Republic's national anthem should be 'toned down and replaced by one which is less patriotic', asking whether the words of 'The Soldier's Song' were 'appropriate to a society which ought to promote non-violence, tolerance and cooperation'. In reply, the Minister for Finance conceded that the anthem's lyrics reflected 'a particular time in this State's history arising out of our quest for independence', but added that there did not seem to be much interest among the general population in changing the anthem.[42]

As part of the Joint Declaration for Peace (the Downing Street Declaration) issued by the Prime Ministers of the Republic of Ireland and the United Kingdom in December 1993, Taoiseach Albert Reynolds pledged that his government would attempt to build trust between the two main traditions in Ireland and try to address unionist fears. To this end, he committed his government to the examination of those 'elements in the democratic life and organisation of the Irish State' which could be represented as a threat to unionists' 'way of life and ethos, or that can be represented as not being fully consistent with a modern democratic and pluralist society', and undertook further to examine ways of removing any such obstacles. He also foreshadowed the creation of a Forum for Peace and Reconciliation 'to make recommendations on ways in which agreement and trust between both traditions in Ireland can be promoted and established', and this Forum was duly created the following year.[43]

The Forum considered the question of the Republic's symbols as part of its discussion of 'Obstacles in the South to Reconciliation'. The Fianna Fáil leader, Bertie Ahern, told the Forum that it was generally better 'to welcome the different symbols of identity rather than to try to expunge them in favour of universal blandness'. He detected no real demand in the Republic for a change to the national anthem, 'though a handful jump up and down every now and again', and in relation to the flag he thought that 'until unionists want to come and negotiate the country's flag with us, I would leave well enough alone in that regard. I think many people would be very unhappy to see us discarding too many of our national symbols and traditions unilaterally, and I personally fall within that category.' By contrast, Mary Harney of the Progressive Democrats, while acknowledging that nationalists had an emotional attachment to 'The Soldier's Song', felt that 'the words of our national anthem are not compatible with peace and reconciliation, the lyrics are militaristic'. She did not necessarily think the anthem should be changed, but 'we should be prepared to look at it' and to consider not playing it at all-Ireland events.[44] No doubt such debates will continue in the Republic, but so far there has been no serious attempt to change the official symbols of the state.

Debate about the use of national symbols at all-Ireland sporting events, especially rugby internationals, has also continued. As noted in Chapter 6, IRFU policy after 1932 was that the flag and anthem of the host state should be used at international rugby matches in Ireland, together with the IRFU flag. This meant that the tricolour was flown and 'The Soldier's Song' played at matches at Lansdowne Road in Dublin, while the Union Jack and 'God Save the King/Queen' were used at Ravenhill in Belfast. For away matches, no anthem was to be played and only the IRFU flag was to be used. However, since 1954, no rugby internationals involving the Irish team have been played in Belfast. According to one account, this was a result of an incident in 1954 when some players from the Republic refused to stand to attention for the British national anthem unless 'The Soldier's Song' was also played and the tricolour flown (a protest which may have been in response to the enactment of the Flags and Emblems Act in that year). It has been claimed that this dispute was resolved when the players agreed to go ahead with the game in exchange for a promise that they would never again have to play international matches in Belfast.[45] However, this account is contradicted by other versions of the story, and in any case it is clear that the decision to play all international matches in Dublin would have been taken anyway because the Lansdowne Road stadium was larger than the Belfast one, so gate receipts could be increased if all games were played there.[46]

In general, the IRFU policy has not caused significant problems or protests. Players and spectators from Northern Ireland (most of whom, it seems fair to assume, are unionists) do not seem to have had problems with respecting the symbols of the Republic at international matches in Dublin. In 1993 the press officer of the Democratic Unionist Party, Sammy Wilson, objected to the use of the tricolour and 'The Soldier's Song' at rugby internationals, since the Irish team was representing the whole of Ireland and rugby fans from Northern Ireland should not have to suffer the 'indignity' of standing for 'The Soldier's Song'. His comments did not receive much public support, however.[47] Some people in the Republic have also raised the question of the appropriateness of using the symbols of the Republic at international matches played in Dublin. Mary Harney told the Forum for Peace and Reconciliation that she found it strange that unionists playing for an all-Ireland team had to 'stand and salute an anthem that they cannot obviously identify with', while Bertie Ahern's willingness to consider the use of another anthem at all-Ireland sporting events was rather undermined by his farcical suggestion that 'A Nation Once Again' might be an anthem more acceptable to unionists.[48] The IRFU has also sought a song which could be used in place of a national anthem at international matches played away from Ireland, and since 1995 a specially commissioned song, 'Ireland's Call', has been used for this purpose.[49]

The Good Friday Agreement and beyond

Since 1994, debates about national symbols in Ireland have taken place in a new context, one in which hopes engendered by the developing 'peace process' have been shadowed at every turn by fears that the process was in imminent danger of collapse. In such a context, there has been an awareness that symbolic issues would have to be addressed and that such sensitive issues would have to be handled carefully lest they destabilise the process. Questions of symbolism have been raised mainly as part of the discourse on 'parity of esteem' between the 'two traditions', with nationalist leaders in both parts of Ireland arguing that the symbolism of the state in Northern Ireland failed to recognise the nationalist tradition.[50] The contentious and potentially divisive nature of symbolism was acknowledged in the 'Good Friday Agreement' which emerged from negotiations involving the political parties of Northern Ireland and the governments of the United Kingdom and the Republic of Ireland. The agreement, endorsed by substantial majorities of voters in referendums held in both parts of Ireland in May 1998, stated under the heading of 'Economic, Social and Cultural Issues' that: 'All participants acknowledge the sensitivity of the use of symbols and emblems for public purposes, and the need in particular in creating the new institutions to ensure that such symbols and emblems are used in a manner which promotes mutual respect rather than division. Arrangements will be made to monitor this issue and consider what action might be required.'[51]

The Northern Ireland Assembly set up under the Good Friday Agreement, and the cross-party, power-sharing Executive formed by that Assembly, have had to grapple with the difficult task of ensuring that 'symbols and emblems are used in a manner which promotes mutual respect rather than division'. The Assembly got off to a promising start, managing to avoid conflict in the choice of a symbol for the Assembly itself. The flax flower emblem adopted by the Assembly won widespread support, but the Assembly was unable to achieve a similar degree of unity when it came to consider policies in relation to the flying of flags from government buildings.

The decision of Sinn Féin ministers in the Executive to order their departments not to fly the Union Jack sparked predictable responses from unionists. Sinn Féin maintained that either no flag should be flown on government buildings, or the tricolour should fly alongside the Union Jack. The Democratic Unionist Party responded by tabling a motion in January 2000 condemning Sinn Féin's stance, and another in June 2000 directing that the Union Jack be flown on Executive buildings on designated days and at Stormont whenever the Assembly was sitting.[52] A range of views were expressed in the debates on these motions, but unionists were united in the view that so long as Northern Ireland remained part of the United Kingdom, the Union Jack should continue to be flown on government buildings, and should be flown alone.[53]

The contentiousness of this issue, and the inability of the parties represented in the Assembly to reach consensus on the question of flags on government buildings, led to the decision being taken out of the Assembly's hands. In May 2000 the UK parliament passed the Flags (Northern Ireland) Order 2000, allowing the Secretary of State for Northern Ireland to make regulations regarding the flying of flags at government buildings (defined as buildings 'wholly or mainly occupied by members of the Northern Ireland Civil Service'). The Order further provided for draft regulations to be referred to the Northern Ireland Assembly, which would then be required to report to the Secretary of State 'the views expressed in the Assembly on the proposed regulations'. Having considered the Assembly's report, the Secretary of State then had to refer the draft regulations to the UK parliament for approval. This Order was brought into operation in September 2000, and draft regulations made under the Order were referred to the Northern Ireland Assembly.

The Flags Regulations (Northern Ireland) 2000 set out the days on which the Union Jack was to be flown at seven specified government buildings.[54] Notably, the seat of the Assembly at Parliament Buildings, Stormont, was not included because it was not mainly occupied by Northern Ireland civil servants. The Union Jack was also to be flown on the specified days at other government buildings 'at which it was the practice to fly the Union flag on notified days in the period of twelve months ending with 30th November 1999'. Seventeen days were specified for flying the Union Jack, most of them royal birthdays or other days associated with the monarchy (the exceptions being Commonwealth Day, St Patrick's Day, Europe Day and Remembrance Day). The regulations brought Northern Ireland into line with the rest of the United Kingdom by dropping Christmas Day, New Year's Day, Easter Sunday and the Twelfth of July from the list of days on which the Union Jack was to be flown. St Patrick's Day, however, was retained, being equivalent to the saints' days marked in the other constituent nations of the UK.

Other matters covered by the regulations were the flying of flags at government buildings on the occasions of visits by the Queen and by other heads of state, and the flying of the Union Jack at half mast at government buildings. With regard to a visit to a government building by a head of state other than the Queen, the regulations provided that the Union Jack could be flown from that building. The national flag of the visiting head of state's country could also be flown at that building or other government buildings, provided that the Union Jack was also flown. On any occasion on which the flying of the Union Jack at particular government buildings was provided for in the regulations, the regulations also provided for discretion to fly the Union Jack at other government buildings. Finally, the regulations prohibited the flying of flags at government buildings except as provided for by the regulations, which meant, among other things, that the Union Jack was not to be flown except on the specified days. There was no mention of the Irish tricolour in the regulations, but one of their effects was to permit the flying of the tricolour (together with the Union Jack) at government buildings on the occasion of a visit by the President of the Republic of Ireland, but to prohibit it on all other occasions.

As required under the Flags (Northern Ireland) Order, the draft regulations were considered by a committee of the Northern Ireland Assembly. The committee was made up of members of the various parties represented in the Assembly, and it was not required to come up with a common view of the regulations but only to report on views of the regulations expressed in the Assembly. This it did by way of summaries of the submissions received from political parties, with the full submissions of the parties and others being published as appendices to the report.[55]

In its submission, the Ulster Unionist Party was broadly supportive of the proposed regulations, and made the point that, under the Good Friday Agreement, the constitutional status of Northern Ireland was not neutral. The flying of the Union Jack from government buildings, in the UUP's opinion, was a clear expression of Northern Ireland's position as part of the United Kingdom, and it would be inappropriate either to stop flying the Union Jack or to give equal status to the tricolour. The UUP also objected to the absence of sanctions for failure to comply with the regulations. The Democratic Unionist Party similarly argued that the Union Jack symbolised Northern Ireland's constitutional position, and that it should have no less standing in Northern Ireland than in the rest of the

UK. The DUP made a number of proposals, including that the Union Jack should be flown from government buildings on all days on which it was the practice to fly it in the twelve months to 30 November 1999 (which would include 12 July); that no other state's flag should be flown from government buildings except with the permission of the Assembly; and that there should be no prohibition on the flying of the Union Jack on government buildings at any other time. Both major unionist parties also called for the Union Jack to be flown at Parliament Buildings, Stormont.

On the nationalist side, the Social Democratic and Labour Party contended that Northern Ireland could not be compared with other parts of the UK, as it was a divided society emerging from many years of conflict. In the SDLP's view, the Union Jack was clearly identified with the unionist community, so flying this flag alone did not promote mutual respect rather than division. As an interim step, the SDLP favoured flying no flags from government buildings, but the party thought that other options (such as flying both the Union Jack and the tricolour, or finding new symbols) should be explored in the longer term. The SDLP also suggested flying both the Union Jack and the tricolour at British-Irish and North-South meetings arising from the Good Friday Agreement. Sinn Féin spoke more strongly of the Union Jack as a sectarian symbol of unionist domination. It maintained that the norms regarding the flying of the Union Jack in Britain were not appropriate in Northern Ireland and that, where British symbols were part of public life, Irish cultural and political symbols should be given equal prominence. If British and Irish symbols were not given equal status, then no symbols should be used. In other words, Sinn Féin believed there should be two flags or none.

These and other submissions showed that, while there were differences within the unionist and nationalist camps, the divisions between nationalists and unionists remained much greater and appeared difficult to overcome. Broadly speaking, unionists saw the Union Jack as a non-political symbol of Northern Ireland's constitutional status within the United Kingdom and thought that the flying of flags from government buildings in Northern Ireland should be on the same basis as in the rest of the UK, while nationalists regarded the Union Jack as a symbol of unionism and believed that rules for the flying of flags in Northern Ireland had to take into account the divided nature of Northern Ireland society. Given the continued lack of consensus displayed in the Assembly's report, it is not surprising that the Secretary of State made no changes to the draft regulations, which were approved by the UK parliament and came into force in November 2000.

Another highly contentious issue facing the people of Northern Ireland in the wake of the Good Friday Agreement, reform of the police service, also has an important symbolic dimension. Expressing the desire of participants in the multi-party talks for 'a police service capable of attracting and sustaining support from the community as a whole', the agreement went on to set out terms of reference for a Commission on Policing in Northern Ireland which, among many other matters, was specifically charged with making recommendations on the symbols of a reformed police service for Northern Ireland.[56] Nationalists and unionists have long held very different attitudes towards the Royal Ulster Constabulary, and this has been both reflected in and reinforced by their different views of the force's symbolism. A 1997 survey found that just over three-quarters of Catholics favoured changes to the RUC's name and symbols, while some 60 per cent of Protestants found such changes unacceptable.[57]

This division of opinion reflected the fact that the symbols of the RUC were strongly unionist. The very name of the force not only linked it to the British monarchy but also employed the name 'Ulster' to refer to Northern Ireland, a usage which most nationalists find offensive and partisan. Pictures of the Queen were displayed in police stations, and until the late 1990s new recruits were required to swear an oath of allegiance to the Queen. The RUC badge (taken over from the pre-partition Royal Irish Constabulary) showed the Crown above the harp, an image which has historically been seen by nationalists as representing British domination of Ireland. In addition, since 1932 (when, as Chapter 4 showed, the Northern Ireland government bowed to loyalist pressure in the wake of the Newry flag dispute) the Union Jack has been flown from police stations on public holidays, including the Twelfth of July. It was not until 1998 that the Chief Constable of the RUC announced that the flag would no longer be flown in honour of the Orange Order's principal marching day.[58]

Criticism of the RUC's symbols was, therefore, made on the grounds that these symbols represented the force as unionist in ethos.[59] In response, defenders of the status quo put forward a number of arguments. Some said that the symbols of the RUC were not important, and were a distraction from the real issues of policing. On the other hand, it was argued that symbols are such a difficult and contentious matter that to interfere with them might create more problems than it solves, simply focusing the attention of both nationalists and unionists on the things that divide them.[60] Another argument, put by the Chief Constable of the RUC, Sir Ronnie Flanagan, was that such symbols as portraits of the Queen and the Union Jack were not offensive or inconsistent with the attempt to create a neutral working environment.[61] However, the most important reason for resistance to proposals to change the name and symbols of the police force in Northern Ireland was undoubtedly that (despite protestations to the contrary) the symbols of the RUC were seen, by unionists as well as by nationalists, as representative of unionist identity. The independent unionist MP Robert McCartney admitted as much in the House of Commons debate on the Police Bill in 1997, declaring that it was because unionists felt their identity and citizenship to be under constant threat that symbols of that identity such as the Crown and the royal appellation of the RUC were so important to them.[62]

The Commission on Policing in Northern Ireland, set up under the terms of the Good Friday Agreement, reported in September 1999. The commission, commonly referred to as the Patten Commission after its Chair, former Governor of Hong Kong Chris Patten, made far-reaching recommendations for transforming the RUC. Among its recommendations were that the force should be renamed the Northern Ireland Police Service, that its crown-and-harp cap badge should be replaced, and that the Union Jack should not be flown from police buildings. These proposals for symbolic change were among the most controversial when the report was released, attracting bitter criticism from unionists and from within the RUC itself. Ulster Unionist Party leader David Trimble described the proposed changes to the RUC's name and symbols as 'a gratuitous insult' to those who had served in the force, while a police reservist complained that the Union Jack and RUC badge 'were good enough for us to die under. Now they are being removed as if they were badges of shame.' 'Is Chris Patten telling us that no symbol of our state can be tolerated, because [Sinn Féin's] Martin McGuinness disapproves?' asked another RUC man.[63] There was a renewed outburst of unionist fury when the Secretary of State for Northern Ireland, Peter Mandelson, announced in January 2000 that most of the Patten Commission's recommendations would be implemented.[64] The Police (Northern Ireland) Act was passed in November 2000, and at the end of 2001 the RUC was replaced by the Police Service of Northern Ireland, with a new badge designed to represent the different traditions of Northern Ireland.

The Patten Commission's report was followed by a review of the criminal justice system in Northern Ireland, also commissioned as part of the implementation of the Good Friday Agreement. This report, released in April 2000, recommended that symbols be removed from courtrooms and that the practice of declaring 'God Save the Queen' when judges enter the courtroom be discontinued, but that the Union Jack should continue to be flown over courthouses and that the Royal Arms should remain on the courthouses' exteriors. In response, Nigel Dodds of the Democratic Unionist Party called the report 'another attack on the British culture and ethos in Northern Ireland, yet more appeasement of an insatiable nationalist appetite to destroy every vestige of the majority community's identity'.[65] Further proposals for change to Northern Ireland's official symbols can be expected as the Good Friday Agreement continues to be implemented, and each new proposal is sure to meet with similar expressions of outrage from those unionists who see the government as caving in to nationalist demands and trampling on unionist identity by changing the symbols of state.

Conclusion

The Good Friday Agreement represents a historic compromise between nationalists and unionists in Northern Ireland, and even if the current agreement collapses, any future settlement would probably be on a similar basis. Nationalists have had to accept that, for the foreseeable future, Northern Ireland will remain part of the United Kingdom. Unionists have had to accept that Northern Ireland will not be governed like any other part of the United Kingdom (not even like the newly devolved government of Scotland) and that the new political structures introduced under the agreement must be acceptable to nationalists. In relation to symbols, this will most likely mean that nationalists will have to live with the continued presence of some symbols which they dislike, while unionists will have to put up with the disappearance of some symbols which they cherish. New symbols will also have to be created to represent the new institutions created by the agreement, and these symbols will have to be ones which, as much as possible, are acceptable to all sections of Northern Ireland society. Finding such symbols will be a difficult task, but if suitable symbols are found, and if the new constitutional arrangements attract widespread public support, they could ultimately provide a focus for a greater sense of common identity among the people of Northern Ireland. At the same time, the people of the Republic of Ireland may also consider changing some of their state's symbols, not only with a view to reaching out to unionists in Northern Ireland, but also with the aim of recognising those political and cultural traditions within the twenty-six counties which were marginalised following the triumph of Sinn Féin.

Debate and conflict over national symbols in Ireland look set to continue well into the twenty-first century. A lasting peace in Northern Ireland would probably lead to a reduction in such conflict, but in the short term the ending of armed conflict may actually increase the level of symbolic conflict, as people use other means to challenge their opponents. Changes to official symbolism in Northern Ireland are also likely to provoke fierce debate, with nationalists seeking the removal of symbols which unionists regard as essential parts of their heritage and identity. Both parts of Ireland have undergone enormous changes over the past decade, and have become significantly more open and tolerant in certain respects. However, the very pace of social change may make people in Ireland more resistant to proposals for change to their symbols. As the society about them changes radically, many may cling all the more tightly to the symbols which provide them with a secure sense of identity.

Conclusion

Viewing his birthplace from England in the late 1930s, the poet Louis MacNeice was scathing about the Irish preoccupation with symbolism and sovereignty:

> Why should I want to go back
> To you, Ireland, my Ireland?
> The blots on the page are so black
> That they cannot be covered with shamrock.
> I hate your grandiose airs,
> Your sob-stuff, your laugh and your swagger,
> Your assumption that everyone cares
> Who is the king of your castle.
> Castles are out of date,
> The tide flows round the children's sandy fancy;
> Put up what flag you like, it is too late
> To save your soul with bunting.[1]

MacNeice saw Ireland's narrow nationalism as an anachronism, his views no doubt coloured by the internationalism prevalent in intellectual circles at the time of the Spanish Civil War and by the belief that all of Europe was soon to be engulfed by a war which would make Ireland's internal conflicts seem trivial by comparison. Yet the world war which seemed imminent in 1938 was itself a spectacular demonstration of the power of nationalism. While it was probably true that few outside Ireland cared who was king of the Irish castle, the Second World War showed that people everywhere cared deeply, not only about who was king of their own castles, but also about which castle enclosed them within its walls, and about which flag flew from its battlements.

Lack of concern about sovereignty and nationhood is generally the privilege of people who live in states where there is a secure and widely shared sense of national identity, where the sovereignty and territorial integrity of the state faces no serious challenge. In such states, nationalism has not disappeared: it has simply become banal. The state's symbols go largely unnoticed and unchallenged, yet they work to remind citizens of their nationality and to reinforce their sense of a stable and secure national identity. In new states and states which have undergone a revolutionary transformation, by contrast, national symbols are still 'hot': they are argued about, defaced, flaunted in opponents' faces. However, in time the political temperature in such states may cool down, and as it does so the relationship of citizens to national symbols will change, as Michael Billig explains: 'One might predict that, as a nation-state becomes established in its sovereignty, and if it faces little internal challenge, then the symbols of nationhood, which might once have been consciously displayed, do not disappear from sight, but instead become absorbed into the environment of the established homeland.'[2] As citizens gradually lose their conscious awareness of these symbols, nationalism becomes banal. This is what happened in the Irish Free State, and what so conspicuously failed to happen in Northern Ireland.

In 1922, nationalism in Ireland was still white hot, and national flags were still waved with passion. The decade leading up to the establishment of the two Irish states had seen widespread political mobilisation and conflict, in which national symbols played an important role. In this period symbols assisted in the creation of a new 'provincial' identity for Ulster unionists; they allowed Sinn Féin to distinguish itself from the Irish Parliamentary Party; and they were used by all parties to rally supporters and challenge opponents. By the time the two Irish states were set up, Irish people were probably more divided over questions of symbolism than ever before.

It is not surprising, then, that national symbols were highly charged politically in the early years of the Irish Free State. Republicans quarrelled with Free Staters over the right to use Sinn Féin's symbols, while ex-unionists and Redmondites lamented the replacement of their symbols by those of Sinn Féin. The Sinn Féin legacy was not the only contentious issue: the debate about the new coinage revealed divisions over how best to represent the nation's ideals and differences of opinion about the position of religion in public life. The debates which occurred in the first decade of the Free State's existence were in part a result of the process of selection of official symbols which went on during the 1920s. But they also reflected the anxieties of people living through a time of political turmoil, in a state which had not yet achieved political stability. Symbols which were felt to be inappropriate might accentuate those anxieties, and the Free State coinage designs seem to have had this effect on many people. However, symbols could also help to assuage anxieties, particularly by providing a comforting sense of continuity. To pro-Treaty Sinn Féiners, for example, the Free State's adoption of the Sinn Féin flag and anthem was a reassuring sign that acceptance of dominion status did not entail an abandonment of separatist principles.

While the official symbols of the Free State were a focus for anxiety and debate in the short term, in the longer term they probably assisted in the political stabilisation of the state. Since the most significant challenge to the state's legitimacy, and the most dangerous threat to its stability, came from the republican opposition, the Cumann na nGaedheal government's attempt to eliminate the symbolic distinction between itself and the republicans assisted the development of political stability. This policy simultaneously denied propaganda opportunities to republicans, isolated republican diehards by giving the lie to their claims that the Free State was still controlled by Britain, and made the Free State seem more compatible with republican ideals, thereby aiding the integration of the bulk of republicans into constitutional politics. At the same time, by selectively using some of the older Irish national symbols such as the harp and the female personification of Ireland (while avoiding the full panoply of nineteenth-century symbols, which would have been too reminiscent of the Irish Parliamentary Party's iconography) the government asserted the state's legitimacy as the inheritor of a long tradition of Irish nationhood.

Alvin Jackson has claimed that 'Cumann na nGaedheal offered the Irish people structures, not symbols', contrasting the pro-Treaty party with its 'symbolically charged' Fianna Fáil opponents.[3] This is a false distinction. By providing the Free State with as many of the symbols of independent nationhood as it could get away with under the Treaty, Cumann na nGaedheal not only helped to stabilise the political structures which it created, but also prepared the way for Fianna Fáil to cut the state's remaining ties with Britain. So successful was Cumann na nGaedheal's symbolic strategy that when Fianna Fáil came to power in 1932 the new government made no changes to the state's official symbols. Since its victory failed to bring about a thirty-two county republic, the Fianna Fáil government had as much cause as its predecessor to identify the state symbolically both with the post-1916 Sinn Féin tradition and with the historic Irish nation.

From 1932 onwards, nationalism in the independent Irish state began to become banal. Once Fianna Fáil took power all but a tiny republican rump fully accepted the state's legitimacy, and moderate republicans could at last feel that the Sinn Féin symbols were being used by a government which lived up to the ideals of 1916. At the same time, the tricolour and 'The Soldier's Song' came increasingly to be seen, not as representing any particular party or political viewpoint, but as symbols of the Irish nation. Debates about the Free State's official symbols had largely died down by the end of 1932, although bitter political conflicts about other issues continued through the 1930s. With militant republicanism sidelined, the remnants of Redmondism largely integrated into Fine Gael, and ex-unionists leaving the country or retreating into political quiescence, there were few independent voices left to challenge the symbolic consensus which, despite their differences on other issues, united the two major parties which had emerged from Sinn Féin.

No such consensus emerged in Northern Ireland because there was no shared sense of national identity. Whereas in the Free State 'the national question' was gradually pushed from the centre of political life, in Northern Ireland the constitutional status of the Six Counties remained the dominant political issue and every election was fought on a 'Union Jack versus tricolour' basis. Thus, nationalism in Northern Ireland never became banal, and the province's people remained very conscious of national symbols. As debates over the display of the tricolour and the Union Jack showed, both nationalists and unionists were quick to notice, and to take offence at, displays of their opponents' symbols. Each group saw the other's symbols as divisive, as emblems of a particular party and community, and took the public display of the other community's symbols as a provocation.

The profound differences between nationalists and unionists also ensured that no symbolic consensus emerged between the Free State and Northern Ireland, and that symbols acted as obstacles to Irish unity. The governments of both states used symbols to define their relationship to Britain, but the nature of that relationship was radically different in each state. While the government of Northern Ireland made every effort to identify the Six Counties symbolically with the rest of the United Kingdom, the Free State government used symbols to distinguish the state from Britain and to demonstrate that the Free State had achieved full independence. There was little symbolic common ground between nationalists and unionists, and the strong attachment of each community to its own symbols helped to entrench partition.

Despite the differences between the Irish Free State and Northern Ireland, there were also a number of striking similarities when it came to questions of national symbolism. Both states chose symbols free of overtly sectarian devices: there was no Sacred Heart on the Free State flag or coins, no Orange emblems in Northern Ireland's coat of arms. In fact, the symbols chosen by both states were remarkably secular for a country where religious feeling was so strong. Governments in both parts of Ireland, it would seem, had no wish to offend their religious minorities by displays of naked sectarianism on symbols which were meant to represent all the people of the state.

However, if religious sectarianism was not entirely respectable (despite notorious instances of religiously sectarian statements by leaders in both states), what might be called 'national sectarianism' was widely endorsed. There was little support on either side of the border for symbolic pluralism, and the idea that minorities in each state could have dual loyalties was neither encouraged nor even considered by the majority communities. Ex-unionists in the Free State who displayed Union Jacks or sang 'God Save the King' were assumed by nationalists to be loyal to

Britain and disloyal to Ireland; nationalists in Northern Ireland were assumed by unionists to be disloyal to the United Kingdom and loyal to the Irish Free State if they waved the tricolour or sang 'The Soldier's Song'. At the same time, such disapproval was combined with a degree of official tolerance of displays of minority national symbols, with the preservation of public order the main concern of both governments.

There was another important respect in which the governments of Northern Ireland and the Free State were alike: neither actively used official symbols in order to promote nation building ('the process whereby the inhabitants of a state's territory come to be *loyal* citizens of that state'[4]). In the period 1870–1914, identified by Eric Hobsbawm as the era in which the requirements of nation building led to the invention of traditions 'with particular assiduity' in Europe and European-derived societies, the governments of such states as Third Republic France, Second Empire Germany and the United States of America consciously used symbols to develop loyalty to the state among the citizenry.[5] The French Third Republic disseminated its symbols widely through the schools, the army, local government, and other state institutions. This was part of the republicanisation of French political culture, an attempt to promote the symbols of the republic as opposed to those of monarchism and Catholicism, but it also played an important role in turning 'peasants into Frenchmen' by providing constant reminders of Frenchness in provinces where this national identity had not yet taken root.[6] In the United States the cult of the flag and its associated rituals (particularly the pledge of allegiance to the flag in schools) became a central part of American civil religion, helping to revive a national identity which could unite North and South after the Civil War and to integrate the large immigrant population into American civil society.[7] Nor did the use of symbols in this way cease after the First World War: on the contrary, the inter-war period produced academic affirmations of the importance of symbols in 'civic training'[8] and saw the rise to power in Italy and Germany of regimes which recognised 'very important matters in these apparent trifles' and accordingly devoted considerable attention to the use of symbols in inculcating allegiance to the state.[9]

While neither the Free State nor Northern Ireland governments followed the example of those states which used official symbols in the nation-building process, the reasons were very different in each case. In the Free State there was little need to use symbols in this way, because, despite the differences among nationalists, they all shared a secure Irish identity. This identity had been built up in the course of a century of nationalist agitation, during which nationalist political organisations had formed a sort of counter-state with its own myths, rituals and symbols. Thus, by the time the Irish Free State was established, a shared national consciousness had already been created among the great bulk of the Irish Catholic population, and the process of turning peasants into Irish men and women was largely complete. The problem, then, was not to convince people that they were Irish, but rather to persuade them that the new state was indeed the inheritor of the tradition of Irish nationhood and that its emblems were appropriate representations of that tradition. Instead of trying to instil loyalty to the state and its symbols, both Cumann na nGaedheal and Fianna Fáil governments concentrated on promoting a particular view of the nation. Both major parties were led by cultural nationalists who were concerned to develop the notion of Ireland as a Gaelic nation, and who were more interested in the teaching of the Irish language and Irish history than in flag rituals or the singing of the national anthem.

The influences on the Northern Ireland government's lack of interest in using symbols in nation building were rather different. For a start, there was less emphasis in the United Kingdom as a whole on using symbols in this way than in some other European states (a factor which probably also influenced the Free State's approach, though its leaders would have been reluctant to admit as much). In addition, the Northern Ireland government did not set out to create or reinforce an 'Ulster' or 'Northern Ireland' identity, preferring to emphasise the province's status as an integral part of the United Kingdom. Perhaps the most important influence on the government's policy, though, was an attitude which could be described as 'political Calvinism'. Writers such as Steve Bruce and Donald Akenson have noted the importance of Calvinism in shaping the outlook of Ulster Presbyterians in particular, but also more generally of Ulster Protestants.[10] As Akenson points out, the Calvinist doctrine of the elect encouraged Ulster Presbyterians to show little interest in proselytising the local Catholic population because, 'vulgarly put, the heathen were predestined to be heathen and that was that'.[11] Whether or not the Calvinist heritage was to blame, unionists in Northern Ireland commonly took a remarkably similar view of nationalists: they were incorrigibly disloyal, and neither political reform nor civic training programs aimed at instilling loyalty to the state would change this. This way of thinking was made explicit following the Newry flag controversy of 1932, in a *Londonderry Sentinel* editorial which used the language of inherence: 'Loyalty is an *instinct* with the Ulster Protestants. It is not, unfortunately, an instinct with the minority of the population. Disrespect for the flag and disloyalty for everything that it symbolises is *ingrained* in this minority'.[12] Protestants, apparently, did not need to be taught to be loyal, while Catholics were simply beyond hope.

If nationalism is to become banal, the nation/state must be seen as a given and its symbols must be considered intrinsic to it: national symbols must become an unchallenged and largely unconsidered part of everyday life. This position was never reached in Northern Ireland. In the remainder of the island, the symbols of the state came to be generally accepted as the symbols of the Irish nation, and largely ceased to be the subject of debate until events in Northern Ireland put them back on the agenda. The violence in Northern Ireland has forced a reassessment of national symbols in both parts of Ireland. In the Republic, the conflict prompted many to reconsider the Sinn Féin tradition, and the association of the state's flag and anthem with that tradition. It also brought home to them the fact that unionists did not see the Republic's symbols as apolitical emblems of a shared Irish nationality. In Northern Ireland, too, questions of symbolism have been re-examined as part of the search for a way to end the political conflict, and there has been growing acceptance of the need to find ways of managing conflict over symbols.

These current debates may be assisted by an understanding of the role of national symbols in Irish politics over the past century. Present-day polemicists themselves refer back to this history: nationalists cite bans on the display of the tricolour as an example of the discrimination which made Northern Ireland a 'failed political entity',[13] while unionists point to the example of the Irish Free State when arguing that attempts to remove British symbols from public life in Northern Ireland are the thin end of a republican wedge.[14] It would be naive to expect that such selective appeals to history will be brought to an end by an examination of the historical evidence, but historians can at least contribute to the ongoing debate by providing a more complex picture of the use of symbols in the past. They can also help to explain why national symbols are so contentious and so important to people.

I have argued that national symbols become the subject of debate because they are crucial to the imagining of nations, because they are ambiguous, and because they are emotionally charged as a result of the associations they have built up. People use debates about national symbols as an opportunity to talk about the nation: its past and future, its values and ideals, its boundaries of inclusion and exclusion. However, while I have sought to challenge the dismissive view of symbols discussed in the introduction to this book, I do not wish to go to the other extreme and argue that symbols are all-important. As Anthony Buckley has usefully reminded us, conflict and division in Northern Ireland are not just about symbolism or about 'culture': there are material realities behind the symbols which cannot be ignored.[15] While my focus in this book has been on symbols, I do not seek to downplay the importance of other dimensions of political conflict in Ireland.

Notwithstanding these cautionary comments, it is clear that symbols are an integral part of political conflict, and that symbolic disputes must therefore be taken seriously if such conflicts are to be resolved.

Frustration at the seeming intractability of Irish political conflicts, like that expressed by Louis MacNeice, is understandable, but dismissing people's concerns about questions of symbolism will not make it any easier to find a solution to the conflict in Northern Ireland. The 1990s saw a growing appreciation of the importance of symbols, and a willingness to be more conciliatory in relation to the symbols of others, on the part of many Irish political leaders. In her inaugural address on becoming President of the Republic of Ireland in 1990, Mary Robinson outlined her own attitude towards the role of symbols in reconciliation:

> As the elected choice of the people of this part of our island I want to extend the hand of friendship and of love to both communities in the other part... As the person chosen by you to symbolise this Republic and to project our self image to others, I will seek to encourage mutual understanding and tolerance between all the different communities sharing this island.
>
> In seeking to do this I shall rely to a large extent on symbols. But symbols are what unite and divide people. Symbols give us our identity, our self image, our way of explaining ourselves to ourselves and to others. Symbols in turn determine the kinds of stories we tell; and the stories we tell determine the kind of history we make and remake. I want Áras an Uachtaráin to be a place where people can tell diverse stories – in the knowledge that there is someone there to listen.[16]

To Mary Robinson's diversity of symbols and stories I would add a diversity of stories *about* symbols. A willingness to admit that the same symbol can be interpreted in radically different ways, and to explore the meanings which symbols have for others, is an essential precondition for reconciliation. An acceptance of diversity need not threaten the attachment of individuals and groups to their own symbols, but such acceptance is vital if there is to be a lasting resolution of the Northern Ireland conflict.

For fifty years the two parts of Ireland, and the nationalist and unionist communities within each state, were largely left to their own devices. Now those devices – the flags, anthems and emblems – must be placed on the table alongside the myths and the memories, the guns and the bombs, to become the subject of dialogue. Symbols are not designed to kill or maim, so there is no need to take them out of commission, but they can be socially explosive: 'as lethal to toy with as a mercury switch booby trap', in the words of Kevin Myers.[17] Although it is still necessary to tread warily, the Good Friday Agreement, with its commitment to using symbols to promote 'mutual respect rather than division', gives cause for hope that these devices will, in time, be defused.

Notes

Notes to Introduction

1 *Northern Ireland Parliamentary Debates: House of Commons*, Vol. 9, 16 October 1928, cols 2326–7.
2 Quoted in S. Nelson, *Ulster's Uncertain Defenders: Protestant Political, Paramilitary and Community Groups and the Northern Ireland Conflict* (Belfast: Appletree Press, 1984), p. 37.
3 See, for example, the comments of the Letters Editor in *Sydney Morning Herald*, 19 August 1996, p. 12.
4 L.M. Danforth, *The Macedonian Conflict: Ethnic Nationalism in a Transnational World* (Princeton: Princeton University Press, 1995), ch. 6.
5 L. Bryson and C. McCartney, *Clashing Symbols? A Report on the Use of Flags, Anthems and Other National Symbols in Northern Ireland* (Belfast: Institute of Irish Studies, 1994).
6 *Independent International*, 29 March–4 April 2000, p. 13.
7 Z. Mach, *Symbols, Conflict and Identity: Essays in Political Anthropology* (Albany: State University of New York Press, 1993), p. 23.
8 R. Firth, *Symbols: Public and Private* (London: George Allen & Unwin, 1973), p. 75; on the importance of symbols in conveying ideas and emotions which cannot easily be represented non-symbolically see Mach, *Symbols, Conflict and Identity: Essays in Political Anthropology*, pp. 32, 35.
9 R. Firth, *Symbols: Public and Private*, pp. 64–5.
10 P. Burke, 'Historians, Anthropologists, and Symbols', in E. Ohnuki-Tierney (ed.), *Culture Through Time: Anthropological Approaches* (Stanford: Stanford University Press, 1990), p. 277.
11 Ibid., pp. 279–281.
12 L. Hunt, *Politics, Culture, and Class in the French Revolution* (Berkeley: University of California Press, 1984), p. 91.
13 Ibid., pp. 90–2.
14 R. Girardet, 'The Three Colors: Neither White Nor Red', in Pierre Nora (ed.), *Realms of Memory: The Construction of the French Past*, Vol. 3, *Symbols*, English language ed. L. D. Kritzman, trans. A. Goldhammer (New York: Columbia University Press, 1998); M. Vovelle, 'La Marseillaise: War or Peace', in Pierre Nora (ed.), *Realms of Memory: The Construction of the French Past*, Vol. 3, *Symbols*, English language ed. L. D. Kritzman, trans. A. Goldhammer (New York: Columbia University Press, 1998). M.

Agulhon, 'Politics, Images, and Symbols in Post-Revolutionary France', in S. Wilentz (ed.) *Rites of Power: Symbolism, Ritual and Politics since the Middle Ages* (Philadelphia: University of Pennsylvania Press, 1985).

15 See generally E. Hobsbawm and T. Ranger (eds), *The Invention of Tradition* (Cambridge: Cambridge University Press, 1983).

16 E. Hobsbawm, 'Introduction',in ibid., pp. 8–9; see also Agulhon, 'Politics, Images, and Symbols in Post-Revolutionary France', p. 194.

17 E. Hobsbawm, 'Mass-Producing Traditions: Europe, 1870–1914', in Hobsbawm and Ranger (eds), *The Invention of Tradition*, pp. 268–9.

18 On the popular use of the term 'tribalism' in relation to Northern Ireland, see J. McGarry and B. O'Leary, *Explaining Northern Ireland: Broken Images*, (Oxford: Blackwell, 1995), p. 216.

19 Even Maurice Agulhon, who certainly takes symbolism seriously, writes of the July Monarchy period, when political symbolism began to be more commonplace and less bitterly contentious, that France 'calmed down and *became civilized*' (Agulhon, 'Politics, Images, and Symbols in Post-Revolutionary France', p. 191 – italics added).

20 B. Anderson, *Imagined Communities: Reflections on the Origin and Spread of Nationalism*, 2nd edn (London: Verso, 1991).

21 D. I. Kertzer, *Ritual, Politics and Power* (New Haven: Yale University Press, 1988), p. 67.

22 Ibid., p. 11.

23 Mach, *Symbols, Conflict and Identity: Essays in Political Anthropology*, pp. 39–40.

24 Kertzer, *Ritual, Politics and Power*, p. 69 and ch. 4 generally.

25 Ibid., p. 71.

26 Hobsbawm, 'Introduction' in *Invention of Tradition*, p. 11.

27 G. A. Birmingham, *The Red Hand of Ulster* (New York: George H. Doran, 1912), p. 157.

28 Firth, *Symbols: Public and Private*, p. 78.

29 Maurice Barrès, *Scènes et Doctrines du Nationalisme*, Vol. 1, 1902, p. 3, quoted in E. Weber, *Peasants into Frenchmen: The Modernization of Rural France 1870–1914* (London: Chatto & Windus, 1977), pp. 440–1.

30 This point is explored and illustrated in D. I. Kertzer, *Politics & Symbols: The Italian Communist Party and the Fall of Communism* (New Haven: Yale University Press, 1996).

31 See Thomas Campbell's poem 'Ye Mariners of England' (quoted in Firth, *Symbols: Public and Private*, p. 343):
     Ye mariners of England
     That guard our native seas
     Whose flag has braved a thousand years
     The battle and the breeze.
   For an example of this poem being quoted in the course of a debate about the Union Jack in Northern Ireland, see Chapter 4.

32 'The Red Flag' in T. Radic, *Songs of Australian Working Life* (Elwood: Greenhouse Publications, 1989), p. 167.

33 M. Billig, *Banal Nationalism* (London: Sage, 1995) pp. 86–7; S. R. Weitman,

'National Flags: A Sociological Overview', *Semiotica* 8 (1973) pp. 328–67.

34　Firth, *Symbols: Public and Private*, pp. 336–7.

35　G. L. Mosse, 'National Anthems: The Nation Militant', in R. Grimm and J. Hermand (eds), *From Ode to Anthem: Problems of Lyric Poetry* (Wisconsin: University of Wisconsin Press, 1989).

36　Firth, *Symbols: Public and Private*, p. 336.

37　Billig, *Banal Nationalism*, pp. 5–6.

38　Ibid., pp. 41, 43.

39　G. Cubitt, 'Introduction', in G. Cubitt (ed.), *Imagining Nations* (Manchester: Manchester University Press, 1998) pp. 5–6. A useful theoretical discussion of conflict over symbols from an anthropological perspective is S. Harrison, 'Four Types of Symbolic Conflict', *Journal of the Royal Anthropological Institute* (N. S.) 1 (1995), pp. 255–72.

40　For convenience, I refer to both parts of Ireland as 'states', although Northern Ireland was part of a larger state (the United Kingdom of Great Britain and Northern Ireland) and is often disparagingly referred to by Irish nationalists as a 'statelet'.

41　Kertzer, *Ritual, Politics and Power*, p. 6.

Notes to Chapter 1

1　'An Irishman' in *Cork Examiner*, 28 December 1928, p. 12.

2　G. A. Hayes-McCoy, *A History of Irish Flags from Earliest Times* (Dublin: Academy Press, 1979) pp. 22–3, 43–7. On the female figure in symbolic harps see B. Boydell, 'The Female Harp: The Irish Harp in 18th and Early-19th-Century Romantic Nationalism', *RIdIM/RMCI Newsletter*, 20, 1 (1995) pp. 10–17. Boydell says that by the early nineteenth century there was 'a clear distinction... between the continued use of the winged-maiden harp to symbolise Ireland when seen from the British or protestant Anglo-Irish viewpoint, and a more realistic portrayal of the harp when seen from the Irish or nationalist perspective' (ibid., p. 12).

3　Hayes-McCoy, *A History of Irish Flags*, pp. 83–99, 109–21.

4　N. Vance, 'Celts, Carthaginians and Constitutions:Anglo-Irish Literary Relations 1780–1820', *Irish Historical Studies,* 22, 87 (1981), pp. 216–38; M. H. Thuente, *The Harp Re-strung: The United Irishmen and the Rise of Irish Literary Nationalism* (Syracuse: Syracuse University Press, 1994), p. 54.

5　B. Loftus, *Mirrors: Orange & Green* (Dundrum: Picture Press, 1994), pp. 70–2; N. O'Connor, *Bringing it all Back Home: The Influence of Irish Music* (London: BBC Books, 1991), p. 167; B. Boydell, 'Iconography of the Irish Harp as a National Symbol', in P. F. Devine and H. White (eds), *Irish Musical Studies, 5, The Maynooth International Musicological Conference 1995 Selected Proceedings: Part Two* (Blackrock: Four Courts Press, 1996), pp. 139–40; Thuente, *The Harp Re-strung: The United Irishmen and the Rise of Irish Literary Nationalism*, p. 29; P. Burke, *Popular Culture in Early Modern Europe* (London: Temple Smith, 1978), pp. 15–17.

6　J. Leerssen, *Remembrance and Imagination: Patterns in the Historical and Literary Representation of Ireland in the Nineteenth Century* (Notre Dame:

University of Notre Dame Press, 1997), pp. 81–2, 175; 'The Harp that once through Tara's Halls', in T. Moore, *Irish Melodies and Songs* (London: George Routledge & Sons, n.d.), p. 21.

7 Held in the collection of Trinity College Dublin.

8 J. Sheehy, *The Rediscovery of Ireland's Past: The Celtic Revival 1830–1930* (London: Thames & Hudson, 1980), p. 12; Boydell, 'The Iconography of the Irish Harp as a National Symbol', pp. 142–4.

9 E. C. Nelson, *Shamrock: Botany and History of an Irish Myth* (Kilkenny: Boethius Press, 1991), pp. 18–22, 27–32, 37, 42, 55–64; Hayes-McCoy, *A History of Irish Flags From Earliest Times*, pp. 100–8.

10 J. R. Hill, 'National Festivals, the State and "Protestant Ascendancy" in Ireland, 1790–1829', *Irish Historical Studies*, 24, 93 (1984), pp. 30–44, 47–51; Nelson, *Shamrock: Botany and History of an Irish Myth*, pp. 71–4.

11 *Northern Whig*, 18 March 1914, quoted in B. Walker, *Dancing to History's Tune: History, Myth and Politics in Ireland* (Belfast: Institute of Irish Studies, 1996), p. 80.

12 Nelson, *Shamrock: Botany and History of an Irish Myth*, pp. 90–114. For mid-century references to 'the shamrock shore' see G. Zimmerman, *Songs of Irish Rebellion: Political Street Ballads and Rebel Songs 1780–1900*, (Dublin: Allen Figgis, 1967), pp. 240, 254; D. Fitzpatrick, *Oceans of Consolation: Personal Accounts of Irish Migration to Australia* (Ithaca: Cornell University Press, 1984), p. 73.

13 Loftus, *Mirrors: Orange & Green*, p. 72; Sheehy, *Rediscovery of Ireland's Past: The Celtic Revival 1830–1930*, p. 13; Lady Morgan, *O'Donnel: A National Tale* (London: Henry Colburn, 1814), Vol. 3, p. 306.

14 On the scholarly debate about round towers see Leerssen, *Remembrance and Imagination: Patterns in the Historical and Literary Representation of Ireland in the Nineteenth Century*, pp. 108–40 (quote at p. 109).

15 T. N. Burke, *Ireland and the Irish: Lectures on Irish History and Biography* (New York: Lynch, Cole and Meehan, 1873), p. 39; *Ritual of the Ancient Order of Hibernians in America* (Saratoga, 1906), pp. 22–31, quoted in Leerssen, *Remembrance and Imagination*, p. 144.

16 Sheehy, *The Rediscovery of Ireland's Past: The Celtic Revival 1830–1930*, pp. 58–60, 62–3, 66, 69, 73.

17 On rising sun symbolism in Australia, for example, see V. Lindesay, *Aussie-osities* (Richmond: Greenhouse Publications, 1988), pp. 44–9; for sun symbolism on flags of the world see W. Smith, *Flags Through the Ages and Across the World* (Maidenhead: McGraw-Hill, 1975), pp. 314–15. On Masonic sun symbolism see M. C. Jacob, *Living the Enlightenment: Freemasonry and Politics in Eighteenth-Century Europe* (New York: Oxford University Press, 1991), pp. 145–6; M. Agulhon, *Marianne into Battle: Republican Imagery and Symbolism in France, 1789–1880*, trans. Janet Lloyd (Cambridge: Cambridge University Press, 1981), p. 86; C. L. Albanese, *Sons of the Fathers: The Civil Religion of the American Revolution* (Philadelphia: Temple University Press, 1976), p. 133.

18 Hayes-McCoy, *A History of Irish Flags from Earliest Times*, pp. 86, 88, 91,

155–7; Thuente, *The Harp Re-strung: The United Irishmen and the Rise of Irish Literary Nationalism*, pp. 90, 152.

19 J. Hutchinson, *The Dynamics of Cultural Nationalism: The Gaelic Revival and the Creation of the Irish Nation State* (London: Allen & Unwin, 1987), ch. 2.

20 Ibid., pp. 79–95; Sheehy, *The Rediscovery of Ireland's Past: The Celtic Revival 1830–1930*, ch. 2.

21 Preface to volume 1 of the *Dublin Penny Journal*, 1832, quoted in Hutchinson, *The Dynamics of Cultural Nationalism: The Gaelic Revival and the Creation of the Irish Nation State*, p. 79.

22 Loftus, *Mirrors: Orange & Green*, p. 72. This illustration had appeared the previous year in another periodical, the *Irish Rushlight*.

23 Loftus, *Mirrors: Orange & Green*, p. 72; F. O'Ferrall, 'Daniel O'Connell the "Liberator", 1775–1847: Changing Images', in R. Gillespie and B. P. Kennedy (eds), *Ireland: Art into History* (Dublin: Town House, 1994), pp. 97–9; 'Erin's King, or Daniel is no More' in Zimmerman, *Songs of Irish Rebellion: Political Street Ballads and Rebel Songs*, p. 232. On the 'Irish crown' and its relationship to the 'repeal cap' or 'cap of liberty' see Hayes-McCoy, *A History of Irish Flags from Earliest Times*, pp. 132–4; G. Owens, 'Constructing the Image of Daniel O'Connell', *History Ireland*, 7, 1, (1999), pp. 33–4.

24 G. Owens, 'Constructing the Repeal Spectacle: Monster Meetings and People Power in Pre-famine Ireland', in M. R. O'Connell (ed.), *People Power: Proceedings of the Third Annual Daniel O'Connell Workshop* (Dublin: Institute of Public Adminstration, 1993); Hayes-McCoy, *A History of Irish Flags from Earliest Times*, pp. 128–33.

25 Hutchinson, *Dynamics of Cultural Nationalism: The Gaelic Revival and the Creation of the Irish Nation State*, pp. 89–90; J. A. Murphy, 'O'Connell and the Gaelic World' in F. B. Nowlan and M. R. O'Connell (eds), *Daniel O'Connell: Portrait of a Radical* (Belfast: Appletree Press, 1984); O. MacDonagh, *States of Mind: Two Centuries of Anglo-Irish Conflict, 1780–1980* (London: Pimlico, 1992), pp. 5–6; G. L. Mosse, *The Nationalization of the Masses: Political Symbolism and Mass Movements in Germany from the Napoleonic Wars through the Third Reich* (New York: Howard Fertig, 1975), p. 4.

26 D. G. Boyce, *Nationalism in Ireland*, 2nd edn (London: Routledge, 1991), p. 159; Sheehy, *Rediscovery of Ireland's Past: The Celtic Revival 1830–1930*, p. 30.

27 See *The Spirit of the Nation: Ballads and Songs by the Writers of 'The Nation' with Original and Ancient Music Arranged for the Voice and Piano-forte*, 2nd edn (Dublin: James Duffy, 1882) – sunburst mentioned on pp. 3, 15, 28, 154, 167; harp or *cláirseach* on pp. 28, 83–4, 91–2, 130, 233, 235; shamrock on pp. 151, 249; also harps and rising sun depicted in frontispiece.

28 Ibid., pp. 235–6. Compare this optimistic view with the gloomy vision of the disillusioned radical William Drennan in his poem 'Glendalloch', written a few years after the Union:

Yon mould'ring pillar, 'midst the gloom,
Finger of Time! shall point her tomb;
While silence of the ev'ning hour
Hangs o'er Glendalloch's ruined tow'r.

(William Drennan, *Fugitive Pieces in Verse and Prose* (Belfast, 1815), p. 115, quoted in Vance, 'Celts, Carthaginians and Constitutions: Anglo-Irish Literary Relations, 1780–1820', p. 231.)

29 Hutchinson, *Dynamics of Cultural Nationalism: The Gaelic Revival and the Creation of the Irish Nation State*, pp. 95–106; Boyce, *Nationalism in Ireland*, pp. 154–64; Leerssen, *Remembrance and Imagination: Patterns in the Historical and Literary Representation of Ireland in the Nineteenth Century*, pp. 147–50; W.B. Yeats, *Autobiographies* (Dublin: Gill & Macmillan, 1955) p. 203.

30 Loftus, *Mirrors: Orange & Green*, p. 72; Sheehy, *The Rediscovery of Ireland's Past: The Celtic Revival 1830–1930*, ch. 5. The importance of mass production in creating a standardised and widely recognised set of symbols is discussed in relation to Irish unionist iconography in A. Jackson, 'Irish Unionist Imagery 1850–1920', in E. Patten (ed.), *Returning to Ourselves: Second Volume of Papers from the John Hewitt International Summer School* (Belfast: Lagan Press, 1995).

31 *United Ireland*, 15 October 1881, quoted in Hayes-McCoy, *A History of Irish Flags from Earliest Times*, p. 170.

32 See Ancient Order of Hibernians membership certificate in R. F. Foster (ed.), *The Oxford Illustrated History of Ireland* (Oxford: Oxford University Press, 1989), opposite p. 241; Irish National Foresters banner in D. Buckley and K. Anderson, *Brotherhoods in Ireland* (Cultra, Ulster Folk and Transport Museum, 1988) (no page number); Home Rule and Land League banners in Hayes-McCoy, *A History of Irish Flags from Earliest Times*, pp. 175–8; photo of Redmond in L. McRedmond (ed.), *Ireland: The Revolutionary Years Photographs from the Cashman Collection: Ireland 1910–30* (Dublin: Gill & Macmillan and Radio Telefís Éireann, 1992), pp. 8–9.

33 *Irish Freedom*, December 1912, p. 4.

34 *Dublin Opinion*, August 1923, p. 156.

35 M. Warner, *Monuments and Maidens: The Allegory of the Female Form* (London: Weidenfeld & Nicolson, 1985), p. 12.

36 J. Th. Leerssen, *Mere Irish & Fíor-Ghael: Studies in the Idea of Irish Nationality, its Development and Literary Expression Prior to the Nineteenth Century* (Amsterdam: John Benjamins, 1986), pp. 255, 474 and ch. 3.

37 See L. P. Curtis, *Apes and Angels: The Irishman in Victorian Caricature* (Newton Abbot: David & Charles, 1971), for the most hostile cartoons of Irishmen; but see also S. Gilley, 'English Attitudes to the Irish in England 1780–1900', in C. Holmes (ed.), *Immigrants and Minorities in British Society* (London: Allen & Unwin, 1978) and R. F. Foster, 'Paddy and Mr Punch', in his *Paddy and Mr Punch: Caricatures in Irish and English History* (London: Allen Lane, 1993) for a more nuanced view.

38 Curtis, *Apes and Angels: The Irishman in Victorian Caricature*, p. 75.
39 For the male figures on 1798 memorials, see G. Owens, 'Nationalist Monuments in Ireland *c*.1870–1914: Symbolism and Ritual', in B. P. Kennedy and R. Gillespie (eds), *Ireland: Art into History* (Dublin: Town House, 1994), pp. 108, 111, 115–17. On the pre-1916 Cúchulainn cult see M. Williams, 'Ancient Mythology and Revolutionary Ideology in Ireland, 1878–1916', *Historical Journal* 26, 2 (1983), pp. 307–28; P. Rafroidi, 'Imagination and Revolution: The Cuchulain Myth', in O. MacDonagh, W. F. Mandle and P. Travers (eds), *Irish Culture and Nationalism 1750–1950* (London: Macmillan, 1983).
40 D. Ó Corráin, 'Prehistoric and Early Christian Ireland', in R. F. Foster (ed.), *The Oxford History of Ireland* (Oxford: Oxford University Press, 1992), p. 24; C.F. Dalton, 'Tradition of Blood Sacrifice to the Goddess Éire', *Studies* 63, 252 (1974), pp. 345–54; J. T. Leerssen, *Mere Irish & Fíor-Ghael*, p. 247; P. S. Dinneen and T. O'Donoghue (eds), *Dánta Aodhagáin Uí Rathaille: The Poems of Egan O'Rahilly* (London: Irish Texts Society, 1911), p. 6, quoted in J. Th. Leerssen, *Mere Irish & Fíor-Ghael*, p. 262.
41 Zimmerman, *Songs of Irish Rebellion: Political Street Ballads and Rebel Songs 1780–1900*, pp. 54–6, 88–91; J. Th. Leerssen, *Mere Irish & Fíor-Ghael*, pp. 282–3.
42 B. Loftus, *Mirrors: William III & Mother Ireland* (Dundrum: Picture Press, 1990), pp. 50–2; Aodh Mac Aingil, *Scáthán Shacramuinte na hAithridhe*, ed. C. Ó Maonaigh (Dublin, 1952), p. 190, quoted in A. Mac Póilin, '"Spiritual Beyond the Ways of Men": Images of the Gael', in E. Patten (ed.), *Returning to Ourselves: Second Volume of Papers from the John Hewitt International Summer School* (Belfast: Lagan Press, 1995), p. 367.
43 For example, Burke, *Ireland and the Irish: Lectures on Irish History and Biography*, p. 60 (my italics): 'I see her rising, emancipated; no trace of blood or persecution on her *virgin* face...I see her in peace and concord with all the nations around her, and with her own *children* within her.' See also Burke's celebration of Irish women for having taken the Virgin Mary as their model (ibid., p. 249): 'The Irish mother alone...displays, by some supernatural grace, the virginal expression of maiden innocence, blended with the beautiful expression of a mother's love.'
44 T.N. Burke, *Lectures on Faith and Fatherland* (Glasgow: Cameron and Ferguson, n.d.), pp. 117–18.
45 On the popular tradition of virgin martyrs in Europe generally, and the admiration of heroines not for what they did but for what they suffered, see Burke, *Popular Culture in Early Modern Europe*, p. 164.
46 Loftus, *Mirrors: William III & Mother Ireland*, pp. 52–6; Hayes-McCoy, *A History of Irish Flags from Earliest Times*, pp. 89, 91–3, 96, 99; C. L. Innes, *Woman and Nation in Irish Literature and Society, 1880–1935* (New York: Harvester Wheatsheaf, 1993), pp. 10–11. On the depiction of liberty as a woman see Agulhon, *Marianne into Battle: Republican Imagery and Symbolism in France*, ch. 1, and on the classical tradition

of symbolic female figures see Warner, *Monuments and Maidens: The Allegory of the Female Form.*

47 Loftus, *Mirrors: William III & Mother Ireland*, pp. 57–61; Hayes-McCoy, *A History of Irish Flags from Earliest Times*, pp. 131–2, 175–8; Sheehy, *The Rediscovery of Ireland's Past: The Celtic Revival 1830–1930*, pp. 52–3.

48 E. Hayes (ed.), *Ballads of Ireland*, 1 (London: A. Fullarton, 1855), p. xxvi, quoted in S. Ryder, 'Gender and the Discourse of "Young Ireland" Cultural Nationalism', in T.P. Foley, L. Pilkington, S. Ryder and E. Tilley (eds), *Gender and Colonialism* (Galway: Galway University Press, 1995), pp. 215–6.

49 Curtis, *Apes and Angels: The Irishman in Victorian Caricature*, pp. 25, 37, 38, 41, 46, 81.

50 Owens, 'Nationalist Monuments in Ireland *c.*1870–1914: Symbolism and Ritual', pp. 114–15; Loftus, *Mirrors: William III & Mother Ireland*, p. 66.

51 Dalton, 'The Tradition of Blood Sacrifice to the Goddess Éire', pp. 351–2; Innes, *Woman and Nation in Irish Literature and Society, 1880–1935*, pp. 44–8.

52 R. Kearney, *Transitions: Narratives in Modern Irish Culture* (Dublin: Wolfhound, 1988), p. 218.

53 'Proclamation of the Republic', in R.F. Foster, *Modern Ireland 1600–1972* (London: Penguin, 1988), pp. 597–8 (my italics).

54 See Agulhon, *Marianne into Battle: Republican Imagery and Symbolism in France, 1789–1880*, p. 39 for Delacroix's famous painting.

55 Innes, *Woman and Nation in Irish Literature and Society*, p. 24.

56 Advertised on the inside cover of P. Ó Cearnaigh, *Camp-fire Songs* (Dublin: Art Depot, n.d.); see also Loftus, *Mirrors: William III & Mother Ireland*, pp. 64–5.

57 S. Gilley, 'Pearse's Sacrifice: Christ and Cuchulain Crucified and Risen in the Easter Rising, 1916', in Y. Alexander and A. O'Day (eds), *Ireland's Terrorist Dilemma* (Dordrecht: Martinus Nijhoff, 1986), pp. 36–7.

58 Loftus, *Mirrors: William III & Mother Ireland*, p. 62. MacNeill's memorandum quoted in C. Townshend, *Political Violence in Ireland: Government and Resistance since 1848* (Oxford: Clarendon Press, 1983), pp. 295–6.

59 B. Ó Cuív, 'The Wearing of the Green' *Studia Hibernica*, 17/18 (1977–78) pp. 107–19; Loftus, *Mirrors: Orange & Green*, pp. 68–70; Zimmerman, *Songs of Irish Rebellion: Political Street Ballads and Rebel Songs 1780–1900*, pp. 41–3; Hayes-McCoy, *A History of Irish Flags from Earliest Times*, pp. 111–13.

60 Hayes-McCoy, *A History of Irish Flags from Earliest Times*, pp. 114–19, 128–9; Owens, 'Constructing the Repeal Spectacle: Monster Meetings and People Power in Pre-Famine Ireland', pp. 86, 90–1; P. Alter, 'Symbols of Irish Nationalism', *Studia Hibernica*, 14 (1974), pp. 106–7; S. Ó Brógáin, *The Wolfhound Guide to the Irish Harp Emblem* (Dublin: Wolfhound Press, 1998), ch. 3.

61 Hayes-McCoy, *A History of Irish Flags from Earliest Times*, p. 192.

62 See the Orange ditty quoted in P. Orr, *The Road to the Somme: Men of the*

Ulster Division Tell Their Story (Belfast: Blackstaff, 1987), p. 58; *Orange Standard* (England), January 1920, p. 7.

63 Hayes-McCoy, *A History of Irish Flags from Earliest Times*, pp. 141–8, 197.

64 For examples see Zimmerman, *Songs of Irish Rebellion: Political Street Ballads and Rebel Songs 1780–1900*.

65 Hill, 'National Festivals, the State and "Protestant Ascendancy" in Ireland, 1790–1829', pp. 43–4, 48; *Dublin Evening Mail*, 5 December 1924, p. 4. For an example of the use of 'St Patrick's Day' in a distinctly imperial context in 1911 see Hayes-McCoy, *A History of Irish Flags from Earliest Times*, p. 189.

66 Leerssen, *Remembrance and Imagination: Patterns in the Historical and Literary Representation of Ireland in the Nineteenth Century*, p. 147. The lyrics of 'A Nation Once Again' can be found in *The Spirit of the Nation: Ballads and Songs by the Writers of 'The Nation' with Original and Ancient Music Arranged for the Voice and Piano-forte*, pp. 238–9.

67 Alter, 'Symbols of Irish Nationalism', pp. 109–12; Boyce, *Nationalism in Ireland*, pp. 184–5, 210. For the lyrics of 'God Save Ireland' see Zimmerman, *Songs of Irish Rebellion: Political Street Ballads and Rebel Songs 1780–1900*, pp. 266–7.

68 Mr Anthony in *Dáil Debates*, vol. 50, 22 November 1933, col. 415; Zimmerman, *Songs of Irish Rebellion: Political Street Ballads and Rebel Songs 1780–1900*, p. 64; F. Callanan, *T.M. Healy* (Cork: Cork University Press, 1996), p. 383. T.D. Sullivan, author of 'God Save Ireland', was both uncle and father-in-law of the anti-Parnellite leader Tim Healy (Callanan, *T.M. Healy*, pp. 7–8).

69 Note on interview with Ó Cearnaigh on Radio Athlone, 2 November 1935, in 101/179, Department of Foreign Affairs, National Archives of Ireland (NAI); D. Fitzpatrick, 'Militarism in Ireland 1900–1922', in T. Bartlett and K. Jeffery (eds), *A Military History of Ireland* (Cambridge: Cambridge University Press, 1996).

70 *Irish Freedom*, September 1912, p. 7; P. de Burca, 'The Story of the Soldier's Song', in W. G. Fitzgerald (ed.), *The Voice of Ireland: A Survey of the Race and Nation From All Angles* (Dublin: Virtue, n.d.), p. 153. As de Burca pointed out (ibid.), the phrase 'Sworn to be free' would have had particular meaning for men like Ó Cearnaigh who had taken an oath to the secret Irish Republican Brotherhood.

71 S. O'Faoláin, *De Valera* (Harmondsworth: Penguin, 1939), p. 37.

72 F. X. Martin, '1916 – Myth, Fact, and Mystery', *Studia Hibernica*, 7 (1967), p. 10. On 'demonstration politics' see Townshend, *Political Violence in Ireland: Government and Resistance since 1848*, p. 312, and on the rising generally see ibid., pp. 277–313.

73 Hayes-McCoy, *A History of Irish Flags from Earliest Times*, pp. 199–203. The O'Rahilly's notes on flags and heraldry can be found in P102/221-224, University College Dublin Archives Department.

74 P.H. Pearse, *Political Writings and Speeches* (Dublin: Talbot Press, 1962),

pp. 149–51. For examples of Pearse's words on symbolism being quoted in the inter-war period see *Irish Press*, 3 February 1932, p. 1; *Irish Independent*, 22 January 1932, p. 12.

75 'The Irish Flag', *Workers' Republic*, 8 April 1916, reprinted in S. Deane (ed.), *The Field Day Anthology of Irish Writing* (Derry: Field Day, 1991), Vol. 3, pp. 732–3.

76 Hayes-McCoy, *A History of Irish Flags from Earliest Times*, p. 208.

77 Hayes-McCoy, *A History of Irish Flags from Earliest Times*, pp. 206–20; Loftus, *Mirrors: Orange & Green*, pp. 84–5.

78 Ó Brógáin, *The Wolfhound Guide to the Irish Harp Emblem*, p. 34.

79 Madge Callanan to James Ryan, 8 June 1916, in P88/19, University College Dublin Archives Department.

80 E. O'Malley, *On Another Man's Wound* (London: Rich & Cowan, 1936), p. 45; see also J. Augusteijn, *From Public Defiance to Guerilla Warfare: The Experience of Ordinary Volunteers in the Irish War of Independence 1916–1921* (Blackrock: Irish Academic Press, 1996), pp. 55, 252.

81 *Irish News*, 10 April 1917, p. 2; Hayes-McCoy, *A History of Irish Flags from Earliest Times*, p. 220; Loftus, *Mirrors: Orange & Green*, p. 86; Inspector-General's report for April 1917 in Box 102, Colonial Office Class CO 904 (viewed on microfilm in the 'British in Ireland' series, reel 64); O'Malley, *On Another Man's Wound*, p. 64; Augusteijn, *From Public Defiance to Guerilla Warfare: The Experience of Ordinary Volunteers in the Irish War of Independence 1916–1921*, p. 228.

82 Augusteijn, *From Public Defiance to Guerilla Warfare*, p. 67; *Nationality*, 9 June 1917, p. 4, 4 May 1918, p. 2.

83 See, for example the ballads in the collection 'Irish Political Song and Poem Leaflets 1915–1932' in the National Library of Ireland.

84 *Nationality*, 26 May 1917, p. 2.

85 'The Boys from the County Cork' in P. Galvin, *Irish Songs of Resistance (1169–1923)* (London: Oak Publications, 1962), p. 70.

86 Hayes-McCoy, *A History of Irish Flags from Earliest Times*, p. 224.

87 Joseph Stanley, 'The Flag of Freedom' in *Songs of Battle* (Dublin: Art Depot, n.d.), p. 5; 'The Tricolour Flag' in *Songs of the Green, White & Gold* (n.p., no publisher, 1919), p. 2; Loftus, *Mirrors: Orange & Green*, p. 86.

88 *What Sinn Fein Must Meet and Beat* (reprinted from *The Irishman*, 10 August 1918); *Under Which Flag?: An Appeal to the Electors of Great Britain* (Dublin: Irish Unionist Alliance, 1918) (both pamphlets held in National Library of Ireland).

89 Statement with reference to the history of 'The Soldier's Song', enclosed with letter from M.A. Walton, 9 October 1931, in S7395A, Department of the Taoiseach, NAI; Peadar Kearney, interview on Radio Athlone, 2 November 1935, summarised in 101/179, Department of Foreign Affairs, NAI.

90 For examples of the singing of 'The Soldier's Song' see *Irish News*, 8 June 1918, p. 2; O'Faoláin, *De Valera*, pp. 46–7. For the use of phrases from the song's lyrics see photo of de Valera addressing a meeting in County Clare

in 1917, standing behind a banner proclaiming 'Soldiers Are We Whose Lives Are Pledged to Ireland' (J. Mackay, *Michael Collins: A Life* (Edinburgh: Mainstream, 1996), between pages 256 and 257); Rev. P. Gaynor, *The Faith and Morals of Sinn Fein* (Dublin: Art Depot, n.d.), p. 4: if God 'meant us to be a slave-nation, why has He made us "children of a fighting race?"'

91 D.J. Murphy (ed.), *Lady Gregory's Journals*, Vol. 1 (Gerrards Cross: Colin Smythe, 1978 and 1987), p. 35.

92 Patrick Pearse linked the bearing of arms to manhood and virility in his writings before the Easter Rising – see Pearse, *Political Writings and Speeches*, pp. 195–6, 204, 206. On young men and the IRA see P. Hart, *The I.R.A. and its Enemies: Violence and Community in Cork, 1916–1923* (Oxford: Clarendon Press, 1998), ch. 8.

93 Hart, *The I.R.A. and its Enemies: Violence and Community in Cork, 1916–1923*, p. 203.

94 *Leader*, 1 September 1917, p. 81, quoted in P. Maume, *'Life That is Exile': Daniel Corkery and the Search for Irish Ireland* (Belfast: Institute of Irish Studies, 1993), p. 63.

95 Murphy (ed.), *Lady Gregory's Journals*, Vol. 1, pp. 215, 317. On the Wren Boys and their connection with 'the boys' of the IRA see Hart, *The I.R.A. and its Enemies: Violence and Community in Cork, 1916–1923*, pp. 178–83.

96 A. Jackson, 'Irish Unionist Imagery, 1850–1920', in E. Patten (ed.), *Returning to Ourselves: Second Volume of Papers from the John Hewitt International Summer School*, p. 353; Nelson, *Shamrock: Botany and History of an Irish Myth*, pp. 115–20, 137–8; Hayes-McCoy, *A History of Irish Flags from Earliest Times*, pp. 188–91; M. Tierney, P. Bowen and D. Fitzpatrick, 'Recruiting Posters', in D. Fitzpatrick (ed.), *Ireland and the First World War* (Dublin: Trinity History Workshop, 1986), p. 51.

97 I use the term 'Redmondite' as convenient shorthand for supporters of the Irish Parliamentary Party, which was led by John Redmond from 1900 until his death in 1918.

98 Gaynor, *The Faith and Morals of Sinn Fein*, p. 1.

99 See bone harp by Sean O'Neill, Ballykinlar internee, 1920, on display in the National Museum of Ireland; bone harp from Tintown camp, 1923, in the collection of Kilmainham Jail Museum; painted handkerchief in Loftus, *Mirrors: Orange & Green*, p. 86; autograph books 19 MS IC 24 08, 19 MS IC 25 03, 19 MS IC 24 07, 19 MS IC 24 01 in the collection of Kilmainham Jail Museum.

100 Memorial card for Tommy Bryan in the collection of Kilmainham Jail Museum; Hayes-McCoy, *A History of Irish Flags from Earliest Times*, p. 222; *Nationality*, 4 May 1918, p. 2. 'My Only Son was Shot in Dublin' quoted in E. Whitfield, 'Another Martyr for Old Ireland: The Balladry of Revolution', in D. Fitzpatrick (ed.), *Revolution?: Ireland 1917–1923* (Dublin: Trinity History Workshop, 1990), p. 66.

101 'The Boys of Kilmichael', quoted in Whitfield, 'Another Martyr for Old

Ireland: The Balladry of Revolution', p. 65.

102 'For Them Who Died' in *The Irish Soldier's Song Book* (Dublin: Fergus O'Connor, n.d.), pp. 15–16; 'The Tricolour Flag' in *Songs of the Green, White & Gold*, p. 2; advertisement for Whelan & Son in *Nationality*, 17 February 1917, p. 4.

103 'I Don't Mind if I do' in 'The Rajah of Frongoch', *Topical Ditties* (Dublin: Art Depot, n.d.), p. 8; *Nationality*, 30 November 1918, p. 1; Sinn Féin handbill headed 'Who are the Traitors to Ireland?', item 127, ILB 300 p1, National Library of Ireland.

104 Recalling Sinn Féin's campaign in the 1917 South Longford by-election, Brighid Lyons Thornton remarked that 'green flags meant the Irish Party' (quoted in K. Griffith and T.E. O'Grady, *Curious Journey: An Oral History of Ireland's Unfinished Revolution* (London: Hutchinson, 1982), p. 109).

105 *Irish News*, 1 April 1918, p. 3; *Freeman's Journal*, 11 December 1918, p. 4.

106 United Irish League handbill headed 'What is Wrong with the Green Flag?', item 80, ILB 300 p2, National Library of Ireland; also published in *Freeman's Journal*, 29 November 1918, p. 1.

107 *Freeman's Journal*, 13 December 1918, p. 4. See also *Freeman's Journal*, 28 November 1918, p. 4, 2 December 1918, p. 5, 3 December 1918, p. 4, 5 December 1918, p. 7, 14 December 1918, p. 4; also the new lyrics to 'The Wearin' of the Green', attacking Sinn Féin's desertion of the green flag, published by the United Irish League and included in 'Irish Political Song and Poem Leaflets 1915–1932' in the National Library of Ireland.

108 *Freeman's Journal*, 5 December 1918, p. 7, 13 December 1918, p. 4; *Irish News*, 3 December 1918, quoted in E. Phoenix, *Northern Nationalism: Nationalist Politics, Partition and the Catholic Minority in Northern Ireland 1890–1940* (Belfast: Ulster Historical Foundation, 1994), p. 52.

109 *Irish News*, 2 April 1918, p. 3.

110 Foster, *Modern Ireland 1600–1972*, p. 490.

111 RIC Inspector-General's Report for March 1919, Box 108, Colonial Office Class CO 904 (viewed on microfilm in 'The British in Ireland' series, reel 69); Phoenix, *Northern Nationalism: Nationalist Politics, Partition and the Catholic Minority in Northern Ireland 1890–1940*, p. 144.

112 'When the Clocks were Striking Noon' in the collection of 'Irish Political Song and Poem Leaflets 1915-1932', National Library of Ireland.

Notes to Chapter 2

1 Sadleir to Kennedy, 25 November 1922; Kennedy to Sadleir, 8 December 1922; Sadleir to Kennedy, 15 December 1922; Kennedy to the President, 18 December 1922, in S3088A, Department of the Taoiseach (DT), National Archives of Ireland (NAI).

2 Minister for Industry and Commerce, memorandum dated 18 February 1925, in S3088A, DT, NAI.

3 Secretary, Department of External Affairs, to Secretary, Executive Council, 7 April 1925, in S3088A, DT, NAI. On the Free State passports see

J. P. O'Grady, 'The Irish Free State Passport and the Question of Citizenship 1921–4', *Irish Historical Studies* 26, 104 (1989) pp. 396–405.

4   *Dáil Debates*, Vol. 15, 29 April 1926, col. 739.

5   Defence Force Regulations, D.F.R. 30/1929, 15 March 1929, 'Flags, Honours, Salutes, etc.', in S3088A, DT, NAI: 'The National Flag of Saorstat Eireann has three upright stripes of green, white and orange. The stripes are of equal dimensions, with the green next to the staff, white in the centre and orange farthest from the staff.'

6   Hayes-McCoy, *A History of Irish Flags from Earliest Times*, p. 231.

7   *An Bhratach Náisiúnta*, p. 6.

8   Memorandum by M. O Muimhneachain, 2 February 1937, and note dated 5 October 1947 (although this date appears to be incorrect) in S6583, DT, NAI; Hayes-McCoy, *A History of Irish Flags from Earliest Times*, p. 226.

9   Lester to McGann, 1 February 1924; Lester to Secretary, Executive Council, 24 April 1924; memorandum dated 27 May 1924, in S3767A, DT, NAI.

10 Lester to Secretary, President's Department, 3 July 1926; extract from minutes of Executive Council, 12 July 1926, in S3767A, DT, NAI.

11 Draft reply in S3767A, DT, NAI; *Dáil Debates*, Vol. 15, 20 July 1926, cols 2196–8.

12 Brase to Adjutant General, Department of Defence, 4 October 1928, in 3/22518, Department of Defence (DD), Military Archives of Ireland (MAI); extract from Executive Council minutes, 12 March 1929, in S3767A, DT, NAI; R. Sherry, 'The Story of the National Anthem' *History Ireland*, 4, 1 (1996), p. 41.

13 M. McDunphy, memorandum dated 31 March 1932, in S7395A, DT, NAI; memorandum from Department of the President, 2 July 1932, and note of Executive Council decision, 11 July 1932, in S3767A, DT, NAI.

14 Statements by Ó Cearnaigh dated 24 August 1926 and 26 August 1926; statement with reference to the history of 'The Soldier's Song', enclosed with letter from M.A. Walton, 9 October 1931; note to the President dated 6 November 1931, in S7395A, DT, NAI.

15 This correspondence is summed up in a memorandum to the Secretary, Department of Finance, 15 December 1932, in S7395A, DT, NAI, and in *Dáil Debates*, vol. 50, 22 November 1933, col. 409.

16 Seán MacEntee in *Dáil Debates*, Vol. 50, 22 November 1933, col. 410; extract from Cabinet minutes, 10 February 1933, and deed of transfer, 20 October 1933, in S7395A, DT, NAI.

17 T. Garvin, *1922: The Birth of Irish Democracy* (Dublin: Gill & Macmillan, 1996), pp. 54–5.

18 *United Irishman*, 21 May 1932, p. 1.

19 Francis J. Bigger in *Irish Independent*, 24 February 1922, p. 4.

20 *Irish Independent*, 19 March 1923, p. 8.

21 *An tÓglach*, 23 December 1922, p. 1.

22 Geo. A. Lyons in *Irish Independent*, 23 August 1926, p. 8; Sean O Coileain in *Irish Independent*, 14 March 1923, p. 6.

23 P. de Burca, 'The Story of the Soldier's Song', p. 153.

24 Lady Gregory, journal entry for 4 November 1928, in Murphy (ed.), *Lady Gregory's Journals*, Vol. 2, p. 334; Eamonn Trinseach in *The Times* (London), 18 June 1929, p. 12; *Round Table*, September 1929, p. 828.

25 D. O'Hegarty to J.W. Dulanty, 26 June 1929, in S6535, DT, NAI.

26 *Freeman*, 9 June 1928, p. 4.

27 Sherry, 'Story of the National Anthem', p. 40.

28 For republican comments pointing out the appropriateness, as they saw it, of this line in 'Let Erin Remember' see *Eire*, 31 May 1924, p. 5; *An Phoblacht*, 29 June 1929, p. 3.

29 *Dublin Opinion*, November 1923, p. 236.

30 Quoted in Boyce, *Nationalism in Ireland*, p. 22.

31 Quoted in Sherry, 'The Story of the National Anthem', p. 40.

32 Dáil Éireann, *Official Report: Debate on the Treaty Between Great Britain and Ireland Signed in London on the 6th December, 1921* (hereafter *Treaty Debate*), pp. 21, 96, 285–6, 384, 385.

33 *Irish Independent*, 6 March 1922, p. 3, 7 March 1922, p. 6, 20 March 1922, p. 6, 10 April 1922, p. 5; see also letter from Cumann na mBan Publicity Department, *Irish Press*, 14 May 1932, p. 6, claiming that such incidents occurred all over the country in 1922; and report in *Irish Independent*, 21 March 1922, p. 5, of tricolours draped in black being hung out the night before pro-Treaty meetings.

34 *Eire*, 14 April 1923, p. 7, 5 May 1923, p. 5.

35 James Ryan, 'Lines Written by a Republican Soldier in 1923', in L. H. Daiken (ed.), *Good-bye, Twilight: Songs of the Struggle in Ireland* (London: Lawrence & Wishart, 1936), pp. 90–1.

36 K. Griffith and T. E. O'Grady, *Curious Journey: An Oral History of Ireland's Unfinished Revolution*, p. 271; Dáil Éireann, *Official Report for Periods 16th August, 1921, to 26th August, 1921, and 28th February, 1922, to 8th June, 1922, with Index*, p. 360.

37 *Republic of Ireland/Poblacht na h-Eireann (Scottish edition)*, 28 October 1922, p. 7. See also the cartoon in *An Phoblacht*, 26 June 1925, p. 1, which shows a tricolour with the Union Jack in the corner flying above the Free State parliament, and the letter by J. Parnell Whity in *Irish Press*, 12 February 1932, p. 6, accusing Cumann na nGaedheal of wanting to place a Union Jack on the tricolour.

38 'The Irish Free State', in P. Galvin (ed.), *Irish Songs of Resistance (1169–1923)* (London: Oak Publications, 1962), p. 72.

39 *Plain People*, 21 May 1922, p. 1.

40 *Irish Times*, 19 November 1925, p. 8; see also George Gilmore quoted in *Cork Examiner*, 1 February 1930, p. 6.

41 *Plain People*, 21 May 1922, p. 1; *Irish Freedom*, November 1926, p. 3.

42 Loftus, *Mirrors: Orange & Green*, p. 86.

43 *Honesty*, 19 April 1930, p. 20; see also Cumann na mBan message calling on people to 'stand once more under the old Flag, the Flag of the Republic' by buying an Easter lily, in *An Phoblacht*, 9 April 1926, p. 1.

44 *Eire*, 31 May 1924, p. 5.

45   Miss J. Moynihan in *Honesty*, 29 June 1929, p. 17.
46   *Irish Freedom*, November 1927, p. 5; William Magennis in *Honesty*, 29 June 1929, p. 8; *Nation*, 16 November 1929, p. 4.
47   *An Phoblacht*, 15 June 1929, p. 3, 29 June 1929, p. 3.
48   *Irish News*, 9 May 1925, p. 6; J. M. Hone, 'The Royal Dublin Society and its Bicentenary', *Quarterly Review*, 256, 507 (1931), p. 76; *Hibernian Journal*, January 1934, p. 8.
49   T.W.E. Drury in *Irish Times*, 19 June 1929, p. 4; 'Ex-Nationalist' in *Irish Times*, 21 June 1929, p. 8; *Round Table*, September 1929, p. 829.
50   M.D. O'Sullivan, 'Eight Years of Irish Home Rule', *Quarterly Review*, 254, 504 (1930), p. 248.
51   *Irish News*, 9 May 1925, p. 6.
52   *Irish Times*, 25 May 1926, p. 4.
53   Dudley Fletcher in *Irish Times*, 26 May 1926, p. 8.
54   *Irish News*, 22 July 1926, p. 6.
55   'A.V.C.' in *Irish Times*, 13 June 1929, p. 7.
56   Purefoy Poe in *Irish Times*, 19 June 1929, p. 4.
57   'Ex-Nationalist' in *Irish Times*, 21 June 1929, p. 8.
58   D.F. Curran in *Irish Independent*, 15 June 1929, p. 10.
59   *Dáil Debates*, Vol. 41, 3 May 1932, col. 1141.
60   *United Irishman*, 21 May 1932, p. 1.
61   Hone, 'The Royal Dublin Society and its Bicentenary', p. 75.
62   See Sir John Keane, 'Ireland: Commonwealth or Republic?', *Quarterly Review*, 262, 519 (1934), pp. 159–60. On ex-unionists' use of the Union Jack and 'God Save the King', see Chapter Five.
63   However, according to Warner Moss, the AOH was 'still a force' in the politics of the Irish Free State: W. Moss, *Political Parties in the Irish Free State* (New York: AMS Press, 1968 [originally published 1933]), pp. 28, 179–80.
64   *Hibernian Journal*, August 1934, p. 77.
65   *Hibernian Journal*, April 1925, p. 38.
66   *Irish Independent*, 21 November 1927, p. 8.
67   Quoted in J.A. Gaughan, *A Political Odyssey: Thomas O'Donnell, M.P. for West Kerry 1900–1918* (Mount Merrion: Kingdom Books, 1983), p. 153.
68   *Star*, 7 December 1929, p. 4.
69   *United Irishman*, 3 November 1923, p. 4.
70   P. M. F. in *Irish Independent*, 21 January 1922, p. 9. See also similar arguments by 'Portlairge' in *Irish Independent*, 8 March 1922, p. 6 and D. Jones in *Irish Independent*, 14 March 1922, p. 8; also the rather convoluted historical argument employed by Maolmhuire MacGarry in defence of the Free State's right to use the tricolour, *Irish Independent*, 9 March 1922, p. 6.
71   *Irish Times*, 30 May 1927, p. 4.
72   *Treaty Debates*, pp. 97, 164.
73   'Saorstát Éireann Abu' poster in Kilmainham Jail Museum, Dublin.
74   *Londonderry Sentinel*, 2 February 1932, p. 7.

75 *Irish Press*, 14 May 1932, p. 6.
76 *United Irishman*, 21 May 1932, p. 1.
77 See, for example, *Irish News*, 9 May 1925, p. 6; 'Main-Top-Man' in *Irish Times*, 28 May 1926, p. 8; *Irish Independent*, 14 August 1926, p. 6; T.F. Harvey Jacob and D.F. Curran in *Irish Independent*, 15 June 1929, p. 10; *Hibernian Journal*, January 1934, p. 8.
78 S2952A, DT, NAI.
79 F.W. Dohery to Provisional Government, 24 January 1922, in S2952A, DT, NAI; Reginald Craig in *Irish Times*, 2 June 1928, p. 5; Dudley Fletcher in *Irish Times*, 16 May 1925, p. 8; 'Innishowen' in *Irish Independent*, 25 January 1922, p. 6; W.H.T. Gahan in *Irish Independent*, 30 January 1922, p. 6.
80 'Gaedheal' in *Irish Independent*, 18 January 1922, p. 6.
81 'Ireland for Ever' in *Irish Independent*, 21 January 1922, p. 9.
82 'Gaedheal' in *Irish Independent*, 18 January 1922, p. 6; 'Patriot' in *Irish Times*, 8 May 1925, p. 5; 'An Irish Antiquary' in *Irish Times*, 13 May 1925, p. 9; Count O'Kelly, Irish Free State representative in Brussels, to the Secretary, Department of External Affairs, 26 April 1927, in S3088A, DT, NAI; 'Nga So' in *Irish Statesman*, 15 September 1928, p. 30; *Limerick Leader*, 17 September 1928, p. 2; James Henry Webb to the Secretary, Executive Council, 14 January 1938, in S2952A, DT, NAI.
83 *Irish Statesman*, 31 July 1926, p. 576. See also extract from *Irish Statesman*, 15 June 1929, in S6535, DT, NAI; Mr Anthony in *Dáil Debates*, vol. 50, 22 November 1933, col. 415.
84 *Dail Debates*, Vol. 50, 22 November 1933, col. 412.
85 Lester to McGann, 1 February 1924, in S3767A, DT, NAI.
86 D.F. Curran in *Irish Independent*, 15 June 1929, p. 10.
87 Mr Anthony in *Dáil Debates*, Vol. 50, 22 November 1933, col. 415; *Hibernian Journal*, May 1937, p. 48; Trench to Governor General, 7 September 1927, in S3262A, DT, NAI.
88 Trench to Governor General, 7 September 1927, in S3262A, DT, NAI; Murphy (ed.), *Lady Gregory's Journals*, vol. 2, p. 334; memorandum dated 27 May 1924 re Executive Council decision, in S3767A, DT, NAI.
89 'Corkman' in *Star*, 16 March 1929, p. 6.
90 *Cork Examiner*, 21 July 1926, p. 8.
91 *Round Table*, September 1929, p. 828.
92 *Irish Statesman*, 31 July 1926, p. 576.
93 *Irish Statesman*, 15 June 1929, extract in S6535, DT, NAI.
94 Murphy (ed.), *Lady Gregory's Journals*, Vol. 2, p. 334.
95 Hone, 'Royal Dublin Society', p. 76.
96 Deputies MacDermot and Anthony in *Dáil Debates*, Vol. 50, 22 November 1933, cols 412, 415.
97 *Irish Independent*, 14 August 1926, p. 6.
98 W. F. Trench to Governor General, 7 September 1927, in S3262A, DT, NAI.
99 Chairman of the Committee of Public Accounts in extract from *Report of the Committee of Public Accounts*, 13 June 1935, p. 100, in S7395A, DT,

NAI; *Hibernian Journal*, May 1937, p. 48; extract from *Daily Express*, 12 September 1930, in S3767A, DT, NAI.

100 Murphy (ed.), *Lady Gregory's Journals*, vol. 2, p. 334.

101 *Irish Press*, 2 November 1935, p. 1.

102 G. Sharp in *Irish Independent*, 15 March 1923, p. 6.

103 H.M. FitzGibbon in *Irish Times*, 5 June 1928, p. 8.

104 W. F. Trench to Governor General, 7 September 1927, in S3262A, DT, NAI.

105 Purefoy Poe in *Church of Ireland Gazette*, 31 May 1929, p. 309.

106 *Dublin Opinion*, October 1928, p. 248.

107 W.F. Trench to Governor General, 7 September 1927, in S3262A, DT, NAI.

108 *Irish Independent*, 14 August 1926, p. 6.

109 W.F. Trench to Governor General, 7 September 1927, in S3262A, DT, NAI.

110 *Irish Independent*, 14 August 1926, p. 6; D.F. Curran in *Irish Independent*, 20 March 1923, p. 6; Mr MacDermot in *Dáil Debates*, Vol. 50, 22 November 1933, cols 411–2.

111 de Burca, 'Story of the Soldier's Song', pp. 151, 153; *Irish Independent*, 13 August 1926, p. 6; O'Faoláin, *De Valera*, p. 47.

112 Geo. A. Lyons in *Irish Independent*, 23 August 1926, p. 8; Malcolm A. Healy in *Irish Times*, 17 June 1929, p. 8.

113 *Dáil Debates*, Vol. 50, 22 November 1933, cols 413, 416–7.

114 Cosgrave to Lord Granard, 19 June 1929, in S7392A, DT, NAI.

115 de Burca, 'Story of the Soldier's Song', p. 151.

116 *Dáil Debates*, Vol. 50, 22 November 1933, cols 413, 418.

117 Lester to McGann, Office of the President, 1 February 1924, and Lester to the Secretary, Executive Council, 24 April 1924, in S3767A, DT, NAI.

118 *Dublin Evening Mail*, 13 June 1924, p. 5.

119 *Dublin Evening Mail*, 16 August 1924, p. 5, 22 October 1924, p. 3. *Dublin Opinion* suggested that, with Yeats as adjudicator, a winning entry would have had to contain 'the right *mélange* of Celtic mysticism and unusual rhymes'; something along the lines of:
> The mist that does be on the bog
> Is lifting, surely, slowly;
> The tail no longer wags the dog
> In Ireland fair and holy.
> The gracious fields of Tir-na-n'*ogg* (poetic license),
> Are gay with gladioli.

(*Dublin Opinion*, November 1924, pp. 308–9.)

120 *Dublin Evening Mail*, 5 December 1924, p. 4.

121 *Dublin Opinion*, November 1923, p. 236.The six contenders for the competition were published in the *Dublin Evening Mail*, 5 February 1925, p. 3.

122 *Dublin Evening Mail*, 5 February 1925, p. 3.

123 *Dublin Evening Mail*, 10 March 1925, p. 5.

124 *Dublin Evening Mail*, 5 February 1925, p. 3.

125 *Dublin Opinion*, July 1924, p. 142.

126 Ibid.

127 H.V. Morton, *In Search of Ireland* (London: Methuen, 1930), p. 11.

128 *Round Table*, September 1929, p. 829.

129 J. Sinclair Stevenson in *Irish Statesman*, 22 June 1929, p. 310.
130 I borrow this memorable phrase from Phillip Adams in *Weekend Australian*, 31 August 1996.
131 T.F. Harvey Jacob in *Irish Independent*, 15 June 1929, p. 10; J. Sinclair Stevenson in *Irish Statesman*, 22 June 1929, p. 310; MacDermot in *Dáil Debates*, Vol. 44, 16 November 1932, col. 1743, and *Dáil Debates*, Vol. 50, 22 November 1933, cols 412–3.
132 *Irish Statesman*, 29 June 1929, p. 325.
133 *Irish Independent*, 14 August 1926, p. 6.
134 G. Sharp in *Irish Independent*, 15 March 1923, p. 6.
135 *Irish Independent*, 14 August 1926, p. 6.
136 *New Ireland*, 28 December 1918, p. 131.
137 *Standard*, 15 September 1928, p. 13; see also Chs. J. Murphy to de Valera, 5/6 June 1937, and G. O Sullivan to de Valera, undated but received 6 July 1938, in S2952A, DT, NAI.
138 Sean O Murcadha in *Sinn Féin*, 23 August 1924, p. 8.
139 *Sinn Féin*, 13 September 1924, p. 1.
140 Mrs P. Farrelly to the President, 21 January 1933, in S2952A, DT, NAI.
141 *Irish Volunteer*, 30 May 1914, quoted in Hayes-McCoy, *A History of Irish Flags from Earliest Times*, p. 201; see also pp. 36–41 on the murky origins of St Patrick's cross.
142 *United Ireland*, 27 January 1934, p. 4, 7 October 1933, p. 5.
143 On national flags and anthems as sacred symbols of nationalism see C. J. H. Hayes, *Nationalism: A Religion* (New York: Macmillan, 1960), pp. 166–7.
144 Dudley Fletcher in *Irish Times*, 26 May 1926, p. 8; G. Crank in *Irish Independent*, 21 August 1926, p. 8; H.M. FitzGibbon in *Irish Times*, 5 June 1928, p. 8; A.A. Luce in *Irish Times*, 19 June 1929, p. 4. As late as 1931 the secretary of the Dublin Rotary Club sought clarification of the legal position of the Free State flag and anthem: F.M. Summerfield to the Secretary, Executive Council, 28 February 1931, in S2952A, DT, NAI.
145 *Dáil Debates*, Vol. 15, 29 April 1926, col. 739; see also letter from Secretary, Cumann Seamus Ui Duibhir, Cumann na nGaedheal, December 1924, and reply from Secretary, Department of Justice, 19 December 1924, in H75/28, Department of Justice, NAI.
146 Memorandum dated 15 June 1928, and memorandum dated 25 February 1943, in S2953A, DT, NAI. The buildings where the tricolour was to be flown daily, according to the 1943 memorandum, were the Harbour Master's Office, Dún Laoghaire; the Government Buildings, North Block; the Courts of Justice (when the Court was sitting); Leinster House (when the Oireachtas was in session); and Áras an Uachtaráin (when the President was in residence).
147 Extract from *Irish Press*, 4 November 1936, p. 11, and extract from Cabinet minutes, 11 September 1936 (probably 9 November 1936), in S9220A, DT, NAI. A very similar argument was made by Fine Gael's Minister for Education Richard Mulcahy in 1949, which suggests that this view of the role of state symbols in education was bipartisan. Mulcahy maintained that

overfamiliarity with such sacred symbols could blunt their appeal, and that it was preferable to develop patriotism in young people through 'instruction in our language, our history, our music and song and our folk-lore'. Respect for the flag would naturally follow and would be more deeply rooted than if it were enforced. (*Dáil Debates*, Vol. 118, 9 November 1949, cols 560–1, extract in S9220A, DT, NAI.)

148 Note from Chief of Staff, 18 August 1927, and extract from minutes of Council of Defence, 18 August 1927, in 3/22518, DD, MAI. See Chapter 5 for further discussion.

149 Extract from minutes of HQ Staff meeting, 31 August 1926, in 3/22518, DD, MAI; Sherry, 'Story of the National Anthem', p. 42.

150 S8607A, DT, NAI.

151 Brase to Adjutant General, Department of Defence, 4 October 1928, in 3/22518, DD, MAI; *Dáil Debates*, Vol. 49, 25 July 1933, col. 442, and Vol. 51, 26 April 1934, col. 2361.

152 D. Gwynn, *The Irish Free State 1922–1927* (London: Macmillan, 1928), p. 61.

153 On the Vatican flag see Smith, *Flags Through the Ages and Across the World*, p. 223.

154 Memorandum dated 25 April 1932 and report of Cabinet decision of 25 April 1932 in S3088A, DT, NAI; see article on the flag in *Irish Press*, 11 May 1932, p. 7. The historical information about the flag came from a statement prepared for the government by R.I. Best of the National Library of Ireland and dated 20 July 1927 (copy in S3088A, DT, NAI).

155 In Desmond Ryan, *Ireland, whose Ireland?*, n.d. but 1939 or 1940, p. 58, quoted in Hayes-McCoy, *A History of Irish Flags from Earliest Times*, p. 224.

156 Brase to Adjutant General, Department of Defence, 4 October 1928, in 3/22518, DD, MAI.

157 *Irish Independent*, 13 August 1928, p. 6.

158 *Irish Times*, 30 June 1932, p. 7.

159 Chairman of the Committee of Public Accounts in extract from *Report of the Committee of Public Accounts*, 13 June 1935, p. 100, in S7395A, DT, NAI; S. Gwynn, *Dublin Old and New* (Dublin: Browne & Nolan, c.1938), p. 170.

160 P.J.D. in *Irish Independent*, 5 January 1932, p. 10; see also Stephen P. Cahalan to Cosgrave, 18 February 1928, in S7392A, DT, NAI; 'Corkman' in *Star*, 16 March 1929, p. 6; *Star*, 1 June 1929, p. 4; *Wicklow People*, 8 June 1929, p. 4.

161 *Irish Press*, 4 April 1932, p. 5.

162 *Irish Independent*, 1 April 1932, p. 9.

163 *United Irishman*, 24 September 1932, p. 1.

164 *Irish Press*, 9 November 1932, p. 6.

165 Sherry, 'Story of the National Anthem', p. 42; draft memorandum by N.S. O N. dated 5 April 1958, in S8607A, DT, NAI.

166 Sean O'Hickey in *Irish Independent*, 10 August 1926, p. 8.

167 Lorcan MacColla in *Irish Press*, 31 March 1932, p. 6; Eris Kilmurry in *Irish Press*, 9 April 1932, p. 6.

168 Stephen P. Cahalan to Cosgrave, 18 February 1928, in S7392A, DT, NAI.

169 'Corkman' in *Star*, 16 March 1929, p. 6.

170 *Freeman*, 30 June 1928, p. 4; *Star*, 22 June 1929, p. 4, 2 November 1929, p. 4.

171 *Star*, 23 February 1929, p. 4, 1 June 1929, p. 4.

172 Edward Bohane, Royal Dublin Society, to Minister for Defence, 30 July 1926, in S2951, DT, NAI; *Freeman*, 30 June 1928, p. 4; *Irish Times*, 11 June 1929, p. 7; see also Chapter Six.

173 For more detail on this controversy see E. Morris, '"God Save the King" Versus "The Soldier's Song"': The 1929 Trinity College National Anthem Dispute and the Politics of the Irish Free State', *Irish Historical Studies*, 31, 121 (1998), pp. 72–90.

174 *Connacht Sentinel*, 11 June 1929, p. 2; *Honesty*, 15 March 1930, p. 4.

175 Hone, 'Royal Dublin Society', p. 75.

176 *Star*, 2 November 1929, p. 4.

177 When President de Valera was to visit Mountjoy School in 1935 it was thought that the school should be instructed to fly the national flag for the occasion and that it could be taken for granted 'that no real opposition will be offered' since 'Bodies of a similar outlook as the Mountjoy School, such as the Baden Powell Boy Scouts, have now adopted the National Flag.' (Memorandum dated 10 April 1935, in S7533, DT, NAI.)

178 *Cork Examiner*, 11 June 1929, p. 7.

179 During the controversy over the Irish Rugby Football Union's failure to fly the tricolour at international matches in Dublin, Cosgrave met with Connacht rugby representatives and told them, among other things, that 'the flag as adopted is really not legalised'. (Note dated 3 February 1932, in S2950, DT, NAI.)

180 In the 1920s and 1930s the tricolour and 'The Soldier's Song' had not yet become widely accepted by nationalists in Northern Ireland (see Chapter 5).

Notes to Chapter 3

1 Ministry of Economic Affairs to Acting Secretary, Provisional Government, 8 August 1922; Acting Secretary, Provisional Government, to Ministry of Economic Affairs, 9 August 1922, in S1587A, Department of the Taoiseach (DT), National Archives of Ireland (NAI).

2 *United Irishman*, 6 October 1923, p. 4.

3 *Freeman*, 27 August 1927, p. 7.

4 Sheehy, *The Rediscovery of Ireland's Past: The Celtic Revival 1830–1930*, p. 92.

5 Yeats, *Autobiographies*, p. 203.

6 S. O'Faoláin, *King of the Beggars: A Life of Daniel O'Connell, The Irish Liberator, in a Study of the Rise of the Modern Irish Democracy (1775–1847)* (London: Thomas Nelson, 1938), p. 329.

7 'The Man and the Echo' in W.B. Yeats, *Selected Poetry*, T. Webb (ed.) (London: Penguin, 1991), p. 221.

8 S. O'Casey, *Three Plays* (London: Pan, 1980), p. 110. See also Seán O'Faoláin's view that republicans were dazzled by their icons, including 'the tears of Dark Rosaleen, [and] the Miseries of the Poor Old Woman', and that this obsession with symbolism led to the Civil War (S. O'Faoláin, *Vive Moi!* [London: Sinclair-Stevenson, 1993], p. 147).

9 N. Jarman, *Material Conflicts: Parades and Visual Displays in Northern Ireland* (Oxford: Berg, 1997), pp. 194–5.

10 On the Tailteann Games wolfhounds see *Irish Times*, 13 August 1928, p. 7; *Irish Independent*, 13 August 1928, p. 3; *Irish Press*, 16 June 1932, p. 2; and photograph of boys with wolfhounds in L. McRedmond (ed.), *Ireland: The Revolutionary Years. Photographs from the Cashman Collection: Ireland 1910–30* (Dublin: Gill & Macmillan and Radio Telefís Éireann, 1992), pp. 102–3. On the Eucharistic Congress round tower see *Irish Press*, 16 June 1932, p. 1, and McRedmond, *Ireland*, p. 122.

11 *Saorstát Éireann Irish Free State Official Handbook* (Dublin: Talbot Press, 1932), p. 135.

12 C. I. Dulin, *Ireland's Transition: The Postal History of the Transitional Period 1922–1925* (Dublin: MacDonnell Whyte, 1992), pp. 140, 178.

13 Extract from Cabinet minutes, 5 December 1922; letter dated 8 December 1922 (author unknown); George Sigerson, suggestions re state seal, 25 December 1922, in S1587A, DT, NAI.

14 Extracts from minutes of Executive Council meetings, 28 December 1922 and 28 August 1923, in S1587A, DT, NAI.

15 Hugh Kennedy to the President, 28 August 1923, item P4/1300, and letter from Conn Ó Curráin, undated, item P4/1306, in Hugh Kennedy papers, University College Dublin Archives Department (UCDAD).

16 Kennedy to C. Roberts, Office of the Revenue Commissioners, 28 December 1923, item P4/1301, in Hugh Kennedy papers, UCDAD. For more on the selection of designs for the state seals see C. Gallagher, 'The Great Seal of Ireland' *Seirbhís Phoiblí*, 14, 3 (1994), pp. 17–27. The Ardagh Chalice (pictured in Sheehy, *Rediscovery of Ireland's Past: The Celtic Revival 1830–1930*, p. 19) had commonly been used as a model for Celtic Revival metalwork.

17 Kennedy to President, 8 January 1924; extract from minutes of Executive Council meeting, 19 January 1924, in S1587A, DT, NAI.

18 *Irish Sketch and Lady of the House*, Christmas 1924, pp. 13–14, copy in S4129A, DT, NAI.

19 *Irish Times*, 6 May 1925, p. 9.

20 *Irish Statesman*, 16 May 1925, p. 292.

21 Extract from Cabinet minutes, 27 August 1937 and 15 September 1937, in S9953A, DT, NAI.

22 S2070A, DT, NAI.

23 Memorandum dated 15 November 1937; memorandum by Sadleir, 15 November 1937; memorandum dated 19 November 1937, S2070A, DT, NAI.

24 Extracts from Provisional Government minutes, 20 January 1922 and 6 March 1922, in S3436A, DT, NAI; D. Scott, *European Stamp Design: A Semiotic Approach to Designing Messages* (London: Academy Editions, 1995), p. 87.

25 Definitives are non-commemorative stamps intended for long-term use.

26 *Irish Times*, 2 February 1922, p. 5.

27 The surviving designs are illustrated in R. Lowe, *1922-Ireland-1972* (Bournemouth: Robson Lowe, n.d.).

28 J. Walsh (Postmaster General) to the President, 29 October 1923, in S3436A, DT, NAI.

29 On the importance of the map of Ireland as a nationalist symbol see J. Bowman, *De Valera and the Ulster Question 1917–1973* (Oxford: Clarendon Press, 1982), p. 13.

30 J. MacKillop, *Dictionary of Celtic Mythology* (Oxford: Oxford University Press, 1998), p. 80; W. I. Thompson, *The Imagination of an Insurrection: Dublin, Easter 1916. A Study of an Ideological Movement* (New York: Oxford University Press, 1967), p. 55. *Irish Times*, 21 April 1923, p. 8.

31 See M. Don. Buchalter, *Hibernian Specialised Catalogue of the Postage Stamps of Ireland 1922–1972* (Dublin: Hibernian Stamp Co., 1972), pp. 29–31 for illustrations and details of the first definitive series.

32 Extract from minutes of Executive Council meetings, 29 March 1924 and 19 June 1924, and P.P. McMenamin to Secretary, the Executive Council, 12 November 1925, in S3436A, DT, NAI.

33 Memorandum from Minister for Posts and Telegraphs to the Executive Council, 21 May 1935, and note of decision by Executive Council, 24 May 1935, in S3436A, DT, NAI.

34 Buchalter, *Hibernian Specialised Catalogue of the Postage Stamps of Ireland 1922–1972*, p. 31; explanation of the stamp in *Irish Times*, 3 September 1937, p. 13.

35 Ibid., pp. 45–8.

36 W. Finlay, *An Illustrated History of Stamp Design* (n.p.: Peter Lowe, 1974), pp. 19, 113, 116–17.

37 D. Scott, *European Stamp Design*. p. 88. Green was used for the 2p. stamps in the definitive series and the 1929, 1932, 1933 and 1934 commemoratives.

38 Memorandum by the Minister for Posts and Telegraphs to the Executive Council, 29 March 1933; memorandum from the Department of Finance to the Executive Council, 8 April 1933; extract from minutes of Executive Council, 18 April 1933, in S3436A, DT, NAI; memorandum to the Minister for Posts and Telegraphs, 21 February 1934, in G13764/34, Postal Division, Department of Communications (PDDC), NAI.

39 Finlay, *An Illustrated History of Stamp Design*, pp. 151–2.

40 The Royal Dublin Society, Eucharistic Congress, Gaelic Athletic Association and Father Mathew commemoratives were suggested by the RDS, the Congress organising committee, the GAA, and a member of Father Mathew's Capuchin order respectively – see S6127, DT, NAI;

G10137/32, PDDC, NAI; G13764/34, PDDC, NAI; G1460/38, PDDC, NAI.

41 Kennedy to President, 4 October 1923, and Cosgrave to Postmaster General, 24 October 1923, in S3436A, DT, NAI.

42 See D.M. Reid, 'Symbolism of Postage Stamps: A Source for the Historian', *Journal of Contemporary History*, 19, 2 (1984), pp. 223–49; D. Altman, *Paper Ambassadors: The Politics of Stamps* (North Ryde: Angus & Robertson, 1991).

43 Republicans in Cork printed their own stamps during the Civil War, but Cork was captured by Free State forces before these stamps were issued (Buchalter, *Hibernian Specialised Catalogue of the Postage Stamps of Ireland 1922–1972*, pp. 151–2).

44 On the importance of the Shannon scheme to the Free State government as a symbol of progress and self-reliance see A. Bielenberg, 'Keating, Siemens & the Shannon Scheme', *History Ireland* 5, 3 (1997) pp. 43–7.

45 Reid, 'The Symbolism of Postage Stamps: A Source for the Historian', p. 241; Altman, *Paper Ambassadors: The Politics of Stamps*, p. 79.

46 G. MacIntosh, 'Acts of "National Communion": The Centenary Celebrations for Catholic Emancipation, the forerunner of the Eucharistic Congress', in J. Augusteijn (ed.), *Ireland in the 1930s: New Perspectives* (Dublin: Four Courts Press, 1999).

47 Memorandum by the Minister for Posts and Telegraphs to the Executive Council (undated, but apparently some time in 1930) in G10137/32, PDDC, NAI.

48 Arnold Marsh, Headmaster of Newtown School, Waterford, wrote to object to the Holy Year stamps: 'I didn't mind the Emancipation Centenary stamp, and indeed welcomed it, and the Eucharistic Congress one appeared to be a mere matter of courtesy to visitors, but this thing is sectarian propaganda pure and simple and I object very strongly, and so do many others.' (Marsh to O'Hegarty, 25 September 1933, in G2333/50, Vol. 2, PDDC, NAI.)

49 James S. Ashe in *Irish Independent*, 21 June 1929, p. 12; *Catholic Bulletin*, July 1929, pp. 592–3; *Hibernian Journal*, August 1932, p. 82.

50 *Irish Independent*, 26 April 1923, p. 4.

51 Yeats in *Seanad Debates*, Vol. 6, 3 March 1926, cols 501–2.

52 *Irish Statesman*, 10 July 1926, p. 480.

53 *Star*, 18 January 1930, p. 4. See also *Star*, 28 June 1930, p. 121; Mr Heffernan in extract from *Dáil Debates*, Vol. 14, 4 February 1926, cols 435–6, in F17/23/29, Department of Finance (DF), NAI.

54 D. Young, *Guide to the Currency of Ireland: Legal Tender Notes 1928–1972* (Dublin: Stagecost Publications, 1972), pp. 6–7.

55 The consolidated banknotes, issued on 6 May 1929, showed a man ploughing with a pair of horses on one side, and various notable places in the Free State on the other: see M. Moynihan, *Currency and Central Banking in Ireland, 1922–60* (Dublin: Gill & Macmillan, 1975), pp. 128–9.

56 J. Brennan to T. Bodkin, 28 November 1927, item 6963/28, Thomas Bodkin papers, Trinity College Library Manuscripts Department (TCDMS).

57 S. McCoole, *Hazel: A Life of Lady Lavery 1880–1935* (Dublin: Lilliput Press, 1996), pp. 74–80.

58 Ibid., pp. 138–9.

59 T. Bodkin to Hazel Lavery, 21 December 1927, quoted in ibid., pp. 139–40 (emphasis in original).

60 Hazel Lavery to T. Bodkin, 26 December 1927, item 6942/578, Thomas Bodkin papers, TCDMS (emphasis in original).

61 John Lavery to T. Bodkin, 30 December 1927, item 6942/547, Thomas Bodkin papers, TCDMS.

62 Brennan to John Lavery, 30 December 1927, in 26,020/3454, Joseph Brennan papers, National Library of Ireland Manuscript Section (NLIMS).

63 McCoole, *Hazel: A Life of Lady Lavery 1880–1935*, p. 141.

64 J. Brennan to John Lavery, 16 January 1928, in 26,020/3454, Joseph Brennan papers, NLIMS.

65 D. Young, *Guide to the Currency of Ireland: Legal Tender Notes 1928–1972*, pp. 8–10.

66 *Irish Times*, 14 September 1928, p. 11.

67 Young, *Guide to the Currency of Ireland: Legal Tender Notes 1928–1972*, p. 9.

68 F17/4/28, DF, NAI.

69 See V. Hewitt, *Beauty and the Banknote: Images of Women on Paper Money* (London: British Museum, 1994), and p. 46 on portraits as a protection against counterfeiting.

70 M.G. Valiulis, 'Power, Gender, and Identity in the Irish Free State', *Journal of Women's History*, 6, 4 and 7, 1 (1995), pp. 117–36.

71 McCoole, *Hazel: A Life of Lady Lavery 1880–1935*, p. 137.

72 Ibid., pp. 141–2, 146–7.

73 Ibid., pp. 77, 83–106, 118–33, 142–3; T.P. Coogan, *Michael Collins: A Biography* (London: Arrow, 1990), pp. 288–94.

74 See the reported comments of Frank Lillis, Chairman of the Munster and Leinster Bank, and Bodkin's response, in McCoole, *Hazel: A Life of Lady Lavery 1880–1935*, p. 140.

75 *Irish Times*, 14 September 1928, p. 7.

76 *Irish Times*, 11 September 1928, p. 7; Brennan to Lavery, 3 December 1928, in 26,020/3454, Joseph Brennan papers, NLIMS.

77 *Leader*, 22 September 1928, p. 175; typescript article by 'Cu Uladh' (undated) and letter from John Lucey, Secretary, Joint Committee of Gaelic Societies, Co. Cork, to Minister for Finance, 9 October 1928, in F17/4/28, DF, NAI.

78 *Leader*, 22 September 1928, pp. 180–1.

79 Moynihan, *Currency and Central Banking in Ireland, 1922–60*, p. 21.

80 Draft memorandum on token coinage by the Department of Finance, sent to members of Executive Council with covering note dated 14 June 1924, in S3875, DT, NAI.

81 Brennan to Robert Johnson (Deputy Master of the Royal Mint), 2 October 1925; Brennan to Minister for Finance, 2 October 1925; Brennan to

Atkinson, 5 October 1925, in F17/23/29, DF, NAI.

82　*Dáil Debates*, Vol. 14, 27 January 1926, col. 159.

83　*Irish Independent*, 20 January 1926, p. 6.

84　*Irish Times*, 20 January 1926, p. 6.

85　Quoted in *Irish Times*, 21 January 1926, p. 7.

86　*Dáil Debates*, Vol. 14, col. 449, quoted in Moynihan, *Currency and Central Banking in Ireland, 1922–60*, p. 27.

87　Moynihan, *Currency and Central Banking in Ireland, 1922–60*, p. 26.

88　*Seanad Éireann Debates*, Vol. 6, 3 March 1926, cols 501–2; L.T. McCauley, 'Summary of Proceedings', in B. Cleeve (ed.), *W.B. Yeats and the Designing of Ireland's Coinage* (Dublin: Dolmen Press, 1972), pp. 25–6.

89　A. Kelly, 'Thomas Bodkin at the National Gallery of Ireland', *Irish Arts Review Yearbook, 1991–92*, p. 172.

90　Yeats to Bodkin, 7 July [probably 1923], item 7001/1731, Thomas Bodkin papers, TCDMS; *Irish Times*, 8 February 1922, p. 4.

91　Moynihan, *Currency and Central Banking in Ireland 1922–60*, p. 32; McCauley, 'Summary of Proceedings', p. 26; Kelly, 'Thomas Bodkin at the National Gallery of Ireland', p. 172.

92　McCauley, 'Summary of Proceedings', pp. 25–7.

93　Letter from the Royal Society of Antiquaries of Ireland, undated, in F17/1/26B, DF.

94　F17/1/26C, DF.

95　Arnold Marsh, 6 August 1926, in F17/1/26C, DF.

96　E.J. French, 14 July 1926, in F17/1/26C, DF.

97　*Dublin Opinion*, February 1926, p. 439.

98　*Irish Statesman*, 10 July 1926, p. 480.

99　*Irish Independent*, 17 August 1926, p. 9.

100　M. O'Callaghan, 'Language, Nationality and Cultural Identity in the Irish Free State, 1922–7: The *Irish Statesman* and the *Catholic Bulletin* Reappraised', *Irish Historical Studies*, 24, 94 (1984), p. 237.

101　*Catholic Bulletin*, August 1926, p. 815.

102　Murphy (ed.), *Lady Gregory's Journals*, Vol. 2, p. 107 (journal entry for 13 June 1926).

103　McCauley, 'Summary of Proceedings', pp. 27–8.

104　Perhaps the committee was being somewhat facetious here; *Dublin Opinion* had earlier mentioned the possibility of coins showing 'a wolf-dog on one side and a rabbit on the other, with the Latin motto: "Attende donec capian" ("Wait till I get him.")' (*Dublin Opinion*, February 1926, p. 439).

105　Committee on Coinage Designs, Interim Report, in F17/23/29, DF, NAI.

106　Memorandum to the Minister for Finance, 9 August 1926, in F17/23/29, DF, NAI.

107　Minister for Finance to the Secretary, Committee on Coinage Designs, 9 August 1926, and report of Executive Council decision, 17 August 1926, in F17/23/29, DF, NAI.

108　Secretary, Committee on Coinage Designs, to the Secretary, Department of Finance, 24 August 1926, in F17/23/29, DF, NAI.

109 McCauley, 'Summary of Proceedings', pp. 35–7.
110 W.B. Yeats, 'What we did or Tried to do', in B. Cleeve (ed.), *W.B. Yeats and the Designing of Ireland's Coinage*, p. 19.
111 *Irish Independent*, 1 December 1928, p. 9; Moynihan, *Currency and Central Banking in Ireland 1922–60*, pp. 35–36. The *Irish Independent*'s report on the coinage exhibition was headlined 'Symbols of Sovereignty'.
112 'Namac' and L. Nic Shamhraidhin in *Nation*, 15 December 1928, pp. 3, 7, took offence at this part of Bodkin's speech, which they considered insulting to the Irish people.
113 T. Bodkin, 'Irish Coinage Designers', in B. Cleeve (ed.), *W.B. Yeats and the Designing of Ireland's Coinage*, p. 43.
114 Ibid., pp. 41–5.
115 *Irish Truth*, 4 December 1926 and 11 December 1926 (copies courtesy of Colm Gallagher).
116 *Irish Independent*, 20 July 1927, p. 7.
117 *Dáil Debates*, Vol. 20, 2 August 1927, col. 1199.
118 Ibid.
119 *Irish Independent*, 15 December 1928, p. 7 and 18 December 1928, p. 13.
120 T. Bodkin, 'Postscript', in B. Cleeve (ed.) *W.B. Yeats and the Designing of Ireland's Coinage*, p. 55.
121 *Connacht Tribune*, 6 August 1927, p. 12; *Cork Examiner*, 7 December 1928, p. 9.
122 'Sagart' in *Irish Independent*, 2 August 1927, p. 8; 'Do Chum Gloire De' in *Irish Independent*, 10 December 1928, p. 8.
123 *Drogheda Argus*, 15 December 1928, p. 5.
124 *Standard*, 8 December 1928, p. 12.
125 *Nation*, 15 December 1928, p. 3.
126 'J.A.G.' in *Standard*, 22 December 1928, p. 9.
127 *Standard*, 29 December 1928, p. 10.
128 Margaret Gibbons in *Irish Independent*, 15 December 1928, p. 7.
129 John Sweetman in *Irish Independent*, 18 December 1928, p. 13.
130 'Daniel' in *Irish Independent*, 19 December 1928, p. 11.
131 *Catholic Bulletin*, January 1928, pp. 20–1.
132 D.O.C. to Thomas Bodkin, item 6963/34, Thomas Bodkin papers, TCDMS.
133 'Beppo' in *Irish Independent*, 5 December 1928, p. 10. On the Irish Catholic obsession with Freemasonry at this time see J.H. Whyte, *Church and State in Modern Ireland 1923–1970* (Dublin: Gill & Macmillan, 1970), pp. 41–2.
134 'Fontenoy' in *Nation*, 30 July 1927, p. 7. Calles was the President of Mexico (1924–28) who challenged the power of the Catholic church.
135 *Catholic Bulletin*, January 1928, p. 19; *Nation*, 8 December 1928, p. 1; *Standard*, 15 December 1928, p. 16; 'J.A.G.' in *Standard*, 22 December 1928, p 9; *Standard*, 29 December 1928, p. 10; *Drogheda Argus*, 15 December 1928, p. 5; O'Byrne in *Irish Independent*, 16 November 1927, p. 8; John Sweetman in *Irish Independent*, 3 December 1928, p. 11; 'Beppo' in *Irish Independent*, 5 December 1928, p. 10; A. Woloman in *Irish*

Independent, 21 December 1928, p. 8.

136 See, for example, the discussion of popular Catholic novelist Canon P.A. Sheehan, who contrasted the 'pagan realism' of English literature with the 'Christian idealism' he wanted to see in Irish literature, in T. Garvin, *Nationalist Revolutionaries in Ireland 1858–1928* (Oxford: Clarendon Press, 1987), p. 60.

137 P. Shepard, *The Others: How Animals Made Us Human* (Washington: Island Press, 1996), p. 227.

138 *Drogheda Argus*, 15 December 1928, p. 5; also John Sweetman in *Irish Independent*, 3 December 1928, p. 11.

139 Dr Corby in *Irish Independent*, 18 December 1928, p. 13.

140 *Standard*, 29 December 1928, p. 10; Beatrice M. Burke in *Irish Independent*, 22 December 1928, p. 8.

141 *Nation*, 8 December 1928, p. 1.

142 *Standard*, 15 December 1928, p. 16. A similar argument was put in the *Wicklow People*, 8 December 1928, p. 4.

143 *Standard*, 29 December 1928, p. 10.

144 *Irish Independent*, 15 December 1928, p. 7.

145 *Nation*, 8 October 1927, p. 8; *Catholic Bulletin*, January 1928, p. 21; *Connacht Sentinel*, 4 December 1928, p. 2; Cecil J. Corby in *Irish Independent*, 5 December 1928, p. 10; 'Namac' and L. Nic Shamhraidhin in *Nation*, 15 December 1928, pp. 3, 7.

146 Yeats to Bodkin, 20 December [1928], item 7001/1740, Thomas Bodkin papers, TCDMS; see also Bodkin, 'Postscript', p. 59.

147 John T. Purcell in *Cork Examiner*, 27 December 1928, p. 2; letter from 'a learned continental priest' quoted in Bodkin, 'Postscript', pp. 57–58; A. Waller in *Cork Examiner*, 2 January 1929, p. 2; 'Small Farmer' in *Irish Independent*, 15 December 1928, p. 7.

148 'Pelican' in *Irish Independent*, 8 December 1928, p. 7; Bodkin, 'Postscript', p. 59.

149 *Irish Statesman*, 15 December 1928, p. 288.

150 T.J. Alexander in *Irish Independent*, 5 December 1928, p. 10; 'L.B.' in *Irish Independent*, 20 December 1928, p. 9; *Enniscorthy Echo*, 15 December 1928, p. 4.

151 L. O'Shea in *Irish Independent*, 19 December 1928, p. 11.

152 *Irish Independent*, 25–27 December 1928, p. 8.

153 *Irish Independent*, 13 December 1928, p. 10.

154 *Enniscorthy Echo*, 15 December 1928, p. 4.

155 *Irish Independent*, 8 December 1928, p. 7.

156 *Dundalk Democrat*, 8 December 1928, p. 4.

157 *Nation*, 22 December 1928, p. 8; *Irish Independent*, 20 December 1928, p. 9; *Irish Independent*, 24 December 1928, p. 8.

158 'Fontenoy' in *Nation*, 30 July 1927, p. 7; 'Namac' in *Nation*, 15 December 1928, p. 3.

159 'Denarius' in *Irish Independent*, 19 December 1928, p. 11; A. Woloman in *Irish Independent*, 21 December 1928, p. 8; *Nation*, 22 December 1928, p. 1.

160 In *The Hidden Ireland* (1924), one of the key Irish-Ireland texts of the Free State period, Daniel Corkery attacked the appropriation of classical forms during the Renaissance as antithetical to the development of genuinely national cultures (see the extract from *The Hidden Ireland* in S. Deane (ed.), *The Field Day Anthology of Irish Writing*, Vol. 3 (Derry: Field Day, 1991) pp. 99–100).

161 'An Irishman' in *Cork Examiner*, 28 December 1928, p. 12; *Nation*, 8 December 1928, p. 1; Archdeacon J. Fallon in *Connacht Tribune*, 15 December 1928, p. 9; 'A Co. Cork Woman' in *Standard*, 22 December 1928, p. 9; Francis Phillips in *Standard*, 29 December 1928, p. 9; *Limerick Leader*, 15 December 1928, p. 7; *Irishman*, 5 January 1929, p. 2; Joseph Dolan in *Irish Independent*, 8 August 1927, p. 2; 'A Sincere Gael' in *Irish Independent*, 12 August 1927, p. 8; 'Beppo' in *Irish Independent*, 11 December 1928, p. 12; Beatrice M. Burke in *Irish Independent*, 15 December 1928, p. 7; M.B. Drapier in *Irish Independent*, 15 December 1928, p. 7; T. Keegan in *Irish Independent*, 18 December 1928, p. 13; 'Lilliput' in *Irish Independent*, 18 December 1928, p. 13.

162 *Irish Independent*, 11 December 1928, p. 12. On round towers as Masonic symbols see J.H. Edge, *A Short Sketch of the Rise and Progress of Irish Freemasonry* (Dublin: Ponsonby & Gibbs, 1913), p. 18; Leerssen, *Remembrance and Imagination: Patterns in the Historical and Literary Representation of Ireland in the Nineteenth Century*, p. 263.

163 *Limerick Leader*, 15 December 1928, p. 7. See also St Brendan Feis Committee in *Connacht Tribune*, 6 August 1927, p. 12; Archdeacon J. Fallon in *Connacht Tribune*, 15 December 1928, p. 9; Francis Phillips in *Standard*, 29 December 1928, p. 9; *Limerick Leader*, 15 December 1928, p. 7; 'Sagart' in *Irish Independent*, 2 August 1927, p. 8; 'A Sincere Gael' in *Irish Independent*, 12 August 1927, p. 8.

164 Joseph Dolan in *Irish Independent*, 8 August 1927, p. 2; Beatrice M. Burke in *Irish Independent*, 15 December 1928, p. 7.

165 O'Byrne in *Irish Independent*, 16 November 1927, p. 8.

166 *Leader*, 22 September 1928, pp. 180–1; 'A Disgusted Irishwoman' in *Cork Examiner*, 1 January 1929, p. 2; Cecil J. Corby and 'Beppo' in *Irish Independent*, 5 December 1928, p. 10.

167 *Irishman*, 5 January 1929, p. 2.

168 *Standard*, 8 December 1928, p. 12; *Limerick Leader*, 15 December 1928, p. 7.

169 L. Nic Shamhraidhin in *Nation*, 15 December 1928, p. 7.

170 *Connacht Tribune*, 15 December 1928, p. 9.

171 *Connacht Tribune*, 6 August 1927, p. 12.

172 *Leader*, 20 August 1927, p. 56; Francis Phillips in *Standard*, 29 December 1928, p. 9; *Limerick Leader*, 15 December 1928, p. 7.

173 *Leader*, 29 December 1928, p. 517.

174 *Cork Examiner*, 22 December 1928, p. 12; see also *Irish Truth*, 11 December 1926.

175 Archdeacon J. Fallon in *Connacht Tribune*, 15 December 1928, p. 9.

176 Beatrice M. Burke in *Irish Independent*, 15 December 1928, p. 7.
177 A. Woloman in *Irish Independent*, 21 December 1928, p. 8.
178 'Denarius' in *Irish Independent*, 19 December 1928, p. 11.
179 'B.M.B.' (presumably Beatrice M. Burke) in *Irish Independent*, 4 January 1929, p. 8.
180 *Nation*, 8 December 1928, p. 1.
181 *Irish Truth*, 4 December 1926.
182 *Irish Truth*, 11 December 1926.
183 Ibid.
184 Maurice Slattery in *Cork Examiner*, 18 December 1928, p. 8.
185 Marie Lynch in *Cork Examiner*, 22 December 1928, p. 12.
186 'A Disgusted Irishwoman' in *Cork Examiner*, 1 January 1929, p. 2. *Catholic Bulletin*, January 1928, p. 19, January 1929, p. 22.
187 'A Disgusted Irishwoman' in *Cork Examiner*, 1 January 1929, p. 2.
188 St Brendan Feis Committee in *Connacht Tribune*, 6 August 1927, p. 12.
189 Archdeacon J. Fallon in *Connacht Tribune*, 15 December 1928, p. 9.
190 'A Co. Cork Woman' in *Standard*, 22 December 1928, p. 9.
191 Francis Phillips in *Standard*, 29 December 1928, p. 9.
192 *Limerick Leader*, 15 December 1928, p. 7.
193 *Irish Freedom*, December 1928, p. 4.
194 'Sagart' in *Irish Independent*, 2 August 1927, p. 8.
195 Joseph Dolan in *Irish Independent*, 8 August 1927, p. 2.
196 'Beppo' in *Irish Independent*, 5 December 1928, p. 10.
197 L.P. Curtis, *Anglo-Saxons and Celts: A Study of Anti-Irish Prejudice in Victorian England* (Bridgeport: University of Bridgeport, 1968), p. 58.
198 Shepard, *The Others: How Animals Made Us Human*, p. 299. On attitudes towards pigs see also P. Stallybrass and A. White, *The Politics and Poetics of Transgression* (Ithaca: Cornell University Press, 1986), pp. 44–59.
199 P76/72, Richard Mulcahy papers, UCDAD.
200 *Leader*, 20 August 1927, p. 56. Stallybrass and White, *The Politics and Poetics of Transgression*, p. 51, note that from the seventeenth century 'The pig was demonized [by the bourgeoisie] less for its supposed evils than for its rustic boorishness from which polite citizens must dissociate themselves.'
201 'A Co. Cork Woman' in *Standard*, 22 December 1928, p. 9.
202 Archdeacon J. Fallon in *Connacht Tribune*, 15 December 1928, p. 9; see also 'Beppo' in *Irish Independent*, 5 December 1928, p. 10; J.J. Hynes in *Nation*, 15 December 1928, p. 8.
203 *Catholic Bulletin*, January 1929, p. 22.
204 *Irish Statesman*, 15 December 1928, p. 288.
205 *Round Table*, March 1929, pp. 388–9.
206 *Irish Statesman*, 8 December 1928, p. 164; *Round Table*, March 1929, p. 388.
207 *Church of Ireland Gazette*, 14 December 1928, p. 723; *Irish Times*, 1 December 1928, p. 8.
208 *Dundalk Democrat*, 8 December 1928, p. 4.
209 *Enniscorthy Echo*, 15 December 1928, p. 4; see also *Leinster Leader*, 8

December 1928, p. 4.

210 *Freeman*, 27 August 1927, p. 7.

211 'Small Farmer' in *Irish Independent*, 15 December 1928, p. 7.

212 Charlotte Dease in *Irish Statesman*, 15 December 1928, p. 298; 'Setanta' in *Irish Independent*, 19 December 1928, p. 11.

213 *Irish Independent*, 15 December 1928, p. 7; see also the poem in *Irish Freedom*, December 1928, p. 4.

214 Purefoy Poe in *Irish Times*, 12 December 1928, p. 11.

215 *Irish Times*, 1 December 1928, p. 8.

216 *Connacht Tribune*, 29 December 1928, p. 4.

217 *Church of Ireland Gazette*, 14 December 1928, p. 723; Dudley Fletcher in *Irish Independent*, 15 December 1928, p. 7.

218 Whyte, *Church and State in Modern Ireland 1923–1970*, pp. 34–9; R. Fanning, *Independent Ireland* (Dublin: Helion Limited, 1983), pp. 53–60; J.J. Lee, *Ireland 1912–1985: Politics and Society* (Cambridge: Cambridge University Press, 1989), pp. 157–60.

219 See, for example, the speech by Professor Alfred O'Rahilly, quoted in *Irish Times*, 15 October 1930, p. 3.

220 On cultural insecurity in the early years of the Irish Free State see O'Callaghan, 'Language, Nationality and Cultural Identity in the Irish Free State, 1922–7'. For another example of this insecurity, manifested in a concern about the 'moral and spiritual degeneration' of Irish people since the war, see P.S. O'Hegarty, *The Victory of Sinn Féin: How it Won it and How it Used it* (Dublin: University College Dublin Press, 1998 [originally published 1924]), pp. 128–31.

221 Francis Phillips in *Standard*, 29 December 1928, p. 9.

222 'A Disgusted Irish Woman', *Cork Examiner*, 1 January 1929, p. 2; *Irish Statesman*, 15 December 1928, p. 288.

223 Yeats, *Selected Poetry*, p. 73.

224 Hewitt, *Beauty and the Banknote: Images of Women on Paper Money*, p. 9. For more on ambivalent feelings towards money see V. Wilson, *The Secret Life of Money: Exposing the Private Parts of Personal Money* (St Leonards: Allen & Unwin, 1999).

225 Hewitt, *Beauty and the Banknote: Images of Women on Paper Money*, p. 9.

226 For another case (in New Zealand) where proposed symbols on coins evidently failed to meet many people's expectations, and where similar concerns about national image and national dignity were expressed, see M. Stocker, 'Muldoon's Money: The 1967 New Zealand Decimal Coinage Designs', *History Now*, 7, 2, (2001), pp. 5–10.

Notes to Chapter 4

1 I will use the term 'provincial' to refer to a Northern Ireland identity, despite the fact that Northern Ireland contained only six of the nine counties of the historic province of Ulster. The term 'national' is not appropriate in this context, since very few people consider Northern Ireland to be a sep-

arate nation. However, my use of 'provincial' should be seen as analogous to 'national', and it is not intended to suggest any of the derogatory connotations of the words 'provincial' and 'provincialism'.

2 R. Rose, *Governing Without Consensus: An Irish Perspective* (Boston: Beacon Press, 1971), p. 208.

3 D. W. Miller, *Queen's Rebels: Ulster Loyalism in Historical Perspective* (Dublin: Gill & Macmillan, 1978), pp. 110–11; P. Clayton, *Enemies and Passing Friends: Settler Ideologies in Twentieth Century Ulster* (London: Pluto Press, 1996), pp. 87, 96–7.

4 A. Jackson, 'Irish Unionist Imagery 1850–1920', p. 353.

5 Nelson, *Shamrock: Botany and History of an Irish Myth*, p. 118.

6 Ibid., p. 138.

7 See Jarman, *Material Conflicts: Parades and Visual Displays in Northern Ireland*, ch. 8, on the symbols used on Orange banners.

8 Such symbolism is also used by the Orange Order's cognate organisations, the Royal Arch Purple Order and the Imperial Grand Black Chapter (or Royal Black Institution), as well as the similar but unrelated Apprentice Boys of Derry.

9 Loftus, *Mirrors: Orange & Green*, pp. 19–32; A.D. Buckley, 'The Chosen Few: Biblical Texts in the Regalia of an Ulster Secret Society', *Folk Life*, 24 (1985–86), pp. 5–9.

10 Rose, *Governing Without Consensus: An Irish Perspective*, p. 257.

11 Buckley, 'Chosen Few', pp. 9–24.

12 Loftus, *Mirrors: William III & Mother Ireland*, pp. 14–38.

13 An upraised hand, very like the red hand, is used in the Black Institution as a symbol referring to the Biblical story of Elijah and the prophets of Baal, and to the 'cloud out of the sea like a man's hand' which was the first sign of the rain which broke the drought proclaimed by Elijah (Buckley, 'The Chosen Few: Biblical Texts in the Regalia of an Ulster Secret Society', p. 19).

14 Loftus, *Mirrors: Orange & Green*, p. 37; S. Ó Brógáin, 'Flags of the Four Provinces' *Irish Vexillology Newsletter* No. 2, 1985, p. 9.

15 Loftus, *Mirrors: Orange & Green*, p. 38; Jackson, 'Irish Unionist Imagery 1850–1920', pp. 354–6; M. Foy, 'Ulster Unionist Propaganda Against Home Rule', *History Ireland*, 4, 1 (1996), pp. 49–53.

16 An example of the red hand being used to suggest a pledge is the postcard with the caption 'Against Home Rule Hands Up!' reproduced in Foy, 'Ulster Unionist Propaganda Against Home Rule', p. 52; a red hand used as a 'Stop' symbol can be seen in the postcard captioned 'Stand Back Redmond' in J. Killen, *John Bull's Famous Circus: Ulster History Through the Postcard 1905–1985* (Dublin: O'Brien Press, 1985), p. 110. Quote from MacDonagh, *States of Mind: Two Centuries of Anglo-Irish Conflict 1780–1980*, p. 14.

17 Loftus, *Mirrors: Orange & Green*, p. 38.

18 R. Rose, *Understanding the United Kingdom: The Territorial Dimension in Government* (London: Longman, 1982), p. 49.

19 Miller, *Queen's Rebels: Ulster Loyalism in Historical Perspective*, p. 119;

on unionist identification with Empire see also Clayton, *Enemies and Passing Friends: Settler Ideologies in Twentieth Century Ulster*, ch. 5; A. Jackson, 'Irish Unionists and the Empire, 1880–1920: Classes and Masses', in K. Jeffery (ed.), *'An Irish Empire'?: Aspects of Ireland and the British Empire*, (Manchester: Manchester University Press, 1996), pp. 123–48.

20 See Miller, *Queen's Rebels: Ulster Loyalism in Historical Perspective*, for an extended argument about the nature of Ulster Protestant loyalism.

21 D. Lister, 'Some Aspects of the Law and Usage of Flags in Britain', *Flag Bulletin* 17, 1 (1978), pp. 15–16.

22 Jackson, 'Irish Unionist Imagery 1850–1920', p. 353.

23 Cecil Kilpatrick, archivist of the Grand Orange Lodge of Ireland, letter to the author dated 12 October 1995.

24 L. Colley, *Britons: Forging the Nation, 1707–1837* (New Haven: Yale University Press, 1992), pp. 44, 209.

25 D. Cannadine, 'The Context, Performance and Meaning of Ritual: The British Monarchy and the "Invention of Tradition", *c*.1820–1977', in E. Hobsbawm and T. Ranger (eds), *The Invention of Tradition* (Cambridge: Cambridge University Press, 1983), p. 130. There were three times as many choral arrangements of the anthem in the period 1890–1910 as in the previous two decades (p. 163).

26 See Hayes-McCoy, *A History of Irish Flags from Earliest Times*, pp. 36–41 for a discussion of the history of the St Patrick's cross.

27 Lister, 'Some Aspects of the Law and Usage of Flags in Britain', p. 15; E. Kwan, 'Which Flag? Which Country?: An Australian Dilemma, 1901–51', PhD thesis, Australian National University (1995), pp. 105–10, 177–8.

28 Reginald, 12th Earl of Meath, *Memories of the Nineteenth Century* (London: John Murray, 1923), pp. 328–32, and *Memories of the Twentieth Century* (London: John Murray, 1924), pp. 103–5.

29 J.M. MacKenzie, *Propaganda and Empire: The Manipulation of Public Opinion, 1880–1960* (Manchester: Manchester University Press, 1984), pp. 231–4; A. Bloomfield, 'Drill and Dance as Symbols of Imperialism', in J.A. Mangan (ed.), *Making Imperial Mentalities: Socialisation and British Imperialism* (Manchester: Manchester University Press, 1990), pp. 74–9, 90–1.

30 W.L. Clowes, 'An Imperial Flag' *Monthly Review*, 1 (Dec. 1900), p. 107.

31 H.L. Swinburne, 'Flag', in *The Encyclopaedia Britannica* Vol. 10, 11 edn. (Cambridge: Cambridge University Press, 1910) p. 458; see also C. Clark, *Flags of Britain: Their Origin and History* (Shrewsbury: Wilding & Son, 1934), p. 8.

32 Loftus, *Mirrors: Orange & Green*, pp. 38-39.

33 *Belfast Newsletter*, 25 May 1904, quoted in D.H. Hume, 'Empire Day in Ireland 1896–1962', in K. Jeffery (ed.), *'An Irish Empire'?: Aspects of Ireland and the British Empire* (Manchester: Manchester University Press, 1996), p. 151 (italics added).

34 John Anderson, Home Office, London, to S.G. Tallents, Imperial Secretary,

Belfast, 5 February 1924; W.B. Spender to Tallents, 11 February 1924; Tallents to Anderson, 26 February 1924; Anderson to Tallents, 28 February 1924, in HO267/77, Public Record Office (PRO), viewed on MIC523/6, Public Record Office of Northern Ireland (PRONI).

35 Wilkinson to Abercorn, 2 January 1924 and Anderson to Tallents, 22 January 1924, in HO267/122, PRO, viewed on MIC523/8, PRONI; Abercorn to Craig, 1 March 1924, in HA8/270, Ministry of Home Affairs (MHA), PRONI.

36 The elaborately decorated grants of arms and supporters are in CAB1/1 and CAB1/2, Cabinet Secretariat (CS), PRONI.

37 Wilkinson to Secretary, Ministry of Home Affairs, 28 September 1928, in HA8/270, MHA, PRONI.

38 Tallents to A. Maxwell, Home Office, London, 13 May 1925, in HO267/122, PRO, viewed on MIC523/8, PRONI; final conclusions of Cabinet meeting, 16 September 1924, in CAB4/121, PRONI.

39 Oscar Henderson to Tallents, 7 May 1925, in HO267/122, PRO, viewed on MIC523/8, PRONI.

40 Final conclusions of Cabinet meeting, 20 April 1926, in CAB4/165, PRONI.

41 Ministry of Home Affairs to Sir Wilson Hungerford, 22 April 1936, in HA8/270, MHA, PRONI.

42 Final conclusions of Cabinet meeting, 20 April 1926, in CAB4/165, PRONI.

43 Memorandum dated 19 October 1928 and final conclusions of Cabinet meeting, 2 November 1928, in CAB4/222, PRONI.

44 Final conclusions of Cabinet meeting, 18 December 1930, in CAB4/274, PRONI.

45 O. Henderson to C.H. Blackmore, Cabinet Secretariat, 15 August 1924, in CAB9T/4/1, CS, PRONI. The Governor's flag consisted of the Union Jack, with the Northern Ireland arms superimposed in the centre of the flag on a golden circle, surrounded by a wreath – see the illustration of the flag in CAB9T/4/1, CS, PRONI

46 Final conclusions of conference of ministers, 15 February 1924, in CAB4/100, PRONI.

47 Final conclusions of Cabinet conference, 29 February 1924, in CAB4/102, PRONI.

48 O. Henderson to W.B. Spender, Secretary to the Cabinet, 22 August 1924, in CAB9T/4/1, CS, PRONI.

49 Memorandum dated 1 September 1924, in HA5/1370, MHA, PRONI; final conclusions of Cabinet meeting, 16 September 1924, in CAB4/121, PRONI.

50 Ministry of Home Affairs memorandum, 17 July 1926, in HA8/270, MHA, PRONI.

51 *Irish News*, 24 October 1932, p. 4.

52 J. Todd, 'Two Traditions in Unionist Political Culture', *Irish Politcal Studies*, 2 (1987), pp. 1–26.

53 Ibid., pp. 5–6.

54 P. Bew, P. Gibbon and H. Patterson, *Northern Ireland 1921–1994: Political Forces and Social Classes* (London: Serif, 1995), pp. 65–7.

55 This analysis of the populist/anti-populist division comes from ibid., pp. 56–72.

56 *The Times*, 24 May 1921, quoted in P. Buckland, *Irish Unionism*, Vol. 2, *Ulster Unionism and the Origins of Northern Ireland 1886–1922* (Dublin: Gill & Macmillan, 1973), p. 131.

57 R. McNeill, *Ulster's Stand for Union* (London: John Murray, 1922), p. 2.

58 John C. Crossle to Montgomery, 2 October 1935, quoted in P. Bew, K. Darwin and G. Gillespie, *Passion and Prejudice: Nationalist–Unionist Conflict in Ulster in the 1930s and the Founding of the Irish Association* (Belfast: Institute of Irish Studies, 1993), p. 30.

59 Hugh Montgomery Irwin to Montgomery, quoted in ibid., p. 33.

60 McNeill, *Ulster's Stand for Union*, p. 3.

61 See for example Rev. William Mitchell in *Belfast Newsletter*, 13 July 1926, p. 10; William C. Cage in *Londonderry Sentinel*, 14 July 1932, p. 2; Rev. S. Chadwick in *Northern Whig*, 18 December 1933, p. 7

62 *Londonderry Sentinel*, 15 August 1933, p. 7.

63 See S. Bruce, *God Save Ulster!: The Religion and Politics of Paisleyism* (Oxford: Oxford University Press, 1986), p. 50. Thanks to my mother for alerting me to the significance of the word 'ransomed'.

64 *Belfast Newsletter*, 11 July 1932, p. 10.

65 *Belfast Newsletter*, 13 July 1932, p. 14.

66 M. Ignatieff, *Blood & Belonging: Journeys into the New Nationalism* (London: BBC Books, 1993), p. 183; see also D. Bell, *Acts of Union: Youth Culture and Sectarianism in Northern Ireland* (London: Macmillan, 1990), p. 20.

67 See Jarman, *Material Conflicts: Parades and Visual Displays in Northern Ireland*, for a comparative study of nationalist and unionist visual displays.

68 Bryson and McCartney, *Clashing Symbols?: A Report on the Use of Flags, Anthems and Other National Symbols in Northern Ireland*, pp. 71–4.

69 See the comments of the unionist political scientist Arthur Aughey on the 'inarticulateness' of Ulster unionism: A. Aughey, 'The Idea of the Union', in J. Wilson Foster (ed.), *The Idea of the Union: Statements and Critiques in Support of the Union of Great Britain and Northern Ireland* (Vancouver: Belcouver Press, 1995), pp. 8–10.

70 Bryson and McCartney, *Clashing Symbols?: A Report on the Use of Flags, Anthems and Other National Symbols in Northern Ireland*, pp. 125–6, 130.

71 See the comments of a loyalist band member to this effect in Bell, *Acts of Union: Youth Culture and Sectarianism in Northern Ireland*, p. 155.

72 N. Jarman, 'Troubled Images: The Iconography of Loyalism', *Critique of Anthropology*, 12, 2 (1992), p. 149.

73 S.S. Larsen 'The Glorious Twelfth: A Ritual Expression of Collective Identity', in A.P. Cohen (ed.), *Belonging: Identity and Social Organisation in British Rural Cultures* (Manchester: Manchester University Press, 1982), pp. 278–9.

74 Lady Craig's diary for 22 June 1921 in D1415/38, PRONI, quoted in Buckland, *Irish Unionism*, Vol. 2, p. 144.
75 *Northern Ireland Parliamentary Debates: House of Commons* (hereafter *Commons Debates*), Vol. 2, 23 May 1922, col. 612.
76 A.F. Colhoun in *Tyrone Constitution*, 14 July 1933, p. 3.
77 Memo from Ministry of Finance, 2 November 1927, in HA8/201, MHA, PRONI; Bryson and McCartney, *Clashing Symbols: A Report on the Use of Flags, Anthems and Other National Symbols in Northern Ireland*, p. 77; submission by Lady Sylvia Hermon in Ad Hoc Committee of the Northern Ireland Assembly, *Report on Draft Regulations Proposed under Article 3 of the Flags (Northern Ireland) Order 2000*, at http://www.ni-assembly.gov.uk/Flags/adhoc1-00r.htm
78 Rev. William Mitchell in *Belfast Newsletter*, 13 July 1926, p. 10 (my italics).
79 This was clearly the situation from 1930; before that the situation was somewhat more complicated: see J. Bardon, *A History of Ulster* (Belfast: Blackstaff Press, 1992), pp. 502–5.
80 Ministry of Education, Northern Ireland, *Final Report of the Departmental Committee*, 19 June 1923, p. 83, quoted in D. Fitzpatrick, *The Two Irelands 1912–1939* (Oxford: Oxford University Press, 1998), p. 219; L. Andrews, 'The Very Dogs in Belfast Will Bark in Irish: The Unionist Government and the Irish Language 1921–43', in A. Mac Póilin (ed.), T*he Irish language in Northern Ireland* (Belfast: Ultach Tust, 1997) pp. 67–8.
81 *Commons Debates*, Vol. 9, 16 October 1928, cols 2326–7.
82 Director of Education, Belfast County Borough, to Secretary, Ministry of Education, 10 November 1927, and Assistant Secretary, Ministry of Education, to Director of Education, Belfast County Borough, 24 November 1927, in ED13/1/12, Ministry of Education (ME), PRONI.
83 Extract from minutes of meeting of the Belfast County Borough Education Committee, 19 June 1931, and note by Ministry of Education official dated 9 July 1931, ED13/1/12, ME, PRONI.
84 Director of Education, Belfast County Borough, to Secretary, Ministry of Education, 1 November 1932, and Assistant Secretary, Ministry of Education, to Director of Education, Belfast County Borough, 5 November 1932, in ED13/1/12, ME, PRONI.
85 See letters in ED13/1/12, ME, and HA8/201, MHA, PRONI.
86 *Commons Debates*, Vol. 12, 12 March 1930, col. 95.
87 *Belfast Telegraph*, 24 September 1932, p. 9.
88 'An Ulster Parent' in *Belfast Telegraph*, 26 September 1932, p. 10. Had the children of Northern Ireland been taught the facts about the Union Jack, this Ulster parent might have been discomfited to discover that the Union Jack was actually much less than a thousand years old, and that Thomas Campbell's poem, from which the line 'Whose flag has braved a thousand years / The battle and the breeze' comes, gives possession of the flag to the 'mariners of *England*', not Britain, much less the United Kingdom ('Ye Mariners of England', quoted in Firth, *Symbols: Public and Private*, p. 343).
89 'Vintondale' in *Belfast Telegraph*, 30 September 1932, p. 4.

90 Secretary, Dungannon Regional Education Committee, to Secretary, Ministry of Education, 3 November 1932, in ED13/1/12, ME, PRONI.

91 Notes dated 29 November 1932 and 6 December 1932 by Ministry of Education officials in ED13/1/12, ME, PRONI.

92 *Commons Debates*, Vol. 12, 12 March 1930, cols 98–9.

93 Bardon, *A History of Ulster*, pp. 499–500.

94 Phoenix, *Northern Nationalism: Nationalist Politics, Partition and the Catholic Minority in Northern Ireland 1890–1940*, p. 270.

95 *Commons Debates*, Vol. 15, 29 November 1932, cols 200–1; *Frontier Sentinel*, 18 June 1932, p. 2.

96 *Irish Times*, 21 September 1932, p. 8.

97 *Frontier Sentinel*, 4 June 1932, p. 5.

98 *Frontier Sentinel*, 17 September 1932, pp. 4–5.

99 *Newry Reporter*, 14 June 1932, p. 3; *Irish News*, 14 June 1932, p. 5; *Irish Times*, 14 June 1932, p. 7.

100 *Belfast Newsletter*, 20 June 1932, p. 7.

101 *Belfast Newsletter*, 21 June 1932, p. 6.

102 John Keith in *Belfast Newsletter*, 13 July 1932, p. 14.

103 Rev. J.C. Taylor in *Belfast Newsletter*, 13 August 1932, p. 9; *Belfast Newsletter*, 14 June 1932, p. 6.

104 *Frontier Sentinel*, 9 July 1932, p. 3.

105 *Belfast Newsletter*, 21 June 1932, p. 7; *Irish Times*, 22 June 1932, p. 13.

106 Bardon, *A History of Ulster*, p. 537.

107 *Irish News*, 24 August 1932, p. 4.

108 *Newry Reporter*, 13 September 1932, p. 3.

109 *Irish Times*, 21 September 1932, p. 8.

110 *Frontier Sentinel*, 18 June 1932, p. 5.

111 Ibid.

112 *Frontier Sentinel*, 4 June 1932, p. 5.

113 *Frontier Sentinel*, 17 September 1932, pp. 4–5.

114 *Irish Times*, 21 September 1932, p. 8.

115 *Irish Times*, 20 June 1932, p. 8.

116 See, for example, the resolution of the County of Belfast Grand Orange Lodge in *Belfast Telegraph*, 30 September 1932, p. 7.

117 *Commons Debates*, Vol. 15, 6 December 1932, cols 311–13.

118 *Northern Whig*, 26 September 1932, p. 7.

119 Editor's note in *Northern Whig*, 29 September 1932, p. 10.

120 *Commons Debates*, vol. 15, 6 December 1932, col. 313.

121 *Northern Whig*, 23 September 1932, p. 11.

122 'M.M.' in *Northern Whig*, 24 September 1932, p. 9; 'No Surrender' and 'Consistent' in *Northern Whig*, 26 September 1932, p. 10.

123 *Northern Whig*, 26 September 1932, p. 9.

124 'T.' in *Northern Whig*, 27 September 1932, p. 9; 'C.' in *Northern Whig*, 24 September 1932, p. 9, and 26 September 1932, p. 10.

125 'J.J.I.' in *Northern Whig*, 27 September 1932, p. 9.

126 'A.W.' in *Northern Whig*, 28 September 1932, p. 3.

127 *Northern Whig*, 26 September 1932, p. 7; *Commons Debates*, Vol. 15, 23 November 1932, col. 80 and 6 December 1932, cols 313–14.

128 *Commons Debates*, Vol. 15, 29 November 1932, col. 194.

129 *Commons Debates*, Vol. 15, 6 December 1932, col. 316.

130 *Commons Debates*, Vol. 15, 29 November 1932, cols 192–4 (my italics).

131 Ibid.

132 *Commons Debates*, Vol. 15, 29 November 1932, cols 185–7, 191.

133 *Belfast Newsletter*, 9 December 1932, p. 11.

134 *Commons Debates*, Vol. 15, 29 November 1932, cols 201–3.

135 *Commons Debates*, Vol. 15, 6 December 1932, col. 321.

136 *Commons Debates*, Vol. 15, 6 December 1932, cols 314–15.

137 *Northern Whig*, 30 November 1932, p. 6.

138 *Londonderry Sentinel*, 1 December 1932, p. 4.

139 Memorandum on 'Flying of the Union Flag' in CAB4/305, PRONI; *Frontier Sentinel*, 17 September 1932, p. 5.

140 Memorandum on 'Flying of the Union Flag' in CAB4/305, PRONI; final conclusion of Cabinet meeting, 5 April 1933, in CAB4/310, PRONI.

141 *Commons Debates*, Vol. 15, 6 December 1932, col. 327.

Notes to Chapter 5

1 W.E. Vaughan and A.J. Fitzpatrick (eds), *Irish Historical Statistics: Population, 1821–1971* (Dublin: Royal Irish Academy, 1978), pp. 49–50.

2 See Phoenix, *Northern Nationalism: Nationalist Politics, Partition and the Catholic Minority in Northern Ireland 1890–1940*, especially chs 9 and 10.

3 *Irish News*, 9 May 1925, p. 6, 22 July 1926, p. 6; *Hibernian Journal*, April 1925, p. 38, September 1928, p. 69, January 1934, p. 8, November 1935, p. 90, May 1937, p. 48.

4 See election reports in the *Derry Journal* in November 1933, and in *Irish Times*, 28 November 1933, p. 7. For songs sung at Hibernian/nationalist rallies see reports in the *Irish News* and the *Hibernian Journal* of the major rallies which took place each year on St Patrick's Day (17 March) and Assumption (15 August).

5 *Londonderry Sentinel*, 23 November 1933, p. 5.

6 *Irish News*, 1 November 1934, p. 7, 9 November 1934, p. 5; *Belfast Newsletter*, 15 November 1934, p. 7.

7 Report of green flags hung out for a Hibernian rally in County Cavan (in the Free State) in *Hibernian Journal*, August 1931, p. 65; use of green flag by Irish National Foresters in Enniskillen in *Irish News*, 18 March 1938, p. 2; emblems used during polling in Derry in *Londonderry Sentinel*, 2 December 1933, p. 10.

8 *Irish News*, 22 January 1934, pp. 5, 10.

9 The portrait is reproduced on the cover of Phoenix, *Northern Nationalism: Nationalist Politics, Partition and the Catholic Minority in Northern Ireland 1890–1940*.

10 *Commons Debates*, Vol. 12, 12 March 1930, col. 99; *Derry Journal*, 29

November 1933, p. 3; *Commons Debates*, Vol. 17, 22 November 1934, col. 176.

11 *Orange Standard* (England), May 1920, p. 54.

12 Quoted in Bardon, *A History of Ulster*, p. 490.

13 L. Donohue, 'Regulating Northern Ireland: The Special Powers Acts, 1922–1972', *Historical Journal*, 41, 4 (1998), pp. 1089–91.

14 Ibid., p. 1113.

15 See report on the removal of Union Jacks from a polling station during the 1925 election, in HA5/1384, Ministry of Home Affairs (MHA), Public Record Office of Northern Ireland (PRONI). A note dated 20 April 1925 on this file by W.A.M. (presumably W.A. Magill, the Secretary of the Ministry of Home Affairs), commented that 'It is of course absurd to regard the Union Jack as a political emblem but at an occasion such as an election when it takes very little to start a bad row it is better policy to remove any possible shadow of an excuse for disturbance.'

16 HA5/486, MHA, PRONI.

17 *Irish Independent*, 14 August 1926, p. 7.

18 *Irish Times*, 24 May 1927, p. 8.

19 *Irish Independent*, 24 May 1927, p. 7.

20 *Irish Times*, 2 June 1927, p. 8.

21 *Irish Times*, 3 June 1927, p. 3; *Irish Independent*, 26 May 1927, p. 7.

22 *Irish News*, 25 May 1927, p. 4.

23 *Commons Debates*, Vol. 9, 1 May 1928, col. 1161; see also *Commons Debates*, Vol. 9, 24 April 1928, cols 954-955. Significantly, a draft of the Minister's reply (in HA23/1/101, MHA, PRONI) referred to the Irish Free State or 'any other friendly people' and to 'a neighbouring friendly State', but these references to the friendliness of the Free State were deleted.

24 Joseph Devlin in *Commons Debates*, Vol. 9, 2 May 1928, cols 1294–5.

25 *Commons Debates*, Vol. 9, 2 May 1928, col. 1291.

26 *Commons Debates*, Vol. 9, 2 May 1928, cols 1292–4. See also the question about a similar incident in *Commons Debates*, Vol. 12, 7 May 1930, cols 1020–2.

27 *Belfast Newsletter*, 2 May 1928, p. 6.

28 On the UPL see G. Walker, '"Protestantism Before Party!": The Ulster Protestant League in the 1930s', *Historical Journal*, 28, 4 (1985) pp. 961–7.

29 *Irish Times*, 13 July 1932, p. 7. See also Bardon, *A History of Ulster*, pp. 537-539; Phoenix, *Northern Nationalism: Nationalist Politics, Partition and the Catholic Minority in Northern Ireland 1890–1940*, pp. 374–6.

30 *Irish News*, 17 April 1933, p. 5, and 19 April 1933, p. 5.

31 *Londonderry Sentinel*, 18 July 1933, p. 5.

32 *Frontier Sentinel*, 19 August 1933, p. 3.

33 Inspector General's Office, Royal Ulster Constabulary, to Secretary, Ministry of Home Affairs, 2 November 1933, in HA23/1/122, MHA, PRONI.

34 *Northern Ireland Parliamentary Debates: Senate* (hereafter *Senate*

Debates), Vol. 15, 2 November 1933, cols 465–6.

35 Ibid., col. 468.

36 *Derry Journal*, 20 November 1933, p. 3, 24 November 1933, p. 7; *Londonderry Sentinel*, 21 November 1933, p. 6, 23 November 1933, p. 5, 25 November 1933, p. 7, 28 November 1933, p. 3.

37 *Londonderry Sentinel*, 25 November 1933, p. 2.

38 Murphy to R. Dawson Bates, 21 November 1933, in HA23/1/122, MHA, PRONI.

39 *Londonderry Sentinel*, 28 November 1933, p. 5.

40 *Londonderry Sentinel*, 14 December 1933, p. 7.

41 Text of the regulation in HA23/1/124, MHA, PRONI.

42 *Belfast Newsletter*, 15 December 1933, p. 7.

43 *Northern Whig*, 22 December 1933, p. 9.

44 *Northern Whig*, 15 December 1933, p. 6.

45 *Londonderry Sentinel*, 14 December 1933, p. 5.

46 *Belfast Newsletter*, 15 December 1933, p. 6.

47 *Irish News*, 15 December 1933, pp. 4, 5; *Frontier Sentinel*, 16 December 1933, p. 4.

48 'Herald' in *Irish News*, 16 December 1933, p. 8.

49 *Frontier Sentinel*, 23 December 1933, p. 5; see also *Derry Journal*, 6 November 1933, p. 4, 18 December 1933, p. 4.

50 T.J. Campbell in *Senate Debates*, Vol. 15, 2 November 1933, col. 466, and vol. 16, 19 December 1933, col. 26.

51 Mr McMahon in *Senate Debates*, Vol. 15, 2 November 1933, col. 467; *Derry Journal*, 6 November 1933, p. 4.

52 *Derry Journal*, 18 December 1933, p. 4.

53 *Derry Journal*, 6 November 1933, p. 4, 18 December 1933, p. 4; *Frontier Sentinel*, 23 December 1933, p. 5.

54 Reported in *Irish News*, 15 December 1933, p. 5.

55 *Irish News*, 16 December 1933, p. 5.

56 *Belfast Newsletter*, 19 December 1933, p. 10.

57 *Derry Journal*, 6 November 1933, p. 8.

58 *Commons Debates*, Vol. 16, 20 December 1933, col. 137.

59 Ibid., col. 138; *Derry Journal*, 27 December 1933, p. 4.

60 Final conclusions of Cabinet meeting, 16 January 1935, CAB4/333, PRONI.

61 Circular from Inspector General, Royal Ulster Constabulary, 12 February 1934, in HA/32/1/603, MHA, PRONI.

62 Donohue, 'Regulating Northern Ireland: The Special Powers Acts, 1922–1972', p. 1108.

63 E. Gilfillan, Chief Inspector, Inspector General's Office, Royal Ulster Constabulary, to Secretary, Ministry of Home Affairs, 23 June 1934, in HA23/1/130, MHA, PRONI.

64 Chief Inspector, Inspector General's Office, Royal Ulster Constabulary, to Secretary, Ministry of Home Affairs, 21 November 1934, in HA23/1/133, MHA, PRONI. The Law Department's advice is not on file.

65 Dawson Bates in *Commons Debates*, Vol. 17, 22 November 1934, col. 109.
66 Murphy to Bates, 20 June 1934, in HA23/1/130, MHA, PRONI.
67 *Commons Debates*, Vol. 16, 26 June 1934, col. 2248.
68 *Commons Debates*, Vol. 17, 22 November 1934, cols 108-109.
69 P. Buckland, *The Factory of Grievances: Devolved Government in Northern Ireland 1921–39* (Dublin: Gill & Macmillan, 1979), p. 18.
70 Secretary, Ministry of Home Affairs, to Inspector General, RUC, 8 November 1935, in HA/32/1/621, MHA, PRONI.
71 CI for Inspector General to Secretary, Ministry of Home Affairs, 9 November 1935, in HA/32/1/621, MHA, PRONI.
72 Secretary, Ministry of Home Affairs, to Minister of Home Affairs, 27 November 1935, in HA/32/1/621, MHA, PRONI. A handwritten note on this memo dated 28 November pointed out that 'The Soldier's Song' was the anthem of the Irish Free State and recognised as such in the British Commonwealth of Nations. 'Dolly's Brae' is a well-known Orange song.
73 Handwritten memo by Attorney General, 9 December 1935, in HA/32/1/621, MHA, PRONI.
74 Matches between these two Belfast teams were notorious for clashes between Catholic Celtic supporters and Protestant Lindfield supporters.
75 Inspector-General, RUC, to Secretary, Ministry of Home Affairs, 19 May 1938, in HA/32/1/621, MHA, PRONI.
76 Donohue, 'Regulating Northern Ireland: The Special Powers Acts, 1922–1972', p. 1111.
77 *Londonderry Sentinel*, 18 July 1933, p. 5; Edward Murphy to Dawson Bates, 21 November 1933, in HA23/1/122, MHA, PRONI; *Belfast Newsletter*, 15 December 1933, p. 6.
78 *Belfast Newsletter*, 21 December 1933, p. 6.
79 *Commons Debates*, Vol. 9, 2 May 1928, col. 1291.
80 L. Paul-Dubois, *Contemporary Ireland* (Dublin: Maunsel, 1908), p. 179.
81 Joyce quoted in C. Townshend, *Ireland: The 20th Century* (London: Arnold, 1999), p. 2.
82 *Freeman*, 19 November 1927, p. 5; Dorothy Macardle in *Nation*, 8 September 1928, p. 3; Seumas Camowen in *Star*, 4 January 1930, p. 2.
83 Macardle in *Nation*, 8 September 1928, p. 3; *Irish News*, 23 June 1932, p. 4.
84 *Irish Independent*, 18 May 1927, p. 6; *Nation*, 18 August 1928, p. 1.
85 'Irish and proud of it always' in *Irish Independent*, 15 August 1924, p. 8.
86 Sean O Gruagain in *Irish Independent*, 12 November 1927, p. 8.
87 T.F. Harvey Jacob in *Irish Independent*, 15 June 1929, p. 10.
88 Examples of forced singing of 'God Save the King' and saluting of the Union Jack in Augusteijn, *From Public Defiance to Guerilla Warfare: The Experience of Ordinary Volunteers in the Irish War of Independence 1916–1921*, p. 275; O'Faoláin, *Vive Moi!*, pp. 141–2; O'Malley, *On Another Man's Wound*, p. 302; Murphy (ed.), *Lady Gregory's Journals*, Vol. 1, p. 201; Coogan, *Michael Collins*, p. 146.
89 D. Gwynn, *Irish Free State*, pp. 62–3; Murphy (ed.), *Lady Gregory's Journals*, vol. 1, p. 518.

90 *Nation*, 22 September 1928, p. 7.

91 *Nation*, 22 June 1929, p. 2. This use of the term 'garrison' to refer to the 'pro-British' was common in Irish nationalist polemic. It carried the implication that unionists were an alien element acting to protect the interests of a foreign power in Ireland.

92 Leo Lehane in *Star*, 23 March 1929, p. 6; Seumas Camowen in *Star*, 4 January 1930, p. 2.

93 *Round Table*, September 1929, p. 828.

94 *Leader*, 19 November 1927, p. 365; *Cross*, August 1929, pp. 110–1.

95 *Church of Ireland Gazette*, 16 November 1928, p. 662.

96 *Cork Examiner*, 18 February 1930, p. 2, 3 March 1930, p. 2, 11 March 1930, p. 10, 24 March 1930, p. 9.

97 For example, general meetings of the Dublin Conservative Workingmen's Club concluded with 'God Save the King' until 1933, and the club observed Armistice Day by flying the Union Jack (M. Maguire, 'The Organisation and Activism of Dublin's Protestant Working Class, 1883–1935', *Irish Historical Studies*, 29, 113 (1994) p. 86); on Armistice Day displays see J. Leonard, 'The Twinge of Memory: Armistice Day and Remembrance Sunday in Dublin since 1919', in R. English and G. Walker (eds), *Unionism in Modern Ireland: New Perspectives on Politics and Culture* (Houndmills: Macmillan Press, 1996), p. 104.

98 For example, 'God Save the King' was still sung at the annual prize-giving at St Andrew's College as late as 1939 (G. Fitzpatrick, *St Andrew's College 1894–1994* (Blackrock: St Andrew's College, 1994), p. 123).

99 R.B. McDowell and D.A. Webb, *Trinity College Dublin 1592–1952: An Academic History* (Cambridge: Cambridge University Press, 1982), pp. 433–4.

100 Memorandum from the Provost and Board of Trinity College, 25 May 1929, included with report by McNeill, 11 June 1929, in S6535, Department of the Taoiseach (DT), National Archives of Ireland (NAI). This incident is considered in detail in Morris, '"God Save the King" Versus "The Soldier's Song"'.

101 *Irish Times*, 7 August 1926, p. 6.

102 *Irish Independent*, 7 August 1926, p. 7.

103 *Irish Times*, 7 August 1926, p. 7.

104 *Irish Times*, 11 August 1928, p. 9.

105 *Leader*, 18 August 1928, p. 53; *Star*, 17 August 1929, p. 1; *Nation*, 17 August 1929, p. 4; *Honesty*, 16 August 1930, p. 8.

106 Secretary to T.A. Smiddy (Irish Free State High Commissioner in London), 4 April 1930, in D5085, Department of Foreign Affairs (DFA), NAI.

107 *Star*, 17 August 1929, p. 1.

108 *Star*, 17 August 1929, p. 1; *Nation*, 17 August 1929, p. 4.

109 See K. Jeffery, 'The Great War in Modern Irish Memory', in T.G. Fraser and K. Jeffery (eds), *Men, Women and War* (Dublin: Lilliput Press, 1993); K. Jeffery, *Ireland and the Great War* (Cambridge: Cambridge University Press, 2000).

110 Leonard, 'Twinge of Memory: Armistice Day and Remembrance Sunday in Ireland since 1919', pp. 101–5.

111 *Church of Ireland Gazette*, 18 November 1927, p. 657; *Irish Times*, 9 November 1927, p. 6, 11 November 1927, p. 6, 12 November 1928, p. 9; 'Pax' in *Irish Statesman*, 3 November 1928, p. 170.

112 See reports in *Irish Times*, 12 November 1928, p. 9, 12 November 1929, p. 9, 12 November 1930, p. 7, 12 November 1931, p. 9.

113 *Cork Examiner*, 11 June 1929, p. 7.

114 D. O'Hegarty to J.W. Dulanty, 26 June 1929, in S6535, DT, NAI.

115 *Leader*, 19 November 1927, p. 365, 18 August 1928, p. 53.

116 *Irish Times*, 9 November 1936, p. 5.

117 *Freeman*, 19 November 1927, p. 5.

118 'Irishman' in *Irish Independent*, 13 June 1929, p. 10.

119 *Limerick Leader*, 15 June 1929, p. 6.

120 *Irish News*, 10 June 1929, p. 4.

121 *Honesty*, 22 March 1930, p. 1.

122 *Nation*, 18 August 1928, p. 4.

123 *Honesty*, 8 March 1930, p. 4; *Nation*, 22 June 1929, p. 2.

124 *Nation*, 22 June 1929, p. 2.

125 *Irish Times*, 9 November 1927, p. 7.

126 *Leader*, 15 June 1929, p. 467; *Nation*, 22 June 1929, p. 2; *Star*, 16 February 1929, p. 4.

127 *Irish Times*, 15 June 1929, p. 10.

128 *Irish Times*, 19 June 1929, p. 4.

129 *Irish Times*, 25 May 1926, p. 4, 12 November 1927, p. 8.

130 Purefoy Poe in *Irish Times*, 12 November 1927, p. 5; Colonel Madden, quoted in *Irish Times*, 15 November 1927, p. 8.

131 *Irish Times*, 15 June 1929, p. 8.

132 *Church of Ireland Gazette*, 14 June 1929, p. 330; Dudley Fletcher in *Irish Times*, 14 June 1929, p. 6.

133 Colonel Madden, quoted in *Irish Times*, 15 November 1927, p. 8. See also Dudley Fletcher's suggestion that adding a Union Jack in the corner of the Free State flag would be 'an enormous step towards union between North and South' (*Irish Times*, 16 May 1925, p. 8); and A.C. Waller's claim that the Union Jack 'is the only flag which at present can represent the whole of Ireland' (*Irish Independent*, 25 May 1926, p. 2).

134 Robert E. Weir in *Church of Ireland Gazette*, 12 April 1929, p. 207.

135 Cyril Jackson in *The Times* (London), 22 June 1929, p. 8; Edward P. Culverwell in *Irish Times*, 15 June 1929, p. 10.

136 'Ignotus' in *Irish Times*, 18 November 1925, p. 9; R.W. Ditchburn in *Irish Times*, 14 November 1930, p. 4.

137 'Not Without Indignation' in *Church of Ireland Gazette*, 22 March 1929, p. 171; see also J.R. O'Rourke in *Church of Ireland Gazette*, 26 April 1929, p. 231 and 'Not Without Indignation' in *Church of Ireland Gazette*, 10 May 1929, p. 261, and letters in support of 'God Save the King' from Robert E. Weir in *Church of Ireland Gazette*, 12 April 1929, p. 207 and Purefoy Poe

in *Church of Ireland Gazette*, 31 May 1929, p. 309.

138 Campbell Brown in *Irish Times*, 14 November 1927, p. 4.

139 *Freeman*, 19 November 1927, pp. 5, 8; *Nation*, 19 November 1927, p. 1, 22 June 1929, pp. 2, 4; also *Leader*, 18 August 1928, p. 53.

140 *An Phoblacht*, 15 October 1926, p. 3.

141 *Irish Times*, 12 November 1926, p. 8, 12 November 1932, p. 10.

142 Raids and removal of flags reported in *Irish Times*, 10 November 1926, p. 7, 18 August 1928, p. 7, 25 August 1928, p. 8, 11 November 1930, p. 5, 22 June 1932, p. 10; *Times* (London), 18 June 1932, p. 12.

143 This incident is outlined briefly in D. O'Sullivan, *The Irish Free State and its Senate: A Study in Contemporary Politics* (London: Faber & Faber, 1940), pp. 255–6.

144 See, for example, the editorial in the *Freeman*, 30 June 1928, p. 4, explaining that there would be no royal visits to the Free State so long as such visits might be used by ex-unionists as an opportunity for 'an offensive exhibition of West Britonism'.

145 *Star*, 15 June 1929, p. 4.

146 Cosgrave to Lady Ardee, 25 June 1929, and O'Hegarty to Dulanty, 26 June 1929, in S6535, DT, NAI; memorandum by Eoin Ua Dubhthaigh, 22 September 1930, in S6077, DT, NAI.

147 *Star*, 15 June 1929, p. 4; Cosgrave to Lord Granard, 19 June 1929, in S7392A, DT, NAI.

148 *Freeman*, 12 November 1927, p. 2; also 19 November 1927, pp. 5, 8.

149 On the political attitudes and economic position of Protestants (who made up the overwhelming majority of the ex-unionist community) in the Free State, see K. Bowen, *Protestants in a Catholic State: Ireland's Privileged Minority* (Kingston: McGill-Queen's University Press, 1983), pp. 55–64, 80–90.

150 *Freeman*, 19 November 1927, pp. 5, 8.

151 *Irish Times*, 11 June 1929, p. 7.

152 Chief of Staff, note dated 18 August 1927, in 3/22518, Department of Defence, Military Archives of Ireland.

153 Extract from minutes of Council of Defence, 18 August 1927, in 3/22518, Department of Defence, Military Archives of Ireland.

154 O'Hegarty to Dulanty, 26 June 1929, in S6535, DT, NAI.

155 Report on the meeting by Inspector Richard O'Connell, 11 November 1930, in S.3/28, Department of Justice (DJ), NAI; also *Irish Times*, 11 November 1930, p. 5.

156 *Irish Times*, 9 November 1927, pp. 7, 8.

157 Ibid.

158 *Nation*, 4 September 1928, p. 4, 27 October 1928, p. 6.

159 Note for the Taoiseach re resolution of the Fianna Fáil Ard-Fheis, September 1943, in S7392A, DT, NAI.

160 Eoin Ua Dubhthaigh to Minister for Justice, 21 September 1932, and extract from Cabinet Minutes, 27 September 1932, in S3370B, DT, NAI.

161 *Irish Times*, 12 November 1932, pp. 9–10; *Irish Press*, 12 November 1932, p. 1.

162 E. O Broithe to Secretary, Department of Justice, 18 October 1933; memo by Domhnall de Brún, 19 October 1933; extract from Cabinet Minutes, 24 October 1933, and Cabinet decisions in subsequent years, in S3370B, DT, NAI.
163 *Irish Press*, 13 November 1933, p. 7.
164 Memorandum from President's Office dated 12 November 1935, in S3370B, DT, NAI; report of discussion with de Valera, 11 November 1936, in S9340, DT, NAI; draft circular re Remembrance Day celebrations, 1936, in S.89/28, DJ, NAI.
165 Handwritten note dated 10 November 1936, in S.89/28, DJ, NAI.
166 *Irish Press*, 13 November 1933, p. 7.
167 *Irish Press*, 12 November 1935, p. 9.
168 Handwritten note dated 7 November 1934, in 1/115, DFA, NAI.
169 In 1933 a Fianna Fáil cumann put a resolution to the party's Ard-Fheis calling for Armistice Day parades to be banned; however, even this resolution (which was not passed) advocated such a ban 'in order to avoid trouble', that is, on security grounds – see *Irish Press*, 3 November 1933, p. 9.

Notes to Chapter 6

1 *House of Lords Debates*, Vol. 59, 8 October 1924, cols 622–5.
2 The painting of the pillar boxes was under way in April 1922 (*Irish Times*, 6 April 1922, p. 5).
3 *Freeman*, 22 September 1928, p. 1.
4 *Manchester Guardian*, 15 March 1922, quoted in Dulin, *Ireland's Transition: The Postal History of the Transitional Period 1922–1925*, p. 64.
5 *Irish Sketch and Lady of the House*, Christmas 1924, p. 13, copy in S4129A, Department of the Taoiseach (DT), National Archives of Ireland (NAI).
6 *Irish Independent*, 1 December 1928, p. 9.
7 Newfoundland was also a dominion until 1934, but is not considered here due to a lack of information about its symbols.
8 On South Africa, where the strength of Afrikaner nationalism made the situation more comparable to the Irish case than any of the other dominions, see J. Lambert, 'Imagining a "South African" Imperial Identity: South Africanism in the 1920s', unpublished paper presented at the Australian Historical Association Conference, Adelaide, 2000.
9 R.A.G. Carson, *Coins: Ancient, Mediaeval & Modern* (London: Hutchinson, 1962), pp. 418, 458–9, 467.
10 A. Nicholson, *Australian Banknote Catalogue* (Melbourne: Hawthorn Press, 1977), pp. 14–37.
11 G. Briggs, *National Heraldry of the World* (London: J.M. Dent, 1973), pp. 8–9, 22–3, 96–7, 118–19.
12 Designs of the settler dominions' stamps can be found in successive editions of *Stanley Gibbons' Simplified Stamp Catalogue* (London: Stanley Gibbons).

13 H. McQueen, 'The Australian Stamp: Image, Design and Ideology', *Arena*, 84 (1988), p. 81.

14 H. Saker, *The South African Flag Controversy 1925–1928* (Cape Town: Oxford University Press, 1985), pp. 22–5.

15 L. Thompson, *The Political Mythology of Apartheid* (New Haven: Yale University Press, 1985), p. 37.

16 Kwan, 'Which Flag? Which Country?: An Australian Dilemma, 1901–1951', p. 78.

17 J.R. Matheson, *Canada's Flag: A search for a Country* (Belleville: Mika Publishing, 1986) ch. 3; A.B. Fraser, 'A Canadian Flag for Canada', *Journal of Canadian Studies*, 25, 4 (1990–91), pp. 64–80.

18 Kwan, 'Which Flag? Which Country?: An Australian Dilemma, 1901–1951'; E. Kwan, 'The Australian Flag: Ambiguous Symbol of Nationality in Melbourne and Sydney, 1920–21', *Australian Historical Studies* 26, 103 (1994), pp. 280–303. C.A. Foley, *The Australian Flag: Colonial Relic or Contemporary Icon?* (Leichhardt: Federation Press, 1996).

19 This account of the flag debate in South Africa is based on Saker, *The South African Flag Controversy 1925–1928*, and P. Rault, 'The South African Flag of 1928–1994', *Flag Bulletin*, 33, 1 (1994), pp. 2–38.

20 South African *Hansard*, Vol. 7, col. 4061, quoted in Saker, *The South African Flag Controversy 1925–1928*, pp. 43-44.

21 'Saor-Statuidhe' in *Irish Independent*, 8 May 1922, p. 6.

22 Gavan Duffy in the Treaty debates, quoted in D.W. Harkness, *The Restless Dominion: The Irish Free State and the British Commonwealth of Nations, 1921–31* (London: Macmillan, 1969), p. 19.

23 Pearse, *Political Writings and Speeches*, p. 151.

24 Finlay, *An Illustrated History of Stamp Design*, pp. 151–2.

25 Dáil Éireann, *Official Report: Debate on the Treaty Between Great Britain and Ireland Signed in London on the 6th December, 1921*, p. 116.

26 A letter from the President's Department, prompted by a question from the author of a book on the flags of the British Empire, said: 'As far as I am aware the Union Jack has not on any occasion been officially flown here since the change of Government arising out of the Treaty. It might, however-er, be no harm for the Department of External Affairs to consider whether any such occasions and if so what occasions, are likely to occur at a future date.' (President's Department to Department of External Affairs, 26 July 1927, in S2952A, DT, NAI.) I have found no indication that the Department of External Affairs did in fact give consideration to the matter.

27 On the Free State government's role in this evolution see Harkness, *The Restless Dominion: The Irish Free State and the British Commonwealth of Nations*; G. Martin, 'The Irish Free State and the Evolution of the Commonwealth, 1921–49', in R. Hyam and G. Martin, *Reappraisals in British Imperial History* (London: Macmillan, 1975), pp. 201–23.

28 *Freeman*, 19 November 1927, p. 5.

29 *Star*, 17 August 1929, p. 6. The article on Canada in the *Star* also used the Canadian example to take a shot at ex-unionists in the Free State: 'As here, so too in Canada, a small but loud-voiced faction endeavour to oppose the

current of nationalism. A minority there, the members of which are foreigners or the children of foreigners, adopt the same tactics towards the manifestation of Canadian nationality as do the anti-Irish minority in the Saorstat, the members of which are also foreigners or the children of foreigners.'

30 Desmond FitzGerald, notes for a speech following the 1926 Imperial Conference, quoted in Harkness, *The Restless Dominion: The Irish Free State and the British Commonwealth of Nations*, p. 255.
31 *Freeman*, 17 December 1927, p. 4.
32 *Freeman*, 12 November 1927, p. 2.
33 *Round Table*, September 1929, p. 829.
34 McNeill to the President, 17 September 1928; note of Executive Council decision, 4 October 1928; J. O'Sullivan to D. O'Hegarty, 7 June 1929; report by McNeill dated 11 June 1929; memorandum dated 28 May 1929 regarding the decision of the Executive Council, in S6535, DT, NAI. For more details of the incident see Morris, '"God Save the King" Versus "The Soldier's Song"'.
35 *Star*, 16 February 1929, p. 4; *Irish Times*, 11 June 1929, p. 7.
36 Irish Free State High Commissioner, London, to the Secretary, Department of External Affairs, 12 June 1929, and Sidney Webb (Lord Passfield, Secretary of State for Dominion Affairs) to T.A. Smiddy (IFS High Commissioner), 5 July 1929, in EA156, Department of Foreign Affairs (DFA), NAI.
37 Draft of letter in EA156, DFA, NAI, marked 'Draft submitted by D/External Affairs'.
38 Cosgrave to Lord Granard, 19 June 1929, in S7392A, DT, NAI.
39 *Freeman*, 18 August 1928, p. 2.
40 Finlay, *An Illustrated History of Stamp Design*, p. 117.
41 See Chapter 5 on ex-unionists and 'God Save the King' and the Union Jack; and see letter from Dudley Fletcher expressing the hope that in time the Union Jack would be added to the Free State's flag (*Irish Times*, 16 May 1925, p. 8).
42 *Irish Independent*, 8 November 1927, p. 11; see also 'Ex-Nationalist' in *Irish Times*, 21 June 1929, p. 8, and defence of the playing of 'God Save the King' at Trinity College by T. Hennessy, TD, in *Star*, 2 March 1929, p. 5.
43 W.F. Trench to Governor General, 7 September 1927, in S3262A, DT, NAI.
44 'The Irish Free State: An Ex-Unionist View', *Round Table*, December 1925, pp. 34–5.
45 *Honesty*, 29 June 1929, p. 8. On Magennis and Clann Éireann see Moss, *Political Parties in the Irish Free State*, pp. 25–6, 148.
46 *Nation*, 16 November 1929, p. 4.
47 *Nation*, 22 June 1929, p. 2.
48 *An Phoblacht*, 29 June 1929, p. 3.
49 *Round Table*, December 1934, p. 34.
50 *Round Table*, March 1937, p. 354.
51 *Northern Whig*, 17 December 1924, quoted in D. Kennedy, *The Widening Gulf: Northern Attitudes to the Independent Irish State, 1919–49* (Belfast:

272 *Our Own Devices*

Blackstaff, 1988), p. 205.

52 'Lux' in *Irish Times*, 29 October 1924, p. 9.

53 *Irish Independent*, 25 June 1929, p. 7.

54 *Belfast Telegraph*, 8 June 1929, p. 6.

55 *Belfast Newsletter*, 13 July 1929, p. 6.

56 *Belfast Newsletter*, 13 August 1929, p. 9; see also the comments of Sir Robert M'Bride, MP, who claimed that the King was taboo in the Free State because he was Protestant (*Belfast Newsletter*, 2 September 1929, p. 12).

57 'A Graduate of Dublin University' in *Belfast Newsletter*, 8 June 1929, p. 5; 'Loyalist' in *Belfast Newsletter*, 10 December 1932, p. 12.

58 *Belfast Newsletter*, 22 July 1926, p. 7.

59 J.M. Andrews, MP, in *Belfast Newsletter*, 13 July 1929, p. 9.

60 *Belfast Newsletter*, 8 June 1929, p. 6.

61 *Belfast Newsletter*, 8 June 1929, p. 7.

62 W.H. Fyffe in *Belfast Newsletter*, 13 July 1929, p. 9.

63 *Belfast Telegraph*, 8 June 1929, p. 6.

64 'An Old Fogey' in *Northern Whig*, 13 June 1929, p. 6.

65 Ibid.

66 *Londonderry Sentinel*, 14 July 1932, p. 2.

67 *Newry Reporter*, 14 July 1932, p. 6; see also similar comments in the editorial of the *Belfast Telegraph*, 21 December 1933, p. 8.

68 J.M. Andrews, MP, in *Belfast Newsletter*, 2 September 1929, p. 12.

69 *Irish Times*, 13 July 1934, p. 8.

70 *Belfast Newsletter*, 29 August 1932, p. 10.

71 *Irish Times*, 19 July 1934, p. 4.

72 The title of chapter 6 of C. O'Halloran, *Partition and the Limits of Irish Nationalism: An Ideology Under Stress* (Dublin: Gill & Macmillan, 1987).

73 Kennedy, *The Widening Gulf: Northern Attitudes to the Independent Irish State, 1919–49*.

74 *Irish Tribune*, 24 December 1926, quoted in O'Halloran, *Partition and the Limits of Irish Nationalism: An Ideology Under Stress*, p. 171.

75 Note on the national flag by Sean Ghall, Oireachtas Library, 7 July 1927, in S3088A, DT, NAI.

76 *Catholic Bulletin*, July 1929.

77 *Irish Times*, 20 January 1926, p. 6.

78 *Irish Times*, 21 July 1934, p. 8.

79 Dudley Fletcher in *Irish Times*, 16 May 1925, p. 8; D.F. Curran in *Irish Independent*, 8 November 1927, p. 11.

80 D.F. Curran in *Irish Independent*, 15 June 1929, p. 10; James S. Ashe in *Irish Independent*, 21 June 1929, p. 12; J. Sinclair Stephenson in *Irish Statesman*, 22 June 1929, p. 310; *Round Table*, September 1929, p. 829.

81 *Irish Independent*, 14 August 1926, p. 6.

82 Article reprinted in the *Star*, 6 July 1929, p. 8.

83 See T. De Vere White, *Kevin O'Higgins* (Dublin: Anvil Books, 1986), ch. 14.

84 Lady Gregory, having got wind of the dual monarchy proposal, commented 'We must hurry on with the new coinage lest that unbeautiful head

should be put on it again.' (Journal entry for 14 February 1927 in Murphy (ed.), *Lady Gregory's Journals*, Vol. 2, p. 169.)

85 Entry for 23 November 1926 in J. Barnes and D. Nicholson (eds), *The Leo Amery Diaries*, Vol. 1, *1896–1929* (London: Hutchinson, 1980), p. 483.
86 See the biographical note on MacDermot in Foster, *Modern Ireland 1600–1972*, p. 549.
87 Bowman, *De Valera and the Ulster Question 1917–1973*, p. 128, and *Dáil Debates*, Vol. 67, 11 May 1937, cols 76–84, quoted in Bowman, p. 152.
88 *Seanad Debates*, Vol. 22, 26 January 1939, col. 819.
89 O'Halloran, *Partition and the Limits of Irish Nationalism: An Ideology under Stress*, pp. 41–50.
90 S. O'Faoláin, *An Irish Journey* (London: Readers Union, 1941), p. 223.
91 O'Faoláin did recognise that various features of life in the independent Irish state were helping to maintain partition (see O'Faoláin, *De Valera*, pp. 156–7).
92 O'Halloran, *Partition and the Limits of Irish Nationalism: An Ideology under Stress*, pp. 159–64.
93 Another individual who challenged the nationalist consensus was Bolton Waller, who wrote that 'one of the most essential things to understand is that the loyalty of the Northern Protestants to the British Empire is absolutely genuine, and one of the chief factors in their mental make-up, a fact and one of the most important of facts'. See B.C. Waller, *Hibernia or the Future of Ireland* (London: Kegan Paul, Trench, Trubner, n.d. [ca. 1928]), p. 82. Waller also recognised that disagreements over symbolic questions represented one of the chief difficulties which would have to be overcome if there was to be a united Ireland (p. 95).
94 *Round Table*, March 1939, p. 366.
95 See J. Sugden and A. Bairner, *Sport, Sectarianism and Society in a Divided Ireland* (Leicester: Leicester University Press, 1993).
96 See S. Harvie, '17 November 1993 – A Night to Remember?', in R. English and G. Walker (eds), *Unionism in Modern Ireland: New Perspectives on Politics and Culture* (London: Macmillan Press, 1996), pp. 192–219; M. Cronin, *Sport and Nationalism in Ireland: Gaelic Games, Soccer and Irish Identity since 1884* (Dublin: Four Courts Press, 1999), pp. 117–24, 170–2.
97 Cronin, *Sport and Nationalism in Ireland: Gaelic Games, Soccer and Irish Identity since 1884*, ch. 4 and pp. 143–69.
98 *Irish Press*, 17 April 1933, p. 9.
99 Memorandum from the Inspector-General's Office, Royal Ulster Constabulary, to the Secretary, Ministry of Home Affairs, 2 November 1933, in HA23/1/122, Ministry of Home Affairs, Public Record Office of Northern Ireland. This report also claimed that the resolution proposed to the 1933 GAA congress had been amended before being passed, so the final version read: 'That the National flag be displayed at all matches *where practicable.*' The *Irish News* reported that the GAA congress had deliberately phrased its decision as a recommendation, not an order, so that it would not create

problems for Northern Ireland clubs (*Irish News*, 4 November 1933, p. 5).

100 Edward Bohane, Royal Dublin Society, to Minister for Defence, 30 July 1926, in S2951, DT, NAI.

101 The Irish Rugby Football Union adopted this approach (see below); the Golfing Union of Ireland also adopted the flag of the four provinces (*Irish Times*, 20 September 1928, p. 4, 22 June 1929, p. 9), as did the Irish Hockey Union (Sugden and Bairner, *Sport, Sectarianism and Society in a Divided Ireland*, p. 63). On the flag of the four provinces see Ó Brógáin, 'The Flags of the Four Provinces'.

102 *Irish Independent*, 22 May 1926, p. 8.

103 *Irish Independent*, 25 May 1926, p. 2; see also letter by A.C. Waller on the same page.

104 *Seanad Debates*, Vol. 7, 22 July 1926, col. 1047.

105 Edward Bohane to Minister for Defence, 30 July 1926, in S2951, DT, NAI.

106 *Freeman*, 18 August 1928, p. 2.

107 *Star*, 23 February 1929, p. 4, 1 June 1929, p. 4.

108 See Sugden and Bairner, *Sport, Sectarianism and Society in a Divided Ireland*, pp. 52–63, for a discussion of rugby in Ireland.

109 *Irish Press*, 1 February 1932, p. 9.

110 *Freeman*, 30 June 1928, p. 4; *Star*, 16 February 1929, p. 7, 23 February 1929, p. 4.

111 *Irish Press*, 4 January 1932, p. 8, 6 January 1932, p. 4.

112 *Irish Press*, 1 February 1932, p. 9.

113 *Irish Press*, 6 January 1932, p. 8.

114 *Irish Press*, 26 January 1932, p. 8.

115 *Irish Independent*, 2 February 1932, p. 12.

116 'Rugger' in *Irish Press*, 6 January 1932, p. 8; P.J. Curran in *Irish Press*, 6 January 1932, p. 6.

117 'Rugger' in *Irish Press*, 26 January 1932, p. 8; resolution of the Connacht branch of IRFU, and comments of Father Cogavin, in *Irish Press*, 2 February 1932, p. 8.

118 M.J. Dennehy in *Irish Press*, 30 January 1932, p. 9; 'Stand off' in *Irish Press*, 4 February 1932, p. 8.

119 'Clash' in *Irish Press*, 2 February 1932, p. 8.

120 *Irish Press*, 2 February 1932, p. 8 (my italics).

121 'C.J.M.' and sports editor's reply in *Irish Press*, 30 January 1932, p. 9.

122 *Irish Press*, 1 February 1932, p. 9.

123 *Irish Press*, 2 February 1932, p. 8.

124 Morris to Cosgrave (undated) in S2950, DT, NAI.

125 Handwritten report of the meeting dated 3 February 1932, in S2950, DT, NAI.

126 *Irish Press*, 3 February 1932, p. 1; *Irish Independent*, 5 February 1932, p. 10.

127 Letter from unidentified author (presumably Minister for External Affairs) to W.A. Clarke, IRFU, 5 February 1932, and Clarke's reply, 6 February 1932, in 1/38, DFA, NAI; *Irish Press*, 6 February 1932, p. 8.

128 Bryson and McCartney, *Clashing Symbols?: A Report on the Use of Flags,*

Anthems and Other National Symbols in Northern Ireland, pp. 84–5.

129 P. O'Sullivan, 'Ireland & the Olympic Games', *History Ireland*, 6, 1 (1998), p. 43.

130 See the summaries of the situation by General O'Duffy in *Irish Times*, 4 April 1932, p. 7, and Dr O'Sullivan in *An Phoblacht*, 16 April 1932, p. 2.

131 *Irish Times*, 29 February 1932, p. 7. Since 1924 the tricolour had been registered as the national flag to be used by the Irish team at the Olympic Games. This fact had itself been the subject of discussion in 1928, when a Northern Ireland representative on the Irish Olympic Council had suggested that the tricolour be replaced by a flag showing a golden harp on a blue background. The President of the Irish Olympic Council promised to look into the matter after the 1928 games, but it seems that no change was made. According to the Belfast correspondent for the *Irish Times*, there was much 'hullabaloo' in Belfast about Northern Ireland athletes being required to compete at the Olympic Games under the tricolour. (*Irish Times*, 30 May 1928, p. 7, 8 June 1928, p. 10; *Irish Independent*, 31 May 1928, p. 9.)

132 Dr O'Sullivan's speech reported in full in *An Phoblacht*, 16 April 1932, p. 2.

133 *Irish Independent*, 4 April 1932, p. 14.

134 *Irish Times*, 6 June 1932, p. 11.

135 *Irish Press*, 14 November 1932, p. 2.

136 O'Sullivan, 'Ireland & the Olympic Games', p. 44.

137 P. Colum, *Cross Roads in Ireland* (New York: Macmillan, 1930), p. 72; Morton, *In Search of Ireland*, pp. 231–2. A more recent example can be found in J. Ardagh, *Ireland and the Irish: Portrait of a Changing Society* (Harmondsworth: Penguin, 1994), p. 388. Seán O'Faoláin, characteristically, claimed not to have been struck by such things, but in making this claim he mentioned them nonetheless (O'Faoláin, *An Irish Journey*, p. 221).

Notes to Chapter 7

1 For analysis of themes and design of the stamps of the independent Irish state see D. Scott, 'Posting Messages', *GPA Irish Arts Review Yearbook, 1990–1991*, pp. 188–96; Scott, *European Stamp Design: A Semiotic Approach to Designing Messages*, ch. 6.

2 S. Ó Brógáin, *The Wolfhound Guide to the Irish Harp Emblem*, ch. 5 (quoting from S13513A, Department of the Taoiseach, National Archives of Ireland).

3 Ibid., ch. 6. In June 1947, following a minor controversy in the newspapers about the number and alignment of the harpstrings in the coat of arms, the government approved a modified design with more strings, which were arranged vertically rather than diagonally.

4 S.Ó Brógáin, 'Irish Naval Flags', *Irish Vexillology Newsletter,* no. 3, 1985, p. 20 (this article also discusses the other flags used by the Naval Service).

5 The flag code can be found in the pamphlet *An Bhratach Náisiunta* [The National Flag], pp. 6–14.

6 'Amhrán na bhFiann' actually translates as 'The Soldiers' Song' or 'The Warriors' Song', not 'The Soldier's Song' ('Fiann' refers to the warrior-

band, the Fianna, in Irish mythology).

7 Sherry, 'The Story of the National Anthem', pp. 42–3. It is also perhaps worth noting that Ó Rinn's translation makes no reference to a *Saxon* foe in the third verse, although this is something of a moot point since the verses are rarely sung anyway.

8 D. Keogh, *Twentieth-Century Ireland: Nation and State* (Dublin: Gill & Macmillan, 1994), pp. 158, 420 (endnote 7); Bardon, *A History of Ulster*, p. 585; letter written by Garret FitzGerald, 10 May 1945, published in *Sunday Independent*, 7 May 1995; see also S9550A, Department of the Taoiseach, National Archives of Ireland.

9 Bryson and McCartney, *Clashing Symbols?: A Report on the Use of Flags, Anthems and Other National Symbols in Northern Ireland*, p. 42, quoting from *Belfast Telegraph*, 2 July 1953.

10 Bryson and McCartney, *Clashing Symbols?*, pp. 144–5; E. Moloney and A. Pollak, *Paisley* (Dublin: Poolbeg Press, 1986), pp. 63–5; H. Patterson, 'Party Versus Order: Ulster Unionism and the Flags and Emblems Act', *Contemporary British History*, 13, 4 (1999), pp. 120–2.

11 Donohue, 'Regulating Northern Ireland: The Special Powers Acts, 1922–1972', pp. 1108–9; Brian Maginess, Minister of Home Affairs, to City of Londonderry and Foyle Unionist Association, 13 April 1951, in HA/32/1/603, Ministry of Home Affairs, Public Record Office of Northern Ireland, quoted in Donohue, p. 1109.

12 Bryson and McCartney, *Clashing Symbols?*, p. 145.

13 Patterson, 'Party Versus Order: Ulster Unionism and the Flags and Emblems Act', pp. 107–9.

14 Bew, Gibbon and Patterson, *Northern Ireland 1921–1994: Political Forces and Social Classes*, p. 105.

15 Moloney and Pollak, *Paisley*, p. 66.

16 *Northern Ireland Parliamentary Debates: House of Commons*, Vol. 38, 10 and 11 February 1954, cols 586–91, 647–50, 722, quoted in T. Hennessey, *A History of Northern Ireland 1920–1996* (Houndmills: Macmillan, 1997), pp. 115–16.

17 Donohue, 'Regulating Northern Ireland: The Special Powers Acts, 1922–1972', p. 1109.

18 Bryson and McCartney, *Clashing Symbols?*, p. 146.

19 Quoted in D.P. Barritt and C.F. Carter, *The Northern Ireland Problem: A Study in Group Relations* (London: Oxford University Press, 1962), p. 126 (see also the comments of Senator J.G. Lennon in 1954 on the Union Jack, quoted on the same page).

20 Bryson and McCartney, *Clashing Symbols?*, p. 149.

21 Moloney and Pollak, *Paisley*, p. 83. Moloney and Pollak also say that in 1959, presumably as a result of this agitation, Belfast Corporation ordered all schools in the city to fly the Union Jack; however, it seems unlikely that the Corporation had the power to make such an order.

22 *Belfast Newsletter*, 9 July 1958, quoted in D. Bryan, *Orange Parades: The Politics of Ritual, Tradition and Control* (London: Pluto Press, 2000),

p. 76.

23 Bryson and McCartney, *Clashing Symbols?*, pp. 146–7.

24 Ibid., pp. 147–8; Moloney and Pollak, *Paisley*, pp. 115–17.

25 The young Bernadette Devlin wore a tricolour pin 'precisely because the Northern Ireland Flags and Emblems Act forbade it', but gave up on the badge when she found that the police would not stop her from wearing it. See B. Devlin, *The Price of My Soul* (London: Pan, 1969), pp. 60–1.

26 Bryson and McCartney, *Clashing Symbols?*, p. 134; Bruce, *God Save Ulster!*, p. 76.

27 Bryson and McCartney, *Clashing Symbols?*, p. 131; Loftus, *Mirrors: Orange & Green*, p. 90.

28 Bryson and McCartney, *Clashing Symbols?*, p. 134.

29 Loftus, *Mirrors: Orange & Green*, p. 41.

30 F. Wright, 'Protestant Ideology and Politics in Ulster', *Archives Européennes de Sociologie (European Journal of Sociology)*, 14, 2 (1973) p. 237 (but note his cautionary comment that the predominance of 'Ulster' flags over Union Jacks may have been due to the fact that 'Ulster' flags were very cheap!); a letter from 1971 saying that the Union Jack no longer represented Ulster Protestantism and unionism, and that 'True Unionists should fly the Ulster flag' is quoted in Clayton, *Enemies and Passing Friends: Settler Ideologies in Twentieth Century Ulster*, p. 131. Although the Northern Ireland flag is popularly referred to as the 'Ulster flag', it should not be confused with the flag of the province of Ulster (see Chapter 4), which has little or no meaning for unionists.

31 McCusker is quoted in Bardon, *A History of Ulster*, p. 757.

32 Loftus, *Mirrors: Orange & Green*, p. 41; Todd, 'Two Traditions in Unionist Political Culture', pp. 5–6, 15; see the mixture of Union Jacks and Northern Ireland flags in the loyalist murals in B. Rolston, *Drawing Support: Murals in the North of Ireland* and *Drawing Support 2: Murals of War and Peace* (Belfast: Beyond the Pale Publications, 1992 and 1995).

33 Hennessey, *A History of Northern Ireland 1920–1996*, p. 273; the full text of the Anglo-Irish Agreement can be found in P. Arthur and K. Jeffery, *Northern Ireland since 1968* (Oxford: Blackwell, 1988), pp. 99–108.

34 Northern Ireland Office, *Proposal for a Draft Order in Council: Public Order: Explanatory Document*, 1986, quoted in Bryson and McCartney, *Clashing Symbols?*, pp. 150–1.

35 Ibid.

36 Joint Group of Unionist MPs, *The Public Order Order: Equality Under the Law?*, n.d., quoted in Bryson and McCartney, *Clashing Symbols?*, p. 151.

37 Quoted in Bryson and McCartney, *Clashing Symbols?*, pp. 162–3.

38 The issue of symbols in workplaces is covered in Bryson and McCartney, *Clashing Symbols?*, ch. 6.

39 Ibid., pp. 104–6.

40 The question of 'representativeness' at Queen's is complicated by the fact that, in recent decades, Catholics have been under-represented among the staff, while Protestants have been under-represented among the students

(Ardagh, *Ireland and the Irish: Portrait of a Changing Society*, pp. 404, 427).

41 *Times Higher Education Supplement*, 5 August 1994, p. 5, 5 May 1995, p. 9.

42 Bryson and McCartney, *Clashing Symbols?*, p. 57.

43 The Downing Street Declaration is reproduced as Appendix A of McGarry and O'Leary, *Explaining Northern Ireland: Broken Images* (Oxford: Blackwell, 1995), pp. 408–13.

44 Forum for Peace and Reconciliation, *Report of Proceedings*, Vol. 7, 24 February 1995, pp. 83–5, 94. For a cautious response to such debates from a unionist academic see A. Aughey, 'Obstacles to Reconciliation in the South', in *Building Trust in Ireland: Studies Commissioned by the Forum for Peace and Reconciliation* (Belfast: Blackstaff Press, 1996), esp. pp. 34–40.

45 Sugden and Bairner, *Sport, Sectarianism and Society in a Divided Ireland*, p. 59.

46 Ibid., p. 60; Bryson and McCartney, *Clashing Symbols?*, pp. 86–7.

47 Bryson and McCartney, *Clashing Symbols?*, pp. 85–6.

48 Forum for Peace and Reconciliation, *Report of Proceedings*, Vol. 7, 24 February 1995, pp. 84, 94.

49 *Irish Times*, 8 April 1995, p. 18; the lyrics of 'Ireland's Call' can be found at http://www.irfu.ie/top/song.shtml

50 See, for example, the comments of Taoiseach John Bruton in *Irish Times*, 13 November 1995, p. 6.

51 *Agreement Reached in the Multi-Party Negotiations*, 10 April 1998.

52 The first motion was passed by the Assembly, but the second failed because it was the subject of a 'petition of concern' by Sinn Féin, the SDLP and the Alliance. This meant that the motion required the support of at least one-third of nationalists in the Assembly to pass, and although a majority of the Assembly voted for the motion, it failed to achieve the necessary cross-community support.

53 *Belfast Telegraph*, 5 June 2000, p. 4; *Irish Times*, 7 June 2000; Assembly debates of 17 January 2000 and 6 June 2000 can be found at http://www.ni-assembly.gov.uk

54 Adelaide House, Castle Buildings (Stormont), Churchill House, Clarence Court, Dundonald House, and Netherleigh House in Belfast, and Rathgael House in Bangor.

55 Northern Ireland Assembly, *Report on Draft Regulations Proposed under Article 3 of the Flags (Northern Ireland) Order 2000*, available at http://www.ni-assembly.gov.uk/Flags/adhoc1-00r.htm

56 *Agreement Reached in the Multi-Party Negotiations*, 10 April 1998.

57 J. McGarry and B. O'Leary, *Policing Northern Ireland: Proposals for a New Start* (Belfast: Blackstaff Press, 1999), p. 67. See also G. Ellison and J. Smyth, *The Crowned Harp: Policing Northern Ireland* (London: Pluto Press, 2000). ch. 9.

58 McGarry and O'Leary, *Policing Northern Ireland: Proposals for a New Start*, pp. 65–6, 133 (endnote 4).

59 See, for example, the summary of a report on policing by the SDLP

(Northern Ireland's largest nationalist party), which referred to the 'historic and symbolic legacy which has wedded policing almost exclusively to a unionist perspective', in *Irish Times*, 14 November 1995, p. 6. This report recommended changing the RUC's name, devising symbols with which both communities could identify, and ending the practice of flying the Union Jack over police stations.

60 McGarry and O'Leary, *Policing Northern Ireland: Proposals for a New Start*, pp. 66–7.
61 Ibid., p. 134 (endnote 8).
62 Ibid., p. 134 (endnote 9).
63 *Independent International*, 15–21 September 1999, pp. 10, 15.
64 *Independent International*, 26 January-1 February 2000, p. 10.
65 *Independent International*, 5–11 April 2000, p. 11.

Conclusion

1 L. MacNeice, 'Autumn Journal' (1938), in E.R. Dodds (ed.), *Collected Poems of Louis MacNeice* (London: Faber & Faber, 1966), pp. 133–4.
2 Billig, *Banal Nationalism*, p. 41.
3 A. Jackson, *Ireland 1798–1998: Politics and War* (Oxford: Blackwell, 1999), pp. 277, 284.
4 W. Bloom, *Personal Identity, National Identity and International Relations* (Cambridge: Cambridge University Press, 1990), p. 55.
5 Hobsbawm, 'Mass-Producing Traditions: Europe, 1870–1914', esp. pp. 263–83.
6 On this process generally see Weber, *Peasants into Frenchmen: The Modernization of Rural France*, and on the use of symbolism in this process see Agulhon, 'Politics, Images, and Symbols in Post-Revolutionary France'; P. Nora (ed.), *Realms of Memory: The Construction of the French Past*, vol. 3, *Symbols* English language ed. L.D. Kritzman, trans. A.Goldhammer (New York: Columbia University Press, 1998).
7 See S.M. Guenter, *The American Flag 1777–1924: Cultural Shifts from Creation to Codification* (Cranbury: Associated University Presses, 1990); C.E. O'Leary, *To Die For: The Paradox of American Patriotism* (Princeton: Princeton University Press, 1999).
8 C. E. Merriam, *Making of Citizens: A Comparative Study of Methods of Civic Training* (Chicago: Chicago University Press, 1931), pp. 145–54, 303–10.
9 Adolf Hitler's comment on the selection of the Nazi flag in Adolf Hitler, *Mein Kampf*, John Chamberlain et al. (eds) (New York: Reynal and Hitchcock, 1939), p. 734, quoted in A. Hill, 'Hitler's Flag: A Case Study', *Semiotica*, 38, 1/2 (1982), p. 128; on fascist Italy see S. Falasca-Zamponi, *Fascist Spectacle: The Aesthetics of Power in Mussolini's Italy* (Berkeley: University of California Press, 1997), esp. ch. 3.
10 See Bruce, *God Save Ulster!*, esp. pp. 9–13; D.H. Akenson, *God's Peoples: Covenant and Land in South Africa, Israel and Ulster* (Ithaca: Cornell

University Press, 1992), ch. 4.

11 Akenson, *God's Peoples: Covenant and Land in South Africa, Israel and Ulster*, p. 120.

12 *Londonderry Sentinel*, 1 December 1932, p. 4 (my italics).

13 See for example G. Adams, *Before the Dawn: An Autobiography* (London: Heinemann, 1996), pp. 51, 54–5.

14 See, for example, *Orange Standard*, September 1995, p. 21.

15 A.D. Buckley, 'Introduction: Daring Us to Laugh: Creativity and Power in Northern Irish Symbols', in A.D. Buckley (ed.), *Symbols in Northern Ireland* (Belfast: Institute of Irish Studies, 1998), pp. 17–19.

16 Mary Robinson, 'The Inaugural Speech', in K. Donovan, A.N. Jeffares and B. Kennelly (eds), *Ireland's Women: Writings Past and Present* (Dublin: Gill & Macmillan, 1994), p. 255. Áras an Uachtaráin is the residence of the President in Dublin.

17 *Irish Times*, 5 March 1985, quoted in B. O'Donoghue (ed.), *Oxford Irish Quotations* (Oxford: Oxford University Press, 1999), p. 89.

Bibliography

Archival sources

'British in Ireland' series on microfilm (copied from records held in the Public Record Office, London)

Royal Irish Constabulary Inspector-General's reports

Kilmainham Jail Museum

Autograph books of internees

Military Archives of Ireland

Department of Defence files

National Archives of Ireland

Department of Finance files
Department of Foreign Affairs files
Department of Justice files
Department of the Taoiseach files
Postal Division, Department of Communications files

National Library of Ireland Manuscript Section

Joseph Brennan papers

Public Record Office of Northern Ireland

Cabinet Secretariat files
Conclusions of Cabinet meetings
Correspondence of the Imperial Secretary (on microfilm, copied from the
Public Record Office, London)
Ministry of Education files
Ministry of Home Affairs files

Trinity College Dublin Library, Manuscripts Department

Thomas Bodkin papers

University College Dublin Archives Department

Hugh Kennedy papers
Richard Mulcahy papers
The O'Rahilly papers
James Ryan papers

Official publications

Agreement Reached in the Multi-Party Negotiations, 1998
Dáil Éireann, *Official Report: Debate on the Treaty Between Great
    Britain and Ireland Signed in London on the 6th December, 1921*
Dáil Éireann, *Official Report for Periods 16th August, 1921, to 26th
    August, 1921, and 28th February, 1922, to 8th June, 1922, with Index*
Dáil Éireann Debates
Forum for Peace and Reconciliation, *Report of Proceedings*, vol. 7, 1995
Northern Ireland Assembly, *Report on Draft Regulations Proposed under
    Article 3 of the Flags (Northern Ireland) Order 2000*, 2000, viewed
    online at   http://www.ni-assembly.gov.uk/Flags/adhoc1-00r.htm
Northern Ireland Assembly Debates, viewed online at
    http://www.ni-assembly.gov.uk
Northern Ireland Parliamentary Debates: House of Commons
Northern Ireland Parliamentary Debates: Senate
Seanad Éireann Debates
United Kingdom House of Lords Debates

Newspapers and periodicals

Belfast Newsletter
Belfast Telegraph
Catholic Bulletin
Church of Ireland Gazette
Connacht Sentinel
Connacht Tribune
Cork Examiner
Cross
Derry Journal
Drogheda Argus
Dublin Evening Mail
Dublin Opinion
Dundalk Democrat
Eire
Enniscorthy Echo
Freeman
Freeman's Journal
Frontier Sentinel
Hibernian Journal
Honesty
Independent International
Irish Freedom (Irish Republican Brotherhood)
Irish Freedom (Sinn Féin)
Irish Independent
Irish News
Irish Press
Irish Statesman
Irish Times
Irish Truth
Irishman
Kerryman
Leader
Leinster Leader
Limerick Leader
Londonderry Sentinel
Nation
Nationality
New Ireland
Newry Reporter
Northern Whig
Orange Standard (England)

Orange Standard (Ireland)
An Phoblacht
Plain People
Republic of Ireland/Poblacht na h-Eireann (Scottish edition)
Round Table
Sinn Féin
Standard
Star
Sunday Independent
Sydney Morning Herald
Times (London)
Times Higher Education Supplement
An tÓglach
Tyrone Constitution
United Ireland
United Irishman
Weekend Australian
Wicklow People

Songbooks and handbills

'Irish Political Song and Poem Leaflets 1915–1932', collection in the National Library of Ireland.
The Irish Soldier's Song Book (Dublin: Fergus O'Connor, n.d.).
Ó Cearnaigh, Peadar, *Camp-fire Songs* (Dublin: Art Depot, n.d.).
'Rajah of Frongoch', *Topical Ditties* (Dublin: Art Depot, n.d.).
Songs of Battle (Dublin: Art Depot, n.d.).
Songs of the Green, White & Gold (n.p.: no publisher, 1919).
Under Which Flag?: An Appeal to the Electors of Great Britain (Dublin: Irish Unionist Alliance, 1918).
'What is Wrong with the Green Flag?', United Irish League handbill (1918), National Library of Ireland.
What Sinn Fein Must Meet and Beat (n.p.: [Sinn Féin], n.d [1918]).
'Who are the Traitors to Ireland?', Sinn Féin handbill, National Library of Ireland.

Books, articles, pamphlets and theses

Adams, Gerry, *Before the Dawn: An Autobiography* (London: Heinemann, 1996).
Agulhon, Maurice, *Marianne into Battle: Republican Imagery and*

Symbolism in France, 1789–1880, trans. Janet Lloyd (Cambridge: Cambridge University Press, 1981).

Agulhon, Maurice, 'Politics, Images, and Symbols in Post-Revolutionary France', in Sean Wilentz (ed.), *Rites of Power: Symbolism, Ritual and Politics since the Middle Ages* (Philadelphia: University of Pennsylvania Press, 1985), pp. 177–205.

Akenson, Donald Harman, *God's Peoples: Covenant and Land in South Africa, Israel, and Ulster* (Ithaca: Cornell University Press, 1992).

Albanese, Catherine L., *Sons of the Fathers: The Civil Religion of the American Revolution* (Philadelphia: Temple University Press, 1976).

Alter, Peter, 'Symbols of Irish Nationalism', *Studia Hibernica*, 14 (1974), pp. 104–23.

Altman, Dennis, *Paper Ambassadors: The Politics of Stamps* (North Ryde: Angus & Robertson, 1991).

Anderson, Benedict, *Imagined Communities: Reflections on the Origin and Spread of Nationalism*, 2nd edn (London: Verso, 1991).

Andrews, Liam, 'The Very Dogs in Belfast Will Bark in Irish: The Unionist Government and the Irish Language 1921–43', in Aodán Mac Póilin (ed.), *The Irish Language in Northern Ireland* (Belfast: Ultach Trust, 1997), pp. 49–94.

Ardagh, John, *Ireland and the Irish: Portrait of a Changing Society* (Harmondsworth: Penguin, 1994).

Arthur, Paul and Keith Jeffery, *Northern Ireland since 1968* (Oxford: Blackwell, 1988).

Aughey, Arthur, 'The Idea of the Union', in John Wilson Foster (ed.), *The Idea of the Union: Statements and Critiques in Support of the Union of Great Britain and Northern Ireland* (Vancouver: Belcouver Press, 1995), pp. 8–19.

Aughey, Arthur, 'Obstacles to Reconciliation in the South', in *Building Trust in Ireland: Studies Commissioned by the Forum for Peace and Reconciliation* (Belfast: Blackstaff Press, 1996), pp. 1–51.

Augusteijn, Joost, *From Public Defiance to Guerilla Warfare: The Experience of Ordinary Volunteers in the Irish War of Independence 1916–1921* (Blackrock: Irish Academic Press, 1996).

Bardon, Jonathan, *A History of Ulster* (Belfast: Blackstaff Press, 1992).

Barnes, John and David Nicholson (eds), *The Leo Amery Diaries*, Vol. 1, *1896–1929* (London: Hutchinson, 1980).

Barritt, Denis P. and Charles F. Carter, *The Northern Ireland Problem: A Study in Group Relations* (London: Oxford University Press, 1962).

Bell, Desmond, *Acts of Union: Youth Culture and Sectarianism in Northern Ireland* (London: Macmillan, 1990).

Bew, Paul, Kenneth Darwin and Gordon Gillespie, *Passion and Prejudice: Nationalist-Unionist Conflict in Ulster in the 1930s and the Founding of the Irish Association* (Belfast: Institute of Irish Studies, 1993).

Bew, Paul, Peter Gibbon and Henry Patterson, *Northern Ireland 1921-1994: Political Forces and Social Classes* (London: Serif, 1995).

An Bhratach Náisiúnta [The National Flag] (Dublin: Stationery Office, n.d.).

Bielenberg, Andy, 'Keating, Siemens & the Shannon Scheme', *History Ireland*, 5, 3 (1997), pp. 43–7.

Billig, Michael, *Banal Nationalism* (London: Sage, 1995).

Birmingham, G.A. (pseudonym of James Owen Hannay), *The Red Hand of Ulster* (New York: George H. Doran, 1912).

Bloom, William, *Personal Identity, National Identity and International Relations* (Cambridge: Cambridge University Press, 1990).

Bloomfield, Anne, 'Drill and Dance as Symbols of Imperialism', in J.A. Mangan (ed.), *Making Imperial Mentalities: Socialisation and British Imperialism* (Manchester: Manchester University Press, 1990), pp. 74–95.

Bodkin, Thomas, 'The Irish Coinage Designers', in Brian Cleeve (ed.), *W.B. Yeats and the Designing of Ireland's Coinage* (Dublin: Dolmen Press, 1972), pp. 40–54.

Bodkin, Thomas, 'Postscript', in Brian Cleeve (ed.), *W.B. Yeats and the Designing of Ireland's Coinage* (Dublin: Dolmen Press, 1972), pp. 55–60.

Bowen, Kurt, *Protestants in a Catholic State: Ireland's Privileged Minority* (Kingston: McGill-Queen's University Press, 1983).

Bowman, John, *De Valera and the Ulster Question, 1917–1973* (Oxford: Clarendon Press, 1982).

Boyce, D. George, *Nationalism in Ireland*, 2nd edn (London: Routledge, 1991).

Boydell, Barra, 'The Female Harp: The Irish Harp in 18th- and Early-19th-Century Romantic Nationalism', *RIdIM/RMCI Newsletter*, 20, 1 (1995), pp. 10–17.

Boydell, Barra, 'The Iconography of the Irish Harp as a National Symbol', in Patrick F. Devine and Harry White (eds), *Irish Musical Studies*, Vol. 5, *The Maynooth International Musicological Conference 1995 Selected Proceedings: Part Two* (Blackrock: Four Courts Press, 1996), pp. 131–45.

Briggs, Geoffrey, *National Heraldry of the World* (London: J.M. Dent, 1973).

Bruce, Steve, *God Save Ulster!: The Religion and Politics of Paisleyism* (Oxford: Oxford University Press, 1986).

Bryan, Dominic, *Orange Parades: The Politics of Ritual, Tradition and Control* (London: Pluto Press, 2000).

Bryson, Lucy and Clem McCartney, *Clashing Symbols?: A Report on the*

Use of Flags, Anthems and Other National Symbols in Northern Ireland (Belfast: Institute of Irish Studies, 1994).

Buchalter, M. Don, *Hibernian Specialised Catalogue of the Postage Stamps of Ireland 1922–1972* (Dublin: Hibernian Stamp Co., 1972).

Buckland, Patrick, *Irish Unionism*, Vol. 2, *Ulster Unionism and the Origins of Northern Ireland 1886–1922* (Dublin: Gill & Macmillan, 1973).

Buckland, Patrick, *The Factory of Grievances: Devolved Government in Northern Ireland 1921–39* (Dublin: Gill & Macmillan, 1979).

Buckley, Anthony D., 'The Chosen Few: Biblical Texts in the Regalia of an Ulster Secret Society', *Folk Life*, 24 (1985–86), pp. 5–24.

Buckley, Anthony D., 'Introduction. Daring Us to Laugh: Creativity and Power in Northern Irish Symbols', in Anthony D. Buckley (ed.), *Symbols in Northern Ireland* (Belfast: Institute of Irish Studies, 1998) pp. 1–21.

Buckley, Anthony D. and Kenneth Anderson, *Brotherhoods in Ireland* (Cultra: Ulster Folk and Transport Museum, 1988).

Burke, Peter, *Popular Culture in Early Modern Europe* (London: Temple Smith, 1978).

Burke, Peter, 'Historians, Anthropologists, and Symbols', in Emiko Ohnuki-Tierney (ed.), *Culture Through Time: Anthropological Approaches* (Stanford: Stanford University Press, 1990), pp. 268–83.

Burke, Thomas N., *Lectures on Faith and Fatherland* (Glasgow: Cameron & Ferguson, n.d.)

Burke, Thomas N., *Ireland and the Irish: Lectures on Irish History and Biography* (New York: Lynch, Cole & Meehan, 1873).

Callanan, Frank, *T.M. Healy* (Cork: Cork University Press, 1996).

Cannadine, David, 'The Context, Performance and Meaning of Ritual: The British Monarchy and the "Invention of Tradition", c. 1820–1977', in Eric Hobsbawm and Terence Ranger (eds), *The Invention of Tradition* (Cambridge: Cambridge University Press, 1983), pp. 101–64.

Carson, R.A.G., *Coins: Ancient, Mediaeval & Modern* (London: Hutchinson, 1962).

Clark, Cumberland, *The Flags of Britain: Their Origin and History* (Shrewsbury: Wilding & Son, 1934).

Clayton, Pamela, *Enemies and Passing Friends: Settler Ideologies in Twentieth Century Ulster* (London: Pluto Press, 1996).

Cleeve, Brian (ed.), *W.B. Yeats and the Designing of Ireland's Coinage: Texts by W.B. Yeats and Others* (Dublin: Dolmen Press, 1972) (mainly reprinted from *Coinage of Saorstát Éireann*, 1928).

Clowes, W. Laird, 'An Imperial Flag', *Monthly Review*, 1 (Dec. 1900), pp. 106–17.

Colley, Linda, *Britons: Forging the Nation, 1707–1837* (New Haven, Yale University Press, 1992).

Colum, Padraic, *Cross Roads in Ireland* (New York: Macmillan, 1930).

Coogan, Tim Pat, *Michael Collins: A Biography* (London: Arrow, 1990).

Cronin, Mike, *Sport and Nationalism in Ireland: Gaelic Games, Soccer and Irish Identity since 1884* (Dublin: Four Courts Press, 1999).

Cubitt, Geoffrey, 'Introduction', in Geoffrey Cubitt (ed.), *Imagining Nations* (Manchester: Manchester University Press, 1998), pp. 1–20.

Curtis, L.P., *Anglo-Saxons and Celts: A Study of Anti-Irish Prejudice in Victorian England* (Bridgeport: University of Bridgeport, 1968).

Curtis, L. Perry, *Apes and Angels: The Irishman in Victorian Caricature* (Newton Abbot: David & Charles, 1971).

Daiken, Leslie H., *Good-bye, Twilight: Songs of the Struggle in Ireland* (London, Lawrence & Wishart, 1936).

Dalton, G.F., 'The Tradition of Blood Sacrifice to the Goddess Éire', *Studies*, 63, 252 (1974), pp. 343–54.

Danforth, Loring M., *The Macedonian Conflict: Ethnic Nationalism in a Transnational World* (Princeton: Princeton University Press, 1995).

Deane, Seamus (ed.), *The Field Day Anthology of Irish Writing*, Vol. 3 (Derry: Field Day, 1991).

de Burca, Padraic, 'The Story of the Soldier's Song', in William G. Fitz-Gerald (ed.), *The Voice of Ireland: A Survey of the Race and Nation from All Angles* (Dublin: Virtue, n.d.), pp. 151–3.

de Vere White, Terence, *Kevin O'Higgins* (Dublin: Anvil Books, 1986) (originally published 1948).

Devlin, Bernadette, *The Price of My Soul* (London: Pan, 1969).

Donohue, Laura K., 'Regulating Northern Ireland: The Special Powers Acts, 1922–1972', *Historical Journal*, 41, 4 (1998), pp. 1089–1120.

Donovan, Katie, A. Norman Jeffares and Brendan Kennelly (eds), *Ireland's Women: Writings Past and Present* (Dublin: Gill & Macmillan, 1994).

Dulin, C.I., *Ireland's Transition: The Postal History of the Transitional Period 1922–1925* (Dublin: MacDonnell Whyte, 1992).

Edge, J.H., *A Short Sketch of the Rise and Progress of Irish Freemasonry* (Dublin: Ponsonby & Gibbs, 1913).

Ellison, Graham and Jim Smyth, *The Crowned Harp: Policing Northern Ireland* (London: Pluto Press, 2000).

Falasca-Zamponi, Simonetta, *Fascist Spectacle: The Aesthetics of Power in Mussolini's Italy* (Berkeley: University of California Press, 1997).

Fanning, Ronan, *Independent Ireland* (Dublin: Helicon Limited, 1983).

Finlay, William, *An Illustrated History of Stamp Design* (n.p.: Peter Lowe, 1974).

Firth, Raymond, *Symbols: Public and Private* (London: George Allen & Unwin, 1973).

Fitzpatrick, David, *Oceans of Consolation: Personal Accounts of Irish Migration to Australia* (Ithaca: Cornell University Press, 1994).

Fitzpatrick, David, 'Militarism in Ireland, 1900–1922', in Thomas Bartlett and Keith Jeffery (eds), *A Military History of Ireland* (Cambridge: Cambridge University Press, 1996), pp. 379–406.

Fitzpatrick, David, *The Two Irelands 1912–1939* (Oxford: Oxford University Press, 1998).

Fitzpatrick, Georgina, *St Andrew's College 1894–1994* (Blackrock: St Andrew's College, 1994).

Foley, Carol A., *The Australian Flag: Colonial Relic or Contemporary Icon?* (Leichhardt: Federation Press, 1996).

Foster, R.F., *Modern Ireland 1600–1972* (London: Penguin, 1988).

Foster, R.F. (ed.), *The Oxford Illustrated History of Ireland* (Oxford: Oxford University Press, 1989).

Foster, R.F., 'Paddy and Mr Punch', in his *Paddy and Mr Punch: Connections in Irish and English History* (London: Allen Lane, 1993), pp. 171–94.

Foy, Michael, 'Ulster Unionist Propaganda Against Home Rule', *History Ireland*, 4, 1 (1996), pp. 49–53.

Fraser, Alistair B., 'A Canadian Flag for Canada', *Journal of Canadian Studies*, 25, 4 (1990–91), pp. 64–80.

Gallagher, Colm, 'The Great Seal of Ireland', *Seirbhís Phoiblí*, 14, 3 (1994), pp. 17–27.

Galvin, Patrick, *Irish Songs of Resistance (1169–1923)* (London: Oak Publications, 1962).

Garvin, Tom, *Nationalist Revolutionaries in Ireland 1858–1928* (Oxford: Clarendon Press, 1987).

Garvin, Tom, *1922: The Birth of Irish Democracy* (Dublin: Gill & Macmillan, 1996).

Gaughan, J. Anthony, *A Political Odyssey: Thomas O'Donnell, M.P. for West Kerry 1900–1918* (Mount Merrion: Kingdom Books, 1983).

Gaynor, P., *The Faith and Morals of Sinn Fein* (Dublin: Art Depot, n.d.).

Gilley, Sheridan, 'English Attitudes to the Irish in England 1780–1900', in C. Holmes (ed.), *Immigrants and Minorities in British Society* (London: Allen & Unwin, 1978), pp. 81–110.

Gilley, Sheridan, 'Pearse's Sacrifice: Christ and Cuchulain Crucified and Risen in the Easter Rising, 1916', in Yonah Alexander and Alan O'Day (eds), *Ireland's Terrorist Dilemma* (Dordrecht: Martinus Nijhoff, 1986), pp. 29–47.

Girardet, Raoul, 'The Three Colors: Neither White Nor Red', in Pierre Nora (ed.), *Realms of Memory: The Construction of the French Past*,

Vol. 3, *Symbols*, English language ed. Lawrence D. Kritzman, transl. Arthur Goldhammer (New York: Columbia University Press, 1998), pp. 3–26.

Griffith, Kenneth and Timothy E. O'Grady, *Curious Journey: An Oral History of Ireland's Unfinished Revolution* (London: Hutchinson, 1982).

Guenter, Scot M., *The American Flag, 1777–1924: Cultural Shifts from Creation to Codification* (Cranbury: Associated University Presses, 1990).

Gwynn, Denis, *The Irish Free State 1922–1927* (London: Macmillan, 1928).

Gwynn, Stephen, *Dublin Old and New* (Dublin: Browne and Nolan, n.d. c. 1938).

Harkness, D.W., *The Restless Dominion: The Irish Free State and the British Commonwealth of Nations, 1921–31* (London: Macmillan, 1969).

Harrison, Simon, 'Four Types of Symbolic Conflict', *Journal of the Royal Anthropological Institute* (NS), 1 (1995), pp. 255–72.

Hart, Peter, *The I.R.A. and its Enemies: Violence and Community in Cork, 1916–1923* (Oxford: Clarendon Press, 1998).

Harvie, Scott, '17 November 1993 – A Night to Remember?', in Richard English and Graham Walker (eds), *Unionism in Modern Ireland: New Perspectives on Politics and Culture* (London: Macmillan Press, 1996), pp. 192–219.

Hayes, Carlton J.H., *Nationalism: A Religion* (New York: Macmillan, 1960).

Hayes-McCoy, G.A., *A History of Irish Flags from Earliest Times* (Dublin: Academy Press, 1979).

Hennessey, Thomas, *A History of Northern Ireland 1920–1996* (Houndmills: Macmillan, 1997).

Hewitt, Virginia, *Beauty and the Banknote: Images of Women on Paper Money* (London: British Museum, 1994).

Hill, Alette, 'Hitler's Flag: A Case Study', *Semiotica*, 38, 1/2 (1982), pp. 127–37.

Hill, Jacqueline R., 'National Festivals, the State and "Protestant Ascendancy" in Ireland, 1790–1829', *Irish Historical Studies*, 24, 93 (1984), pp. 30–51.

Hobsbawm, Eric and Terence Ranger (eds), *The Invention of Tradition* (Cambridge: Cambridge University Press, 1983).

Hobsbawm, Eric, 'Introduction: Inventing Traditions', in Eric Hobsbawm and Terence Ranger (eds), *The Invention of Tradition* (Cambridge: Cambridge University Press, 1983), pp. 1–14.

Hobsbawm, Eric, 'Mass-Producing Traditions: Europe, 1870-1914', in

Eric Hobsbawm and Terence Ranger (eds), *The Invention of Tradition* (Cambridge: Cambridge University Press, 1983), pp. 263–307.

Hone, J.M., 'The Royal Dublin Society and its Bicentenary', *Quarterly Review*, 256, 507 (1931), pp. 63–77.

Hume, David H., 'Empire Day in Ireland 1896-1962', in Keith Jeffery (ed.), *'An Irish Empire'?: Aspects of Ireland and the British Empire* (Manchester: Manchester University Press, 1996), pp. 149–68.

Hunt, Lynn, *Politics, Culture, and Class in the French Revolution* (Berkeley: University of California Press, 1984).

Hutchinson, John, *The Dynamics of Cultural Nationalism: The Gaelic Revival and the Creation of the Irish Nation State* (London: Allen & Unwin, 1987).

Ignatieff, Michael, *Blood & Belonging: Journeys into the New Nationalism* (London: BBC Books, 1993).

Innes, C.L., *Woman and Nation in Irish Literature and Society, 1880–1935* (New York: Harvester Wheatsheaf, 1993).

Jackson, Alvin, 'Irish Unionist Imagery, 1850–1920', in Eve Patten (ed.), *Returning to Ourselves: Second Volume of Papers from the John Hewitt International Summer School* (Belfast: Lagan Press, 1995), pp. 344–59.

Jackson, Alvin, 'Irish Unionists and the Empire, 1880–1920: Classes and Masses', in Keith Jeffery (ed.), *'An Irish Empire'?: Aspects of Ireland and the British Empire* (Manchester: Manchester University Press, 1996), pp. 123–48.

Jackson, Alvin, *Ireland 1798–1998: Politics and War* (Oxford: Blackwell, 1999).

Jacob, Margaret C., *Living the Enlightenment: Freemasonry and Politics in Eighteenth-Century Europe* (New York: Oxford University Press, 1991).

Jarman, Neil, 'Troubled Images: The Iconography of Loyalism', *Critique of Anthropology*, 12, 2 (1992), pp. 133–65.

Jarman, Neil, *Material Conflicts: Parades and Visual Displays in Northern Ireland* (Oxford: Berg, 1997).

Jeffery, Keith, 'The Great War in Modern Irish Memory', in T.G. Fraser and Keith Jeffery (eds), *Men, Women and War* (Dublin: Lilliput Press, 1993), pp. 136–57.

Jeffery, Keith, *Ireland and the Great War* (Cambridge: Cambridge University Press, 2000).

Keane, Sir John, 'Ireland: Commonwealth or Republic?', *Quarterly Review*, 262, 519 (1934), pp. 154–70.

Kearney, Richard, *Transitions: Narratives in Modern Irish Culture* (Dublin: Wolfhound, 1988).

Kelly, Anne, 'Thomas Bodkin at the National Gallery of Ireland', *Irish Arts Review Yearbook* (1991–92), pp. 171–80.

Kennedy, Dennis, *The Widening Gulf: Northern Attitudes to the Independent Irish State, 1919–49* (Belfast: Blackstaff Press, 1988).

Keogh, Dermot, *Twentieth-Century Ireland: Nation and State* (Dublin: Gill & Macmillan, 1994).

Kertzer, David I., *Ritual, Politics and Power* (New Haven: Yale University Press, 1988).

Kertzer, David I., *Politics and Symbols: The Italian Communist Party and the Fall of Communism* (New Haven: Yale University Press, 1996).

Killen, John, *John Bull's Famous Circus: Ulster History Through the Postcard 1905–1985* (Dublin: O'Brien Press, 1985).

Kwan, Elizabeth, 'The Australian Flag: Ambiguous Symbol of Nationality in Melbourne and Sydney, 1920–21', *Australian Historical Studies*, 26, 103 (1994), pp. 280–303.

Kwan, Elizabeth, 'Which Flag? Which Country?: An Australian Dilemma, 1901–1951', PhD thesis, Australian National University, 1995.

Lambert, John, 'Imagining a "South African" Imperial Identity: South Africanism in the 1920s', unpublished paper presented at the Australian Historical Association Conference, Adelaide, 2000.

Larsen, Sidsel Saugestad, 'The Glorious Twelfth: A Ritual Expression of Collective Identity', in Anthony P. Cohen (ed.), *Belonging: Identity and Social Organization in British Rural Cultures* (Manchester: Manchester University Press, 1982), pp. 278–91.

Lee, J.J., *Ireland 1912–1985: Politics and Society* (Cambridge: Cambridge University Press, 1989).

Leerssen, Joseph Th., *Mere Irish & Fíor-Ghael: Studies in the Idea of Irish Nationality, its Development and Literary Expression Prior to the Nineteenth Century* (Amsterdam: John Benjamins, 1986).

Leerssen, Joep, *Remembrance and Imagination: Patterns in the Historical and Literary Representation of Ireland in the Nineteenth Century* (Notre Dame: University of Notre Dame Press, 1997).

Leonard, Jane, 'The Twinge of Memory: Armistice Day and Remembrance Sunday in Dublin since 1919', in Richard English and Graham Walker (eds), *Unionism in Modern Ireland: New Perspectives on Politics and Culture* (Houndmills: Macmillan Press, 1996), pp. 99–114.

Lindesay, Vane, *Aussie-osities* (Richmond: Greenhouse Publications, 1988).

Lister, David, 'Some Aspects of the Law and Usage of Flags in Britain', *Flag Bulletin*, 17, 1 (1978), pp. 14–23.

Loftus, Belinda, *Mirrors: William III & Mother Ireland* (Dundrum: Picture Press, 1990).

Loftus, Belinda, *Mirrors: Orange & Green* (Dundrum: Picture Press, 1994).

Lowe, Robson, *1922-Ireland-1972* (Bournemouth: Robson Lowe, n.d.).

McCauley, Leo T., 'Summary of the Proceedings', in Brian Cleeve (ed.), *W.B. Yeats and the Designing of Ireland's Coinage* (Dublin: Dolmen Press, 1972), pp. 25–39.

McCoole, Sinéad, *Hazel: A Life of Lady Lavery 1880–1935* (Dublin: Lilliput Press, 1996).

MacDonagh, Oliver, *States of Mind: Two Centuries of Anglo-Irish Conflict, 1780–1980* (London: Pimlico, 1992 [originally published 1983]).

McDowell, R.B. and D.A. Webb, *Trinity College Dublin 1592–1952: An Academic History* (Cambridge: Cambridge University Press, 1982).

McGarry, John and Brendan O'Leary, *Explaining Northern Ireland: Broken Images* (Oxford: Blackwell, 1995).

McGarry, John and Brendan O'Leary, *Policing Northern Ireland: Proposals for a New Start* (Belfast: Blackstaff Press, 1999).

MacIntosh, Gillian, 'Acts of "National Communion": The Centenary Celebrations for Catholic Emancipation, the Forerunner of the Eucharistic Congress', in Joost Augusteijn (ed.), *Ireland in the 1930s: New Perspectives* (Dublin: Four Courts Press, 1999), pp. 83–95.

Mackay, James, *Michael Collins: A Life* (Edinburgh: Mainstream, 1996).

MacKenzie, John M., *Propaganda and Empire: The Manipulation of Public Opinion, 1880–1960* (Manchester: Manchester University Press, 1984).

MacKillop, James, *Dictionary of Celtic Mythology* (Oxford: Oxford University Press, 1998).

MacNeice, Louis, *The Collected Poems of Louis MacNeice*, ed. E.R. Dodds (London: Faber & Faber, 1966).

McNeill, Ronald, *Ulster's Stand for Union* (London: John Murray, 1922).

Mac Póilin, Aodán, '"Spiritual Beyond the Ways of Men": Images of the Gael', in Eve Patten (ed.), *Returning to Ourselves: Second Volume of Papers from the John Hewitt International Summer School* (Belfast: Lagan Press, 1995), pp. 360–83.

McQueen, Humphrey, 'The Australian Stamp: Image, Design and Ideology', *Arena*, 84 (1988), pp. 78–96.

McRedmond, Louis (ed.), *Ireland: The Revolutionary Years. Photographs from the Cashman Collection: Ireland 1910–30* (Dublin: Gill & Macmillan and Radio Telefís Éireann, 1992).

Mach, Zdzislaw, *Symbols, Conflict and Identity: Essays in Political Anthropology* (Albany: State University of New York Press, 1993).

Maguire, Martin, 'The Organisation and Activism of Dublin's Protestant Working Class, 1883–1935', *Irish Historical Studies*, 29, 113 (1994), pp. 65–87.

Martin, F.X., '1916 – Myth, Fact, and Mystery', *Studia Hibernica*, 7, (1967), pp. 7–124.

Martin, Ged, 'The Irish Free State and the Evolution of the Commonwealth, 1921-49', in Ronald Hyam and Ged Martin, *Reappraisals in British Imperial History* (London: Macmillan, 1975), pp. 201–23.

Matheson, John Ross, *Canada's Flag: A Search for a Country* (Belleville: Mika Publishing, 1986).

Maume, Patrick, *'Life That is Exile': Daniel Corkery and the Search for Irish Ireland* (Belfast: Institute of Irish Studies, 1993).

Merriam, Charles Edward, *The Making of Citizens: A Comparative Study of Methods of Civic Training* (Chicago: University of Chicago Press, 1931).

Miller, David W., *Queen's Rebels: Ulster Loyalism in Historical Perspective* (Dublin: Gill & Macmillan, 1978).

Moloney, Ed and Andy Pollak, *Paisley* (Dublin: Poolbeg Press, 1986).

Moore, Thomas, *Irish Melodies and Songs* (London: George Routledge & Sons, n.d.) (originally published 1808–1834).

Lady Morgan, *O'Donnel: A National Tale* (London: Henry Colburn, 1814 [facsimile edn New York: Garland Publishing, 1979]).

Morris, Ewan, '"God Save the King" Versus "The Soldier's Song": The 1929 Trinity College National Anthem Dispute and the Politics of the Irish Free State', *Irish Historical Studies*, 31, 121 (1998), pp. 72–90.

Morton, H.V., *In Search of Ireland* (London: Methuen, 1930).

Moss, Warner, *Political Parties in the Irish Free State* (New York: AMS Press, 1968 [reprint of 1933 edition]).

Mosse, George L., *The Nationalization of the Masses: Political Symbolism and Mass Movements in Germany from the Napoleonic Wars through the Third Reich* (New York: Howard Fertig, 1975).

Mosse, George L., 'National Anthems: The Nation Militant', in Reinhold Grimm and Jost Hermand (eds), *From Ode to Anthem: Problems of Lyric Poetry* (Wisconsin: University of Wisconsin Press, 1989), pp. 86–99.

Moynihan, Maurice, *Currency and Central Banking in Ireland, 1922–60* (Dublin: Gill and Macmillan, 1975).

Murphy, Daniel J. (ed.), *Lady Gregory's Journals*, 2 vols (Gerrards Cross: Colin Smythe, 1978 and 1987).

Murphy, John A., 'O'Connell and the Gaelic World', in Kevin B. Nowlan and Maurice R. O'Connell (eds), *Daniel O'Connell: Portrait of a Radical* (Belfast: Appletree Press, 1984), pp. 32–52.

Nelson, E. Charles, *Shamrock: Botany and History of an Irish Myth* (Kilkenny: Boethius Press, 1991).

Nelson, Sarah, *Ulster's Uncertain Defenders: Protestant Political, Paramilitary and Community Groups and the Northern Ireland Conflict* (Belfast: Appletree Press, 1984).

Nicholson, Alan, *Australian Banknote Catalogue* (Melbourne: Hawthorn Press, 1977).

Nora, Pierre (ed.), *Realms of Memory: The Construction of the French Past*, Vol. 3, *Symbols,* English language ed. Lawrence D. Kritzman, transl. Arthur Goldhammer (New York: Columbia University Press, 1998).

Ó Brógáin, Séamas, 'The Flags of the Four Provinces', *Irish Vexillology Newsletter*, 2 (1985), pp. 9–10.

Ó Brógáin, Séamas, 'Irish Naval Flags', *Irish Vexillology Newsletter*, 3 (1985), pp. 20–21.

Ó Brógáin, Séamas, *The Wolfhound Guide to the Irish Harp Emblem* (Dublin: Wolfhound Press, 1998).

O'Callaghan, Margaret, 'Language, Nationality and Cultural Identity in the Irish Free State, 1922-7: The *Irish Statesman* and the *Catholic Bulletin* Reappraised', *Irish Historical Studies*, 24, 94 (1984), pp. 226–45.

O'Casey, Seán, *Three Plays* (London: Pan, 1980).

O'Connor, Nuala, *Bringing it all Back Home: The Influence of Irish Music* (London: BBC Books, 1991).

Ó Corráin, Donnchadh, 'Prehistoric and Early Christian Ireland', in R.F. Foster (ed.), *The Oxford History of Ireland* (Oxford: Oxford University Press, 1992), pp. 1–43.

Ó Cuív, Brian, 'The Wearing of the Green', *Studia Hibernica*, 17/18 (1977–78), pp. 107–19.

O'Donoghue, Bernard (ed.), *Oxford Irish Quotations* (Oxford: Oxford University Press, 1999).

O'Faoláin, Seán, *King of the Beggars: A Life of Daniel O'Connell, the Irish Liberator, in a Study of the Rise of the Modern Irish Democracy (1775–1847)* (London: Thomas Nelson, 1938).

O'Faoláin, Seán, *De Valera* (Harmondsworth: Penguin, 1939).

O'Faoláin, Seán, *An Irish Journey* (London: Readers Union, 1941).

O'Faoláin, Seán, *Vive Moi!* (London: Sinclair-Stevenson, 1993 [originally published 1963]).

O'Ferrall, Fergus, 'Daniel O'Connell, the "Liberator", 1775–1847: Changing Images', in Raymond Gillespie and Brian P. Kennedy (eds), *Ireland: Art into History* (Dublin: Town House, 1994), pp. 91–102.

O'Grady, Joseph P., 'The Irish Free State Passport and the Question of Citizenship, 1921–4', *Irish Historical Studies*, 26, 104 (1989), pp. 396–405.

O'Halloran, Clare, *Partition and the Limits of Irish Nationalism: An Ideology Under Stress* (Dublin: Gill & Macmillan, 1987).

O'Hegarty, P.S., *The Victory of Sinn Féin: How it Won it and How it Used it* (Dublin: University College Dublin Press, 1998 [originally published 1924]).

O'Leary, Cecilia Elizabeth, *To Die For: The Paradox of American Patriotism* (Princeton: Princeton University Press, 1999).

O'Malley, Ernie, *On Another Man's Wound* (London: Rich & Cowan, 1936).

Orr, Philip, *The Road to the Somme: Men of the Ulster Division Tell Their Story* (Belfast: Blackstaff Press, 1987).

O'Sullivan, M.D., 'Eight Years of Irish Home Rule', *Quarterly Review*, 254, 504 (1930), pp. 230–49.

O'Sullivan, Donal, *The Irish Free State and its Senate: A Study in Contemporary Politics* (London: Faber and Faber, 1940).

O'Sullivan, Patrick, 'Ireland & the Olympic Games', *History Ireland*, 6, 1 (1998), pp. 40–5.

Owens, Gary, 'Constructing the Repeal Spectacle: Monster Meetings and People Power in Pre-Famine Ireland', in Maurice R. O'Connell (ed.), *People Power: Proceedings of the Third Annual Daniel O'Connell Workshop* (Dublin: Institute of Public Administration, 1993), pp. 80–93.

Owens, Gary, 'Nationalist Monuments in Ireland, *c*.1870–1914: Symbolism and Ritual', in Brian P. Kennedy and Raymond Gillespie (eds), *Ireland: Art into History* (Dublin: Town House, 1994), pp. 103–17.

Owens, Gary, 'Constructing the Image of Daniel O'Connell', *History Ireland*, 7, 1 (1999), pp. 32–6.

Patterson, Henry, 'Party Versus Order: Ulster Unionism and the Flags and Emblems Act', *Contemporary British History*, 13, 4 (1999), pp. 105–29.

Paul-Dubois, L., *Contemporary Ireland* (Dublin: Maunsel, 1908).

Pearse, Pádraic H., *Political Writings and Speeches* (Dublin: Talbot Press, 1962).

Phoenix, Eamon, *Northern Nationalism: Nationalist Politics, Partition and the Catholic Minority in Northern Ireland 1890–1940* (Belfast: Ulster Historical Foundation, 1994).

Radic, Thérèse, *Songs of Australian Working Life* (Elwood: Greenhouse Publications, 1989).

Rafroidi, Patrick, 'Imagination and Revolution: The Cuchulain Myth', in Oliver MacDonagh, W.F. Mandle and Pauric Travers (eds), *Irish Culture and Nationalism, 1750–1950* (London: Macmillan, 1983), pp. 137–48.

Rault, Philippe, 'The South African Flag of 1928-1994', *Flag Bulletin*, 33, 1 (1994), pp. 2–38.

Reginald, 12th Earl of Meath, *Memories of the Nineteenth Century* (London: John Murray, 1923).

Reginald, 12th Earl of Meath, *Memories of the Twentieth Century* (London: John Murray, 1924).

Reid, Donald M., 'The Symbolism of Postage Stamps: A Source for the

Historian', *Journal of Contemporary History*, 19, 2 (1984), pp. 223–49.

Rolston, Bill, *Drawing Support: Murals in the North of Ireland* (Belfast: Beyond the Pale Publications, 1992).

Rolston, Bill, *Drawing Support 2: Murals of War and Peace* (Belfast: Beyond the Pale Publications, 1995).

Rose, Richard, *Governing Without Consensus: An Irish Perspective* (Boston: Beacon Press, 1971).

Rose, Richard, *Understanding the United Kingdom: The Territorial Dimension in Government* (London: Longman, 1982).

Ryder, Sean, 'Gender and the Discourse of "Young Ireland" Cultural Nationalism', in Timothy P. Foley, Lionel Pilkington, Sean Ryder and Elizabeth Tilley (eds), *Gender and Colonialism* (Galway: Galway University Press, 1995), pp. 210–24.

Saker, Harry, *The South African Flag Controversy 1925–1928* (Cape Town: Oxford University Press, 1980).

Saorstát Éireann Irish Free State Official Handbook (Dublin: Talbot Press, 1932).

Scott, David, 'Posting Messages', *GPA Irish Arts Review Yearbook*, 1990–1991, pp. 188–96.

Scott, David, *European Stamp Design: A Semiotic Approach to Designing Messages* (London: Academy Editions, 1995).

Sheehy, Jeanne, *The Rediscovery of Ireland's Past: The Celtic Revival 1830–1930* (London: Thames and Hudson, 1980).

Shepard, Paul, *The Others: How Animals Made us Human* (Washington: Island Press, 1996).

Sherry, Ruth, 'The Story of the National Anthem', *History Ireland*, 4, 1 (1996), pp. 39–43.

Smith, Whitney, *Flags Through the Ages and Across the World* (Maidenhead: McGraw-Hill, 1975).

The Spirit of the Nation: Ballads and Songs by the Writers of 'The Nation' with Original and Ancient Music Arranged for the Voice and Pianoforte, 2nd edn (Dublin: James Duffy, 1882 [1st edn 1845]).

Stallybrass, Peter and Allon White, *The Politics and Poetics of Transgression* (Ithaca: Cornell University Press, 1986).

Stanley Gibbons' Simplified Stamp Catalogue (London: Stanley Gibbons).

Stocker, Mark, 'Muldoon's Money: The 1967 New Zealand Decimal Coinage Designs', *History Now*, 7, 2 (2001), pp. 5–10.

Sugden, John and Alan Bairner, *Sport, Sectarianism and Society in a Divided Ireland* (Leicester: Leicester University Press, 1993).

Swinburne, H. Lawrence, 'Flag', in *The Encyclopaedia Britannica*, Vol. 10, 11th edn (Cambridge: Cambridge University Press, 1910), pp. 454–63.

Thompson, Leonard, *The Political Mythology of* Apartheid (New Haven: Yale University Press, 1985).

Thompson, William Irwin, *The Imagination of an Insurrection: Dublin, Easter 1916. A Study of an Ideological Movement* (New York: Oxford University Press, 1967).

Thuente, Mary Helen, *The Harp Re-Strung: The United Irishmen and the Rise of Irish Literary Nationalism* (Syracuse: Syracuse University Press, 1994).

Tierney, Mark, Paul Bowen and David Fitzpatrick, 'Recruiting Posters', in David Fitzpatrick (ed.), *Ireland and the First World War* (Dublin: Trinity History Workshop, 1986), pp. 47–58.

Todd, Jennifer, 'Two Traditions in Unionist Political Culture', *Irish Political Studies*, 2 (1987), pp. 1–26.

Townshend, Charles, *Political Violence in Ireland: Government and Resistance since 1848* (Oxford: Clarendon Press, 1983).

Townshend, Charles, *Ireland: The 20th Century* (London: Arnold, 1999).

Valiulis, Maryann Gialanella, 'Power, Gender, and Identity in the Irish Free State', *Journal of Women's History*, 6, 4/7, 1 (1995), pp. 117–36.

Vance, Norman, 'Celts, Carthaginians and Constitutions: Anglo-Irish Literary Relations, 1780–1820', *Irish Historical Studies*, 22, 87, (1981), pp. 216–38.

Vaughan, W.E. and A.J. Fitzpatrick (eds), *Irish Historical Statistics: Population, 1821–1971* (Dublin: Royal Irish Academy, 1978).

Vovelle, Michel, 'La Marseillaise: War or Peace', in Pierre Nora (ed.), *Realms of Memory: The Construction of the French Past*, Vol. 3, *Symbols*, English language ed. Lawrence D. Kritzman, trans. Arthur Goldhammer (New York: Columbia University Press, 1998), pp. 29–74.

Walker, Brian, *Dancing to History's Tune: History, Myth and Politics in Ireland* (Belfast: Institute of Irish Studies, 1996).

Walker, Graham, '"Protestantism Before Party!": The Ulster Protestant League in the 1930s', *Historical Journal*, 28, 4 (1985), pp. 961–67.

Waller, Bolton C., *Hibernia, or the Future of Ireland* (London: Kegan Paul, Trench, Trubner, n.d. [c. 1928]).

Warner, Marina, *Monuments and Maidens: The Allegory of the Female Form* (London: Weidenfeld and Nicolson, 1985).

Weber, Eugen, *Peasants into Frenchmen: The Modernization of Rural France, 1870–1914* (London: Chatto & Windus, 1977).

Weitman, Sasha R., 'National Flags: A Sociological Overview', *Semiotica*, 8 (1973), pp. 328–67.

Whitfield, Éimear, 'Another Martyr for Old Ireland: The Balladry of Revolution', in David Fitzpatrick (ed.), *Revolution?: Ireland 1917–1923* (Dublin: Trinity History Workshop, 1990), pp. 60–8.

Whyte, J.H., *Church and State in Modern Ireland 1923–1970* (Dublin:

Gill & Macmillan, 1970).

Williams, Martin, 'Ancient Mythology and Revolutionary Ideology in Ireland, 1878–1916', *Historical Journal*, 26, 2 (1983), pp. 307–28.

Wilson, Valerie, *The Secret Life of Money: Exposing the Private Parts of Personal Money* (St Leonards: Allen & Unwin, 1999).

Wright, Frank, 'Protestant Ideology and Politics in Ulster', *Archives Européennes de Sociologie (European Journal of Sociology)*, 14, 2 (1973), pp. 213–80.

Yeats, W.B., 'What we did or Tried to do', in Brian Cleeve (ed.), *W.B. Yeats and the Designing of Ireland's Coinage* (Dublin: Dolmen Press, 1972), pp. 9–20.

Yeats, W.B., *Autobiographies* (Dublin: Gill & Macmillan, 1955).

Yeats, W.B., *Selected Poetry*, ed. Timothy Webb (London: Penguin, 1991).

Young, Derek, *Guide to the Currency of Ireland: Legal Tender Notes, 1928–1972* (Dublin: Stagecost Publications, 1972).

Zimmerman, Georges-Denis, *Songs of Irish Rebellion: Political Street Ballads and Rebel Songs 1780–1900* (Dublin: Allen Figgis, 1967).

Index